Georg August Schweinfurth

The Heart of Africa

Three Years' Travels and Adventures in the Unexplored Regions of Central Africa -

Vol. 2

Georg August Schweinfurth

The Heart of Africa
Three Years' Travels and Adventures in the Unexplored Regions of Central Africa - Vol. 2

ISBN/EAN: 9783744760188

Printed in Europe, USA, Canada, Australia, Japan

Cover: Foto ©Andreas Hilbeck / pixelio.de

More available books at **www.hansebooks.com**

THE
HEART OF AFRICA.

THREE YEARS' TRAVELS AND ADVENTURES
IN THE UNEXPLORED REGIONS OF CENTRAL AFRICA.
FROM 1868 TO 1871.

By DR. GEORG SCHWEINFURTH.

TRANSLATED BY ELLEN E. FREWER.
WITH AN INTRODUCTION BY WINWOOD READE.

IN TWO VOLUMES.
VOL. II.

WITH MAPS AND WOODCUT ILLUSTRATIONS.

Third and Cheaper Edition.

LONDON:
SAMPSON LOW, MARSTON, SEARLE, & RIVINGTON,
CROWN BUILDINGS, 188, FLEET STREET.
1878.

[All Rights reserved.]

CONTENTS.

CHAPTER IX.

                                                                     PAGE

MOHAMMED's friendship for Munza—Invitation to an audience—Solemn escort to the royal halls—Waiting for the king—Munza makes his toilet—Architecture of the hall—Display of ornamental weapons—Fantastic attire of the monarch—Features and expression—Stolid composure—Offerings to royalty—Simple attire of the ladies—Munza's mode of smoking—The cola-nut—Musical performances—The eunuch—The court-fool—Munza's oration—Monbuttoo chorus—Munza's gratitude—A present of a house—Curiosity of natives—A skull-market—Ambassadors from the Niam-niam—Bunza—Visit from the royal ladies—Triumphal procession—A bath under *surveillance*—The sword-bean—Munza's castle—Reserve on geographical matters—A dog for a Pygmy—Momvoo-goats—Extract of meat—Khartoomers' settlements—Mohammed's plan—Disappointed hopes—Means and good-luck—A festival—Munza dances—A royal visit—Guinea-hog 1

CHAPTER X.

THE MONBUTTOO—Previous accounts of the people—Population—Surrounding nations—Aspect of country—Neglect of agriculture—Products of the soil—Produce of the chase—Forms of salutation—Preparation of food—Prevalence of cannibalism—Warlike spirit—The state officers—The royal household—The palace—Advanced culture of the people—Prevalence of light hair—Analogy with the Fulbe—Preparation of bark—Costume of the men—Nudity of the women—Tattooing and painting—Coiffure—Piercing the ears—Weapons—Iron-smelting—Early knowledge of copper—Excellence of tools—Wood-carving—Benches and stools—Shields—Pottery—Architecture—Ornamental trees—Conception of a Supreme Being 33

CHAPTER XI.

THE AKKA—Nubian stories—Ancient classical allusions—My incredulity about Pygmies—Visit from a Pygmy—Adimokoo's information—His war-dance—Mummery's Pygmy *corps*—Nsewue—African dwarf races—Analogy of Akka and Bushmen—Height and complexion—Hair and beards—Shape of body—Elegance of hands—Formation of skull—Projecting lips—Animated gestures—Language—Nsewue's cruelty to animals—Hunting propensities of the Akka—Protection by Munza—History of Miani's Akka . . 65

CHAPTER XII.

Return to the north—Tikkitikki's reluctance to start—Passage of the Gadda—Sounding the Keebaly—The Kahpily—Antelope-hunt—Cataracts of the Keebaly—Kubby's refusal of boats—Possibility of fording—Origin of the Keebaly—Division of highland and lowland—Return to Nembey—Bivouac on the frontier—Eating wax—Declaration of war—Parley with the enemy—My mistrust of the guides—Treacherous attack on Mohammed—A dangerous wound—Open war—Detruncated heads—Effect of arrows—Mohammed's defiance—Attack on the abattis—Pursuit of the enemy—A mysterious procession—Wando's bad omen—Consulting the oracle—The Farookh—Mohammed's favourable progress—Capture of Niam-niam women—Lamentations of the husbands—Cruelty to dogs—The calamus—Another capture—Upper course of the Mbrwole—Composure of the captive—Change of scenery—Arrival at the Nabambisso 86

CHAPTER XIII.

Solitude and hunger—Productive ant-hill—Diversion in the woods—Excursion to the east—A papyrus-swamp—Disgusting food of the Niam-niam—Merdyan's Seriba—Losing the way—Kind reception in Tuhamy's Seriba—Scenery of Mondoo—Mount Baginze—Source of the Dyoor—Mountain vegetation—Cyanite gneiss—Mohammed's campaign—Three Bongo missing—History of three skulls—Indifference of Nubians to cannibalism—Building a grass-hut—Crossing the Sway—Evil tidings—Successful chase—Bendo—Badry's recital—With Nganye—Suspension-bridge over the Tondy—Division of the caravan—Détour to the east—Elands—Bamboo-jungles—The Seriba Mbomo—Abundance of corn—The Babuckur—Crossing the Lehssy—Wild buffaloes—Return to Sabby—Home news—Hunger on the march—Passage of the Tondy 120

CONTENTS.   v

CHAPTER XIV.
PAGE

Flourishing condition of Ghattas's establishments—Arrival of stores—
Trip to Kurkur—Hyena dogs—Dislike of the Nubians to pure
water—Present of a young elephant—Cattle-plagues—Meteorology
—Trip to the Dyoor—Bad news of Mohammed—Preparations for
a Niam-niam campaign—A disastrous day—Loss of my property—
Burnt Seriba by night—A wintry scene—Rebuilding the Seriba—
Cause of the fire—Bad news of the Niam-niam expedition—Start
to the Dyoor—Counting steps—Kind reception by Khalil—My new
wardrobe—Low temperature—Maintenance of Egyptian troops—
The army and the slave-trade—Suggestions for means of transport
—Defeat of Khartoomers by Ndoruma—Hippopotamus-hunt—
Birds on the Dyoor—Hippopotamus-lard—Khalil—Character of
the Nubians—Strife in the Egyptian camp—Commencement of a
new tour—Crocodiles in the Ghetty—Memorials of Miss Tinné—
Dirt and disorder—The Baggara—The Pongo—Frontiers of the
Bongo and Golo—Idrees Wod Defter's Seriba—Corn-magazines of
the Golo—The Kooroo—The goats' brook—Arrival at Seebehr's
Seriba 164

CHAPTER XV.

Increasing level of country—Seebehr's Seriba—Dehm Nduggo—Help-
lessness of the Turks—A loathsome scene—Seebehr's court—Ibra-
him Effendi—Establishment of Dehms—Ivory-trade and slave-trade
—Population of Dar Ferteet—The Kredy—Overland route to
Kordofan—Raw copper—Rough mining—Underwood of Cycadeæ—
Kredy huts and mills—The Beery—Inhospitality at Mangoor—
Numerous brooks—Dehm Gudyoo—Scorbutic attack—A dream
and its fulfilment—Remnants of mountain-ridges—Upper course
of the Pongo—Information about the far west—The Bahr-Aboo-
Dinga—Barth's investigations—Primogeniture of the Bahr-el-Arab
—First break in the weather—Elephant-hunters from Darfoor—
The Sehre—Abundance of game—A magic tuber—Deficiency of
water—A comfortless night—Cheerfulness of the Sehre—Lower
level of land—A miniature mountain chain—Norway rats—A giant
fig-tree—An evil eye—Return to Khalil's quarters. 211

CHAPTER XVI.

Tidings of war—Hunting on the Dyoor—Reed-rats—Transport of corn
—Dyoor fishing—River-oysters—Ignorance of the Soudanese—
Change of weather—An execution—Return to Ghattas's Seriba—
Allagabo—Start to the Meshera—Strange evolutions of antelopes

—Cattle-raids—Traitors among the natives—Needless alarm—
Remains of old Shol—Lepers on board—Ambiguous slave-dealing
—Down the Gazelle—A horrible night—A false alarm—Taken in
tow—The Mudir's camp—Crowded boats—Confiscation of slaves
—A pleasant surprise—Slave-caravans on the bank—Arrival in
Khartoom—Telegram to Berlin—Seizure of my servants—Remon-
strance with the Governor-General—Mortality in the fever season
—Tikkitikki's death—Θάλαττα, θάλαττα 252

LIST OF ILLUSTRATIONS.

(ENGRAVED BY J. D. COOPER.)

	PAGE
KING MUNZA IN FULL DRESS	*Frontispiece*
MUNZA'S RESIDENCE	*to face* 19
BREED OF CATTLE FROM THE MAOGGOO COUNTRY	20
GOAT OF THE MOMVOO	24
KING MUNZA DANCING BEFORE HIS WIVES	*to face* 28
KING MUNZA'S DISH	31
MONBUTTOO WARRIORS	50
MONBUTTOO WOMAN	51
WEAPONS OF THE MONBUTTOO	53
SPEAR-HEADS	56
HATCHET, SPADE, AND ADZE, OF THE MONBUTTOO	57
WOODEN KETTLE-DRUM	58
SINGLE SEAT USED BY THE WOMEN	*ib.*
SEAT-REST	59
WATER-BOTTLES	60
BOMBY THE AKKA	71
NSEWUE THE AKKA	74
VIEW ON THE KEEBALY, NEAR KUBBY	*to face* 94
A GALLERY-FOREST	*to face* 99
MOHAMMED DEFIES HIS ENEMIES	*to face* 107
DAILY LIFE IN CAMP	*to face* 120
SUSPENSION-BRIDGE OVER THE TONDY	*to face* 147
HORNS OF CENTRAL AFRICAN ELAND	150
BABUCKUR SLAVE	156
GOLO WOMAN	207
CORN-MAGAZINE OF THE GOLO	208
SLAVE-TRADERS FROM KORDOFAN	*to face* 209

	PAGE
KREDY HUT	226
KREDY CORN-MAGAZINE	*ib.*
SLAVE AT WORK	231
"KARRA," THE MAGIC TUBER	244
A BONGO CONCERT	248
HUNTING REED-RATS	254
FAR-EL-BOOS. (*Aulacodus Swinderianus*)	256

THE HEART OF AFRICA.

CHAPTER IX.

Mohammed's friendship for Munza—Invitation to an audience—Solemn escort to the royal halls—Waiting for the king—Munza makes his toilet—Architecture of the hall—Display of ornamental weapons—Fantastic attire of the monarch—Features and expression—Stolid composure—Offerings to royalty—Simple attire of the ladies—Munza's mode of smoking—The cola-nut—Musical performances—The eunuch—The court-fool—Munza's oration—Monbuttoo chorus—Munza's gratitude—A present of a house—Curiosity of natives—A skull-market—Ambassadors from the Niam-niam—Bunza—Visit from the royal ladies—Triumphal procession—A bath under *surveillance*—The sword-bean—Munza's castle—Reserve on geographical matters—A dog for a Pigmy—Momvoo-goats—Extract of meat—Khartoomers' settlements—Mohammed's plan—Disappointed hopes—Means and good-luck—A festival—Munza dances—A royal visit—Guinea-hog.

Munza was impatiently awaiting the arrival of the Khartoomers. His storehouses were piled to the full with ivory and hunting booty of an entire year, which he was eager to exchange for the produce of the north or to see replaced by new supplies of the red ringing metal which should flow into his treasury.

This was Mohammed's third visit to the country, and not only interested motives prompted the king to receive him warmly, but real attachment; for the two had mutually pledged their friendship in their blood, and called each other by the name of brother. During his absence in Khartoom, Mohammed had entrusted the command of the expedition of the previous year to his brother Abd-el-fetah, a Mussulman of the purest water and a hypocritical fanatic, who had greatly offended the king by his arrogance and unsympathetic reserve. He considered himself defiled by contact with a "Kaffir," and would not allow a nigger to approach within ten steps of his person; he refused to acknowledge either African king or prince, and always designated the ladies of the court as slaves. But Mohammed was entirely different. By all the natives he was known by his unassuming title of "Mbahly," *i.e.*, the little one, and in all his dealings with them he was urbanity itself. He won every heart by adopting the national costume, and attired in his native rokko-coat and scarlet plume, he would sit for hours together over the brimming beer-flasks by the side of his royal *confrère*. No wonder, then, that Munza's daily question to Mohammed's people had been: "When will Mbahly come?" and no wonder that, as we were preparing to cross the great river, his envoys had met us with a cordial greeting for his friend. Nor was the attachment all on Munza's side. Immediately on our arrival, Mohammed, leaving the organisation of our encampment entirely to the discretion of his lieutenants, had gathered up his store of presents, and hastened to convey them to the king. The interview was long, and our large encampment was complete and night was rapidly approaching before Mohammed returned to his quarters. He came accompanied by the triumphal strain of horns and kettle-drums, and attended by thousands of natives bearing the ample store of provisions which, at the king's commands, had been instantly forthcoming. He announced that I was invited to an audience of the king on the following morning, and that a state reception was to be prepared in honour of my visit. It need hardly be said that it was with feelings of wonder and curiosity that I lay down that night to rest.

The 22nd of March, 1870, was the memorable date on which my introduction to the king occurred. Long before I was stirring, Mohammed had once more betaken himself to the royal quarters. On leaving my tent, my attention was immediately attracted to the opposite slopes, and a glance at the wide space between the king's palace and the houses of his retinue was sufficient to assure me that unusual animation prevailed. Crowds of swarthy negroes were surging to and fro; others were hurrying along in groups, and ever and anon the wild tones of the kettle-drum could be heard even where I was standing. Munza was assembling his courtiers and inspecting his elephant-hunters, whilst from far and near streamed in the heads of households to open the ivory-mart with Mohammed, and to negotiate with him for the supply of his provisions.

Somewhat impatiently I stood awaiting my summons to the king, but it was already noon before I was informed that all arrangements were complete, and that I was at liberty to start. Mohammed's black body-guard was sent to escort me, and his trumpeters had orders to usher me into the royal presence with a flourish of the Turkish *réveil*. For the occasion I had donned a solemn suit of black. I wore my unfamiliar cloth-coat, and laced up the heavy Alpine boots, that should give importance to the movements of my light figure; watch and chain were left behind, that no metal ornament might be worn about my person. With all the solemnity I could I marched along; three black squires bore my rifles and revolver, followed by a fourth with my inevitable cane-chair: for it is the rule of the country that no one shall sit upon the ground. Next in order, and in awestruck silence, came my Nubian servants, clad in festive garments of unspotted whiteness, and bearing in their hand the offerings that had been so long and so carefully reserved for his Monbuttoo majesty.

It took us half an hour to reach the royal residence. The path descended in a gentle slope to the wooded depression of the brook, then twisted itself for a time amid the thickets of the valley, and finally once more ascended, through extensive plantain-groves, to the open court that was bounded by a wide semicircle of motley dwellings. On our arrival at the low parts of the valley we found the swampy jungle-path bestrewn with the stems of fresh-hewn trees and a bridge of the same thrown across the water itself. The king could hardly have been expected to suggest such peculiar attention of his own accord, but this provisionary arrangement for keeping my feet dry was made in compliance with a kindly hint from Mohammed, who, knowing the nature of my boots, and the time expended in taking them off and on, had thus thoughtfully insured my ease and comfort; moreover, these boots were unique in the African world, and must be preserved from mud and moisture. Unfortunately all these arrangements tended to confirm the Monbuttoo in one or other of their infatuated convictions: either that my feet were like goats' hoofs, or, according to another version, that the firm leather covering was itself an integral part of my body. The idea of goat's feet had probably arisen from the comparison of my hair and that of a goat; and doubtless the stubbornness with which I always refused to uncover my feet for their inspection strengthened them in their suspicion.

As we approached the huts, the drums and trumpets were sounded to their fullest powers, and the crowds of people pressing forward on either hand left but a narrow passage for our procession. We bent our steps to one of the largest huts, which formed a kind of palatial hall open like a shed at both ends. Waiting my arrival here was one of the officers of state, who, I presume, was the master of the ceremonies, as I afterwards observed him presiding over the general festivities. This official took me by the right hand, and without a word, conducted me to the interior of the hall. Here, like the audience at a concert, were arranged according to their rank hundreds of nobles and courtiers, each occupying his own ornamental bench and decked out with all his war equipments. At the other end of the building a space was left for the royal throne, which differed in no respect from the other benches, except that it stood upon an outspread mat; behind this bench was placed a large support of singular construction, resting as it seemed upon three legs, and furnished with projections that served as props for the back and arms of the sitter: this support was thickly studded with copper rings and nails. I requested that my own chair might be placed at a few paces from the royal bench, and there I took up my position, with my people standing or squatting behind me, and the Nubian soldiers forming a guard around. The greater number of the soldiers had their guns, but my black squires, who had never before been brought face to face with so mighty a potentate, subsequently confessed to me that their hearts beat fast, and that they could not help trembling to think how a sign from Munza could have brought all our limbs to the spit.

For a considerable time I had to sit waiting in expectation before the empty throne. My servants informed me that Munza had attended the market in his ordinary costume, but that he had been seen to hasten home to his private apartments, where he was now undergoing a process of anointing, frizzling, and bedizening at the hands of his wives, in order that he should appear before me in the imposing splendour of his state attire. I had thus no other alternative than patiently to abide my time; for what could be more flattering to a foreign guest than for a king to receive him in his costliest toilet?

In the interval of waiting there was a continuous uproar. The fitful beating of kettle-drums and the perpetual braying of horns resounded through the airy building until it shook again, and mingling with the boisterous strains rose the voices of the assembled courtiers as they whiled away the time in loud and eager conversation. There was no doubt that I was myself the main cause of their excitement; for although I sat with my back to the majority, I could not be otherwise than quite aware that all eyes were intently fixed upon me. All, however, kept their seats at a respectful distance, so that I could calmly look about me and note down my observations of what I saw.

The hall itself was the chief object that attracted my attention. It was at least a hundred feet in length, forty feet high, and fifty broad. It had been quite recently completed, and the fresh brightness of the materials gave it an enlivening aspect, the natural brown polish of the wood-work looking as though it were gleaming with the lustre of new varnish. Close by was a second and more spacious hall, which in height was only surpassed by the loftiest of the surrounding oil-palms; but this, although it had only been erected five years previously, had already begun to show symptoms of decay, and being enclosed on all sides was dark, and therefore less adapted for the gathering at a public spectacle. Considering the part of Africa in which these halls were found, one might truly be justified in calling them wonders of the world; I hardly know with all our building resources what material we could have employed, except it were whalebone, of sufficient lightness and durability to erect structures like these royal halls of Munza, capable of withstanding the tropical storms and hurricanes. The bold arch of the vaulted roof was supported on three long rows of pillars formed from perfectly straight pine-stems; the countless spars and rafters as well as the other parts of the building being composed entirely of the leaf-stalks of the wine-palm (*Raphia vinifera*).* The floor was covered with a dark red clay plaster, as firm and smooth as asphalt. The sides were enclosed by a low breastwork, and the space between this and the arching roof, which at the sides sloped nearly to the ground, allowed light and air to pass into the building. Outside against the breastwork stood crowds of natives, probably the "great unwashed" of the Monbuttoo, who were unable to obtain places within, and contented themselves with eagerly gazing through this opening at the proceedings. Officials with long sticks went their rounds and kept order among the mob, making free use of their sticks whenever it was necessary; all boys who ventured uninvited into the hall being vigorously beaten back as trespassers.

I had probably been left for an hour, and was getting lost in the contemplation of all the wonders, when a louder sound of voices and

* This palm is found in every bank-forest in the Monbuttoo country, and its leaves vary from 25 to 35 feet in length: the midrib of the leaf (rhachis) is of a bright brown colour, and furnishes the most popular building material throughout Central Africa.

an increasing clang of horns and kettle-drums led me to suppose that there was an announcement of the approach of the king; but, no, this was only a prelude. The sovereign was still being painted and beautified by the hands of his fair ones. There was, however, a fresh and increasing commotion near the entrance of the hall, where a number of ornamental weapons was being arranged. Posts were driven into the ground, and long poles were fastened horizontally across them; then, against this extemporised scaffolding were laid, or supported crosswise, hundreds of ornamental lances and spears, all of pure copper, and of every variety of form and shape. The gleam of the red metal caught the rays of the tropical noontide sun, and in the symmetry of their arrangement the rows of dazzling lance-heads shone with the glow of flaming torches, making a background to the royal throne that was really magnificent. The display of wealth, which, according to Central African tradition, was incalculable, was truly regal, and surpassed anything of the kind that I had conceived possible.

A little longer and the weapons are all arranged. The expected king has left his home. There is a running to and fro of heralds, marshals, and police. The thronging masses flock towards the entrance, and silence is proclaimed. The king is close at hand. Then come the trumpeters flourishing away on their huge ivory horns; then the ringers swinging their cumbrous iron bells; and now, with a long firm stride, looking neither to the right nor to the left, wild, romantic, picturesque alike in mien and in attire, comes the tawny Cæsar himself! He was followed by a number of his favoured wives. Without vouchsafing me a glance, he flung himself upon his unpretending chair of state, and sat with his eyes fixed upon his feet. Mohammed had joined the retinue of his royal friend, and took up his position opposite me on the other side of the king on a stool that was brought for his accommodation. He also had arrayed himself in a suitable dress in honour of the occasion, and now sat in the imposing uniform of a commander of Arnauts.

I could now feast my eyes upon the fantastic figure of the ruler. I was intensely interested in gazing at the strange weird-looking sovereign, of whom it was commonly reported that his daily food was human flesh. With arms and legs, neck and breast, all bedizened with copper rings, chains, and other strange devices, and with a kind of copper crescent at the top of his head, the potentate gleamed with a shimmer that was to our ideas unworthy of royalty, but savoured far too much of the magazines of civic opulence, reminding one almost unavoidably of a well-kept kitchen! His appearance, however, was decidedly marked with his nationality, for every adornment that he had about him belonged exclusively to Central Africa, as none but the fabrications of his native land are deemed worthy of adorning the person of a king of the Monbuttoo.

Agreeably to the national fashion a plumed hat rested on the top of his chignon, and soared a foot and a half above his head: this hat was a narrow cylinder of closely-plaited reeds; it was ornamented with three layers of red parrots' feathers, and crowned with a plume of the same; there was no brim, but the copper crescent projected from the front like the vizor of a Norman helmet. The cartilage of Munza's ears was pierced, and copper bars as thick as the finger inserted in the cavities. The entire body was smeared with the native unguent of powdered cam-wood, which converted the original bright brown tint of his skin into the colour that is so conspicuous in ancient Pompeian halls. With the exception of being of an unusually fine texture, his single garment differed in no respect from what was worn throughout the country; it consisted of a large piece of fig-bark impregnated with the same dye that served as his cosmetic, and this, falling in graceful folds about his body, formed breeches and waistcoat all in one. Round thongs of buffalo-hide, with heavy copper balls attached to the ends, were fastened round the waist in a huge knot, and like a girdle held the coat, which was neatly hemmed. Around the king's neck hung a copper ornament made in little points which radiated like beams all over his chest; on his bare arms were strange-looking pendants in the shape of cylinders bound with rings. Just below the knee were three bright, horny-looking circlets cut out of hippopotamus-hide, likewise tipped with copper. As a symbol of his dignity Munza wielded in his right hand the sickle-shaped Monbuttoo scimitar, in this case only an ornamental weapon, and made of pure copper.

As soon as the king had taken his seat, two little tables, beautifully carved, were placed on either side of his throne, and on these stood the dainties of which he continually partook, but which were carefully concealed by napkins of fig-bark; in addition to these tables, some really artistic flasks of porous clay were brought in, full of drinking water.

Such was Munza, the autocrat of the Monbuttoo, with whom I was now brought face to face. He appeared as the type of those half-mythical potentates, a species of Mwata Yanvo or Great Makoko, whose names alone have penetrated to Europe, a truly savage monarch, without a trace of anything European or Oriental in his attire, and with nothing fictitious or borrowed to be attributed to him.

He was a man of about forty years of age, of a fair height, of a slim but powerful build, and, like the rest of his countrymen, stiff and erect in figure. Although belonging to a type by no means uncomely, his features were far from prepossessing, but had a Nero-like expression that told of *ennui* and satiety. He had small whiskers and a tolerably thick beard; his profile was almost orthognatic, but the perfectly Caucasian nose offered a remarkable contrast to the thick and protruding negro lips. In his eyes gleamed the wild light of animal sensuality, and around his mouth lurked an expression that I never saw in any other Monbuttoo, a combination of avarice, violence, and love of cruelty that could with the extremest difficulty relax into a smile. No spark of love or affection could beam forth from such features as his.

A considerable time elapsed before the king looked directly at the pale-faced man with the long hair and the tight black clothes who now for the first time appeared before him. I held my hat in my hand, but no greeting had as yet taken place, for, observing that everyone kept his seat when the king entered the hall, I had done the same, and now waited for him to address me. The wild uproar of the cannibals still continued, and Munza, sitting in a careless attitude, only raised his eyes now and then from their fixed stare upon the ground as though to scan the whole assemblage, but in reality to take stray glances at my person, and in this way, little by little, he satisfied his curiosity. I could not help marvelling at the composure of this wild African, and wondering where in the world he could have learnt his dignity and self-possession.

At length the monarch began to ask me some questions. They were fluently translated into the Zandey dialect by the chief interpreter, who always played a principal part in our intercourse with the natives. The Niam-niam in their turn rendered the sense to me in Arabic. The conversation, however, was of the most commonplace character, and referred neither to the purpose of my coming nor to the country from which I came. Munza appeared extremely anxious to keep up to an Oriental measure the principle of *nil admirari*; nothing could disturb his composure, and even at my subsequent visits, where there was no state ceremonial, he maintained a taciturnity nearly as resolute.

My servants now produced the presents I had brought and spread them at the king's feet. These consisted, in the first place, of a piece of black cloth, a telescope, a silver platter, and a porcelain vase; the silver was taken for white iron, and the porcelain for carved ivory. The next gift was a real piece of carved ivory, brought as a specimen to show the way in which the material is employed; there was a book with gilt edges; then came a double mirror, that both magnified and reduced what it reflected; and last, though by no means least, was a large assortment of beads of Venetian glass, including thirty necklaces, each composed of thirty distinct pieces, so that Munza was in possession of more than a thousand separate beads.* The universal principle followed by the Nubians forbade that any presents of firearms should be made to native rulers. Munza regarded all these offerings with great attention, but without committing himself to any audible expression of approval. Not so his fifty wives, who were seated on stools arranged behind his throne; they gave frequent half-suppressed utterances of surprise, and the double mirror was passed admiringly from hand to hand, its contortions eliciting shouts of delight.

There were fifty of these ladies present: they were only the most intimate, or wives of the first rank, the entire number of court ladies being far larger. Except in the greater elegance of their style, they departed in no way from the fashion of the country.

The sole attire of the Monbuttoo women is a huge chignon and a pattern painted in black all over their bodies which stands out in bold relief against their bright yellow skins. All garments are rejected as useless appendages, and even ornaments are very little worn; beads are scarcely used at all, and copper is reserved for the adornment of the men.

After a time Munza turned his attention to his refreshments. As far as I could distinguish them, they consisted of lumps of plantain-meal and tapioca piled on leaves, of dried plantains, and of a fruit which to my surprise I immediately recognised as the cola-nut of the west. From this rosy-shelled kernel the king cut a few slices, and chewed them in the intervals of smoking his tobacco. His pipe, in the shape of an iron stem six feet long, was handed to him by a chibbukchak, who was in attendance for that purpose. Very

* I had obtained these little works of art from my Venetian friend Miani, to whom they had been presented some years previously by his fellow-citizens, when he was preparing to undertake a new expedition. The enterprise had failed from no other cause than from the jealousy shown by the Egyptian Government.

remarkable was the way in which Munza smoked. To bring himself into the correct position he threw himself far back in his seat, supported his right elbow on the arm-rest, put one leg across the other, and with his left hand received the pipe-stem. In this attitude he gravely took one long inhalation, then, with a haughty gesture, resigned his pipe to the hands of his attendant and allowed the smoke slowly to re-issue from his mouth. It is a habit among Turks of rank to smoke thus by taking only two or three inhalations from a pipe handed to them by their servants; but where, again, may I ask, could this cannibal prince have learnt such a custom?

To my request for a cola-nut the king responded by graciously passing me a specimen with his own hand. Turning to Mohammed, I expressed my surprise at beholding this fruit of the far west amongst the Monbuttoo; I told him of its high value* as a spice in Bornoo, where it is worth its weight in silver, and I went on to say that it confirmed my impression that the Welle was identical with the river of Baghirmy, called the Shary, and that this nut accordingly came to me like a key to a problem that I was seeking to solve. Then again addressing Munza, I made him understand that I knew the fruit, and pointing in the direction of Lake Tsad, I told him that there it was eaten by the great people of the country. I hoped in this way to induce him to give me some information on the subject; but he had made up his mind to be astonished at nothing, nor could I ever even on future occasions draw him into a geographical discussion. All that I could learn was that the cola-nut grew wild in the country, and that it was called "nangweh" by the natives, who were accustomed to chew it in the intervals of their smoking.

The performances that had been prepared for our entertainment now commenced. First of all a couple of horn-blowers stepped forward, and proceeded to execute solos upon their instruments. These men were advanced proficients in their art, and brought forth sounds of such power, compass, and flexibility that they could be modulated from sounds like the roar of a hungry lion, or the trumpeting of an infuriated elephant, down to tones which might be compared to the sighing of the breeze or to a lover's whisper. One of them, whose ivory horn was so huge that he could scarcely hold it in a horizontal position, executed rapid passages and shakes

---

* According to Liebig the cola-nut contains more coffeine than the most potent coffee-berries.

with as much neatness and decision as though he were performing on a flute.

Next appeared a number of professional singers and jesters, and amongst them a little plump fellow, who acted the part of a pantomine clown, and jumped about and turned somersaults till his limbs looked like the arms of a windmill; he was covered from head to foot with bushy tufts and pigtails, and altogether his appearance was so excessively ludicrous that, to the inward delight of the king, I burst into a hearty fit of laughter. I called him a court fool, and in many respects he fully deserved the title. The Nubians drew my attention, as though to something quite new, to the wooden Monbuttoo scimitar that he wore in his girdle. His jokes and pranks seemed never-ending, and he was permitted to take liberties with everyone, not excepting even Munza himself; and amongst other tricks he would approach the king with his right hand extended, and just as Munza had got hold of it, would start backwards and make off with a bound.

The next episode consisted of the performances of a eunuch, who formed a butt for the wit of the spectators. How Munza had come into possession of this creature, no one seemed to know, and I could only learn that he was employed in the inner parts of the palace. He was a fat grotesque-looking figure, and when he sang looked exactly like a grunting baboon; to add to the oddity of his appearance, Munza, as though in mockery of his Nubian guests, had had him arrayed in a red fez, and thus he was the only one in all the immense concourse of natives who had anything foreign in his attire.

But the most important part of the programme was reserved for the end: Munza was to make an oration. Whilst all the audience remained quietly seated on their stools and benches, up jumped the king, loosened his coat, cleared his throat, and commenced his harangue. Of course I could not understand a single word, and a double interpretation would have been worse than useless: but, from what I could see and hear, it was evident that Munza endeavoured to be choice and emphatic in his language, as not only did he often correct himself, but he made pauses after the sentences that he intended to be impressive, to allow for the applause of his auditors. Then the shout of " Ee, ee, tchupy, tchupy, ee, Munza, ee," resounded from every throat, and the musical instruments caught up the strain, until the uproar was truly demoniacal. Several times after this chorus, and as if to stimulate the tumult, Munza uttered a stentorian "brrr - -"* with a voice so sonorous that the very roof vibrated, and the swallows fled in terror from their nests in the eaves.

The kettle-drums and horns now struck up a livelier and more rythmical strain, and Munza assumed a new character and proceeded to beat time with all the solemnity of a conductor. His *bâton* was something like a baby's rattle, and consisted of a hollow sphere of basket-work filled with pebbles and shells, and attached to a stick.†

The discourse lasted full half an hour, during which time I took the portrait of the king that forms the frontispiece to this book. Hunger at length compelled me to take my leave of the sovereign and retrace my steps to the camp. At parting Munza said to me, "I do not know what to give you in return for all your presents; I am sorry I am so poor and have nothing to offer you." Fascinated by his modesty and indulging the idea that it was only a preface to a munificent gift worthy of royalty, I replied, "Don't mention that: I did not come for what I could get; we buy ivory from the Turks, and pay them with yellow lead and white iron, and we make white stuffs and powder and guns for ourselves. I only ask for two things: a pig (*Potamochœrus*) and a chimpanzee."

"You shall certainly have them," said Munza; but I was thoroughly deceived, and, in spite of my repeated reminders, neither pig nor chimpanzee ever appeared.

As I left the hall the king commenced a new oration. As for myself, I was so thoroughly fatigued with the noise and tumult, that I was glad to spend the remainder of this memorable day quietly in my tent.

Early on the following morning I was aroused by my people, who begged me to come out and see what the king was sending me. Looking down the road I perceived a group of Monbuttoo, who with a good deal of shouting were lugging up the hill something that I could not make out. Mohammed presently hurried up with the surprising announcement that he had made Munza comprehend that

---

* It may interest the reader to learn that in the Shamane prayers "brrr - -" is synonymous with "hail," and I have little doubt that it here meant some sort of applause, as it was always the signal for the repetition of the hymn in celebration of the glories of Munza.

† A similar contrivance is used on the river Gaboon on the West Coast. Rattles seem to have been introduced into religious performances by people in almost every portion of the world. Here, like the sistrum of the Isis, the rattle served the purpose of scaring away evil spirits.

my valuables were all lying out in the open air and exposed to the rain, and that the king was now sending me a house as his first present. I thought at first that he was jesting, but a few minutes sufficed to convince me of the truth of his statement. About twenty natives were carrying on their shoulders the substructure of a small quadrilateral house, while others were following with the roof. A very short time elapsed before they had mounted the hill and placed the erection in close juxtaposition to my tent. The light structure, woven together with the Spanish reed, looked exactly like a huge hamper, with the roof for a lid. It was about twenty feet long, and sufficiently commodious to contain all my goods, and was especially useful for protecting my paper packets.

I was thus elevated to the rank and enjoyed the rights of a householder among the Monbuttoo, and my intercourse with the natives became more intimate every day. My tent was continually besieged by a host of curious spectators, of whom the more well-to-do brought their benches, and, ranged in rows before the opening, watched in silent eagerness my every movement. Their chief interest seemed absorbed in contemplating my person, although many of the utensils and implements that surrounded me must have been quite as strange and incomprehensible to them. These frequent visitors at first afforded me great amusement, and I received them with friendly gestures, and combed my hair and shaved *in conspectu omnium*. Nor was the wonder all on their side; every moment revealed some novelty to myself, and I found full employment in sketching and taking notes. The great difficulty to our intercourse was in not understanding one another's language. Now and then, however, I managed to get hold of some people who could speak the Zandey dialect; and then, with the help of my Niam-niam interpreters, I could ask them questions and get my wishes conveyed to the general multitude.

"Bring your weapons," I would say; "bring your weapons, and the produce of your handicraft, your ornaments and tools, and I will give you beautiful things in return. Bring the fruit of your forests, and the leaves of the trees on which they grow. Bring the skins and skulls of animals. But above all bring the human skulls that remain over from your meals; they are of no use to you—bring them, and I will give you copper in exchange."

I had rarely occasion to repeat my request, but almost before my wish was uttered there was opened a regular curiosity mart; goods were bartered, and a flourishing trade was done.

The stock of bones that was thus brought to me in one day was quite astonishing, and could not do otherwise than remove any lingering hesitation I might have in believing the cannibal propensities of the people. There were piles of every kind—fragments of skulls, and lower jaw-bones from which the teeth had been extracted to serve as ornaments for the neck. The belief seemed to be that I had no intention of dealing otherwise than wholesale. Proofs enough were before me; sufficient, I should suppose, to silence even the most stubborn scepticism. It cost me some trouble to convince the people that my requirements only extended to such skulls as were perfectly uninjured, and that for such only could I be content to pay. For a perfect skull I promised an armlet of copper, but I found that nearly all that were brought to me had been smashed for the purpose of extracting the brains. Out of the two hundred skulls that were produced, I was able to select no more than forty, each of which I carefully labelled for consignment to Europe. The people who brought them professed to give full particulars about them, as to where they had come from, and whether they were male or female—details which of course enhanced the value of the collection. The great majority of those which the Monbuttoo brought me had been procured from the people who inhabited the districts south of their own land, and were the result of the raids that had been made upon them; hardly any were the skulls of the Monbuttoo themselves. The condition in which I received many of the fragments afforded indubitable proof that they had been boiled in water and scraped with knives; and some, I suspect, came straight from the platters of the natives, inasmuch as they were still moist, and had the odour of being only just cooked. A good many had all the appearance of being raked out of old dust-heaps, whilst some few had been found in the streams, and had manifestly been laved by the water.

To those who brought the skulls, I thought it expedient to explain that we wanted them, so that in our far-off country we could learn all about the people who dwelt here, and that we were able, from the mere shape of the head, to tell all about people's tempers and dispositions, their good qualities and their bad; and that for this purpose we gathered skulls together from every quarter of the globe. When the Khartoomers saw that the collection was now going on for a second year, they were only the more confirmed in their belief that I submitted them to a certain process by which I obtained a subtle poison. From the more dense and stupid natives, the idea could not be eradicated that I wanted all the bones for my food.

Among those who day after day entered the camp to pay me a visit, were several who had come from a great distance, and amongst them the ambassadors of the neighbouring Niam-niam king, Kanna, whose territories lie to the west and north-west of the Monbuttoo. The district had been part of the kingdom of Keefa, a powerful prince, whose enormous stores of ivory had ever constituted a great attraction for the expeditions of the Khartoomers, though they seldom travelled as far as his dominions. Keefa, whose surname was Ntikkima, about two years before our arrival had lost his life in a campaign against the Mabode, a black negro people to the south-west of the Monbuttoo. His four eldest sons had partitioned his extensive power between them, and the largest share of land had fallen to the lot of Kanna, who now sent the deputation to invite Mohammed to visit his country. Mohammed, meanwhile, had already determined that the land of Kanna should be the limit of the southward march of a corps that he detached; but time would not permit us ourselves to make so wide a *détour*. It would occupy the space of several months.

From these Niam-niam envoys I derived several scraps of information about the western regions, which threw some light upon the lower course of the Welle, and of that other stream to the north of it, which, from the union of several streams that rise in the district of Wando, appears very soon to become a large and copious river. Between these two rivers (the Welle and the so-called Bahr-el-Wando, which joins it in Kanna's district) was situated the residence of the deceased Keefa, which, owing to its position, was described in the Arabic way as being on an island. It was represented as being to the N.N.W. of Munza's residence, from which, according to their accounts, it was distant some forty miles.

I made inquiries amongst them about the white man Piaggia, whom the Nubians had brought into the country, and who was affirmed to have visited Keefa's residence; but my respondent replied that, though they had heard of him by report, he had never been into the country; and this corresponded exactly with what had been told me by Ghattas's company that had brought Piaggia as far as Tombo.

Many as were the visitors that I received at my tent, none awakened greater interest than one of the sons of Munza. The name of this distinguished personage was Bunza, and he was about the lightest-skinned individual that I had here beheld. His complexion could not have been fairer if he had been a denizen of Central Egypt. His hair was equally pale and grizzly; his tall chignon being not unlike a bundle of hemp, and standing in marked contrast to the black tresses which were stretched across the brow. As the hair about the temples does not grow sufficiently long for this purpose, the Monbuttoo are accustomed to use false hair; and as fair heads of hair are somewhat uncommon, false hair to match the original is difficult to purchase. This young man, of whom I was successful in taking a deliberate sketch, exhibited all the characteristics of pronounced albinism, and in truth to a degree which can be often seen in a fair individual of the true Semitic stock, either Jew or Arabian.

Of the other members of the royal family, several of Munza's wives and his eldest sister came to inspect our camp. This latter woman was repulsive-looking enough, and did not appear to possess any of the warlike virtues attributed to one of her sisters named Nalengbe, who is since dead, but who had once arrayed herself in a man's dress, and entered into personal conflict with the Nubians. This weak woman's vanity made her the laughing-stock of strangers and acquaintances alike; she perambulated the camp, displaying the grossest familiarity with the soldiers. She begged me to make her a present of some lead, which the Nubians from motives of policy had withheld. Lead was still in this region as much of a rarity as though it was just discovered and produced among them for the first time. Munza's sister used to hammer bright ear-rings out of whatever musket-balls she could procure.

One morning about thirty of the royal ladies came, all together, into the camp to receive the presents which Mohammed had provided for them. They all had comely, youthful, well-knit figures, and were for the most part tall, but much cannot be said in favour of their expression. They emulated each other in the extent of their head-gear and in the profusion with which they adorned the body. Two of them submitted to have their portraits taken; the whole party sat in a circle, taking up their position during the time that I was sketching the likenesses on the little single-stemmed stools which they had brought with them; when they took their seats they threw their hands across their laps. Some of the group stood out in marked contrast to the rest by their light complexion and fair hair, whilst others approximated very nearly to the colour of *café-au-lait*. When I had finished my drawing, I was anxious to show my appreciation of the ladies' patience, and accordingly offered to present them with some beads, but they at once begged to refuse the proffered necklace, explaining that they were not at liberty to accept presents from any one but " Mbahly " (Aboo Sammat). These they had come to fetch, but they had had no orders to receive anything from " Mbarik-pah ; " it might arouse suspicion, and suspicion with Munza, the interpreters insisted, was tantamount to death.

However interested I might be, just at first, in the vivacious movements of the people as they thronged around me, it did not take long to make me feel that they were a weariness and a nuisance. On the very next day after our arrival I was obliged to encircle my tent with a thorn-hedge to keep off the press of the inquisitive crowds. Full many, however, there were who would not be deterred by any obstacle of this kind ; regardless of the obstruction, they penetrated right into my presence. It seemed as if nothing could keep the curious crowds at a distance, and, at my wits' end what to do, I applied to Mohammed for assistance. He assigned me a guard of men; but even this scheme only partially succeeded; it answered very well as long as I kept within the bounds of my asylum, but I had only to venture beyond, and I found my retinue as large as ever. The majority of those who harassed me in this way were women, who, by keeping up with me step by step, thoroughly baffled me in all my attempts to botanize ; and if perchance I managed to get away into the wood, they would find me out, and trample down the rare flowers I had laboriously collected, till I was almost driven to despair. When thus escorted by about a hundred women I was marching down to the streams in the depth of the valleys, I might indulge the fancy that I was at the head of a triumphal procession, and as often as our path led us through villages and farms the numbers in the train were swollen prodigiously.

Sometimes I was in a better mood, and indulged in a little joke. I had picked up some of their words, and when I shouted one of these out loud it was taken up merrily by the whole party, and passed on from mouth to mouth. Their word " hosanna," for instance, means " it is not," and on one occasion having happened to shout out this, I proceeded for a quarter of an hour while the women around me paused not a moment in making the air resound with the triumphal cry " Hosanna."

These Monbuttoo women, who were so intolerably obtrusive whilst I was amongst other folks, were reserved enough about themselves; however anxious I might be to investigate their domestic habits, I had but to present myself at the entrances of their huts, and off they were in an instant to the interior, and their doors barred against all intrusion.

There were delicious places where, encircled by the luxuriance of a tropical vegetation, the clear and sparkling pools invited me to the enjoyment of a safe and refreshing bath, an irresistible attraction after the numberless mud baths of the Niam-niam country. Everything seemed to conspire to render the scenery perfect in its bewitching grace; each winding of the brook would be overarched by a magnificent canopy of gorgeous foliage; the waving pendants of the blooming shrubs would shadow the secluded stream; a fantastic wreath of elegant ferns growing up amongst the goodly leaves of the aroideæ and the ginger-plants would adorn the banks; gigantic stems, clothed with accumulated moss, would rise upwards in majestic height and reach down like steps in romantic beauty to the bathing-place. But, alas! even this nook, where the delights of Paradise seem almost to be perpetuated, may not be secure from the torment of humanity. It happens here according to the teaching of the poet, that

"every prospect pleases,
And only man is vile."

Nature is only free and perfect where man comes not with his disturbing foot. In my romantic bathing, this disturbance, ever and again, would come in the shape of some hideous and inquisitive Monbuttoo woman, who had posted herself on the overlooking heights, either to enjoy the picturesque contrast of light and shade, or to gratify her curiosity by getting a peep at my figure through the openings of the foliage as I emerged from the dim obscurity of the wood.

A day seldom passed without my making some addition to my botanical store. Beside a pathway in the wood I chanced to come upon the great seeds of a legumen which hitherto was quite unknown to me; the natives, when I showed them to them, told me that the name of the plant which bore them was the "morokoh;" after a while I succeeded in getting an entire pod, and recognised it as the produce of the *Entada scandens*, known in the West Indies as the sword-bean. These seed-vessels attain a length of five feet, and are about as wide as anyone could span, the seeds themselves being flat, and having their corners rounded off, and (with the exception of the produce of some palms) are the largest that are known, their

MUNZA'S RESIDENCE.

flattened sides not unfrequently measuring three square inches. Their size gives them a great capability for resisting the influence of the sea, and they retain their germinating power for many months, so that, carried by the ocean currents, they are borne to every quarter of the globe. They have been observed in the Arctic regions and on the northern shores of Nova Zembla, and within the tropics they have found their way to both the Indies and to many islands of the Pacific. These enormous beans bear signal witness to the course of the Gulf Stream. Their proper home would seem to be the tropical regions of Africa, as their occurrence in the Monbuttoo lands, equally distant from either ocean, manifestly witnesses. Anxious to investigate where the "morokoh" could really be found, I devoted a special excursion to the search, and went out for a couple of leagues or more in a south-westerly direction from the camp. Crossing several brooks and passing through many a grove of oil-palms, we reached some farmsteads that were erected in a welcome shade. All along our steps we were followed by a group of people who continually fell out and squabbled with the Bongo and other natives belonging to our caravan, but who towards myself personally were as courteous and amiable as could be wished. It might be expected that my bean-pods, five feet long, would be found upon some enormous trees of corresponding growth, but in truth the *Entada scandens* is a weak deciduous creeper, which climbs along the underwood that abounds in the depressions of the brooks.

The twenty days of our residence in this interesting spot slipped away only too quickly. There was, however, a series of fresh surprises awaiting me. How I made acquaintance with the Pygmies is a tale that must be told in a later chapter. High festivities in the court of the king; the general summons of the population to take their share in the hunt as often as either buffaloes or elephants came within sight; the arrival of vassals conveying their tribute and making a solemn entrance with their attendant warriors—all these events succeeded each other in rapid order, and gave me ample opportunity of studying the peculiarities of the people from many different points of view.

I paid repeated visits to the king, sometimes finding him in his granaries engaged in distributing provisions to his officers, and sometimes in the inner apartments of his own special residence. One afternoon I received permission, in company with Mohammed, to inspect all the apartments of the royal castle. The master of the ceremonies and the head-cook escorted us round. Mohammed was already familiar with all the arrangements, and was consequently able to call my attention to anything worthy of particular notice. What I call "the castle" is a separate group of huts, halls, and sheds, which are enclosed by a palisade, and which may be entered only by the king and by the officers and servants of the royal household. All official business is transacted in the outer courts. Trees were planted regularly all round the enclosure, and contributed to give a comfortable and homelike aspect to the whole. Not only did the oil-palms abound, but other serviceable trees were planted round the open space, and declared the permanency of the royal residence, in contradistinction to the fluctuating and unsettled dwelling-places of the Niam-niam chieftains.

I was next brought to a circular building with an imposing conical roof, which was appropriated as the arsenal, and was full of weapons of every variety. Sword-blades and lances were especially numerous, and I was at liberty to make my selection out of them, as the king had chosen in this way to make his return for the presents he had received from me.

BREED OF CATTLE FROM THE MAOGGOO COUNTRY.

The same day I had the opportunity of seeing the splendid oxen which Munza had received from the friendly king in the south-east, and to which I have already had occasion to refer. A representation of one of these animals is now introduced, showing the great fat hump, which is larger than any that I had hitherto seen.

All attempts to elicit any information about the country to the south of their own were quite unavailing; the people were silent as the tomb. Nor did I succeed much better when I came to inquire of King Munza himself. Every inquiry on my part was baffled by the resolute secrecy of African state policy, and the difficulties of the duplicate interpretation gave Munza just the pretext he wanted for circumlocution and evasive replies.

I was most anxious to obtain correct information as to whether the great inland lake to which Piaggia had referred had any real existence in the district or not, and I satisfied myself by positive testimony that the natives had no actual knowledge about it. But it was really very difficult to convey to them any notion whatever of what was intended; there was an utter absence of any simile by which the idea of a lake, a great inland expanse of fresh water, could be illustrated, and the vocabularies of the interpreters (Arabic and Zandey), however copious they might be, were yet inadequate in this particular matter. Neither in Egypt nor in the Egyptian Soudan is there a proper term for a lake. There are indeed the terms "birket," "foola," and "tirra," but these only signify respectively a pond, a rainpool, and a marsh; and Piaggia, who, as I have pointed out, did not actually reach Keefa, spoke only from hearsay, either from the reports of the Nubians, to whom probably some vague information of Baker's discoveries had reached, or by an erroneous conception of the explanation of the natives when they described the "great water," which in reality was the river flowing past Keefa's residence.* Monbuttoo and Niam-niam alike are entirely incapable of comprehending what is meant by an ocean. Anything contrary to this statement which may have been spread

---

* When, two years after my visit to Monbuttoo-land, my unfortunate friend, the Italian traveller Miani, visited the district, he was informed by Bakangoi, a Niam-niam king to the west of Kanna, that beyond his western neighbours, the Amakara, there flowed three rivers, the largest of which was named the Birma-Makongo. A notice, found amongst his papers, also speaks of a piece of water called Ghango, which was described by the natives as a great lake, and by their accounts was situated about latitude 1° N. These statements would seem to refer to the Congo-Lualaba spoken of by the natives on the Welle, and in my opinion tend to prove the independence of the two streams.

abroad by Khartoom adventurers* I do not think I need hesitate to describe as sheer nonsense or as idle fancy. The tales of steamers and of ships with crews of white men, which are said to have been described by the natives as having come along their rivers, and the stories that pictures of these ships have been found in their dwellings, are doubtless circulated amongst travellers to the Niam-niam lands, but without any assignable grounds.

After much demurring and waiving the question, the king's interpreter did affirm that he knew of such standing water in the country: he pointed towards the direction of the W.S.W., and said its name was "Madimmo," and that it was Munza's own birth-place. The place was called "Ghilly" by the Niam-niam; but when I inquired more accurately, and began to investigate its extent, I received an answer, which set my mind entirely at rest, that it was as large as Munza's palace!

I nurtured the silent hope that by mentioning certain names that perchance might be known to the Monbuttoo, I should succeed in breaking down their reserve. I asked the king if he knew anything of the land of Ulegga and of its king Kadjoro, or whether he knew King Kamrasi, whose dominions were beyond the "great water," and behind the mountains of the Malegga; and I pointed at the same time towards the S.E. Then I mentioned Kamrahs, repeating the word and saying "Kamrahs, Kamrahs," in the way that the Nubians are accustomed to do, but both Munza and his interpreter were silent, or proceeded to speak of other matters. But while this conversation was going on, a significant look that Munza gave his interpreter did not escape my notice, and very much confirmed my suspicion that he was not altogether unacquainted with Kamrasi.

Some time afterwards, Munza, in the most off-hand way, complained that I had not given him enough copper. Knowing the general expectations of an African king, I was only surprised that he had not urged his demand before. He reminded me of the quantity of copper that Mohammed had given him: "Mohammed," he said, "is a great sultan; but you are also a great sultan." When I reminded him that I did not take any of his ivory, he seemed to acquiesce in my excuse; but he very shortly afterwards sent me some messengers to request that I would make him a present of the two dogs which I had brought with me. They were two common Bongo curs of very small growth, but by contrast

* Compare Dr. Ori's letter to the Marquis Antinori in the 'Bolletino della Soc. Geogr. Ital.,' i. p. 184.

with the meagre breed of the Monbuttoo and the Niam-niam they were attractive enough to excite the avidity of Munza. He had never seen dogs of such a size, and did not want them as dainty morsels for his table, but really wished to have them to keep. However, he had long to beg in vain; I assured him that the creatures had grown up with me till I was truly fond of them; they were, as I told him, my children; I was not disposed to part with them at any price, and might as well be asked to give the hair off my head. But my representations had no effect upon Munza; he had made up his mind to have the dogs, and did not pass a day without repeating his request, and enforcing it by sending fresh relays of presents to my tent. Nothing, however, moved me. At last some slaves, both male and female, were sent, and the sight of these suggested a new idea. I resolved to give way, and to exchange one of my dogs for a specimen of the little Akka people. Munza acceded at once, and sent me two of them. He could not suppress his little joke. "You told me," said he, "not long since, that the dogs were your children; what will you say if I call these my children?"

I accepted the smallest of the Akka, a youth who might be about fifteen years of age, hoping to be able to take him to Europe as a living evidence of a truth that lay under the myth of some thousand years. His name was Nsewue, and I received him as an adopted son. I had him well clothed, and he was waited on and treated in every respect by my attendants as though he had been my own child.

It had become high time for me to give way, and not to put the cannibal ruler's patience to too severe a test. The exchange which had been effected restored me to the royal favour, and a prohibition which had been issued to the natives, warning them not to have any transactions with me by selling me produce or curiosities, was withdrawn. I received now such quantities of ripe plantains that I was able to procure an abundance of plantain-wine, an extremely palatable and wholesome drink, which is obtained after being allowed to ferment for twenty-four hours.

During this time Mohammed had begun to find that the supply of provisions was growing inadequate, and that he would have some difficulty in meeting the necessities of his numerous bearers and of his heterogeneous caravan. He accordingly resolved to make a division of the entire company, and to send a detachment back to Izingerria beyond the Welle, where they might get corn and other supplies. In my own case, I was obliged to do without proper bread; no eleusine was to be had, and I was reduced to a flat tough cake made of manioc and plantain-meal.

As no cattle-breeding is practised among the Monbuttoo, I should have been fastened down to a uniform diet of vegetables if I had not happened to be aware that in the last raid against the Momvoo a very considerable number of goats had been driven into

GOAT OF THE MOMVOO.

the country. I induced the king to become my agent for getting me some of them, and sent him three large copper bracelets, weighing about a pound, for every goat that he would let me have. In this way I gradually obtained about a dozen fat goats, and more beautiful creatures of the kind I had never seen since I left Khartoom. They were of two different breeds: one of them was singularly like the Bongo race, which has been before described, and which is remarkable for the long hair that hangs from their neck and shoulders; the other differed from any type that I had previously seen in having an equally-distributed drooping fleece, which serves as a covering for its short-haired extremities, and in its nose being very considerably arched. The ordinary colour of these graceful animals is a uniform glossy black. They are fed almost exclusively upon plantain-leaves, a food which makes them thrive admirably. When I had got half-a-dozen of them together I had them all killed at once. I had the flesh all taken off the bones, the sinews carefully removed, and then made my bearers, who had no other work to do, mince it up very fine upon some boards. The entire mass was next thrown into great vessels and boiled; it was afterwards strained, and when it had got cold it was freed from all fat and finally steamed until it was a thick jelly. The extract of meat obtained in this way had to serve throughout our return journey, and in the sequel proved a very remunerative product. It was not liable to decomposition, and its keeping so well made it an excellent resource in time of want, and postponed the evil day of our actual suffering from hunger.

Besides the company of Mohammed Aboo Sammat, there were two other companies that for some years had been accustomed to carry their expeditions into the Monbuttoo country, namely, Agahd's and that of the Poncets, which was afterwards transferred to Ghattas. It was a matter of arrangement that these should confine their operations to the eastern districts, where Degberra was king. At their departure they always left a small detachment in charge to look after their business interests and to prevent any competition. Agahd's and Poncet's soldiers had been left in the garrisons in the districts that were under the control of Degberra's generals, Kubby and Benda, and they were only too glad to embrace the present chance (as we were only distant a two days' journey) of coming to see their friends and acquaintance from Khartoom and to hear the news.

To all appearance the Monbuttoo air agreed excellently with them all, which is more than can be said of those who reside in some of the northern Seribas. They had wives and families in the country, and made no other complaint than that their life was somewhat lonely and monotonous and their food so different to what they had been accustomed to; but what the fanatical Mohammedans had most readily to avow was that they really held the natives in admiration and respect, notwithstanding their intense detestation of the cannibalism which was attributed to them. Mohammed also left some of his people in the neighbourhood of Munza; and these strangers had permission to erect Seribas and to plant their environs with sweet potatoes, manioc, and plantains. Their prerogative extended no further than this, and they had no authority at all over the natives; however small might be their number in any place (sometimes not a score of men altogether) they were sure to be sufficient to restrain the inhabitants from any attempt at surprise. The African savages are not like the American Indians, who are always prepared to see a few of their party killed at the outset, provided that they can only make sure of ultimate success and can get their plunder at last; not that the Africans underrate the advantage they possess in the superiority of their numbers, nor that they entertain too high an estimate of the bravery of the Nubians, but they are conscious that no attack could be ventured without one or two of them having to pay the penalty of their lives. No one is ready for his own part to run the risk of his own being the life that must be sacrificed; and thus it happens that the prospect of a few deaths is sufficient to deter them, though they might be reckoned by thousands, from making that outbreak which their numerical strength might guarantee would be finally successful.

As soon as Mohammed became aware that he had got to the end of the king's store of ivory he began to think of his ways and means, and contemplated pushing on farther to the south and opening a new market for himself. With the greatest enthusiasm I entered into his design, and taking up his cry, "To the world's end!" I added, "Now's the time, and onward let us go!" But, unfortunately, there were insuperable obstacles in the way. In the first place, there was the decided opposition of the king, who entertained the very natural belief that the farther progress of the Khartoomers to the south would interfere with his monopoly of the copper trade; and in the next place there was the impossibility of Mohammed being able, without Munza's co-operation, to procure sufficient provisions for so arduous an undertaking. To put the former difficulty to the test, Mohammed despatched his nephew with the conduct of an expedition just sufficiently large to venture the attempt. For three days this expedition pressed on, until upon the river Nomayo, an affluent of the Welle, they reached the residence of one of Munza's sub-chieftains, whose name was Mummery. Half-way upon their route they had rested at the dwelling-place of another chieftain, named Nooma. Both Mummery and Nooma, it should be said, were Munza's own brothers; but neither of them would venture to open commercial transactions of any kind without the express orders of the king, and consequently the expedition had to return at once and leave its object unaccomplished.

The disappointment was very keen: it was a bitter grief to see one's most cherished projects melt thus thoroughly away. Nor was it a much smaller matter of regret that Mohammed felt himself obliged to curtail even our few weeks' residence with Munza; he might propose, indeed, to advance to the south from the eastern portion of the Monbuttoo country, but that was a project that was little likely to be accomplished.

For a long period I held fast to my intention of remaining behind alone in Munza's country with the soldiers who would be left in charge of the Seriba; and I indulged the fascinating hope that I should find an opportunity of penetrating into that farther south which I longed so earnestly to investigate; but my protector would not acquiesce in this for a moment, nor did any of my own people show an inclination to support my wishes. It was very doubtful if we could be relieved during the next year, or the year after, if at all; my resources even now were hardly enough to take me home again; the wherewithal for further enterprise was altogether wanting; if I should entrust my collection, which I had so laboriously gathered, to the care of others, there was every risk of its becoming wet and even spoiled; the prospect, too, of penetrating into the interior under the escort of the Monbuttoo themselves was not altogether inviting: I should only have accompanied their plundering raids, where I should have been compelled to be a daily witness of their cruelties and cannibalism; thus upon serious deliberation I was driven to the conviction that my scheme was not feasible.

No doubt a very different vista would have opened itself before me into the untraversed interior of the continent if I had chanced to be one of those favoured travellers who have unlimited command of gold. But fortune and money appear, with regard to African travel, to stand very much in the same relation to one another as force and time in physics; what you gain in one, you lose in the other. The fortunate and healthy travellers, like Karl Mauch and Gerhard Rohlfs, have generally been very limited in their means; whilst rich travellers, such as the Baron von der Decken and Miss Tinné, have succumbed to difficulties, sickened, or died. Any expedition that was fitted out with a liberality proportioned to that of Speke's would have been capable of advancing from Munza's to the south, defiant of opposition; enough copper would have neutralised the resistance of the king: if force could be opposed by force, and threats could be met by threats, the native princes would all declare themselves to be friends, and, like Mtesa and Kamrasi, would meet them with open arms. But, as I say, the resources must be adequate. With two hundred soldiers from Khartoom, not liable to fever, and capable of existing upon food of any sort, and who were up to all the dodges and chicaneries of the African chieftains, any one could penetrate as far as he chose. If I had possessed 10,000 dollars in my purse, or had them invested properly in Khartoom, I would have guaranteed to bring my leader on to Bornoo. The sum would have sufficed to keep his soldiers up to their duty; and under those circumstances I should have been master of the situation, and Mohammed would have had means to get as much ivory as he could desire.

These intimations may suffice to show that, in my opinion, with the aid of the Khartoom merchant companies, access could be had to the remotest parts of the continent without any exorbitant outlay of money; but conditions so favourable for prosecuting the work as those which then fell to my lot, I fear may be long before they occur again.

Munza's visits made a diversion in our camp life. The finest entertainment, however, which chanced to occur was the celebration of the victory which Mummery had obtained over the Momvoo. As the produce of his successful raid, Mummery brought the due contributions of ivory, slaves, and goats, to lay before the feet of the king, and the occasion was taken to institute a festival on the grandest scale. In consequence of Munza's establishment being already taxed with the entertainment of so many strangers, Mummery only stayed for a single night. The morning after his arrival was appointed for the feast.

The early part of the day was cold and rainy; but quite betimes, the shouts and cheers that rang around the camp told us that the rejoicing had already begun. Towards mid-day the news was brought that the excitement was reaching its climax, and that the king himself was dancing in the presence of his numerous wives and courtiers. The weather was still chill and drizzly; but, putting on a long black frock-coat as being the most appropriate costume for the occasion, I bent my steps to the noble saloon, which resounded again with the ringing echoes of uproarious cheers and

KING M'UNZA DANCING BEFORE HIS WIVES.

clanging music. The scene that awaited me was unique. Within the hall there was a spacious square left free, around which the eighty royal wives were seated in a single row upon their little stools, having painted themselves in honour of the occasion with the most elaborate care; they were applauding most vigorously, clapping their hands with all their might. Behind the women stood an array of warriors in full accoutrement, and their lines of lances were a frontier of defence. Every musical accompaniment to which the resources of the court could reach had all been summoned, and there was a *mêlée* of gongs and kettle-drums, timbrels and trumpets, horns and bells. Dancing there in the midst of all, a wondrous sight, was the king himself.

Munza was as conspicuous in his vesture as he was astounding in his movements. It is ever the delight of African potentates on occasions of unusual pomp to present themselves to their subjects in some new aspect. Munza's opportunities in this way were almost unlimited, as he had a house full of skins and feathers of every variety: he had now attired his head in the skin of a great black baboon, giving him the appearance of wearing a grenadier's bearskin; the peak of this was dressed with a plume of waving feathers. Hanging from his arms were the tails of genets, and his wrists were encircled by great bundles of tails of the guinea-hog. A thick apron, composed of the tails of a variety of animals was fastened round his loins, and a number of rings rattled upon his naked legs. But the wonder of the king's dress was as nothing compared to his action. His dancing was furious. His arms dashed themselves furiously in every direction, though always marking the time of the music; whilst his legs exhibited all the contortions of an acrobat's, being at one moment stretched out horizontally to the ground, and at the next pointed upwards and elevated in the air. The music ran on in a wild and monotonous strain, and the

women raised their hands and clapped together their open palms to mark the time. For what length of time this dance had been going on I did not quite understand; I only know that I found Munza raving in the hall with a mad excitement worthy of the most infatuated dervish that had ever been seen in Cairo. Moment after moment it looked as if the enthusiast must stagger, and, foaming at the mouth, fall down in a fit of epilepsy; but nervous energy seems greater in Central Africa than among the "hashishit" of the north: a slight pause at the end of half an hour, and all the strength revived; once again would commence the dance, and continue unslackened and unwearied.

So thoroughly were the multitude engrossed with the spectacle, that hardly any attention at all was given to my arrival, and a few who noticed it did not permit themselves to be diverted from the enjoyment of their pleasure. I had an opportunity, therefore, of transferring the scene to paper, and of finishing a sketch which embraces its prominent features.

But above the tumult of men was heard the tumult of the elements. A hurricane arose, with all the alarming violence of tropical intensity. For a little while the assembly was unmoved and disposed to take no notice of the storm; but soon the wind and pelting rain found their way into the openings of the hall; the music ceased, the rolling drum yielding to the thunder; the audience in commotion rose, and sought retreat; and in another instant the spectacle was over; the dancing king was gone.

The floods of rain compelled me to remain upon the spot, and I took advantage of the opportunity to make an undisturbed inspection of the other and larger hall, which was situated just opposite to the one in which I was. A low doorway led into the edifice, which was 150 feet long and not less than fifty feet high. It was lighted only by narrow apertures, and the roof was supported on five rows of columns. On one side of it was a wooden partition which divided from the spacious edifice a small apartment, where the king was accustomed, according to the imperial wont of altering the sleeping-place, occasionally to pass the night. An enormous erection, ponderous enough to support an elephant, served as a bedstead; on each side of this were several posts, each encircled by forged iron rings that could not weigh less than half a hundredweight. In this royal bedchamber I noticed a large number of barbarous decorations, and I observed that the pillars and the timberwork were rudely painted with numerous geometrical designs, but that the artists seem to have had only three colours at their command; blood-red, yellow-ochre, and the white from dogs' dung (*album græcum*).

During the earlier hours of the morning and the later hours of the afternoon, I spent the time, day after day, in continual excursions, which enabled me to add to the novelties of my collection. The middle of the day I devoted to the necessary supervision of my household. The periodic washing-day had come, and I was at a loss to find a washing-tub that could contain the accumulated linen. Mohammed's ingenuity came once more to my aid. He borrowed King Munza's largest meat-dish for my use. A lordly dish it was; more like a truck than an article for the table. It was five feet long, and hewn from a single block.

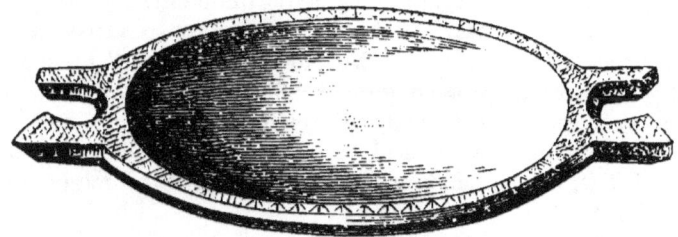

KING MUNZA'S DISH.

Munza twice honoured our camp with a visit. His majesty's approach was announced long beforehand by the outcries of the teeming people that thronged along his way. On entering the encampment he found the German flag waving from a tall flagstaff that I had erected in the immediate proximity of my tent; he was curious to know what it meant, and had to be initiated into the object of a national symbol, and to be informed of the tragical experiences of King Theodore in Abyssinia. It was a great relief to me that he did not require to enter either into my tent or into a large grass-shed which had been recently erected for me. Altogether the monarch displayed much less covetousness than I had reason to expect. Recognising this moderation on his part, I endeavoured to entertain him by showing him my collection of pictures, and amongst others I submitted to him the one of himself in the copper habiliments which he had worn on the day of our first audience. They were the only portraits he had ever seen, and his astonishment was very great; the play of the muscles of his face displayed the interest he took, and, according to the custom of the land, he opened his mouth quite wide, and covered it with his open hand, betraying thereby his surprise and admiration. I had afterwards to open my bosom for his inspection, and when I turned up my shirt-sleeves, he could not suppress a cry of amazement. The interview ended, as such visits generally did, by his expressing a wish, with which I had not the least intention to comply, that I would take off my boots.

The date of our departure was now drawing near, and yet neither my promised chimpanzee nor guinea-hog* had appeared. About the chimpanzee the truth was that not one could be found in the district, which was far too densely populated, the woods upon the river-banks being very light and traversed by frequent pathways. But with regard to the guinea-hog it was quite different: they were to be found in the nearest environs of the royal residence, and, if only Munza had been inclined, he could have redeemed his promise and secured me a specimen without difficulty. He left me, consequently, to get one, if I could, for myself; but this, to a novice in the chase, was more easily said than done, and I had to ramble in the thickets, rifle in hand, under the vain hope that I might secure a specimen.

Only once, and that was just when evening was coming on to close a cloudy day, and a drizzling mist was giving obscurity to the woods, I caught sight of one of these animals. Its red bristly head and long pointed ears peered out from behind the prostrate stem of a great tree, and I was just concluding that it was within gunshot, when at the very instant two of my native attendants were seen beside it rolling on the ground and bleeding at the nose. My people were not remarkable for pluck, and nothing would induce them to a second venture with the beast. Thus I was compelled to renounce my hope of getting a guinea-hog.

* The Guinea-hog (*Potamochœrus penicillatus*) is called "Napezzo," or "fat," by the Monbuttoo, and its flesh is considered very choice. These animals, which are not nearly so wild as the wart-hogs (the blabark of the South African Boërs), and are indeed capable of being partially tamed, are found throughout the tropical regions of Africa, from the west coast to Zanzibar. Burton met with them in Ugogo. In early times they were already introduced into Brazil.

CHAPTER X.

THE MONBUTTOO—Previous accounts of the people—Population—Surrounding nations—Aspect of country—Neglect of agriculture—Products of the soil—Produce of the chase—Forms of salutation—Preparation of food—Prevalence of cannibalism—Warlike spirit—The state officers—The royal household—The palace—Advanced culture of the people—Prevalence of light hair—Analogy with the Fulbe—Preparation of bark—Costume of the men—Nudity of the women—Tattooing and painting—Coiffure—Piercing the ears—Weapons—Iron-smelting—Early knowledge of copper—Excellence of tools—Wood-carving—Benches and stools—Shields—Pottery—Architecture—Ornamental trees—Conception of a Supreme Being.

It was in December 1868, just before starting from Khartoom, that I received, in a somewhat circuitous way, the first intelligence of a people called the Monbuttoo, who were said to dwell to the south of the Niam-niam. Dr. Ori, the chief official physician at Khartoom, in a letter to the Marquis Antinori, had detailed all the most recent particulars of the ivory traffic in the remote districts south of the Gazelle, and had specially referred to the transactions of Jules Poncet. These particulars were published without much delay in the journal of the Geographical Association of Paris; and I chanced to find Dr. Ori's letter quoted entire in the Italian Geographical Society's 'Bolletino,' which was transmitted to me by the Marquis Antinori himself just before I was setting out on my expedition.

Although the intelligence conveyed by Ori and Poncet failed utterly in giving either clearness or consistency to the confused depositions of those ignorant and uninformed men who had been their authorities, it still had the intrinsic merit of enlarging the domain of geographical knowledge by some matters of fact which it was reserved for me individually to confirm by my own observation. It laid down as facts, first, that to the south of the Niam-niam territory there is a river flowing towards the west;* secondly, that

* Heuglin, in 1863, had received intelligence of what was now proved, viz., that the same district from which issues the White Nile also gives birth to another stream.

this river is not tributary to the Nile; and, thirdly, that its banks are populated by a race quite distinct from the ordinary negro race, its inhabitants being of a brownish complexion, and exhibiting a grade of civilization which is considerably in advance of what is elsewhere found in Central Africa.

These people were designated by the name of the Monbuttoo, and by the ivory-traders they were known as Gurrugurroo, a definition that is derived from an Arabic word which refers to their universal habit of piercing their ears.

No sooner had I really reached the district of the Gazelle than I discovered, from my conversation and intercourse with the leaders of the ivory traffic, that the Monbuttoo were regarded as holding a very peculiar and prominent place. Their country never failed to furnish a theme of general praise. It was declared to be prolific in ivory; it was profuse in its natural products; the pomp of its sovereign was unrivalled; but, above all, the skill of its people, in the fabrication alike of their weapons for war and their utensils for peace, was assumed to be so striking that they were comparable to the denizens of the civilized west, and that in some respects the Franks themselves did not surpass them in the exercise of an æsthetic faculty.

That I might succeed in making my way onwards to the territory of this problematical people, naturally became more and more my impatient and ardent desire; and it will readily be understood how eagerly I recognised Aboo Sammat as offered by a propitious fate to be the conductor upon whom I might rely for being introduced to a closer view of this undefined race, which might be likened in a way to a nebula in the geographical firmament. Very much I now rejoice at being in a position to submit, upon the evidence of my own observation, a somewhat detailed account of this race, who may be described as constituting a sort of remote island of humanity. Surrounded as it is by the waves of fluctuating nationalities, it is, as it were, an "*ultima Thule*" of geographical research; or perhaps still more appropriately it might be likened to a boulder thrown up from a lower formation, and exhibiting a development of indigenous culture, entirely different to what can be witnessed all around.

The territory of the Monbuttoo, as it lies in the heart of Africa, does not cover an area of more than 4000 square miles, but the ratio of the census of its population is hardly exceeded by any region of the entire continent. Estimating the density of the people by the districts through which we travelled, and observing that cultivated farms followed upon cultivated farms, without a barren spot between, I suppose that there are at least 250 inhabitants to the square mile, which would give an aggregate population of about a million. The position of the country is embraced very nearly between the parallels of 3° and 4° N. latitude, and 28° and 29° E. longitude from Greenwich. To the north of the country there is a large river, usually copious in its stream, called the Keebaly. This is joined by the Gadda, which flows from the south-east. After the junction it is known as the Welle, and has a breadth of about 800 feet, whilst never, even in the driest season, does its depth diminish to less than fifteen feet. It proceeds to the west along the southern portion of the adjoining Niam-niam district, and being swollen by the accession of numerous tributaries from the southern districts of the Monbuttoo, it very rapidly assumes its large dimensions. Beyond a doubt it is the upper course of the most easterly of the two arms which, after they have united in Baghirmy, flow onwards under the name of the Shary, that river to which Lake Tsad owes its existence.

There are two chieftains who, with regard to the extent of their dominions and the numerical strength of their armed forces (for their sway extends far beyond the populous districts of the Monbuttoo), may well be designated as kings. They have partitioned the sovereignty between them : the eastern division being subject to Degberra, the western division is governed by Munza,* who exercises a much more powerful control; he is a son of King Tikkiboh, who had once enjoyed the undivided rule over the entire Monbuttoo land, but thirteen years previously had been murdered by his brother Degberra.

Sub-chieftains or viceroys are distributed over various sections of the country, and these are accustomed to surround themselves with a retinue and state little inferior to those of the kings themselves. In Munza's realms there are three of these dignitaries; viz., his brothers Izingerria, Mummery, and Nooma ; subordinate to Degberra there are his four sons, Kubby, Benda, Koopa, and Yangara.

The country of the Niam-niam constitutes the northern and north-western boundaries of the Monbuttoo. This comprises the territories of Kanna and Indimma, sons of the once powerful Keefa, and, farther on, the district of Malingde or Marindo, which approaches

---

* Munza concluded the year 1870 with a conflict with Ghattas's company, which had entered his country. I have not received any detailed account of the occurrence.

in an easterly direction more towards the territory of Wando ; each of these countries is, however, separated by wildernesses which it requires two days to cross. On the west is the territory of the Niam-niam chief, Mandshy, of whom a sub-chieftain, named Manshyah was visited by Miani in 1872. According to that traveller's computation, his territory was only about four leagues to the west of Munza's. The southern limits of the Monbuttoo are enclosed, as it were, by a semicircle of typical negroes, whom they embrace in the comprehensive definition of " Momvoo," a disdainful epithet implying the extremity of their degradation. From this category we are possibly called upon to exclude in this quarter (as perchance in every other region of Africa) those isolated races of dwarfs, familiarly known as " Pygmies," of which the Akka, who reside in the S.S.W., and have their abodes close to the confines of the kingdom of Munza, may be quoted as examples. According to the depositions of some Nubians who have been stationed for some years past in the Monbuttoo country, the language of the Babuckur is spoken among the Momvoo. To support their opinion the Nubians affirm that women-slaves brought from Babuckur have always been found able to converse with the natives of the land just to the south of the Monbuttoo; a circumstance which is not without its signification as explaining the most recent migration of nations into this part of Africa. Since the two *enclaves* of Babuckur on the eastern boundaries of the Niam-niam appear only to be removed from each other by an interval of sixty miles, and to be hemmed in by hostile neighbours, the fact, taken in connection with the above, may serve to demonstrate that Monbuttoo and Niam-niam alike must have been advancing in an easterly direction.

Munza's neighbours towards the south-west and south of the kingdom of Kanna are the Mabohde. This is a people whom Keefa, Kanna's father (known also as Ntikkima), was accustomed to harass in war till he met with his own death. Farther on towards the S.S.W., and separated from Munza by the Mabohde and the Akka, there lies the district of the Massanza, a tribe which is held in subjection by the formidable hand of Kizzo. To the south and south-east are found the Nemeigeh, the Bissangah, and the Domondoo, tenanting a mountainous region, which not improbably is the western declivity of that important mountainous formation to which Baker, in describing the north-west of Lake Mwootan, has referred under the name of the Blue Mountains. The settlements of the Domondoo are the usual limits to which the Monbuttoo are accustomed to carry their plundering expeditions. Some Nubian soldiers who had been quartered in the country of Munza, and who had accompanied him in some of his marauding exploits have given a description of the general mountainous character of the land, and, moreover, have asserted that goats, which are known neither to the Niam-niam nor to the Monbuttoo, have been captured there in great numbers. The Babuckur also, notwithstanding the frequent incursions which their neighbours, ever greedy of animal diet, have made upon their over-populated and oppressed communities, are always found in possession of herds of goats so numerous that they might be described as inexhaustible. Many days' journey to the south and south-east of Munza's realms are the abodes of the Maoggoo, over whom a powerful sovereign exercises his authority, and who seems to have various transactions with Munza, if I may judge from the splendid cattle which had been sent him as a present. Maoggoo is not improbably the same as Malegga, the appellation of a people, which appears in Paker's map to the west of the Blue Mountains in an extensive country (Ulegga), of which it is affirmed that the king is named Kadjoro, and that the population is especially devoted to the breeding of cattle.

Having thus minutely taken a survey of the surroundings of the Monbuttoo, we may in the next place proceed to observe the land itself, regarding it as the substance of the picture of which we have been thus accurately surveying the background.

The Monbuttoo land greets us as an Eden upon earth. Unnumbered groves of plantains bedeck the gently-heaving soil; oil-palms, imcomparable in beauty, and other monarchs of the stately woods, rise up and spread their glory over the favoured scene; along the streams there is a bright expanse of charming verdure, whilst a grateful shadow ever overhangs the domes of the idyllic huts. The general altitude of the soil ranges from 2500 to 2800 feet above the level of the sea: it consists of alternate depressions, along which the rivulets make their way, and gentle elevations, which gradually rise till they are some hundred feet above the beds of the streams below. Upon the whole the soil may be described as far more diversified in character than what is observed in the eastern parts of the Niam-niam land. Like that, it is rich in springs, wherever there are depressions; it has a network of "desaguaderos" associated with the watercourses, and justifies the comparison that has already been suggested between the entire land and a well-soaked sponge, which yields countless streams to the pressure of the hand. Belonging to one of the most recent formations, and still in process of construction, the ferruginous swamp-ore is found very widely diffused over the Monbuttoo country, and indeed extends considerably farther to the south, so that the red earth appears to be nearly universal over the greater part of the highlands of Central Africa. The denser population has involved, as might be expected, more frequent clearances for the sake of establishing plantain-groves, and promoting the culture of maize and sugar-canes, but even here in the deeper valleys trees grow to such a prodigious height, and exhibit such an enormous girth, that they could not be surpassed by any that could be found throughout the entire Nile region of the north. Beneath the imposing shelter of these giants other forms grow up and, rising one above another, stand in mingled confusion. In its external and general aspect the country corresponds with the description which Speke has given of Uganda; but the customs of the inhabitants of that land, their difference of race, and their seclusion from all intercourse with commercial nations stamp them as being of a type which is of a very contrasted character.

It seems almost to involve a contradiction to give the title of agriculturists to a people whose existence indeed depends upon the easy securing of fruits and tubers, but who abhor the trouble of growing cereals. Sorghum and penicillaria, which are the common food of the population in nearly the whole of Central Africa, are absolutely uncared for amongst the Monbuttoo; eleusine is only grown occasionally, and maize, which is known as "Nendoh," is cultivated quite as an exception in the immediate proximity of their dwellings, where it is treated as a garden vegetable. The growth of their plantain (*Musa sapientium*) gives them very little trouble; the young shoots are stuck in the ground after it has been slackened by the rain; the old plants are suffered to die down just as they are; and this is all the cultivation that is vouchsafed. They are not accustomed to bestow any greater amount of attention to the planting either of the tubers of their manioc (or cassava), their sweet potatoes, their yams (neggoo), or their colocasiæ. A very limited range of plants embraces the whole of what they take the pains to cultivate, and that cultivation is all accomplished in the narrowest bounds. The entire produce is summed up in their sesame (mbellemoh), their earth-nuts, their sugar-canes, and especially their tobacco. The Virginian tobacco is the only kind which is seen; it is called Eh Tobboo, its name betraying its

American origin. The *Nicotiana rustica*, which is of such constant growth amongst the Bongo, Dyoor, and Dinka, is here entirely unknown.

Very little care, moreover, is given to the sugar-cane, which may be found amid the thinned woods that line the banks of the rivers. It is grown only as a sort of delicacy, being found nowhere in any great quantity, and its quality is far from good. One ever-thriving supply, which is of the utmost importance for maintaining the population, is provided in all the valleys by the cassava (*Manihot utilissima*); but the cultivation of the sweet potato, equally extensive as it is, demands a somewhat more careful attention, requiring the sunny soil of the upper slopes of the valleys above the line of the plantain-groves and nearest to the edge of the depressions. Both sweet potatoes and cassava here attain the very fullest standard of perfection, as far as regards either size or quality. But the staple food is the plantain. This is generally gathered in a green condition, dried, ground into meal, and boiled to a pulp; occasionally, but not so often, it is dried after it is ripe for the purpose of being kept for a longer time. The fruit when dried is a very choice delicacy, but any fermented drink made from plantains I found to be almost unknown among the Monbuttoo.

On the south of the Welle there is a very extensive cultivation of the oil-palm (*Elais guineensis*). It is a tree that, although common to the west coasts, has not hitherto been found in the Nile districts, and consequently, like the cola-nuts, which the wealthier of the Monbuttoo are accustomed to chew, it yields a significant evidence of the western associations of the people.

Every kind of cattle-breeding is quite unfamiliar to them; and if the common little dogs known as the "nessy" of the Niam-niam breed be excepted, and no account be taken of their poultry ("naahle"), the Monbuttoo may be said to be absolutely without domestic animals at all. In a half tame state they keep, as I have said, the potamochœrus, which is their only representative of the swine family. From the marauding excursions with which they harass their southern neighbours they bring back a prodigious number of goats, but they make no attempt to rear them for themselves. Their hunting expeditions supply them with meat enough for their requirements, their taste leading them to give the preference to the flesh of elephants, buffaloes, wild boars, and the larger kinds of antelopes. Although the denseness of the population precludes any such increase of game of this kind as is universal in the more northern and less cultivated regions of Central Africa, yet the yield of their chase would be adequate for their own wants, because the abundance of their supply at certain seasons is very great, and they have the art of preserving it so that it remains fit for food for a very considerable time. With this fact capable of being substantiated, it is altogether a fallacy to pretend to represent that the Monbuttoo are driven to cannibalism through the lack of ordinary meat. To judge from Munza's accumulated store of ivory, which is the result of the combined exploits of all the men in his dominions capable of bearing arms, the provision of elephant-meat alone must be sufficient to keep his people amply supplied. Nor should the immense quantity of poultry be forgotten, as there is hardly a dwelling that is not conspicuous for having a considerable stock.

A bird very common in the Monbuttoo lands is the grey parrot (*Psittacus erythacus*), which is very eagerly sought by the natives, who not only adorn their heads with the bright red feathers from its tail, but have a great relish for its savoury flesh. Other sport in the way of birds is very inconsiderable, guinea-fowls, francolins, and bustards being all caught by means of snares. The herb *Tephrosia Vogelii** is cultivated in nearly all the villages for the purpose of poisoning fish, and the fish that is thus secured forms a very considerable addition to the supply of food.

Whilst the women attend to the tillage of the soil and the gathering of the harvest, the men, unless they are absent either for war or hunting, spend the entire day in idleness. In the early hours of the morning they may be found under the shade of the oil-palms, lounging at full length upon their carved benches and smoking tobacco. During the middle of the day they gossip with their friends in the cool halls, which serve for general concourse, where they may be seen gesticulating vigorously to give full force to their sentiments. The action of the Monbuttoo in speaking exhibits several singularities, as, for example, their manner of expressing astonishment by putting their hand before their open mouth, very much in the same way as a person does when he is gaping. It has been said that the North American Indians have the habit of showing their surprise in the same way.

Smiths' work, of course, is done by the men, but, just as in most other parts of Africa, the pottery is exclusively made by the

---

* A kindred plant of this genus is used in the West Indies, where the practice is generally carried on by slaves.

women. Wood-carving and basket-weaving are performed indifferently by either sex. Musical instruments are not touched by the women.

The universal form of salutation consists in joining the right hands, and saying, "Gassiggy," at the same time cracking the joints of the middle fingers.

The two sexes conduct themselves towards each other with an excessive freedom. The women in this respect are very different to the modest and retiring women of the Niam-niam, and are beyond measure obtrusive and familiar. Towards their husbands they exhibit the highest degree of independence. The position in the household occupied by the men was illustrated by the reply which would be made if they were solicited to sell anything as a curiosity, "Oh, ask my wife: it is hers."

Polygamy is unlimited. The daily witness of the Nubians only too plainly testified that fidelity to the obligations of marriage was little known. Not a few of the women were openly obscene. Their general demeanour surprised me very much when I considered the comparative advance of their race in the arts of civilisation. Their immodesty far surpassed anything that I had observed in the very lowest of the negro tribes, and contrasted most unfavourably with the sobriety of the Bongo women, who are submissive to their husbands and yet not servile.

Carved benches are the ordinary seats of the men, but the women generally use stools that have but one foot. On the occasion of paying a visit or going to a public gathering the men make their slaves carry their benches for them, as it is their custom never to sit upon the ground, not even when it has been covered with mats.

The care that is given to the preparation of their food is very considerable, and betokens their higher grade of culture. The unripe produce of the plantain and the manioc, that in all districts is ready at their hand without the trouble of cultivation, make good the deficiency of corn. Their mode of treating manioc is precisely the same as that which is adopted in South America for the purpose of extracting the fine flour called tapioca. For spices they make use of the capsicum, the malaghetta pepper, and the fruit of two hitherto unspecified Solaneæ, and for which I regret that I cannot select the name of *S. anthropophagorum*, because it has been already assigned to the "cannibal salad" of the Fiji Islanders. The flavour of both these is very revolting, having a detestable twang, something between a tomato and melongena. Mushrooms are also in common use for the preparation of their sauces.

All their food is prepared by the admixture of oil from the oil-palms. In its unpurified condition, when first expressed from the pods, this oil is of a bright red colour, and of a somewhat thick consistency; for a few days it has an agreeable taste, which, however, soon passes off and leaves a decided rankness. By subsequently submitting the kernels to fire, a coarse, inflammable oil is obtained, which is used for the purpose of lighting their huts. Other vegetable oils in considerable abundance are obtained from earth-nuts, from sesame, and from the fruit of a forest-tree, *Lophira alata*. From the fat thick bodies of the male white ants they boil out a greasy substance which is bright and transparent, and has a taste perfectly unobjectionable.

But of most universal employment amongst them is human fat, and this brings our observations to the climax of their culinary practices. The cannibalism of the Monbuttoo is the most pronounced of all the known nations of Africa. Surrounded as they are by a number of people who are blacker than themselves, and who, being inferior to them in culture, are consequently held in great contempt, they have just the opportunity which they want for carrying on expeditions of war or plunder, which result in the acquisition of a booty, which is especially coveted by them, consisting of human flesh. The carcasses of all who fall in battle are distributed upon the battle-field, and are prepared by drying for transport to the homes of the conquerors. They drive their prisoners before them without remorse, as butchers would drive sheep to the shambles, and these are only reserved to fall victims on a later day to their horrible and sickening greediness. During our residence at the court of Munza the general rumour was quite current that nearly every day some little child was sacrificed to supply his meal. It would hardly be expected that many opportunities should be afforded to strangers of witnessing the natives at their repast, and to myself there occurred only two instances when I came upon any of them whilst they were actually engaged in preparing human flesh for consumption. The first of these happened by my coming unexpectedly upon a number of young women who had a supply of boiling water upon the clay floor in front of the doorway of a hut, and were engaged in the task of scalding the hair off the lower half of a human body. The operation, as far as it was effected, had changed the black skin into a fawny grey, and the disgusting sight could not fail to make me think of the soddening and scouring of our fatted swine. On another occasion I was in a hut and observed a human arm hanging over the fire, obviously with the design of being at once dried and smoked.

Incontrovertible tokens and indirect evidences of the prevalence of cannibalism were constantly turning up at every step we took. On one one occasion Mohammed and myself were in Munza's company, and Mohammed designedly turned the conversation to the topic of human flesh, and put the direct question to the king how it happened that just at this precise time while we were in the country there was no consumption of human food. Munza expressly said that being aware that such a practice was held in aversion by us, he had taken care that it should only be carried on in secret.

As I have said, there was no opportunity for strangers to observe the habits of the Monbuttoo at their meals; the Bongo and Mittoo of our caravan were carefully excluded by them as being uncircumcised, and therefore reckoned as "savages;" whilst the religious scruples of the Nubians prevented them from partaking of any food in common with cannibals. Nevertheless the instances that I have mentioned are in themselves sufficient to show that the Monbuttoo are far more addicted to cannibalism than their hunting neighbours, the Niam-niam. They do not constitute the only example of anthropophagi who are in a far higher grade of culture than many savages who persistently repudiate the enjoyment of human flesh (for example, the Fiji Islanders and the Caraïbs). It is needless for me to recount the personal experiences of the Nubian mercenaries who have accompanied the Monbuttoo on their marauding expeditions, or to describe how these people obtain their human fat, or again to detail the processes of cutting the flesh into long strips and drying it over the fire in its preparation for consumption. The numerous skulls now in the Anatomical Museum in Berlin are simply the remains of their repasts which I purchased one after another for bits of copper, and go far to prove that the cannibalism of the Monbuttoo is unsurpassed by any nation in the world. But with it all, the Monbuttoo are a noble race of men; men who display a certain national pride, and are endowed with an intellect and judgment such as few natives of the African wilderness can boast; men to whom one may put a reasonable question, and who will return a reasonable answer. The Nubians can never say enough in praise of their faithfulness in friendly intercourse and of the order and stability of their national life. According to the Nubians, too, the Monbuttoo were their superiors in the arts of war, and I often heard the resident soldiers contending with their companions and saying, " Well, perhaps you are not afraid of the Monbuttoo, but I confess that I am; and I can tell you they are something to be afraid of."

As matter of fact the Khartoom traders, some years before, had had a definite trial of arms with the Monbuttoo. Shortly after his accession to power, Munza had of his own accord and by a special embassy invited Aboo Sammat to extend his transactions beyond their present limits in Nganye's and Wando's territories; but in the year previous to that, the Nubian merchant Abderahman Aboo Guroon, having endeavoured to penetrate from Keefa's dominions into the Monbuttoo lands, was attacked on the north of the Welle by the Monbuttoo forces, who opposed his advances upon their territory. At that time Munza's father, Tikkiboh, had absolute rule in the country, and the achievements of his daughter Nalengbe, a sister of the present king, are still fresh in the memory of all who were present at the engagement; eye-witnesses gave me detailed accounts of the exploits of this veritable Amazon, whom I have mentioned before, and related how, in full armour, with shield and lance, and girded with the rokko apron of a man, she had with the utmost bravery led on the Monbuttoo troops, who then for the first time came in contact with firearms; and how her exertions were attended with a complete success, the adventurous Aboo Guroon being repulsed with considerable loss, and forced to relinquish altogether his design of entering the country. In the following year, 1867, Mohammed Aboo Sammat, invited as I have said by the king himself, crossed the Welle and entered the land, thus, as the first explorer, opening the ivory traffic under conditions of peace, which have ever since remained undisturbed.

The Monbuttoo potentates enjoy far higher prerogatives than the Niam-niam princes. Besides the monopoly of the ivory, they claim regular contributions from the products of the soil. In addition to his special body-guard, the sovereign is always surrounded by a large body of courtiers, whilst an immense number of civil officers and local overseers maintain the regal dignity in the various districts of the land.

Next in rank to the sub-chieftains, who are generally chosen from the numerous members of the blood-royal, are the principal officers of state. These are five in number: the keeper of the weapons, the master of the ceremonies, the superintendent of the commissariat stores, the master of the household to the royal ladies, and the interpreter for intercourse with strangers and foreign rulers.

The royal ladies are divided, according to age and seniority, into several classes. The elder matrons occupy villages built for their accommodation at some distance from the residence; their number amounts to several hundred, for, besides his own wives of the first and second rank, Munza is bound to maintain the ladies inherited from his father, and even those belonging to a deceased brother. It is a long-established African custom that at a king's death his wives should fall to the lot of his successor, who never fails to annex to their number a large addition of his own. In the seventeenth century the wives of the King of Loango were estimated at 7000.

Whenever at night the king leaves his private apartments to visit his wives, the place re-echoes with the shouts of the courtiers, accompanied by the strains of horns and kettle-drums, and then, too, may be heard the Monbuttoo hymn, "Ee, ee, Munza, tchuppy, tchuppy, ee." Besides the courtiers, the royal household contains many officials appointed to some peculiar functions; there are the private musicians, trumpeters and buglers, whose productions testify to the time and labour spent upon their acquirement; there are eunuchs and jesters, ballad-singers and dancers, who combine to increase the splendour of the court, and to provide general amusement for the festal gatherings.

The king's private residence consists of a group of several large huts, each of which is set apart for one of his daily occupations. They are enclosed, like a Seriba, with a palisade, and are shaded by plantations of well-kept trees. The king's food is always prepared by one of his wives, who perform the office in turn, relieving one another at stated intervals. Munza invariably takes his meals in private; no one may see the contents of his dish, and everything that he leaves is carefully thrown into a pit set apart for that purpose. All that the king has handled is held as sacred, and may not be touched; and a guest, though of the highest rank, may not so much as light his pipe with an ember from the fire that burns before his throne. Any similar attempt would be considered as high treason and punished with immediate death.

As permission was granted me to inspect the internal arrangements of the royal palace, I was enabled to survey the whole series of huts. The king's wardrobe alone occupied several apartments. In one room I saw nothing but hats and feathers of every variety, special value being laid upon the red parrots' feathers, which are arranged in great round tufts. One hut there was in which were suspended whole bundles of the tails of civets, genets, potamochœri, and giraffes, together with skins and thousands of the ornaments with which the king was accustomed to adorn his person. I observed also long strings of the teeth of rare animals captured in the chase. One ornament alone, composed of more than a hundred lions' fangs, must have been a costly heirloom to be handed on from father to son. For the first time I noticed the skin of the *Galago Demidoffi*, an animal hitherto only observed in Western Africa.

A little conical hut that I was shown was set apart for the privacy of the royal retiring-room, the only one of the kind that I came across in Central Africa. The internal arrangements of this corresponded exactly with what is seen in Turkish dwelling-houses. The heathen negroes are generally more observant of decorum in this respect than any Mohammedan.

On another occasion I was conducted through the armoury. The store of weapons consisted principally of lances tied up in bundles of two or three hundred together, which in times of war are distributed amongst the fighting force; there are also piles of the knives and daggers which are borne by Monbuttoo warriors. In the same place were kept the ornamental weapons which are used for decorating the royal halls on festal occasions, consisting for the most part of immense spears, formed head and shaft alike of pure copper, and brightly polished.

The storehouses and corn-magazines were provided with well-made, water-tight roofs, and Munza spends a portion of every day in the several sections, personally superintending the distribution and arrangement of the stores.

From these details it may be understood that the Monbuttoo are subject to a monarchical government of an importance beyond the average of those of Central Africa; and in its institutions it appears to correspond with the descriptions of negro empires long since passed away. The half mythical empire of the powerful Mwata Yanvo, whose influence doubtless extended to the Monbuttoo lands, may probably, to a certain extent, have furnished the type for many of these institutions; but be that as it may, it is an indisputable fact, that of all the known nations of Central Africa, the Monbuttoo, without any influence from the Mohammedan or Christian world, have attained to no contemptible degree of external culture, and their leading characteristics prove them to belong to a group of nations which inhabit the inmost heart of Africa, and which are being now embraced in the enlarging circle of geographical knowledge.

In turning to the national characteristics of this people, we may notice in the first place that their complexion is of a lighter tint than that of almost all the known nations of Central Africa, the colour of whose skins may be generally compared, by the test I have frequently adopted, to that of ground coffee. It is this peculiarity that forms a great distinction between the Monbuttoo and the Niam-niam, whose complexions are more aptly compared to cakes of chocolate or ripe olives. It cannot fail to strike the traveller as remarkable that in all African nations he meets with individuals with black, red, and yellow complexions, whilst the yellow tribes of Asia and the copper-coloured tribes of America each present a remarkable uniformity in the tone and shade of their skins.

The Monbuttoo have less fulness of muscle than the Niam-niam, without, however, any appearance of debility. The growth of the hair is much the same, and the beard is much more developed than that of the Niam-niam.*

But there is one special characteristic that is quite peculiar to the Monbuttoo. To judge from the hundreds who paid visits of curiosity to my tent, and from the thousands whom I saw during my three weeks' sojourn with Munza, I should say that at least five per cent. of the population have light hair. This was always of the closely frizzled quality of the negro type, and invariably associated with the lightest skins that I had seen since leaving Lower Egypt. Its colour was by no means like that which is termed light hair amongst ourselves, but was of a mongrel tint mixed with grey, suggesting the comparison to hemp. All the individuals who had this light hair and complexion had a sickly expression about the eyes, and presented many signs of pronounced albinism; they recalled a description given by Isaac Vossius, in his book upon the origin of the Nile, of the white men he saw at the court of the King of Loango: he says that "they were sickly-looking and wan of countenance, with their eyes drawn as though they were squinting." In the previous chapter I have given a similar description of one of the

* Long beards are said to be found amongst the Niam-niam to the south of the Welle, and amongst Miani's papers there is a notice in which he described a man with a beard half as long as his own, which was of a remarkable length.

king's sons, named Bunza. This combination of light hair and skin gives the Monbuttoo a position distinct from all the nations of the northern part of Africa, with the single exception of the various inhabitants of Morocco, amongst whom fair-haired individuals are far from uncommon.

It has been already observed that in the physiognomical form of the skull the Monbuttoo in many ways recall the type of the Semitic tribes; and they differ from the ordinary run of negroes in the greater length and curve of the nose. All these characteristics betoken an affinity with the Fulbe, and as such the Monbuttoo may probably be included amongst the " Pyrrhi Æthiopes " of Ptolemy. This would, however, be but a vague supposition if it were not supported by the fact that the Fulbe are of eastern origin, although in later times a portion of them have made a retrograde movement from Senegal towards the east. It must be understood that I do not intend by these remarks to offer a bridge for carrying over Eichwaldt's theory of the affinity of the Fulbe with the Malays, nor do I intend by such a national migration to add a new link to what he declares to be accomplished in the case of Meroe. Barth considers these Fulbe to be the issue of a double cross, a cross between the Arabs and people of Barbary on the one hand and the people of Barbary and the negroes on the other. This hypothesis, I believe, would also hold good for the Monbuttoo; but altogether it is a question too vague to be capable of being here discussed with any justice.

On account of the loss of the specimens of the Monbuttoo dialect, which I had been at great pains to collect by means of a double interpretation, I am unfortunately not in a position to give much information about the dialect; this, much, however, I can confidently assert, that it is a branch of the great African language-stock north of the equator, the greater number of the words belonging to the Nubio-Lybian group.

With the Zandey dialect it has nothing in common, being entirely deficient of nasal sounds. Only a prolonged residence in each other's country would enable a Niam-niam and a Monbuttoo mutually to understand one another.

Still more than in the colour of their skin do the Monbuttoo differ from the neighbouring nations in dress and habits. This appears to be a land where costume is a settled matter of rule, for the uniformity of attire is as complete as it is rapidly becoming under the sway of fashion in all classes of our civilized communities.

Owing to their complete seclusion,* until quite recently, from the Mohammedan, as well as the Christian world, weaving is an art unknown to the Monbuttoo, and their only material for clothing is obtained from their fig-tree (*Urostigma Kotschyana*), the "rokko" of the Niam-niam, the bark of which is found to be in a condition most serviceable for the purpose when the trunk of the tree is about as thick as a man's body; the stem is then peeled in rather a remarkable manner: two circular incisions, four or five feet apart, are made right round the trunk, and the bark is removed entire; strange to say, this does no harm to the tree, and in a very short time a peculiar growth or granulation takes place along the edge of the upper incision in the form of little fibres, which gradually descend along the bare cambium or sap-wood, until the tree is once more clothed with a fresh layer of bast. The only explanation that can be offered for this unusual growth is, that in peeling off the bark the entire layer of bast is not removed, but that some portion of it is left hanging to the wood and retains its vitality.† In the course of three years the fresh growth is complete, and the bark is in a condition to be again removed; apart from this property, the rearing of these rokko-trees would not compensate the natives for the trouble of planting them.

The rokko-bark has a certain resemblance to the lime-bast, which is so important an article of commerce in Russia; its fibres, however, have not the smoothness and paper-like thinness of the Russian product, but are tangled together almost like a woven mass. By a partial maceration and a good deal of threshing, the Monbuttoo contrive to give the bark the appearance of a thick close fabric, which, in its rough condition, is of a grey colour, but after being soaked in a decoction of wood acquires a reddish-brown hue, something like ordinary woollen stuff. Fastened at the waist with a girdle, one of these pieces of bark is sufficient to clothe the body, from the breast downwards to the knees, with a very effective substitute for drapery.

Representations of two Monbuttoo warriors in full array are given in the next page.

---

* According to the statements of the natives, at the time of my visit to the Monbuttoo none of the contagious diseases of civilized countries had reached their land. I was, however, rather inclined to doubt their non-acquaintance with small-pox, but can positively assert that syphilis was unknown throughout the district.

† Livingstone observed a similar new growth of bark on the trunk of the Baobab (*Adansonia*), from which the Matabele obtain material for cord.

The women go almost entirely unclothed; they wear nothing but a portion of a plantain-leaf or a piece of bark about the size of their

MONBUTTOO WARRIORS.

hand attached to the front of their girdle; the rest of the body being figured in laboured patterns by means of a black juice obtained from the fruit of the Blippo (*Randia malleifera*). Whilst the Dinka women, leaving perfect nudity as the prerogative of their husbands, are modestly clothed with skins—whilst the Mittoo and Bongo women wear their girdle of foliage, and the Niam-niam women their apron of hides, the women of the Monbuttoo—where the men are more scrupulously and fully clothed than any of the nations that I came across throughout my journey—go almost entirely naked.

MONBUTTOO WOMAN.

Whenever the women go out, they carry over their arm a strap which they lay across their laps on sitting down. These straps or scarves are about a foot wide, and something like a saddle-girth, and as they form their first attempt in the art of weaving, their texture is of the clumsiest order, possessing no other recommendation than their durability; they are appropriated to the further use of fastening infants to their mothers' backs.

The women can be distinguished from one another by the different tattooed figures running in bands across the breast and back along the shoulders; their bodies, moreover, are painted with an almost inexhaustible variety of patterns. Stars and Maltese crosses, bees and flowers, are all enlisted as designs; at one time the entire body is covered with stripes like a zebra, and at another with irregular spots and dots like a tiger; I have seen these women streaked with veins like marble, and even covered with squares like a chess-board. At the great festivals every Monbuttoo lady endeavours to outshine her compeers, and accordingly applies all her powers of invention to the adornment of her person. The patterns last for about two days, when they are carefully rubbed off, and replaced by new designs.

Instead of this paint the men use a cosmetic prepared from pulverised cam-wood, which is mixed with fat and then rubbed over the whole body. The Niam-niam also make use of this powder, but they only apply it partially in irregular spots and stripes, delighting especially in staining the breast and face to increase the ferocity of their appearance.

The *coiffure* of both sexes is alike; the hair of the top and back of the head is mounted up into a long cylindrical chignon, and being fastened on the inside by an arrangement made of reeds, slopes backwards in a slanting direction. Across the forehead, from temple to temple, the hair is twisted in thin tresses, which lie one above another, closely fitting the skull until they reach the crown of the head. Their own hair is rarely long enough to form this portion of the head-gear, but the deficiency is supplied from the heads of those who have fallen in war, or, since hair is an article of traffic in the country, it is procured from the market. On the top of their chignon, the men wear the cylindrical straw-hats so often referred to. These are without brims, square at the top and circular at the base, and are adorned either with the tufts of red parrots' feathers that I have described in connection with Munza's wardrobe,* or with the long feathers of eagles and falcons. The hats, of course, follow the slanting directions of the chignon, and fall back diagonally to the head, and altogether the head-gear is remarkably similar to that worn by the Ishogo women in Western Africa. The Monbuttoo women wear no hat on their chignon, which is merely adorned with little hair-pins attached to combs made of the quills of porcupines.

These details may suffice to give a fair notion of the external appearance of the Monbuttoo, and if I add that their only mutilation of the body consists in boring the inner muscle of the ear for the

* In the woodcut which represents Munza in full dress, the king has one of these clusters of feathers in his hat.

purpose of inserting a bar about the size of a cigar, I shall have described all the fashions in vogue, from which no individual is at liberty to make marked deviation. They neither break out their lower incisor teeth, like the black nations on the northern river plains, nor do they file them to points, like the Niam-niam; neither do they imitate the Bongo and Mittoo women in the hideous perforation of their lips; and I repeat that, if we except circumcision (which, according to the accounts of all the heathen negroes of equatorial Africa, is a custom they have received from their remote ancestors), this piercing of the ear is the one disfigurement of nature adopted by the Monbuttoo.

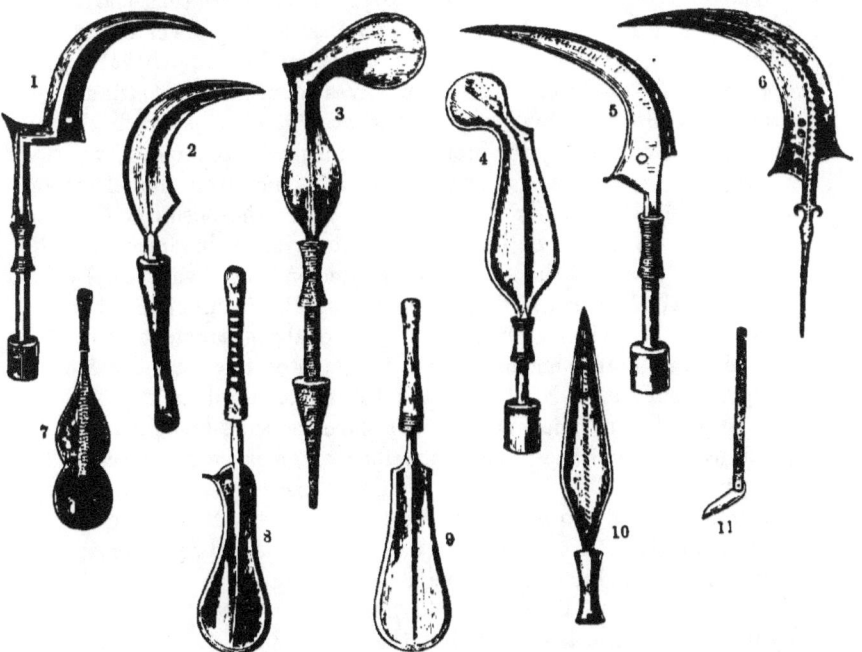

WEAPONS OF THE MONBUTTOO.

Figs. 1–9. Various scimitars.   10. Large dagger.   11. Hand-knife, for carving and peeling bark.

The weapons of the Monbuttoo warriors are very numerous. Besides shields and lances, they also carry bows and arrows, a combination somewhat rare amongst Africans; in addition to these, in their girdles they are accustomed to have scimitars with curved blades like sickles, whilst some of them use daggers and spatular knives of all shapes and sizes. The projectiles which are in use among the Niam-niam are not included in the equipment of the Monbuttoo.

Since the Monbuttoo dwell upon the red ferruginous soil extending from the Gazelle over a large portion of Central Africa, it may be assumed as a matter of course that smiths' work must play an important part in their industrial pursuits, and indeed in this respect they excel all other natives of the districts through which I travelled, whilst in other branches of their manufacture they surpassed even the Mohammedans of Northern Africa.

The smelting-process is of the most primitive description, and is the same that has been described by travellers in all parts of Africa. The simplicity of the arrangement is caused by the ventilating apparatus; for as the construction of valves is unknown, a continual draught is produced by means of two clay vessels, of which the openings are covered by the Monbuttoo smiths with plantain-leaves, which have been allowed to simmer in hot water until they have become as flexible as silk: other nations cover the openings with soft skins. Although entirely without our pincers, hammers, and files, the Monbuttoo have a set of implements of their own, by means of which their iron-work is more carefully manipulated than that of any of their neighbours. Instead of the usual stone anvil, they use a miniature one of wrought iron, and on this each separate weapon is cut out with a chisel, and hammered until an approximate degree of sharpness is attained; the edge being brought to its finish by a piece of fine-ground sandstone or gneiss, which answers the purpose of a file. As a general rule, no special form is given to the iron used as a medium of exchange, unless indeed the great semicircular bars in the royal treasury be considered as currency, and which remind one of the rough copper rings that are brought from the mines of Darfoor.[*] Neither plates of iron nor round spades (melots) are in vogue, but the smiths have to work from great lumps of iron as large as the fist. The dexterity of these artificers is wonderful, and the short space of time in which they will convert the raw material into spades and lances is, I should think, unrivalled. The Monbuttoo smiths often joined our Bongo workmen at their forges in our camp, and as I had frequent opportunity of observing and comparing the two, I do not hesitate

[*] Iron rings of the heaviest calibre are current in Wandala, south of Bornoo.

in asserting the decided superiority of the workmanship of the Monbuttoo.

The masterpieces, however, of these Monbuttoo smiths are the ornamental chains which, in refinement of form and neatness of finish, might vie with our best steel chains. The process of tempering is quite unknown to them, the necessary hardness being attained by continual hammering.

Copper was already known, and the king was in possession of large quantities of the metal, before the Nubians set foot in the country; and as previously to that event the Monbuttoo (if we except the great raid which Barth reports to have been made upon them by the Foorians in 1834) had had no intercourse with the Mohammedan world, there is every reason to conclude that they must have received their supply either from the copper-mines of Angola and Loango, or from some other region of the north-western portion of South Africa.

Almost all the ornaments worn by the Monbuttoo are made of copper, so that it may be easily understood that the demand for the metal is not small. One of the most frequent uses to which it is applied is that of making flat wires many yards long, to wind round the handles of knives and scimitars, or round the shafts of lances and bows. Copper, as well as iron, is used for the clasps which are attached to the shields, partly for ornament and partly to prevent them from splitting. Copper necklaces are in continual wear, and copper fastenings are attached to the rings of buffalo-hide and to the thick thongs of the girdles. The little bars inserted through the ear are tipped with the same metal; in fact there is hardly an ornament that fails in an adjunct of copper in some form or other. All other metals being unknown, iron and copper are estimated by the Monbuttoo as silver and gold by ourselves. Lead and tin have been introduced as curiosities by the Nubians, but previous to their arrival had never been seen. Information, however, which was incidentally dropped by a Niam-niam, led me to suppose that fragments of platinum about the size of peas have been found in these lands: he told me that a white metal, as hard as iron and as heavy as the lead of which the Nubians made their bullets, had been discovered, but that its existence was always carefully concealed from the strangers. I see no reason to doubt the truth of this statement, since it originated from a people who in no other way could have become aware of the existence of such a metal, which has been hitherto as unknown to the Nubians as silver and gold to the Monbuttoo.

It would require many illustrations to convey an adequate idea of the various forms of the heads of the arrows and lances: suffice it to say, that the symmetry of the various barbs, spikes, and prongs with which they are provided is always perfect. The prevailing forms of the spear-heads are hastate, whilst the arrows are generally made flat or spatular, as inflicting a deeper and wider wound than the pointed tips. All weapons of the Monbuttoo and the Niam-niam are provided with blood-gutters, a mark which serves to distinguish them at once from those of the Bongo and Mittoo. The shafts of the Monbuttoo arrows are made of reed-grass, and differ from all others of the Bongo territory by being winged with pieces of genet's skin or plantain leaves. The bows are rather over three feet in length, and in form and size correspond very nearly with those used by the Mittoo and Bongo; the bow-strings being made of a strip of the split Spanish reed, which possesses more elasticity than any cord. These bows are provided with a small hollow piece of wood for protecting the thumb from the rebound of the string. The arrow is always discharged from between the middle fingers.

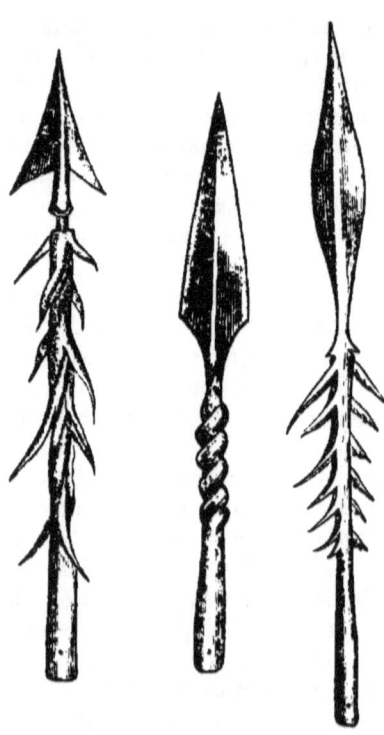

SPEAR-HEADS.

The perfection of their instruments gives the Monbuttoo a great advantage in the art of wood-carving, and they are the only African nation, including even the modern Egyptians, who make use of a graving-tool with a single edge, an instrument which, by supporting the forefinger, enables the workman to give a superior finish to the

TOOLS OF THE MONBUTTOO.

details of his productions. The wood used for carving is generally that of the stem of one of the Rubiaceæ (*Uncaria*), of which the soft close texture resembles that of poplar-wood. The felling of these giant trees, which vary from six to eight feet in diameter, and often shoot up to a height of forty feet without throwing forth a single branch, is performed by means of their small hatchets, with a most tedious amount of labour. The hatchets are like those which are used in other parts of Central Africa, and consist of a sharpened iron wedge inserted through the thick end of a knotted club; thus every blow tends to fix the blade firmer in its socket.

HATCHET, SPADE, AND ADZE, OF THE MONBUTTOO.

The first crude form is given to the larger blocks of wood by means of a tool something like a cooper's adze.* When first hewn, the wood of the Uncaria is white, but it is afterwards blackened by exposure to fire, or still more frequently by being allowed to lie in the dark soil of the brooks.

Platters, stools, drums, boats, and shields constitute the chief items of their handicraft. Upon the Lower Shary, the boats which are in common use are manufactured by fastening together wooden planks, but here, on the Welle, canoes are hewn out of a solid stem, and are in every way adapted for their purpose. I saw some of them upwards of thirty-eight feet long and five feet wide, quite large enough for the conveyance of horses and cattle.†

The large signal-drums of the Niam-niam are to be seen in every

* One of these tools is represented in the accompanying illustration.
† A boat of this kind is seen in the view of the rapids of the Keebaly, in Chap. XII.

Monbuttoo village. They stand sometimes upon four, and sometimes upon two feet, and are like the instruments which are seen upon the West Coast. Another smaller kind is made in a semi-

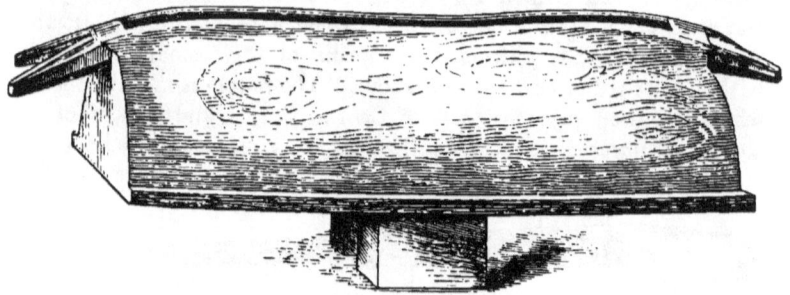

WOODEN KETTLE-DRUM.

circular shape, very compressed, and fitted with a handle at the top; the opening for the sound is below, and the instrument may be compared to a flattened bell.

Benches and stools, such as are used exclusively by the women, are made in every diversity of shape. They are carved out of a

SINGLE SEAT USED BY THE WOMEN.

single block, for, to say the truth, no people of Central Africa seems to have acquired the art of joining one piece of wood to another, so that the craft of the cabinet-maker may be said to be unknown.

The seats of these stools are circular and somewhat hollowed out, surmounting a prettily carved stem, which rises from a circular or polygonal base. Close to the edge of the seat is a triangular aperture, which serves as a handle. They are usually made from twelve to sixteen inches high, and are hardly to be distinguished from certain contrivances for meal-times, which are here made so as to serve at once for table and plate. Wooden platters there are of every possible size: one kind of them has two open ring-shaped handles; another stands upon four feet, and both are patterns quite worthy of our own factories at home. Besides the single seats they are in the habit of making long benches also with four feet. The practice of making all their utensils to stand upon feet is all but universal among the Niam-niam and the Monbuttoo, even the little cylindrical boxes covered with bark for storing away their knick-knacks being finished off in this fashion. The ordinary seats of the men are made exclusively from the leaf-stalks of the Raphia palm: they always keep to precisely the same form, and in their manufacture appear to indicate a first attempt at the joiner's art. The benches of the Monbuttoo men are about five feet long and of corresponding width; they are made of such lightness that one of our bearers, without any apparent exertion, carried six of them at once; but they are nevertheless of very extraordinary firmness, and the way in which the separate parts are fixed together is really very ingenious. The Monbuttoo do not fasten their benches or any of their structures by means of nails or pegs, but they sew them, as it were, together by fine split Spanish reeds, which by their unyielding toughness answer as admirably as the material of our cane chairs.

Backs are not attached to the Monbuttoo seats; but as some support of the kind is clearly indispensable, they endeavour to supply its place by placing by the side of their benches a singular sort of crutch. This is obtained by taking a young tree and cutting a section of it, where what botanists call its "verticillate ramification" has de-

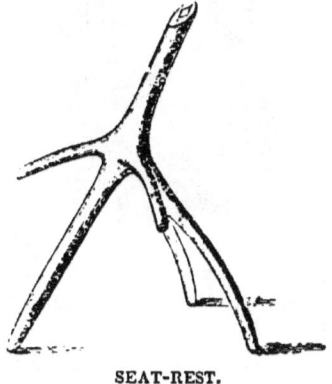

SEAT-REST.

veloped itself into four additional separate limbs: the main stem and two of the boughs supply the three feet, the other two boughs serving, with the continuation of the stem, to make the arms and back. No wood is so available for the purpose as that of the cotton-tree (*Eriodendron*).

The shields of the warriors are hewn out of the thickest stems by means of the axe, and consist of perfectly smooth rectangular boards, not more than half an inch thick, but which are long enough to cover two-thirds of the person. These inelegant instruments of defensive warfare, in which the recommendation of solidity is ill sacrificed for the sake of their lightness, require to be protected from splitting or starting, and to secure this a number of parallel seams of rotang are fixed across the width, and both the upper and lower edges are provided with a strong border of rotang twist, and a strong rib run across the middle gives them an additional firmness. They are generally decorated with tails of the guinea-hog (*Potamochœrus*), and are invariably stained quite black. If any fissures or cracks should be detected, they are at once drawn together by iron and copper braces.

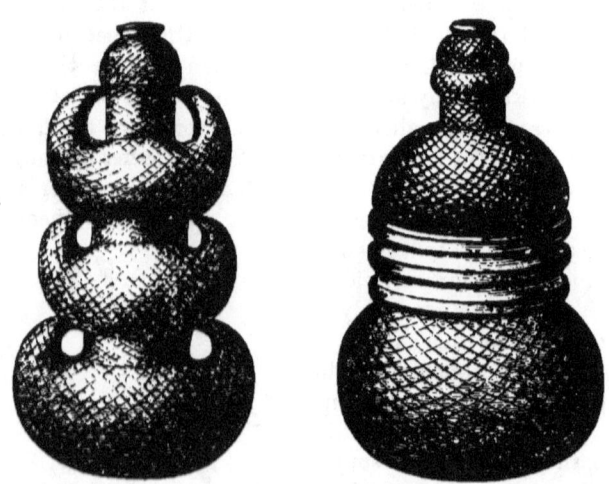

WATER-BOTTLES.

Contrasted with the rest of Africa, and even with the Bongo, whose comparative skill was noticed on a previous page, the district shows a very considerable advance in the manufacture of pottery. Although they remain as unacquainted as other races with the use of the wheel, their productions, besides being of a superior quality, are of a more perfect symmetry than any which are elsewhere observed. All the vessels and drinking-cups of the Africans in general have the character of urns, being made without handles and never otherwise than spherical in form; but those of the Monbuttoo exhibit a manifest improvement, and by having the surface decorated either with some raised symmetrical pattern (which is especially the case upon their oil-vessels) or with some ornamental figures, they afford a firm hold to the hand, and thus make good the lack of handles for lifting them.*

For clay pipe-bowls, upon which others of the natives lavish so much care, the Monbuttoo have no use. They smoke only the Virginian tobacco, and for this purpose use pipes of a primitive, but really very serviceable description, made from the midrib of a plantain-leaf. This is bored all through with a stick, and near the extremity a small opening is made, into which is inserted a plantain-leaf, twisted up into a cornet and filled with tobacco. This is changed as often as the pipe is lighted. It is a contrivance that modifies the rankness of the tobacco almost as perfectly as if it had been inhaled through the water-reservoir of a narghileh. The upper classes occasionally smoke iron or copper pipes made on the same principle, but always prefer the inserted cornets to a solid bowl.

They are very ignorant of the art of leather-dressing, and are no more acquainted with the use of tan than any of the rest of the tribes that have their homes in the Bahr-el-Ghazal district.

Their baskets and nets are woven out of rotang, the baskets in which they bear burdens on their backs being very similar to those which are seen amongst the Thuringians. Their mode of dressing their hair necessarily prevents them from ever carrying a load upon their heads.

They are in the habit of twisting ornaments for themselves out of reeds and grass, which they wear like rings round their arms and legs, and which make a rustling sound as they walk. They bestow a great amount of care in weaving the fine webs which hold on their hats and chignons. The rattles filled with shells and pebbles that are used for beating time to the music of the drums and horns at the great festivals are also woven from reeds.

The Monbuttoo musical instruments require no particular description. They do not include the pretty little mandolins of the Niam-niam, nor any other stringed instruments, and their horns,

* The two examples of water-bottles given in the engravings are copies of the originals. To the one in three compartments handles are attached, being the only instance of the kind that I ever saw.

trumpets, and drums may be said to be little short of universal throughout Africa. Wooden dulcimers (Marimba) are met with neither here nor in South Africa.

But the artistic versatility of the people reveals itself more than anywhere else in their architectural skill. It would hardly be credited that Africa would be capable of rearing any erection so spacious and well proportioned as the hall of Munza's palace. This was little short of 150 feet in length and 60 feet in breadth, and rose to the height of about 50 feet. Combined with these imposing dimensions were a lightness of character and solidity of structure that were quite remarkable. The ever-useful leaf-stalks of the wine-palm form the principal building-material, and its natural polish and bright brown colour give every building for which it is used an aspect of finished grace. The flat horizontal roofs of their huts, as distinguished from the conical roofs which we have hitherto observed as almost universal throughout the rest of Central Africa, mark out these Monbuttoo in a fresh respect as being allied to the natives of the west, viz., the Ishogo, the Ashango, the Bakalai, the Ashiva, the Camma, the Mpongwe, and the Fan— a relation that is further confirmed by the physical character of the land, the streams of which flow to the west instead of to the north. Some of the huts, however, have conical roofs, and these are generally used, either as kitchens, because they allow better escape for the smoke, or as granaries, because they throw off the rain more rapidly.

The dwellings of the ordinary population are by no means large, being seldom more than thirty feet long, and twenty feet wide; the roofs project considerably, and are slightly rounded with a bend corresponding to the natural curvature of the palm-leaves from which they are made, and which furnish the ribs of the roof. They are rendered water-tight by a lining of plantain-leaves, which is frequently covered again with grass, straw, or skin. The walls are built up to a height of five or six feet, and are lined like the roof and bound together by the split Spanish reed. This, again, is the mode of erecting the huts upon the West Coast. It offers an astonishing power of resistance to the fury of the elements, which, left to play upon rows of posts or to range through open halls, might be expected to work complete destruction; yet such is the stability with which the Monbuttoo huts are raised, that they never totter in a storm, and only show by a slight trembling in the walls that they are exposed to the violence of a hurricane.

A spacious doorway is the only aperture for light and air, the door itself being made in one piece; the interior is divided into two apartments, the more remote of which is reserved for the stores.

Plantations of trees are frequent, and still more frequent are patches of shrubs, which are intentionally suffered to grow, and which, as being serviceable, are permitted to survive the extirpation of the ancient forests. These are generally to be seen in the immediate vicinity of the unenclosed farms. In addition to them, many trees are allowed to stand for the sake of the shelter they afford; and some are kept because of their useful products, as for example, the *Tephrosia Vogelii*, which furnishes the powder for poisoning fish; or the *Gardenia malleifera*, which produces the pigment for the staining of the skin, and of which the white funnel-shaped blossoms are a striking ornament to the bushes; and some are retained merely for ornament and for increasing the pleasantness of the external aspect of their dwellings. As examples of this superfluous indulgence I may refer to the marvellous *Mussaenda*, with its glowing bracts, and to the variety of resplendent orchids. Here, too, I noticed what I must not omit to mention, the turf-like *Chlorophytum*, with its variegated leaves of mingled white and green, which is employed among the Niam-niam as a charm to detect a thief, much in the same way as the *Canavalia ensiformis*, known as the "overlook" or horse-bean, is employed in Jamaica and Haiti, where it is sown in the negro-plantations for that purpose.*

The huts are arranged in sets following the lines of the brooks along the valleys, the space between each group being occupied by plantations of oil-palms. The dwellings are separated from the lowest parts of the depressions by the plantain-grounds, whilst above, on the higher and drier soil, extend the fields of sweet potatoes and colocasiæ.

No one could seriously expect a traveller, after a transient residence of five weeks, to pass anything like a decided judgment upon the religious ideas of a people like the Monbuttoo. A wide

---

* The maize-fields, as requiring more culture than the native, with his dislike to hard work, cares to bestow on them, are generally supposed to be the most liable to the encroachment of thieves, and for this reason are usually placed in close proximity to the huts. Thieves adopt a peculiar device for concealing their foot-prints in the soft soil. They attach to their ankles a kind of crutch or stilt, which is called "ballaroo" by the Niam-niam.

scope for speculation is undoubtedly opened, but it would ill become a stranger to pretend to pronounce a conclusive verdict. I must be excused, therefore, from drawing any very definite inference from the fact that they adopt the rite of circumcision so far as to have it performed on boys when they come to an age of puberty, a period of life which is neither in accordance with the original prescription, nor with the doctrine of Mohammed. I may say, however, that I never allowed myself to be unconcerned with regard to the opinions of any of the people amongst whom I journeyed about a presiding Deity, but, by collecting all the proofs I could from their habitual speech, I endeavoured to learn what were their conceptions about the sovereignty of an invisible power, and its influence upon the destinies of men.

The Monbuttoo have undoubtedly very intelligent ideas of what the Nubians mean by their bowing of the knee, their prostrations, and their cry of "Allah!" The very designation which they use to express their conception of God as the concentration of the Supreme Being, opens a long vista into the kindred association of African people. In the district of the Mahas, the word now employed for the God of the Nubians is "Nor," and, upon the authority of my interpreters, I may state that "Noro" was the term by which, after the double interpretation, "Allah" was rendered to me. When the question was put as to where "Noro" resided, the Monbuttoo, who was familiar with the Niam-Niam dialect, pointed upwards to the sky; but when he was further pressed with the inquiry whether he could see him, he only answered with a smile. Whether the Monbuttoo are in the habit of consulting oracles, or whether they have any reliance upon auguries from fowls, or any fortune-telling apparatus corresponding to the "damma" of the Niam-niam, my residence among them was not long enough to permit me to ascertain.

CHAPTER XI.

THE AKKA—Nubian stories—Ancient classical allusions—My incredulity about Pygmies—Visit from a Pygmy—Adimokoo's information—His war dance—Mummery's Pygmy *corps*—Nsewue—African dwarf races —Analogy of Akka and Bushmen—Height and complexion—Hair and beards—Shape of body—Elegance of hands—Formation of skull—Projecting lips — Animated gestures — Language — Nsewue's cruelty to animals—Hunting propensities of the Akka—Protection by Munza— History of Miani's Akka.

WHENEVER two or three Egyptians are found in company, the chances are very great that their conversation, if it could be overheard, would be found to relate to the market prices of the day, or to some fluctuations in the state of trade. With the romantic sons of the Nubian Nile-valley the case would be very different. Ample opportunity of making this comparison was continually afforded me during the long evenings which I passed in my transit over the waters of the Upper Nile; and even now I can recall with vivid interest the hours when, from my detached compartment on the stern of the boat, I could, without being observed, listen to the chatter by which the Nubians on the voyage beguiled their time. They seemed to talk with eagerness of all the wonders of the world. Some would expatiate upon the splendours of the City of the Caliphs, and others enlarge upon the accomplishment of the Suez Canal and the huge ships of the Franks; but the stories that ever commanded the most rapt attention were those which treated of war and of the chase; or, beyond all, such as described the wild beasts and still wilder natives of Central Africa.

It is not with stories in the sense of 'The Thousand and One Nights' that this people entertained each other; neither did they recite their prolix histories as though they were reading at the celebration of Ramadan in Cairo, amidst the halls where night after night they abandoned themselves to the enjoyment of their coffee. These things I had now long ago left far behind; however, occasionally, as the expiring strain of Arabia, I might still hear the song of Abd-el-Kader the sheikh, or of Aboo Zeyd the hero. My whole style of living seemed now to partake of the character of an Odyssey; it appeared to be adapted for the embellishment of an Homeric episode, and such an episode in truth was already awaiting me.

Of the Nile itself, which had the appearance, day by day, of becoming wider as farther and farther we progressed towards the south, they affirmed that it issued from the ocean by which Africa was girt; they would declare that we were on the route which would lead us, like the cranes, to fight with the Pygmies; ever and again they would speak of Cyclopes, of Automoli, or of "Pygmies," but by whatever name they called them, they seemed never to weary of recurring to them as the theme of their talk. Some there were who averred that with their own eyes they had seen this people of immortal myth; and these—men as they were whose acquaintance might have been coveted by Herodotus and envied by Aristotle—were none other than my own servants.

It was a fascinating thing to hear them confidently relate that in the land to the south of the Niam-niam country there dwelt people who never grew to more than three feet in height, and who wore beards so long that they reached to their knees.* It was affirmed of them that, armed with strong lances, they would creep underneath the belly of an elephant and dexterously kill the beast, managing their own movements so adroitly that they could not be reached by the creature's trunk. Their services in this way were asserted to contribute very largely to the resources of the ivory-traders. The name by which they are known is the "Shebber-digintoo," which implies the growth of the disproportioned beard.

I listened on. The more, however, that I pondered silently over the stories that they involuntarily disclosed—the more I studied the traditions to which they referred—so much the more I was perplexed to explain what must either be the creative faculty or the derived impressions of the Nubians. Whence came it that they could have gained any knowledge at all of what Homer had sung? How did it happen that they were familiar at all with the material which Ovid and Juvenal, and Nonnus and Statius worked into their verse, giving victory at one time to the cranes, and at another to the Pygmies themselves?

* It may be remarked that the people of the Soudan when they depict a dwarf, ordinarily, like we should ourselves, represent him as a diminutive man with a long beard.

My own ideas of Pygmies were gathered originally only from books, but the time seemed now to have come when their existence should be demonstrated in actual life.

Legends of Pygmies had mingled themselves already with the earliest surviving literature of the Greeks, and the poet of the Iliad, it will be remembered, mentions them as a race that had long been known:—

> "To warmer seas the cranes embodied fly,
> With noise, and order, through the midway sky;
> To pygmy nations wounds and death they bring,
> And all the war descends upon the wing."
>
> *Pope's* 'Homer's Iliad,' iii. 6–10.

But not the classic *poets* alone; sober historians and precise geographers have either adopted the poetic substance of the tradition or have endeavoured, by every kind of conjecture, to confirm its accuracy. Nothing, for instance, can be more definite than the statement of Herodotus about the Nasamonians after they had crossed the Libyan deserts: "They at length saw some trees growing on a plain, and having approached they began to gather the fruit that grew on the trees; and while they were gathering it some diminutive men, less than men of middle stature, came up and seized them and carried them away."* The testimony of Aristotle is yet more precise when he says plainly: "The cranes fly to the lakes above Egypt, from which flows the Nile; there dwell the Pygmies, and this is no fable, but the pure truth; there, just as we are told, do men and horses of diminutive size dwell in caves;"† a quotation this, which would seem to imply that the learned Stagyrite was in possession of some exact and positive information, otherwise he would not have ventured to insist so strongly upon the truth of his assertion. Very likely, however, we should be justified in surmising that Aristotle mentions cranes and Pygmies together only because he had the passage of the Iliad floating in his memory, and because he was aware of the fact that cranes do pass the winter in Africa.

But all that concerns us, with regard to the present topic, is that three or four centuries before the Christian era the Greeks were aware of the existence of a people inhabiting the districts about the sources of the Nile, who were remarkable for their stunted growth. The circumstance may warrant us, perhaps, in employing the desig-

---

* Herodotus, ii. 32.
† Aristotle's 'Hist. Animal,,' lib. viii. cap. 2.

nation of "pygmy," not for men literally a span long, but in the sense of Aristotle, for the dwarf races of Equatorial Africa.

Throughout the time that I had resided in the Seribas of the Bongo territory, of course I had frequent opportunities of enlarging my information, and I was continually hearing such romantic stories that I became familiarised in a way with the belief that the men about me had really been eye-witnesses of the circumstances they related. Those who had been attached to the Niam-niam expeditions, whenever they described the variety of wonders and the splendour of the courts of the cannibal kings, never omitted to mention the dwarfs who filled the office of court buffoons; every one outvying another in the fantastic embellishment of the tales they told. The general impression that remained upon my mind was that these must be some extraordinary specimens of pathological phenomena that had been retained by the kings as natural curiosities. The instance did not escape my recollection that Speke had given the description and portrait of a dwarf, Kimenya, with whom he had become acquainted at the court of Kamrasi;* but that there could be a whole series of tribes whose height was far below an average never really found a reception in my understanding, until at the court of Munza the positive evidence was submitted to my eyes.

Several days elapsed after my taking up my residence by the palace of the Monbuttoo king without my having a chance to get a view of the dwarfs, whose fame had so keenly excited my curiosity. My people, however, assured me that they had seen them. I remonstrated with them for not having secured me an opportunity of seeing for myself, and for not bringing them into contact with me. I obtained no other reply but that the dwarfs were too timid to come. After a few mornings my attention was arrested by a shouting in the camp, and I learned that Mohammed had surprised one of the Pygmies in attendance upon the king, and was conveying him, in spite of a strenuous resistance, straight to my tent. I looked up, and *there*, sure enough, was the strange little creature, perched upon Mohammed's right shoulder, nervously hugging his head, and casting glances of alarm in every direction. Mohammed soon deposited him in the seat of honour. A royal interpreter was stationed at his side. Thus, at last, was I able veritably to feast my eyes upon a living embodiment of the myths of some thousand years!

* 'Speke's Travels,' p. 550.

Eagerly, and without loss of time, I proceeded to take his portrait. I pressed him with innumerable questions, but to ask for information was an easier matter than to get an answer. There was the greatest difficulty in inducing him to remain at rest, and I could only succeed by exhibiting a store of presents. Under the impression that the opportunity before me might not occur again, I bribed the interpreter to exercise his influence to pacify the little man, to set him at his ease, and to induce him to lay aside any fear of me that he might entertain. Altogether we succeeded so well that in a couple of hours the Pygmy had been measured, sketched, feasted, presented with a variety of gifts, and subjected to a minute catechism of searching questions.

His name was Adimokoo. He was the head of a small colony, which was located about half a league from the royal residence. With his own lips I heard him assert that the name of his nation was Akka, and I further learnt that they inhabit large districts to the south of the Monbuttoo, between lat. 2° and 1° N. A portion of them are subject to the Monbuttoo king, who, desirous of enhancing the splendour of his court by the addition of any available natural curiosities, had compelled several families of the Pygmies to settle in the vicinity.

My Niam-niam servants, sentence by sentence, interpreted to me everything that was said by Adimokoo to the Monbuttoo interpreter, who was acquainted with no dialects but those of his own land.

In reply to my question to Adimokoo as to where his country was situated, pointing towards the S.S.E., he said, "Two days' journey and you come to the village of Mummery; on the third day you will reach the River Nalobe; the fourth day you arrive at the first of the villages of the Akka."

"What do you call the rivers of your country?"

"They are the Nalobe, the Namerikoo, and the Eddoopa."

"Have you any river as large as the Welle?"

"No; ours are small rivers, and they all flow into the Welle."

"Are you all one people, or are you divided into separate tribes?"

To this inquiry Adimokoo replied by a sudden gesture, as if to indicate the vastness of their extent, and commenced enumerating the tribes one after another. "There are the Navapukah, the Navatipeh, the Vabingisso, the Avadzubeh, the Avagowumba, the Bandoa, the Mamomoo, and the Agabundah."

"How many kings?" I asked.

"Nine," he said; but I could only make out the names of Galeema, Beddeh, Tindaga, and Mazembe.

My next endeavour was to discover whether he was acquainted in any way with the dwarf races that have been mentioned by previous travellers, and whose homes I presumed would be somewhere in this part of Africa. I asked him whether he knew the Malagilagé. My question, however, only elicited a comical gesture of bewilderment and a vague inquiry, "What is that?" Nor did I succeed any better in securing any recognition of the tribes of the Kenkob or the Betsan. Equally unavailing, too, were all my efforts to obtain answers of any precision to the series of questions which I invented, taking my hints from Petermann and Hassenstein's map of Central Africa, so that I was obliged to give up my geographical inquiries in despair and turn to other topics. But in reality there did not occur any subject whatever on which I obtained any information that seems to me to be worth recording. At length, after having submitted so long to my curious and persistent questionings, the patience of Adimokoo was thoroughly exhausted, and he made a frantic leap in his endeavour to escape from the tent. Surrounded, however, by a crowd of inquisitive Bongo and Nubians, he was unable to effect his purpose, and was compelled, against his will, to remain for a little longer. After a time a gentle persuasion was brought to bear, and he was induced to go through some of the characteristic evolutions of his war-dances. He was dressed, like the Monbuttoo, in a rokko-coat and plumed hat, and was armed with a miniature lance as well as with a bow and arrow. His height I found to be about 4 feet 10 inches, and this I reckon to be the average measurement of his race.

Although I had repeatedly been astonished at witnessing the war-dances of the Niam-niam, I confess that my amazement was greater than ever when I looked upon the exhibition which the Pygmy afforded. In spite of his large, bloated belly and short bandy legs —in spite of his age, which, by the way, was considerable— Adimokoo's agility was perfectly marvellous. The little man's leaps and attitudes were accompanied by such lively and grotesque varieties of expression that the spectators shook again and held their sides with laughter. The interpreter explained to the Niam-niam that the Akka jump about in the grass like grasshoppers, and that they are so nimble that they shoot their arrows into an elephant's eye and drive their lances into its belly.

Adimokoo returned home loaded with presents. I made him

understand that I should be glad to see all his people, and promised that they should lose nothing by coming.

On the following day I had the pleasure of a visit from two of the

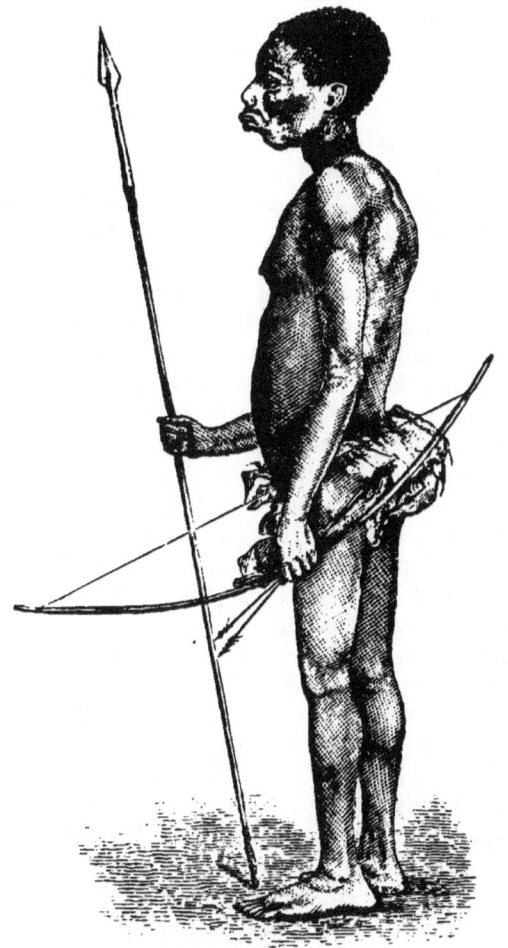

BOMBY THE AKKA.

younger men. I had the opportunity of sketching their likenesses, and as one of the portraits has been preserved it is inserted here.

After they had once got over their alarm, some or other of the Akka came to me almost every day. As exceptional cases, I observed that some individuals were of a taller stature; but upon investigation I always ascertained that this was the result of intermarriage with the Monbuttoo amongst whom they resided. My sudden departure from Munza's abode interrupted me completely in my study of this interesting people, and I was compelled to leave before I had fully mastered the details of their peculiarities. I regret that I never chanced to see one of the Akka women, and still more that my visit to their dwellings was postponed from day to day until the opportunity was lost altogether.

I am not likely to forget a *rencontre* which I had with several hundred Akka warriors, and could very heartily wish that the circumstances had permitted me to give a pictorial representation of the scene. King Munza's brother Mummery, who was a kind of viceroy in the southern section of his dominions, and to whom the Akka were tributary, was just returning to the court from a successful campaign against the black Momvoo. Accompanied by a large band of soldiers, amongst whom was included a corps of Pygmies, he was conveying the bulk of the booty to his royal master. It happened on the day in question that I had been making a long excursion with my Niam-niam servants, and had heard nothing of Mummery's arrival. Towards sunset I was passing along the extensive village on my return to my quarters, when, just as I reached the wide open space in front of the royal halls, I found myself surrounded by what I conjectured must be a crowd of impudent boys, who received me with a sort of bravado fight. They pointed their arrows towards me, and behaved generally in a manner at which I could not help feeling somewhat irritated, as it betokened unwarrantable liberty and intentional disrespect. My misapprehension was soon corrected by the Niam-niam people about me. "They are Tikkitikki,"[*] said they; "you imagine that they are boys, but in truth they are men; nay, men that can fight." At this moment a seasonable greeting from Mummery drew me off from any apprehension on my part, and from any further contemplation of the remarkable spectacle before me. In my own mind I resolved that I would minutely inspect the camp of the new-comers on the following morning; but I had reckoned without my host: before dawn Mummery and his contingent of Pygmies had taken their departure, and thus,

"Like the baseless fabric of a vision,"

---

[*] Tikkitikki is the Niam-niam designation of the Akka.

this people, so near and yet so unattainable, had vanished once more into the dim obscurity of the innermost continent.

Anxious, in my contact with this mythical race, to lose or pass over nothing which might be of interest, I very diligently made memoranda after every interview that I had with the Akka. I measured six full-grown individuals, none of whom much exceeded 4 feet 10 inches in height, but, unfortunately, all my notes and many of my drawings perished in the fire.

A brief account may now be given of the little Pygmy that I carried off and kept with me during the remainder of my wanderings till I was again in Nubia, who for a year and a half became my companion, thriving under my care and growing almost as affectionate as a son.

I have already explained in a previous chapter the circumstances under which the little man came into my keeping. I succeeded tolerably well in alleviating the pain of the lad's parting from all his old associates by providing him with all the good living and bestowing upon him all the attention that lay in my power. To reconcile him to his lot I broke through an old rule. I allowed Nsewue, as I called him, to be my constant companion at my meals —an exception that I never made in favour of any other native of Africa. Making it my first care that he should be healthy and contented, I submitted without a murmur to all the uncouth habits peculiar to his race. In Khartoom at last I dressed him up till he looked like a little pasha in his black coat and Turkish fez. The Nubians could not in the least enter into my infatuation, nor account for my partiality towards the strange-looking lad. When he walked along the thoroughfares at my side they pointed to him, and cried, with reference to his bright-brown complexion, "See, there goes the son of the Khavaga!" Apparently they overlooked the fact of the boy's age, and seemed not to be in any way familiarised with the tradition of the Pygmies. In the Seribas all along our route the little fellow excited a still greater astonishment.

Notwithstanding all my assiduity and attention, I am sorry to record that Nsewue died in Berber, from a prolonged attack of dysentery, originating not so much in any change of climate, or any alteration in his mode of living, as in his immoderate excess in eating, a propensity which no influence on my part was sufficient to control.

During the last ten months of his life, my *protégé* did not make any growth at all. I think I may therefore presume that his height would never have exceeded 4 feet 7 inches, which was his measurement at the time of death. The accompanying portrait may be accepted as a faithful representation of one who was a fair type of his race.

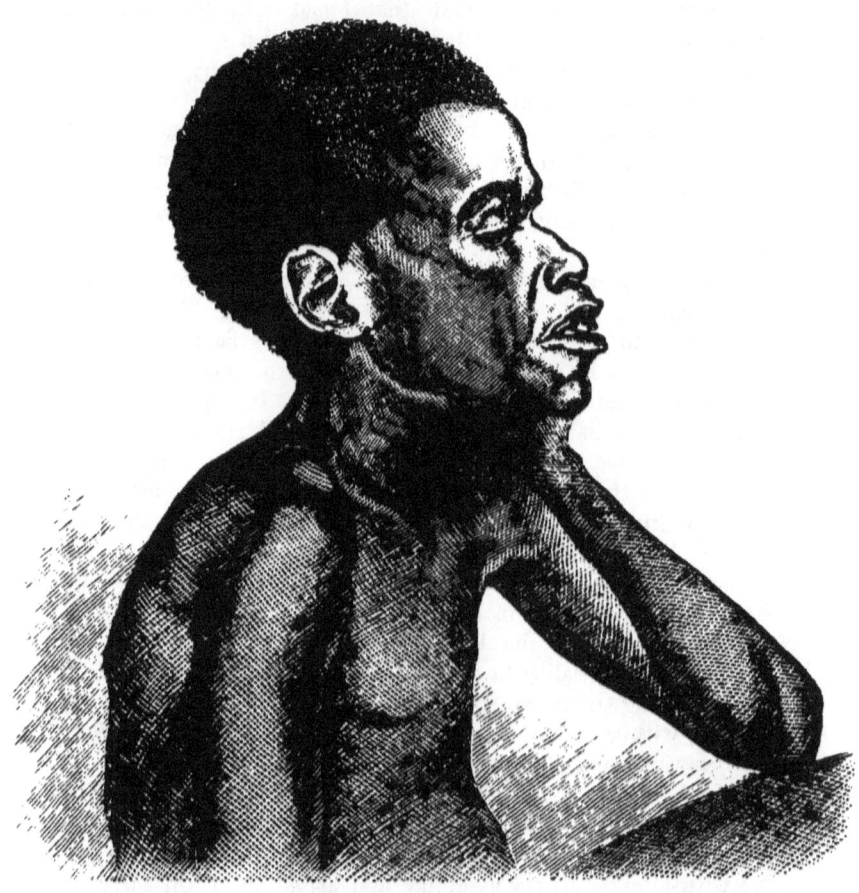

NSEWUE THE AKKA.

Altogether very few examples of the Akka came under my notice; but so ample was my opportunity of studying in detail the peculiarities of this individual specimen, that, in the course of any observations that follow, I shall feel justified in referring to Nsewue, when the rest of my experience furnishes no other illustration.

The Akka would appear to be a branch of that series of dwarf races which, exhibiting all the characteristics of an aboriginal stock, extend along the equator entirely across Africa. Whatever travellers have penetrated far into the interior of the continent have furnished abundant testimony as to the mere fact of the existence of tribes of singularly diminutive height; whilst their accounts are nearly all coincident in representing that these dwarf races differ from the surrounding nations in hardly anything excepting in their size. It would be entirely an error to describe them as dwarfs either in the sense of the ancient myths, or in the way of *lusus naturæ*, such as are exhibited as curiosities amongst ourselves; most of the accounts, moreover, that have been given, concur in the statement that these undersized people are distinguished from their neighbours by a redder or brighter shade of complexion; but they differ very considerably in the reports they make about the growth of the hair. The only traveller, I believe, before myself that has come into contact with any section of this race is Du Chaillu, who, in the territory of the Ashango, discovered a wandering tribe of hunters called Obongo, and took the measurements of a number of them. He describes these Obongo as "not ill-shaped," and as having skins of a pale, yellow-brown, somewhat lighter than their neighbours; he speaks of their having short heads of hair, but a great growth of hair about their bodies. Their average height he affirms to be 4 feet 7 inches. In every particular but the abundance of hair about the person, this description is quite applicable to the Akka. According to Battel,[*] there was a nation of dwarfs, called the Matimbos or Dongo, to the north-east of the land of Yobbi, which lies to the north of the Sette River, and consequently in the same district as that in which Du Chaillu discovered the Obongo. Portuguese authorities, moreover, quite at the beginning of the seventeenth century, contain a distinct reference to a dwarf nation called Bakka-bakka. Dapper furnishes corresponding information on the same subject; and all that he relates about the dwarfs coincides very accurately with what is known about the Akka, whose name had penetrated even at that date to the western equatorial coasts. It is to be understood that districts were known by the name of the people who chanced to be occupying them, and not by any permanent name of the soil itself. After Dapper, in his compilation, had told the history of the Yagas, who are said in olden time to have spread fear and destruction as far as the coasts of the Loango, a hundred miles away, so that it took three months for caravans to come and go, he proceeds to state

[*] *Vide* Battel, 'Purchas his Pilg.,' II., p. 983. London, 1625.

that the greater part of the ivory was obtained still farther inland, and was brought from a people who were tributary to the great Makoko, and called Mimos or Bakke-bakke. "These little men," he writes,* "are stated by the Yagas to have the power of making themselves invisible, and consequently can slay an elephant with little trouble." And this dexterity in killing elephants seems to be implied in another place,† where, in describing the court of Loango and the dwarfs who took up their positions before the throne, he says, "the negroes affirm that there is a wilderness inhabited by those dwarfs, and where there are many elephants; they are generally called Bakke-bakke, but sometimes Mimos." Farther on again ‡ he speaks of the empire of the great Makoko (described as lying beyond the kingdom of Congo, and some 200 miles or more inland, north of the river Zaire), and proceeds to specify that "in the wilderness of this country there are to be found the little people that have been mentioned before, who carry on the greater part of the ivory trade throughout the kingdom." Besides this it is expressly stated that the ivory was bartered for the salt of Loango. Now in none of the countries that I visited in Central Africa was either sea salt or common salt ever an article of commerce, but each separate nation produced its own supply from ashes: but whilst I was at the court of Munza I learnt from the Khartoomers who had settled there that, as matter of fact, king Munza did receive tribute from the Akka in the shape of "*real good salt*," which was brought from the far south. Taken in connection with Dapper's account, this statement would seem to justify the hypothesis that even at this day there may be commercial transactions between the very heart of Africa, where the Akka dwell, and the western coasts.

Still more demonstrative than any reports about Matimbos and Bakke-bakke, as proving the identity of my Akka with the abnormally-formed folks previously named, is the evidence that is furnished by the natives of the Upper Shary districts. Escayrac de Lauture § was told of a Lake Kocidabo, which was said to be a two months' journey to the S.S.E. of Masena, the capital of Baghirmy, and to unite the source-affluents of the Shary just at the spot where, according to the Monbuttoo, the Welle widens into a boundless expanse of water. Somewhat to the west of this lake, he was informed, were the dwellings of the Mala-gilageh (literally, men with tails), who were of a small stature and reddish complexion, and

* Dapper, Germ. ed., Amsterd., p. 571. † Ib., p. 527. ‡ Ib., p. 573.
§ 'Bulletin de la Soc. de Géograph. de Paris,' tom. x., 1855.

covered with long hair. The fabulous tails must be supposed to be added by a kind of poetic licence, or as a concession to the belief in the marvellous stories that were rife throughout the Soudan. It may with much probability be assumed that the same districts in Central Africa must be the homes of the Kenkob and Betsan, of whom Kölle,* residing in Sierra Leone, heard reports from those who professed to have actually seen them. In these reports the great lake was very often referred to. One of Kölle's informants called it "Leeba," and said that he had on one occasion personally accompanied an embassy that was commissioned to convey a present of salt to the king who ruled over the territories by the shores of the lake; and he distinctly affirmed not only that the Kenkob lived in close proximity to the same lake, but that they were a people only three or four feet in height, but who nevertheless possessed great strength and were excellent hunters. Another witness informed Kölle that he only knew of "a river Reeba" in that part of the country; but it is extremely likely that in reality he was referring to the same Lake Leeba which, by repeated geographical investigation, has been proved to be a part of the Shary : † he went on to describe that by this river Reeba there dwelt a diminutive race called Betsan, varying from three feet to five feet in height, and stated that they had very long hair and very long beards, adding that they supported themselves entirely by the produce of the chase.

Both these witnesses agreed in describing the hair of the dwarfs as long; and I always found that the Niam-niam laid particular stress upon their having long beards; but I must confess I never observed this characteristic in any of the Akka who came under my notice.

Nor is east Tropical Africa without its representatives of people of this stunted growth. Of these I may especially mention the Doko, who are reported to dwell to the south of Enarea and Kaffa on the Upper Juba. Krapf, who has with much diligence compared the various accounts of many slaves who have been carried away to Shoa from the district in question, fixes the habitation of the Doko as being below the latitude of 3° N. Their height is compared with that of boys ten years of age. Even those who have

* 'Polyglotta Africana,' p. 12.

† In nearly all the negro dialects the letters *l* and *r* are used indifferently; and Africans, as a rule, very much confound the ideas of lake and river.

seen them and (like A. d'Abbadie) deny that they are *dwarfs*, yet admit that they are under the medium stature. On the coast itself, in Zanzibar and at Brava, where, occasioned by the Mohammedan Somali, there is a considerable intercourse with the districts said to be populated by the Doko, stories of these dwarfs are in every one's mouth, and they are termed the "Berikeemo," *i.e.* people two feet high.

This rapid summary of the dwarf races that are known in Africa would be incomplete without a passing reference to the Kimos of Madagascar, of whom, from the middle of the seventeenth century down to our own time the most contradictory reports have been in circulation. Any detailed accounts of these would of course be here entirely out of place. Madagascar, too, from its isolation, must ever be treated independently. The relation of its inhabitants to the inhabitants of Central Africa is very doubtful. It will now suffice to say generally that the evidence appears to lie open before us of there being a series of unestablished and imperfectly developed nations which, although they are now in their decline, extend from ocean to ocean across the entire equatorial zone of Africa.

Scarcely a doubt can exist but that all these people, like the Bushmen of South Africa, may be considered as the scattered remains of an aboriginal population now becoming extinct; and their isolated and sporadic existence bears out the hypothesis.* For centuries after centuries Africa has been experiencing the effects of many immigrations: for thousands of years one nation has been driving out another, and as the result of repeated subjugations and interminglings of race with race, such manifold changes have been introduced into the conditions of existence that the succession of new phases, like the development in the world of plants, appears almost as it were to open a glimpse into the infinite.

Incidentally I have just referred to the Bushmen, those notorious natives of the South African forests, who owe their name to the likeness which the Dutch colonists conceived they bore to the ape, as the prototype of the human race. I may further remark that their resemblance to the equatorial Pygmies is in many points very striking. Gustav Fritsch, the author of a standard work upon the natives of South Africa, first drew my attention to the marked similarity between my portraits of the Akka and the general type

---

* Some ethnographists consider the African dwarf tribes as the degenerate remnant of other negro-races, but their distinct existence and peculiar mode of life completely belies the assertion.

of the Bushmen, and so satisfied did I become in my own mind, that I feel quite justified (in my observations upon the Akka) in endeavouring to prove that all the tribes of Africa whose proper characteristic is an abnormally low stature belong to one and the self-same race.

According to Fritsch the average height of the genuine Bushmen is 1·44 metre, or about 4 feet 8½ inches; the height of the two Akka, whose portraits I have inserted, were 4 feet 1 inch and 4 feet 4 inches respectively; and, as I have said, I never saw any instance in which the height materially exceeded 4 feet 10 inches. The skin of the Akka is of a dull brown tint, something of the colour of partially roasted coffee. As far as I can remember, the colour would correspond nearly with Nos. 7 and 8 in the table of skin-tints in Plate 49 of Fritsch's work, and these are the numbers by which he indicates the complexion of the Bushmen. It is somewhat difficult to discriminate between the complexion of the Akka and that of their neighbours the Monbuttoo, since the latter exhibit a variety of shades of the same tint; but I should be inclined to say that the distinction lies in the somewhat duller hue of the Akka, such as might be understood by comparing No. 2 with No. 8 in the table to which I have referred.

The hair and beard are but slightly developed. All the Akka that I saw wore the ordinary costume and cylindrical straw hat of the Monbuttoo; but, in consequence of their hair being short as well as woolly, they are unable to form a chignon like their neighbours. The colour of their hair corresponds with their complexion; in texture it may best be compared with the waste tow from old cordage. The absence of the beard is characteristic also of the Bushmen. The Nubians indeed used to tell me of the dwarfs about the courts of the Niam-niam princes being noted for long hair, and they affirmed that some of them, in the fashion of the West Africans, were in the habit of stiffening out the long pointed tufts of hair on their chin with pitch; no doubt, too, their common designation for this people (Shebber digintoo) has reference to this characteristic; but I could never succeed in getting any accurate or more definite information about dwarfs of this species. The Akka resemble the majority of the Monbuttoo in having brown hair, other nations of a reddish tone of complexion not sharing this peculiarity.

Taking, as I have said, my little *protégé* Nsewue as a fair type of the Akka in general, I will proceed to enumerate the most prominent marks in their appearance.

The head of the Akka is large, and out of proportion to the weak, thin neck on which it is balanced. The shape of the shoulders is peculiar, differing entirely from that of other negroes in a way that may probably be accounted for by the unusual scope required for the action of the shoulder-blades; the arms are lanky; and altogether the upper portion of the body has a measurement disproportionately long. The superior region of the chest is flat and much contracted, but it widens out below to support the huge hanging belly, which gives them, however aged, the remarkable appearance of Arabian or Egyptian children. The look of the Akka from behind is very singular, their body seeming then to form a curve so regular and defined that it is almost like a letter S; this is probably to be accounted for by an exceptional suppleness in the lower joints of the spine, since after a full meal the centre of gravity is shifted, and the curve of the back accordingly becomes more or less concave. All the various personal traits of the Akka to which I have thus referred are illustrated very plainly in Fritsch's work by the figure (No. 69) which represents an old Bushman.

The joints of the legs are angular and projecting, except that the knees are plump and round. Unlike other Africans, who ordinarily walk with their feet straight, the Akka turn them somewhat inward. I hardly know how to describe their waddling; every step they take is accompanied by a lurch that seems to affect all their limbs alike; and Nsewue could never manage to carry a full dish for any distance without spilling at least a portion of its contents.

Of all their members their hands were undoubtedly the best formed. These might really be pronounced elegant, although I do not mean that they were in the least like the long narrow ladies' hands that are so lauded in romance, but which Carl Vogt has characterised as appropriate to the monkey type. Nothing about my poor little favourite ever excited my admiration to the same degree as his pretty little hands.

But all the peculiarities of the race culminate in the shape of the skull and in the physiognomical character of the head. As matter of fact, history has not shewn that any general degeneracy in a nation has ever been attended by a general decrease in a people's stature; but still it is quite possible that the peculiarities I have already mentioned might originate in some modification of the way of living. Any attempt, however, to attribute the formation of the skull to the effects either of circumstance, of food, or of climate must at once be rejected as inadmissible. The most noticeable points in the structure of the heads of the Akka is their high degree of *prognathy*. The two portraits that are given exhibit facial angles of 60° and 66° respectively. Besides this, they are remarkable for the snout-like projection of the jaw with an unprotruding chin, and for the wide skull which is almost spherical, and which has a deep indentation at the base of the nose. These leading resemblances indubitably exist between the Akka and the Bushmen; and where the general similarity is so great, all minor discrepancies must sink into insignificance.

All the accounts of the South African Bushmen agree in representing that their eyes are small and their eyelids contracted. "Their eyes," says Lichtenstein, "are small, deeply set, and so compressed as to be scarcely visible." Fritsch lays special stress upon this peculiarity of the Bushmen, but at the same time draws attention to the similarity of expression between them and the Hottentots, who otherwise differ from them so widely. Now the Akka, on the other hand, have large eyes, wide open, so as to give them the bird-like appearance of Azteks. Amid the multitude of resemblances this may be said to be the only important difference between the Akka and the Bushmen, and probably even this may be accounted for as being the effect either of food or climate, in the same way as the weather-beaten countenance of the mariner may be attributed to the life of exposure that he has led.*

Setting aside, however, this diversity with regard to the eyes, the heads of the Akka and the Bushmen will be found to present various points of similarity in other respects. The Akka are distinguished from all other nations of Central Africa by the huge size of the ear. Now, however small, in an æsthetic sense, the negroes' pretentions to any beauty may ordinarily be supposed to be, it must be conceded that they can vie with any race whatever in the elegance and symmetrical shape of their ears; but no share of this grace can be assigned either to the Bushmen or to the Akka.

The lips project in a way that corresponds completely with the projecting jaw. They are long and convex: they do not overlap, and are not so thick as those of the generality of negroes. What really suggests the resemblance to an ape is the sharply defined outline of the gaping mouth; for the pouting lips of most negroes convey no idea at all of relationship with inferior animals. These

---

* It should also be mentioned that the skin of the Akka has not the withered wrinkled look which is observable in the Bushmen.

gaping lips, again, are possessed by the Akka in common with the Bushmen, whose profiles may be seen in the illustrations given by Fritsch; they are not found at all amongst the Monbuttoo.

The continual changes of expression which, as Lichtenstein observes, play upon the countenance and render the Bushmen like apes rather than human beings are exhibited to a very remarkable degree by the Akka. The twitching of the eyebrows (in this case still more animated by the brightness of the eyes), the rapid gestures with the hands and feet while talking, the incessant wagging and nodding of the head, all combine to give a very grotesque appearance to the little people, and serve to explain the fund of amusement derived from the visit of Adimokoo.

Of the language of the Akka I must confess my entire ignorance, having lost the few notes that I possessed. I remember that I was much struck by the inarticulateness of the pronunciation.* During the year and a half that my *protégé* was domesticated with me, he was unable to learn sufficient Arabic to make himself understood; in this respect he was very different to the other natives about me, who made themselves masters of a copious vocabulary. He never advanced beyond stammering out a few Bongo phrases, which no one except myself and a few of my own people could comprehend.

Although I was informed that circumcision was practised by the Akka, I could never ascertain whether it was really an indigenous custom, or whether it was merely borrowed from the Monbuttoo, and so adopted by such of the Akka as had settled near the court of Munza.

In acuteness, dexterity, and it must be added in cunning, the Akka far surpass the Monbuttoo. They are κατ' ἐξοχήν, a nation of hunters. The cunning, however, which they display is but the outward expression of an inner impulse which seems to prompt them to find a delight in wickedness. Nsewue was always fond of torturing animals, and took a special pleasure in throwing arrows at the dogs by night. Such a people as this would naturally excel in the inventive faculty for laying traps and snares for game.

Like the Obongo and the Bushmen, as I myself experienced

---

* On account of the apparent dissimilarity of the languages of the Akka and Bushmen, some ethnographists have endeavoured to confute my assumption of the common origin of the two nations. But the truth is that the Akka dialect is not really known. The specimens of the conversation of the two Akka who were brought to Europe, were found to consist of Monbuttoo words, mixed with the Arabic of the Soudan.

during my first *rencontre* with Adimokoo, the Akka are extremely shy with other men.

Their only domestic animals are poultry; and it struck me as a coincidence somewhat curious that one of the Pompeian mosaics which I saw in the National Museum at Naples represents the Pygmies in the midst of their little houses, which are depicted as full of common fowls.

It is notorious that the natives of South Africa in general have vowed death and destruction against the Bushmen, reckoning them as incorrigibly wild and in no way superior to apes of the most dangerous character. Now the dwarfs of Central Africa, although they fall little short of the Bushmen in natural maliciousness, are not regarded as mischievous fiends who must be exterminated like a brood of adders, but they are considered rather as a race of benevolent spirits or mandrakes who are in no way detrimental. They are of assistance to the Monbuttoo in securing them a more abundant produce from the chase, and so they enjoy the protection of their neighbours very much in the same way as (according to Du Chaillu) the Obongo enjoy the protection of the Ashango. These amicable relations, however, would not be possible but for the reason that the Monbuttoo possess no herds. If the Monbuttoo were a cattle-breeding people, it cannot be doubted that the Akka would consider all their animals as game, and could not deny themselves the delight of driving their spears into the flanks of every beast they could get near, and by these tactics would very soon convert their guardians into enemies.

Munza supplies all the Akka who have settled near him with the best of diet, and Nsewue was never weary of descanting in praise of the flasks of beer, the plantain-wine, the ears of corn, and all the other delicacies with which his people were feasted.

I will only add that a debt of gratitude is due from the students of ethnology to the Monbuttoo king, who has been instrumental in preserving this remnant of a declining race until the time has come for the very heart of Africa to be laid open.

In the same way as he had given me Nsewue, did Munza, two years later, present my ill-fated successor, the Italian explorer Giovanni Miani, with a couple of Akka boys, true types of their race. My pygmy died, and I reached home in safety: with Miani it was just the reverse; in November, 1872, he succumbed to the effects of the Niam-niam climate and to the fatigue of his journey, whilst his two Akka reached Rome in perfect health in June, 1874.

Having been bequeathed by the unfortunate traveller to the Italian Geographical Society, the young Africans were entrusted to the charge of Count Miniscalchi Erizzo,* a man well known for his Oriental researches, with whom they found a kind home and received a careful training. Thus for nearly four years have these sons of Equatorial Africa been nurtured beneath the sunny skies of Italy.

In the autumn of 1876 I had the pleasure of an interview with these wonderful young strangers in the Miniscalchi Palace at Verona. They were in excellent health and spirits, and when I was introduced to them as one who had visited their distant home, greeted me without the least touch of awkwardness or embarrassment. Their attainments were quite surprising; each of them wrote his name in a firm, bold hand, and read fluently from a book with a perfectly good Italian accent; and the elder of the two, although he was almost entirely self-taught, and had received scarcely any regular instruction, played a little air upon the piano with great correctness. His tiny fingers could barely reach three quarters of an octave. Later in the day I saw the two youths walking happily on the broad pavements of the Corso Cavour in company with a young European friend, and I could not help contrasting their present life in the ancient palace of a Veronese nobleman with their early existence, when at any moment they might have been consigned to the flesh-pots of the Monbuttoo.

No one, after witnessing the healthy, vigorous condition of the two young Akka, could suppose them to be the scions of a degenerate race, but must rather be compelled to acknowledge them as well-developed types of a highly distinctive stock, and it is greatly to be hoped that, under the kind care and treatment which they are still receiving in the house of the Countess Miniscalchi, they will long be spared, and that many experts in the science of comparative anthropology may be enabled to make their acquaintance.

According to the measurements I took on the day of my visit (October 1st, 1876), I found that Tibo Francesco, the elder of the two Akka, was 4 feet 6 inches in height, and Cheirallah Luigi, the younger, about 4 feet 2 inches; thus neither of them had attained the 4 feet 10 inches which I had hitherto found to be the average height of their tribe. Francesco, whose upper lip began to show signs of a moustache, I reckoned at 16 years of age; Luigi, from 13½ to 14. Both of them exhibited the same remarkable breadth

* He died in April, 1876.

of shoulder in comparison with their height, which I had noticed in all other Akka, and which I consider one of the distinctive marks of their race.

Some few of the anatomists who have examined Miani's Akka have pronounced them to be of dissimilar nationality; this judgment I believe to be erroneous, for although the physiognomy may differ, there is a marked resemblance in the shape of the skull. Francesco certainly has a more projecting jaw than Luigi, but this may be accounted for by the difference in age: their hair, noses, eyes and ears, are very much alike, and both of them have the deep indentation at the top of the nose and the nearly spherical skull which I noticed as peculiar to all the Akka with whom I came in contact during my residence near the court of Munza. Like my own Nsewue, both Francesco and Luigi had hands that were remarkably small and delicate.

In accordance with the general desire to know something of the female portion of this remarkable race, in 1876 Romolo Gessi, another Italian traveller, brought to Europe a slave-girl who had been offered to him as an Akka at one of the markets on the Bahr-el-Gebel. She is now at Trieste, where she is said to be thriving admirably. According to Mateucci,* however, the genuineness of her nationality is very doubtful.

* 'Gli Akkah e le razze Africane.' Bologna, 1877.

CHAPTER XII.

Return to the north—Tikkitikki's reluctance to start—Passage of the Gadda—Sounding the Keebaly—The Kahpily—Antelope-hunt—Cataracts of the Keebaly—Kubby's refusal of boats—Possibility of fording—Origin of the Keebaly—Division of highland and lowland—Return to Nembey — Bivouac on the frontier — Eating wax — Declaration of war—Parley with the enemy—My mistrust of the guides—Treacherous attack on Mohammed—A dangerous wound—Open war—Detruncated heads—Effect of arrows—Mohammed's defiance—Attack on the abattis—Pursuit of the enemy—A mysterious procession—Wando's bad omen—Consulting the oracle — The Farookh — Mohammed's favourable progress — Capture of Niam-niam women — Lamentations of the husbands—Cruelty to dogs—The calamus—Another capture—Upper course of the Mbrwole—Composure of the captive—Change of scenery—Arrival at the Nabambisso.

AFTER a sojourn of three weeks, the 12th of April was fixed for the raising of our camp and for the departure of our caravan from the residence of the Monbuttoo king.

For myself it was with a sad and heavy heart that I had to begin retracing my steps towards the north. How bitter was my disappointment may well be imagined. I could not be otherwise than aware that I was leaving behind my only chance of answering some of those important questions that might be propounded to me; and my regret was aggravated by the conviction that a journey comparatively short would now have brought me to the sources of the three great rivers of the west, the only streams that are absolutely closed to our geographical knowledge, viz., the Benwe, the Ogawai, and the Congo. Distant as I was hardly more than 450 miles from the limit that had been reached by Livingstone, I could discern, as I fondly imagined, from Munza's residence, a path clearly open towards the south-west which would conduct me to the Congo and to the states of the mighty Mwata Yanvo; it appeared to me to be a path that, once explored, would solve the remaining problems of the heart of Africa as decidedly as the sword of Alexander severed the Gordian knot, and now, just when there was only one more district to be traversed, and that not larger than what we had already passed since leaving the Gazelle, to be obliged to abandon further progress and to leave the mysterious secrets still unravelled was a hardship to which it was impossible patiently to submit. But there was no alternative, and, however reluctantly, I had to yield.

I have already spoken of the various obstacles to any further advance; I must, however, again insist upon my conviction that any single traveller, provided he had not an undue proportion of flesh (for to be fat would be fatal), might march on unhindered down the Welle as far as Baghirmy, since the population was all well disposed enough as far as regards the white man. But any attempt to carry on an entire caravan in that direction would have met with the most strenuous opposition on the part of King Munza.

The first event of the morning of our start occasioned no small stir amongst the Nubians. Mohammed Aboo Sammat had established a Seriba in the place, for the garrisoning of which twenty-eight men had to be left behind, and several hours elapsed before the necessary conscription could be accomplished. Apart from myself, depressed as I was by my disappointment, every one was elated at the prospect of returning, so that no penalty could be considered much heavier than being compelled to tarry in this remote region for one or two years, and possibly longer, to be the associates of cannibals; each man accordingly upon whom the unlucky destiny chanced to fall received his orders to remain with the loudest murmurs of dissatisfaction, and the outcry and contention threatened to be interminable. At length, by cajoling, by bribing, by promises of ample pay, and, it must be. added, by the representation of the lives of frolic they would lead with the Monbuttoo women, the malcontents were persuaded unwillingly to acquiesce in their fate.

It was noon before the column was actually in motion. The Nubians parted from their companions with the most touching embraces; the crowds of chattering Monbuttoo surrounded the encampment and watched with vivid interest the thousand gestures of farewell, whilst the negro bearers, silent and stolid as ever, set forward on their way.

During this parting scene my little Tikkitikki (as the Niam-niam called the Pygmy who had been presented to me a few days previously) was seized with an apparent fit of home-sickness; he set up such a dismal howling and sobbed so bitterly that I confess I was for a while undecided whether I would really carry him away; but I soon discovered that it was only the uninitiated who could be imposed upon by his behaviour. He was not bewailing the loss of his home, for he was utterly ignorant as to where that home had been; neither was he deploring his separation from his kinsfolk, for they stood by, gesticulating wildly, and only mocked at his distress. The fact was, he was influenced solely by his dread of strangers. He was in mortal fear of being eaten up. It very rarely happens among the Monbuttoo that natives are surrendered to the Nubians for slaves: the occasion therefore of a present being made of a human creature would only too readily suggest the thought that some ulterior destination for cannibal purposes was in view. Altogether inadequate to appease Tikkitikki's fears as to his approaching fate was the gorgeous silk jacket in which I arrayed him, and it was with no little satisfaction that I found I could pacify him by offering him the choicest morsels that I could procure for him to eat. After spending a few days with me in my tent, and finding himself treated with all the dainties that the country could produce, he forgot his troubles, laid aside his apprehensions, and became as happy as a little prince.

For about five miles we followed the route by which we had arrived, proceeding in a north-easterly direction until we reached the mounds of gneiss that lay before the third stream. Making a little *détour* to the left I mounted the eminences, which were crowned with some fine fig-trees, whence I could watch our long caravan winding amongst the plantain-groves; now and then my view of the *cortége* would be obstructed by some rising oil-palms, and finally the train would disappear in the obscurity of the gallery-forest. The streams were now much swollen, and their passage entailed not only a considerable loss of time but some trial of strength. The paths were so narrow that we were compelled to proceed in single file, not unfrequently being obliged to halt in places where the shadows of the forest were far too light to afford us any protection from the raging heat. Altogether, however, in spite of its inconveniences, the journey was through scenery so charming that it could not be otherwise than enjoyable.

After crossing the third brook we made a turn to the right, thus entering upon a way that was new to us. Having traversed an open steppe along the edge of a gallery extending to the north-east, we encamped at nightfall at a farmstead near the river Gadda. Half-an-hour's march in the morning brought us to the river-bank.

In its dimensions the Gadda resembles the Wow just above its junction with the Dyoor, but it does not exhibit the same periodical changes in the volume of its waters; its bed remains full throughout the year, and at this date (April 13th) I found that it was 155 feet wide and 3 feet deep, its velocity being 57 feet in a minute. The banks were bounded by light woods, and the soil not being subject to any further inundations had only a gentle slope; the flood-marks on the shore proved the difference between the highest and lowest conditions of the river to be 20 feet. The Gadda has its source far to the south-east, and, flowing across the dominions of the Monbuttoo king Degberra, joins the Keebaly: the united streams then receive the name of the Welle.

Without unnecessary loss of time we forded the sandy river-bed, and, continuing our march for about another half hour, arrived at the left bank of the Keebaly. The river here exhibited much the same character as the Welle at the spot where we had forded it upon our outward journey, but I presume it was somewhat narrower, as by trigonometrical measurement I found that its width was only 325 feet.

By the orders of the king, boats were in readiness to convey the caravan across, and the ferrymen did their work so well and quickly that the entire passage was accomplished in three hours. While the transit was being effected I took the opportunity of embarking in a canoe for the purpose of estimating the depth and velocity of the stream, an operation in which I was materially assisted by the greater experience of my servant Mohammed Ameen. In the same way as I noticed on the Welle, the current was much stronger on the northern or right shore; by throwing a gourd upon the flood and observing the number of feet it progressed in a minute, I estimated the ratio of the currents upon the opposite banks to be as 15:19. The depth was between 12 and 13 feet, and there were neither rocks nor sand-banks in this part of the river-bed.

As I stood in the long grass superintending the stowage of the baggage, I was considerably inconvenienced by the inquisitiveness of the natives, who persisted in thronging close around.

Northward again. We passed the farmsteads of the local overseer Parra, crossed the brook Mboolah, and pitched our camp at a hamlet but a few miles from the stream. The remainder of the day I spent in botanizing. I made my way into the thickets, and found some splendid representatives of such large-leaved plants as the Philodendra, Calladia, and Marantha, which gleamed with a metallic sheen. The overseer was very liberal; he supplied us freely with beer, and the greater part of the night was spent in friendly intercourse with the natives, who found, as ever, my hair and my lucifers to be an unfailing source of interest. Myself the people designated as "a good man," and, satisfied that I had come from the skies, they interpreted my arrival as a token of peace and happiness.

Our road on the following day lay through a country that was generally open, and we had no stream to cross until we reached the brook Bumba, near the village of Bongwa. Here we regained our former route. The country was perfectly safe, and I was accordingly able to march with my own people in the rear of the caravan, and devote my attention to my botanical researches. The hamlets that we passed were pleasant resting-places, and as we halted under the welcome shade of the foliage, the natives rarely failed to hasten out and bring fresh plantains for our refreshment.

At Bongwa we made a halt for a whole day, for the purpose of giving the smiths an opportunity of working, as it was necessary for our copper bars to be transformed into some thousands of rings. For my own part I found ample employment in sketching, and in adding what I could to my store of curiosities. The victualling of the caravan, moreover, had become a matter of increased difficulty; it was now the season for planting out, and all the roots and tubers which the natives had spared from the preceding year had just been put into the ground, so that there was a general scarcity of provisions; a fact that was brought home to our own experience, when we found that the yams that were supplied to us had already commenced throwing out their fresh sprouts.

Retracing our former track we forded the six approximate streams that it may be remembered I noticed on our advance. On our arrival at Nembey's residence, we at once found shelter in the camphuts that had been erected at our last visit, and which were still in a very fair state of preservation. I took a long ramble and made a careful inspection of the plantations of sugar-cane in the adjoining wilderness upon the river-banks; my first impression was that the canes were a rank spontaneous growth, but I was distinctly and repeatedly assured that they were nowhere, by any chance, found wild, and would not thrive without the aid of man.

Wando's territory was before us. It now became a matter of serious consideration how our progress across that hostile district should be accomplished. Mohammed's first suggestion was that we should take a circuitous route far to the east, and then that he should himself return with his armed forces strengthened by a complement from his head Seriba on the Nabambisso, and thus proceed to rescue the store of ivory that had been entrusted to Wando's care. To this scheme no doubt there were various objections. The new route would be entirely unknown to the Nubians, and as, beyond a question, it would lead across wildernesses utterly void of population, the caravan would necessarily have to endure no small measure of privation. In any case trustworthy guides would be necessary in order that the caravan might arrive at its destination in any seasonable time. Notwithstanding all difficulties, Mohammed resolved to attempt to penetrate to the eastern Monbuttoo country, although for this purpose we should be obliged to recross the Keebaly. Nembey was tributary to Degberra, the king of the eastern Monbuttoo, and it had been necessary for Mohammed thus to proceed in the first place to his village; the fact being that the enmity between Munza and Degberra was so bitter that there was no possibility of passing *directly* from the territory of one to that of the other. We started accordingly, and the whole train having crossed the brook Kussumbo, we turned to the south-east along an open steppe, and proceeded for about half a league until we reached a deep hollow from which there issued one of the smaller tributaries of the Kussumbo. This hollow was formed by one of the landslips so common in this part of Africa, caused by the gradual washing away from below of the ferruginous swamp-ore, which was here at least 50 feet thick. The depth of the defile itself was about 80 feet; its sides were enveloped in dense bushes, and the masses of rock, which were quite homogeneous, were adorned with a covering of hitherto unknown fern of the genus adiantum, which, in spots like this, clothes the reeking stones with a complete down of feathery fronds.

Another half league across the steppe and I was surprised to find that we were on the banks of a copious river that about eight miles to the south-west joined the Keebaly. Astonished at the sight of the rushing waters I turned to my Monbuttoo guide, and, availing myself of the few words in his dialect with which I was familiar, I asked him "*Na eggu rukodassi?*" (What do you call that river?) From his reply I discovered that it was the Kahpily, not the Keebaly. The similar sound of the names of these two collateral streams warned me afresh how carefully the traveller should render the names of rivers which he hears;* time passes on and the names of places are changed with their chiefs, but the names of their rivers are handed on by the Africans from generation to generation as long as their language and nationality remain unaltered;† only where these change do the names of the rivers fall into oblivion. The Kahpily has a rapid current from north-east to south-west; its depth here was only 4 feet, but its bed, 40 feet in width, and its steep rocky walls, 40 feet in height, demonstrated that this important stream must be subject to a considerable increase in its volume. In my own mind I was convinced that all these rivers, meeting within so limited an area, must have their sources in some mountain region at no great distance, little as the aspect of the surrounding country seemed to warrant the supposition. It was evident to my mind that the Kahpily must rise near the source-streams of the Dyoor, and from a mountain-chain extending to the south-east from Baginze, a district which would appear to be the nucleus of a whole series of source-streams that flow thence to the north and west.

While the caravan was being carefully conducted across the river by means of an immense stem of a tree that stretched over from bank to bank, I enjoyed a refreshing bath in the foaming waters. Proceeding next in the direction of E.S.E., we passed over a level steppe. As we approached the river that next intercepted us we found that we were on the recent track of a lion; the vestiges in the red clay were all so well-defined that the natives, with their keen hunting instinct, pronounced without hesitation that they had been made by an aged male. The steppes extend for a long distance along the right bank of the Keebaly without being relieved by human habitations, and the district naturally abounds with game. Herds of leucotis antelopes animated the plain and tempted me to devote an hour to the chase. Drenched with perspiration, almost as if I were in the tumult of a battle, and

---

* See 'Livingstone's Last Journal,' ii. pp. 63, 64.

† It may be objected that this theory does not hold good for many parts of Central Africa. Barth (vol. iii. p. 266) gives twelve instances to prove that all the tribes of the Central Soudan have no other distinctions for any of their streams beyond the general terms of " water " or river. But I must be permitted to urge that the Arabs of the Eastern Soudan have their Atbara, Sobat, &c. At any rate, the people amongst whom I travelled, especially the Niam-niam and the Monbuttoo, formed remarkable exceptions, for they invariably gave all localities the names of the adjacent rivers or brooks.

aimlessly following the impulse of the moment, I pushed my way through the tall savannah-grass. Hunting in Africa may be fairly described to be one continual whirl and scramble; the very abundance of game confuses the vision; one object of attraction rises rapidly after another, and baffles any attempt at deliberation. After considerable perseverance I succeeded in bringing down a buck antelope, much to the astonishment of the natives, who were watching my movements from the road, and persisted to the last in questioning the efficiency of my firearms. I hit a second antelope, but did not kill it. It was pursued by the natives for many miles, and only just before sunset did they succeed in surrounding it so that they could despatch it by means of their lances. In the middle of the night I was called up, and naturally supposed that something serious had transpired, but I soon discovered that the reason why my rest had been disturbed was merely that I might be shown the mark of my bullet in the animal's thigh. The men insisted upon my feeling the depth of the wound with my finger, and seemed unable to comprehend that they were showing me nothing that was new.

A little rivulet, called the Kambeley, wound down a hollow incline of which the sides were indented with many a vale of different level. The sides of the hollow were covered for a considerable height with a tangled jungle from which the great leaves of the trumpet-tree (*Cecropia*) rose like brilliant fans; and interwoven amongst its thickets there was a new species of palm, something akin to the rotang, of which every leaf terminated in a long spray, armed with prickles, like a pike-hook. From this palm the Monbuttoo cut canes as thick as their arms, which are reputed to be so difficult to break that they are not unfrequently used as a criterion in testing strength. Above the primeval wood the narrow valley was crowned with a number of small and graceful huts. Altogether the spot was so romantic and wild, and yet withal it had an air of so much snug and cosy comfort, that it seemed to entice one to choose it for his home.

At this point our caravan was joined by a party of people sent by Kubby, one of Degberra's sub-chieftains, from beyond the Keebaly, to open ivory transactions with Mohammed, a circumstance that boded us no good, and forbade us from being in any way sanguine of a hospitable reception from Kubby. This half-way meeting was only a blind; it was a pretext to prevent us from alleging that his subsequent refusal to allow us to cross the river was actuated by any hostile motive. An African chief always likes to have a loophole as long as it is doubtful whether peace is preferable to war.

The ground, with its continual indentations, slanted gradually downwards as we approached the great river. Several ravines and clefts with their flowing source-springs had to be traversed before we reached the river-bank, and even then, with the roar of the cataract close beside us, we were obliged to trace and retrace our steps up and down the shore before we could find a suitable place for an encampment.

At this date (April 18th) the Keebaly filled a bed more than 1200 feet in width. The main current followed the left or southern shore, along which a great bank of gneiss lay exposed, now stretched out in wide flats, and now piled up in countless fragments like huge lumps of ice. The extreme height of this bank never exceeded fifty feet, while the northern bank, on which we had our station, was covered with the most splendid forest and rose to a height of at least a hundred feet. Higher up, the stream was parted into numerous channels, and amidst these was a profusion of woody islands, against which the foaming waters broke, throwing the sparkle of their spray into the darkness of the thicket.* The channels appeared to be all quite navigable, although the sound of the rapids could be distinctly heard. "Kissingah" is the general name by which these rapids are distinguished; but the Monbuttoo are accustomed simply to refer to them as "the islands." We could observe the conical roofs of the fishing-huts peeping out from amidst the foliage, and noticed the canoes of the unfriendly natives darting rapidly across from one islet to another. Not one, however, of these fishing-boats came near us; nor was there the least indication of the coming of any of Kubby's messengers to assist us in our passage across the stream. We became aware only too soon of a resolution to obstruct our progress, the cause of which was readily to be explained. Poncet's (subsequently Ghattas's) company had a Scriba in Kubby's district, and the Nubians who had been left in charge had succeeded in inducing the chief to refuse us the assistance of his boats, for no other reason whatever than that they feared Mohammed's competition with themselves, and that they were eager to monopolize the entire ivory-trade of the district.

For the next day we waited on. No boats arrived. This waste of time suited the plans neither of Mohammed nor of myself. Our

* The accompanying drawing, taken on the spot, will convey a correct idea of the scene.

VIEW ON THE KEERALY, NEAR KUBBY.

provisions, moreover, were getting low. There was no prospect of revictualling. Accordingly our resolution was taken: without delay we would return to Nembey.

During the day of indecision, I exerted myself as best I could to explore the wildernesses of the Keebaly.

An infallible proof of the size and copiousness of the river was afforded by the number of hippopotamuses that were floundering about.

The waters of the Keebaly have the repute of affording a home to a very remarkable animal that has never been observed in any of the streams that rise from the Nile basin. The Nubians, who have a habit of calling anything with which they are not familiar by whatever name may come uppermost at the moment, have given this animal the designation of a "Kharoof-el-bahr," or river-sheep; they describe it in such a way that there can be little doubt that it is a manatus or lamantin (probably M. Vogellii), which is so frequently found in the rivers of Western Africa that flow into the Atlantic. My short and unsettled sojourn on the Keebaly prohibited me from securing, out of these tropical source-streams, a specimen of this strange representative of the Sirenia family.

I am perfectly certain that if Mohammed had pleased he could have forced his way across the river. The dexterous Nubians had but to swim over with their guns upon their heads, and they could readily have taken possession of the canoes which, too large and cumbrous to be transported by land, were concealed in the thickets upon the opposite shore. I merely mention this to illustrate my opinion that, with a company of Nubians, the great African rivers in themselves offer no insuperable obstacles to a resolute traveller.

As already affirmed, the Keebaly is to be considered as the mainstream of the river that, in its lower course, is known as the Welle. Before quitting it we may do well to give our brief attention to the geographical questions that are associated with this discovery.

In the accounts collected from his agents, and published by Poncet, the river is called the Boora or Baboora;* but as I never heard this name, I can only surmise that Poncet's informants had somehow misunderstood or misinterpreted the regular name Keebaly or Keebary. In the same way I never heard anything of a king mentioned under the name of Kagooma, or of a tribe called the Onguroo. The Nubians seem never to recollect the native names

* In many Central African dialects, such as the Baghirmy and Bongo, the monosyllable " ba " means " river."

of rivers, and invariably pronounce all names whatever most incorrectly; the information derived from that quarter is of little value to the geographer, and it is very much to be regretted that the most travelled and experienced leaders of the Khartoom expeditions should have failed so much in acquiring definite details; had it been otherwise, their knowledge would have been of great assistance in laying down more complete and accurate maps of the country.

The probability that the Keebaly and the Welle are identical with the upper course of the Shary appears to become at once almost a positive certainty when we ask the counter-question, "If this is not the Shary, whence does the Shary come?" All that we know and all that we do not know about the north and north-western districts conspire to satisfy us that in that direction there is neither a sufficient reservoir, nor an adequate space, for the development of a network of streams large enough to form a river which is half a mile broad at its mouth, and which fills a lake as large as the whole of Belgium. The waters of the Welle, however, do not rise till April, while the Shary occasionally rises in March. In order to explain this earlier rising of the lower river, we seem to be compelled to adopt the supposition that there must be some *second* main-stream which issues from a latitude more southerly than the Keebaly. Quite insignificant are the two affluents, the Nalobey and the Nomayo, which the river receives on the left from the south of Munza's territory.

There can be little doubt about the real origin of the Keebaly. Although, as delineated on my map, the river has a position as though it issued directly from the north-west angle of the Mwootan Lake (Albert Nyanza), nothing was more remote from my intention than to jump to such a precipitate conclusion; there was nothing either in the nature of the river and its tributaries, or in the information received from the various natives, which could, in any way, justify such a hypothesis. On the contrary, I am quite convinced of the correctness of Baker's statement. I entirely concur with his view that Lake Mwootan is the great basin of the Nile, and that the Bahr-el-Gebel is its only outlet. That Lake Mwootan, simply on account of its abundance of water, must necessarily have *several* outlets, and that the Ayi (the river which Baker calls the Yè) is one of those outlets, is only a geographical chimera which, in the Old World at least, has no analogy, and which would only be admitted to the theories of *dilettanti*. The missing link in the river-course between Lake Mwootan and the mouth of the Asua has since been explored by Gessi in his voyage in March, 1876. He navigated an arm of the Bahr-el-Gebel that took a N.N.E. direction as far as Duffele, but neither he* nor his companion Piaggia was able to make any satisfactory investigation of another branch, that after issuing from the lake turned N.N.W., and was by the accounts of the natives also an arm of the Bahr-el-Gebel. The streams in this part of Africa so often lose themselves in wide grass-plains, or are broken up by such countless floating islands, that what at first is a strong open current becomes apparently choked up or diverted before entering the main stream, and a traveller may often be tempted to regard it as a mere bifurcation. The true nature of such streams can only be discovered by a land journey along both banks. According to Baker's measurement, Lake Mwootan (Albert Nyanza) is 2720 feet above the level of the sea. But by comparing the rapids of the Keebaly with the height of Munza's residence (2707 feet), which has been verified by the most rigid scientific appliances, I have ascertained that they are almost on the same level as the lake. The river and the lake being thus at the same altitude constitutes decisive evidence that the Keebaly does not issue from the lake, from which it is distant about 180 miles.

All the rivers that were embraced within the compass of my journey appeared to me to have their source in the spur of the Galla-Abyssinian highlands, through which the Bahr-el-Gebel passes in the Madi country. Those which belong to the Nile system would seem to spring from the mountains of Koshi on the north of Lake Mwootan, whilst those which are tributary to the Shary have their source in what Baker designates the Blue Mountains, which he observed to the north-west of the lake. Including the Mfumbiro group on the north of Lake Tanganyika—that group which under Speke's name of " the Mountains of the Moon," has obtained a certain geographical notoriety—this mountain system apparently forms a section of that conspicuous terrace-chain which (with the only exceptions of the Niger source-territory and the lofty isolated coast ranges by the equator) divides the continent of Africa, not according to the prevailing idea into a northern and southern, but into an eastward and westward half of highland and lowland. The highland embraces a large number of inland lakes, some of which allow their waters to escape most diffusely, whilst others appear to have no outlet at all. Many of these lakes are found close to the western ridge of the high ground. Besides the Keebaly, the Lualaba amongst other rivers may be named as forcing its way through the mountains of

* 'L'Esploratore,' 1877, p. 105.

Rua, and apparently flowing in a westerly direction towards the lowland. If we imagine a prolonged line to cut the entire continent from Massowa to Mossamedes, it would coincide almost precisely with the terrace-chain of which I have spoken; it would answer very much to a corresponding line of division between the highlands and lowlands of South America which, like an Africa turned right over, has its coast-chain on the western side.

We made our way back to Nembey by the same route that we had come. Before regaining the place we very narrowly escaped coming into collision with the inhabitants of some hamlets through which we passed. The entire caravan for some days past had been placed upon reduced rations, and when some of the bearers caught sight of the manioc-roots that had been planted close to the dwellings, the temptation of pulling them up was too great to be resisted. The women were highly indignant, assailed the offenders lustily, and shrieked at them with the loudest imprecations. The caravan came to a standstill. As those in the rear never knew what was happening in front, Mohammed, attended by his body-guard, hurried up to inquire into the cause of the disturbance. Having ascertained the circumstances, he came to the resolution that it would be his best policy to make an example of the thieves. Accordingly he gave his instructions, and the delinquents received a sound thrashing with the kurbatch, while the injured women looked on with mingled satisfaction and derision.

On arriving at Nembey we found our grass camp-huts in flames, the inhabitants having set fire to them as a token of their sense of having had enough of our company. They had evidently no wish for us to tarry among them any longer. Without halting, therefore, we continued our march, recrossed the Kussumbo, and, towards dark, reached the last of the villages before the frontier wilderness, where I and my people found comfortable accommodation in a large shed belonging to the local chief. We were here informed that Wando was bent upon our destruction, the entire population of the frontier being already in arms, and the women and children having been removed to a place of safety.

Mohammed by this time had been driven, however unwillingly, to the conclusion that he had neither competent guides nor adequate provisions to enable him to carry out his original project of avoiding the enemy's territory by taking a circuitous route to the east. There was no alternative for us than to continue our old road over the wilderness that bounded the frontier. Meanwhile, repeated showers

A GALLERY-FOREST.

of rain had fallen, and had contributed very much to the difficulty of crossing the swamps by making them unusually humid. So much time was occupied in conveying the caravan across the brook that bounded the Monbuttoo district that I had leisure to make a sketch of the gallery-forest, which, however, very inadequately represents the splendour of its luxuriance.*

The sun was still high when we made our first camp in the wilderness. We were upon the third of the gallery-brooks. Since our former visit new blossoms had unfolded themselves, and seemed to give a fresh aspect to the scene. In every quarter of the thickets, gleaming like torches, there rose the imposing clusters of the Combretum, with its large bright-red bracteæ; and, as if to rival them in splendour, every branch of the Spathodea put forth a *thyrsus* of large orange-coloured balls.

In the midst of my enjoyment, as I was admiring the beauties around me, I was startled by a cry, like a shout of triumph, that came from a party of our negroes who were scouring the woods in the hope of securing something good to eat. I hurried in the direction of the sound, and found the men all clustered round the stem of a tree, to which they were busily applying firebrands. Having discovered a quantity of honey in a hollow tree, they adopted the most effectual measures to secure their treasure, and very soon the honey, the wax, and the very bodies of the bees themselves were indiscriminately devoured. If any one could persuade the inhabitants of Central Africa to desist from their habit of consuming this wax, he would do no small service towards accelerating the civilization of the continent. At present, with the exception of ivory, no article of traffic from these districts repays its transport: but the inexhaustible supply of wax from them might be made the object of a productive trade. Hitherto Abyssinia and Benguela have been the only countries that have supplied any considerable quantities of this valuable product; yet the demand for real beeswax in the lands alone that are subject to

* The annexed woodcut is too minute to represent the details, but it may give some idea of the plantain-groves in the obscurity of these forests. The cumbrous stems are thickly overgrown with wild pepper, and the spreading branches are loaded with long beard moss (*Usnea*), and with that remarkable lichen to which I have given the name of elephant's ear: high among the boughs are the huge dwellings of the tree-termes. Some stems, already decayed, serve as supports for immense garlands of Mucuna, and, overhung by impenetrable foliage, form roomy bowers where dull obscurity reigns supreme. Such is the home of the chimpanzee.

the orthodox Greek Church, where it is the only material allowed for church lights, is almost unbounded.

The ruins of the grass-huts beside the broad meadow-water brought back to our recollection the melancholy night of rain which we had to endure upon our outward journey. The spot was, if possible, more miserable and dejected now. Neither leaves nor grass could be obtained in sufficient quantity for our need. Trees had to be felled to make a path across the swamp, and even then, go carefully as we would, the mud was much above our knees. If the enemy had been sagacious enough to attack us under those adverse circumstances, we should have fallen an easy prey.

In another two days we should pass the enemy's border. The very expectation seemed to awaken our impatience, and we started off at early dawn. Towards noon we came to the official declaration of war, consisting, as I have previously described, of the maize, the feather, and the arrow, hung across our path, as the emblems of defiance. There was something of the anxiety of suspense as we found ourselves at the partition brook which marked off Wando's territory. Aware of the danger of venturing rashly into the pathless thickets, our cautious leader ordered a general halt. Small detachments were first despatched to reconnoitre and to clear the way. As soon as they had satisfied themselves that all was safe, the signal was given by the trumpets, and the column of bearers was set in motion. The crowd of women was not permitted to march as usual in single file, but for the sake of compactness was gathered in a mass and strode on, trampling down whatever vegetation came in its way.

Safely through the wood, we reached an open steppe. We were in sight of the enemy's position, and once again a halt was called. The occasional gleaming of a spear in the grass, or the waving of a plume upon a Niam-niam's hat, made us aware that we were not far from the presence of the foe. They seemed to be in a wide semicircle, that embraced the front of our halting-ground. There was, however, something in their demeanour that appeared to indicate a desire on their part for a parley. The interpreters therefore were sent forward, the trumpeter Inglery at their head; Mohammed himself followed, and a conference ensued. The natives all this time took careful cognizance of the range of the Khartoomers' guns, and did not seem disposed to approach nearer than was requisite to understand what was said.

As the parley proceeded, and we saw the parties draw nearer to each other, we began to expect a favourable termination of the interview. It turned out that the men with whom Mohammed was treating were representatives of the districts adjoining the A-Banga, the Nabanda Yuroo. They declared that though they were subject to Wando they had really no share in his hostile intentions; they were anxious to guard themselves against the mischief that might befall them from their proximity to the scene of war, and consequently were only pleading "for their hearths and homes." Mohammed was inclined to listen to their plea, although he was reckoning without his host. Meanwhile some of the actual belligerents arrived, and professed that they could give us a safe-conduct across the country, declaring that they were well aware where Wando had deposited Mohammed's ivory, and upon these pretexts they urged Mohammed to accept them as guides.

I could not resist making my way up to Mohammed as he stood surrounded by his guard, and giving his instructions to the interpreters, in order that I might point out to him the advantage of his position. I wanted him to understand how much better it would be to secure all these men as hostages than to trust to their promises and proposals; but he made light of my apprehensions, affirming that savages were all cowards and afraid of war, and that he had no doubt everything would come right at last.

Without further delay the A-Banga were then permitted to escort us to their villages on the other side of the brook, where, in spite of the suspicious absence of all the women and children, we received an abundant supply of provisions, and I was presented with a good store of the flesh of some eland-antelopes, which the natives had killed on the day before. In reality, these people amply deserved a thorough chastisement at our hands for the massacre of our women slaves during our outward journey, but Mohammed, under the hope of obtaining a safe transit and recovering his ivory, thought it more diplomatic to overlook the offence.

Before sunrise next morning all were in readiness to proceed. To myself the day proved to be one of the few unlucky days that marred the general good fortune that attended my enterprise. A slight mishap befell me in crossing the first brook, which was but the precursor of a more serious trouble to come. In crossing a swamp I fell into a deep quagmire, from which I scrambled out with everything upon me except my hat covered with the blackest and filthiest of mire. With all my might I shouted to my servants to bring me clean dry clothes. My outcry raised an alarm that spread to the rear. There arose an impression that I had been wounded, and in a short time half the caravan had crowded round. Order having been restored, we proceeded on our way, deviating, however, a little from our previous route, and passing numerous villages and cultivated spots. Owing to irregularities in the soil our caravan became somewhat broken, and it was deemed advisable to make a halt near the huts of the next local overseer, for the double purpose of gathering the stragglers and of allowing an interval for the morning meal.

Starting afresh, Mohammed led the way. He was himself unarmed, but he was attended by his young armour-bearers, and followed by a detachment of his black body-guard. Next in order and close behind were the men whose mediation and offers of guidance had yesterday been accepted. Somehow or other I could not get rid of my presentiment that these fellows were not to be trusted, and accordingly, contrary to my custom, I took good care to keep my trusty rifle in my hand. It struck me as very remarkable that in the villages which we passed the men, women, and children were all assembled in crowds, and calmly watched our progress, just as though there was no rumour or thought of war.

After about half a league I was at the head of a column of bearers, but I had fallen some hundred paces behind Mohammed. All at once several shots fired in rapid succession made me aware that something unusual had happened in front. Looking to the right I saw some natives rushing away at full speed across the steppes; a hasty fire was opened upon the fugitives, and their savage yells of pain betrayed that some of them were wounded, although they contrived to make good their escape. Another moment and I caught sight of Mohammed being carried back towards us with a broad streak of blood across his white sash, and close beside were the two little armour-bearers writhing with their faces to the ground, their backs pierced by the native lances. It was a ghastly sight. Dashing up to Mohammed I ripped up his clothes, and discovered at a glance that my poor friend had received a deep spear-cut in his thigh. I did not lose an instant in adopting what measures I could. As fate would have it, I had a box of insect-needles in my pocket. Water, of which we were always careful to have a supply, was close at hand. Mohammed's own muslin scarf was just the thing for a bandage. Having been carefully washed, and then bound together with half-a-dozen of the strongest of the needles, and finally enveloped in the scarf and tied with yarn, the gaping wound was completely dressed, and began to heal almost as soon as it was closed.

The sad event had occurred in this way. One of the pretended guides forced his way between Mohammed and his young shield-bearers, and brandishing his lance cried out, "The people of Yuroo are for peace; *we* are for war." Mohammed instinctively made a sidelong movement to escape the falling blow, and thus probably saved his life. Meanwhile the other natives attacked the boys and stabbed them between the shoulders. Although Mohammed had escaped the direct blow that was intended, the huge lance, with its head a foot and a half in length, had sunk deep into his flesh. With the fortitude of desperation he dragged the murderous weapon from the wound, hurled it after the fugitive assassin, and then fell senseless to the earth. The injury caused by the barbs of the spear (which were an inch long) was miserably aggravated by the impetuous fury with which the weapon was extracted. The wound was broad and deep enough to admit my whole hand, and had only just escaped the kidney, which was visible through the open flesh.

In their first surprise at the sudden attack, Mohammed's personal retinue had fired almost at random after the fugitive traitors; but as their guns were only loaded with deer-shot, they for the most part hit the enemy without killing them. Immediately there ensued a general chase, and during the time that I was engaged in binding up Mohammed's wound, I could hear the reports of firearms along the whole line of our procession.

And now again a halt was ordered, the columns of bearers were collected, their loads were deposited in piles upon the ground, and the signal was given for a general plunder. Joyfully enough was the order hailed; it was especially welcome to the hungry Bongo after their scanty fare on the previous days.

As a proof that the natives were in league together, I noticed that directly after the treacherous attack upon Mohammed, all spectators disappeared from the road; and although the Nubians, considering themselves perfectly justified in taking what slaves they could, went in pursuit of women and children, I did not see that their exertions were attended with any success. They secured a number of unfortunate boys, but they let them loose again, persecuting them with gun-shot and lances as they took to flight. The air rung with their shrieks, and it was only the long grass, I cannot doubt, that prevented my seeing not a few of these undeserving victims sink and die upon the earth.

Within an hour not only were the granaries of the villages around effectually ransacked and abundance of corn piled up around our quarters, but the villages themselves were involved in flames. With an expedition quite astonishing, the conical roofs were removed from the nearest huts and employed in the construction of an improvised camp for ourselves, which was subsequently surrounded by a substantial abattis. The woodwork from the adjacent dwellings furnished the material for this defence, which we presumed might be necessary in case of attack.

Meantime our fighting force was adequate to keep the natives, who had assembled to do battle with us as intruders, at a safe distance from our camp, where our own negroes were busily storing whatever they had captured. While this was going on some of the fighting-men came in, and approaching their chieftain, who, wrapped in wet bandages, was reclining on a couch beneath a tree, laid at his feet their first trophies of war, consisting of several heads of the A-Banga. It was in the first excitement of battle that these heads had been taken off the bodies of the fallen, and in revenge for the slaughterous attack upon Mohammed; but throughout the whole period of hostility, although some twenty natives were killed, this was the first and last instance that came under my notice of the barbarous custom. All the negroes attached to our caravan had a superstitious horror of the practice of decapitating the dead, and the Nubians would have deemed themselves defiled by touching the corpse of a heathen.

The scene of these adventures was within gunshot of a bank thicket, through the deep hollow of which flowed a copious brook that a little farther north joined the Assika. On the opposite bank, which was considerably higher than the side on which we were encamped, there were several groups of hamlets scattered about the open plain, and between these, numbers of armed men could be distinguished hurrying about, the precise object of whose activity we were at a loss to determine. Amongst the Nubians who were with us were some of the stoutest and most resolute men in the whole of Aboo Sammat's corps, and these had come to the resolution that they would force their way through the natives who might be hidden in the jungle, cross the brook, and carry an attack over to the opposite bank. All the ivory that had been purchased on the outward route and deposited in the land seemed to be in peril of being lost, and it was the conviction of the Nubians that their only chance now of recovering their property was by capturing some of the native women, who would have to be redeemed. Things seemed to promise favourably for the undertaking. The soil was suitable, the network of brooks and trenches interspersed with grass plots opened certain facilities for encompassing an adversary, and if the Nubians had acted with greater determination they could hardly have failed to secure the desired hostages; but the passage across the woods on the river-banks was their first difficulty. They had to contend at a great disadvantage, for they could only squander their bullets uselessly or at random among the trees; while the natives from their lurking-places could do good and sure execution with their spears and arrows.

I accompanied our party of assailants for some distance, and had a better opportunity than had ever presented itself before of observing the effect of the native arrows. The arrows that had wooden heads I observed to have a range of at least 300 paces, and to fall with scarcely a sound; such as had iron tips on the contrary came whizzing through the air, but would not carry half the distance; these appeared only to be used when the natives felt tolerably sure of their aim.

The A-Banga have a war-dress and equipments that would seem to be entirely derived from the Monbuttoo: they dance and jump about behind the bushes as if they were taking part in a pantomime, generally trying to keep a crouching posture, and only rising to discharge their arrows. The storm of arrows which they hurled against us as we advanced fell like strays from a waggon-load of straw, and yet our enemy could not be detected anywhere, except that at intervals a form would be seen to rush across as it changed its place of ambush. Just at the beginning of the fray one of our side was struck by a wooden arrow in rather a remarkable way; the point, which was some inches long and as hard as iron, having caught the inner corner of his eye, remained sticking close to the side of the lachrymal cavity; the fellow roared out lustily, but he was found to have sustained no serious hurt. It was said that a casualty of this kind was by no means unusual, because the natives always aimed at the eye as the most vulnerable quarter; but as the arrows are very light, and have to describe a curve before they can reach their mark, I should presume their destination is altogether a matter of chance.

On the border of the wood, close to the pathway as it emerged, some of the more courageous of the natives made a stand and received our people with gestures of defiance, brandishing their weapons, and tossing their plumed heads. From the thickets beyond, the war-cries of those who were less venturesome could be distinctly heard, and from the distance, beyond again, resounded the clang of the kettledrums. One of the savages sprang forward towards us, and holding up his shield denounced us with a volley of maddened imprecations. A bullet quickly pierced alike his shield and his breast, and he sank mute and senseless to the earth. A second ventured forward, but only to succumb to the same fate. Then the savages thought it was time to retreat, and accordingly wheeling round they disappeared into the obscurity of the wood, where the rustle of the foliage gave witness to a general flight. Now was the opportunity to cross, of which the Nubians took advantage, but though they reached the farmsteads without opposition they could only fire into the air without an aim, as though they were greeting the new moon after the fast of Ramadan.

For myself curiosity alone had led me on. I had no warlike ardour, I had no feeling of vengeance against the natives, and consequently I took no personal share in this mild skirmish, but those who were present delighted afterwards in telling wonderful stories of the daring prowess I had displayed in penetrating the enemy's ranks. Such reports often follow a traveller's reputation for years, and whoever repeats them is pretty sure to append some marvel of his own fancy. " *When Fame paints a serpent, she attaches feet to its body.*"

The savages had no idea of the velocity of a bullet; they invariably ducked their heads as often as they could hear a ball whistling in the air; and it was a very ludicrous spectacle when hundreds of black heads that had been peeping from behind the trees would simultaneously disappear.

By sundown the whole region about us was clear of the enemy, and as darkness came on the bearers returned within the shelter of our abattis, laden richly with spoils that they had secured in the adjacent villages. Sentries and watch-fires were established, and the night was passed in a stillness that was rarely broken by a stray and distant shot. With the exception of a few Bongo-bearers who, yielding to their marauding propensities, had pushed too far into the hamlets, we had suffered no loss. Two of the Nubians, however, had received severe lance-wounds, and had to be carried back to the camp on litters.

It was currently reported among the natives that Mohammed was mortally wounded. Encouraged by the accession of fresh contingents

MOHAMMED DEFIES HIS ENEMIES.

To face p. 107.

during the night, they once again made the woods re-echo with their savage war-cries, amidst which could be heard the vilest and most abusive Arabic invectives that they seemed to have learnt for the mere purpose of vituperating their enemies. Mbahly's death, however, was the burden of their chorus. "Mbahly! Mbahly! Give us Mbahly. We want meat." Mohammed would not submit to these taunts. In spite of his weakness he insisted upon showing himself. With his wound firmly bandaged, he was conveyed beyond the camp to a white-ant hill, from whence he could be seen far around. For nearly a quarter of an hour he stood upon this elevation swinging his scimitar, and shouting with the full strength of his voice, "Here I am, Mbahly is not dead yet." He then challenged them to come with a hundred lances if they dare, and retorted upon them in jeering scorn their cry of, "Pushyo! pushyo!" (meat, meat), always using the Niam-niam dialect, in which he was tolerably fluent.*

Mohammed was at once to be recognised by his Monbuttoo straw hat, with its bright-red feathers. Although all his compatriots would have considered it a degradation to adopt a savage costume, he always delighted, in these expeditions, to dress himself like a native chieftain. In order to give the natives a still further demonstration of his safety, in the course of the afternoon he made his nephew array himself in his own state attire, his flowing rokko-coat, and his stately plumes, and sent him to conduct a sally towards the north. This party, however, returned without coming to any engagement.

I spent the whole day in my own tent preparing the ammunition which I supposed would be requisite for my people if the state of warfare should last. Deer-shot, with some of a heavier description, I considered would be of the greatest service in the hands of unskilful marksmen. I had another occupation, which made me feel like a very Nemesis. I manipulated the heads of the A-Banga men which I had so recently appropriated. Probably with their own eyes these heads had watched the stewing of other human heads, but now they had to simmer in my caldron. Although I was quite aware that the Nubians reckoned the bones of all heathens and unbelievers as entitled to no more respect than the bones of brute beasts, yet for decency's sake I preferred performing the operation

* In the woodcut that depicts this scene, the background gives a representation of the splendid forest scenery that marked the spot.

in the seclusion of my tent. Notwithstanding that my dogs had not had any animal food for several days, they could not be induced to eat a morsel of the boiled human flesh.

Just as it was growing dark we were startled, if not alarmed, by the appearance of a great troop of natives. The attack was not made, as hitherto, from the dense dark woods at our feet, but proceeded from our old path upon the south. Only the foremost ranks were visible, the rear being hidden by the high grass and bushes; but the wild cries, like the howling of a coming storm, testified to the overwhelming numbers of the aggressors. Half of our armed force issued from the camp in a compact line, and fired a volley straight upon the nearest of the assailants, five of whom were seen to fall dead upon the ground. The altered tone of the war-cry proved that many more were wounded, and as all the guns were loaded with a good handful of heavy shot this was sure to be the case; but this time the conflict came to such close quarters that two more of our men were severely wounded by the native lances. As soon as the attack was thus diverted, and the front ranks of the enemy began to retreat, the negroes of our caravan, who had been placed in reserve immediately behind the soldiers, started off at full speed in pursuit of the fugitives, and their lances made far greater havoc than all the bullets of the Nubians. Before leaving Munza's residence our bearers had all been provided with new weapons, and thus our little negro-band was able to hold its own against greatly preponderating numbers of the enemy.

The weight and diversity of the weapons of the A-Banga, added to the inconvenience of their costume, necessarily prevented them from making a rapid flight; they were consequently obliged to keep throwing off one impediment after another until the ground was strewn with shields, lances, clothes, and sometimes with their false chignons, ornaments and all. When the negroes returned to camp, bringing in their spoil and swinging the chignons on the points of their lances, they were greeted alike with the glad shout of triumph and the loud ring of laughter.

It was near midnight when the pursuers came back. They had prosecuted their chase to the frontier wilderness; they had found the villages all deserted by their inhabitants, and had obtained such stores of plunder that enough was accumulated to keep our whole caravan for a month.

This had been the most energetic attack that the enemy had yet attempted; it was made exclusively by the A-Banga, no Niam-niam having as yet appeared upon the scene. The arrival of Wando, with all his force, was expected the next day.

Early, therefore, on the following morning, half of our little armament was sent forward to the north, not merely to anticipate any movement on Wando's part, but, if possible, to accomplish the object of obtaining some women as hostages, who might be exchanged for the still undiscovered ivory. Mohammed was annoyed at the previous failures to secure any women, knowing by experience that hardly any ransom is accounted too large by the Niam-niam for the recovery of their wives.

About two hours after the departure of our soldiers a singular sight arrested our attention. Marching along in single file upon the top of the opposite slope, which was separated from our camp by the woody depression and the brook, we saw a lengthened train of armed natives, who by their large quadrangular shields gleaming in the sun could be at once recognised as A-Banga. The procession seemed unending; it occupied fully three hours in passing, and at the lowest computation must have consisted of 10,000 or 12,000 men. It was at first the general impression that the chieftain had arrived with the main body of his troops. It was conjectured that he intended to make a circuit to the west, and, having crossed the brook, to attack us at nightfall from the same quarter as our assailants of the previous day. But our fears were not realised, and we remained utterly unable to reconcile the manœuvres we had witnessed with the absence of Wando, which was still a mystery to us, as he might have been joined by all his allies in the course of a single day. Everything, however, was made clear to us when our soldiers returned at night from their plundering expeditions. They told us that on arriving in the morning at the hamlets, they had found the fighting force of the A-Banga all drawn up, evidently waiting in anxious suspense for the assistance of Wando, but that on their approach this large body of men immediately vacated their post. Thus the long train that had caused us so much bewilderment was simply the 10,000 natives retreating at the advance of a detachment of forty or fifty of our soldiers.

Upon the gradual slope on which our camp-enclosure was situated, the white ant-hills, that often rise to an altitude of ten feet, were the only eminences whence any extended view could be obtained across the long grass of the steppe. These were nearly always occupied by the natives, who mounted them for the purpose of getting a better vantage-ground for shouting their menaces and invective insults, but occasionally they answered another end: they served to allow the outposts of the contending parties to hold communication with each other. Amongst Mohammed's trained soldiers he had no less than forty Niam-niam, who were greatly devoted to him. These would appear to have held some correspondence with the enemy, and from them we learnt that the A-Banga were much irritated at the conduct of Wando, who, after urging them to attack us, had left them in the lurch. They complained that all they had got from their acquiescence in his wish was that the "Turks" had killed their fellow-comrades and laid waste their land. Wando himself, they said, had had an unpropitious augury at the beginning of the fray, and, intimidated at the prospect, had abandoned his scheme; he had withdrawn to the recesses of the forest, and, in spite of the remonstrances of the A-Banga, he now refused to render them any aid.

The little wooden bench, the "boroo," which I have already described, was also consulted in our own camp. My two Niam-niam, who were no great heroes, although they had an almost unlimited confidence in Wando's power, had a still more unbounded reliance upon the answers of their wooden oracle. The test had been very unfavourable for one of them, but I was told that it had promised a safe escape for myself, a circumstance that once again confirmed my people in their opinion of my unchangeable good luck. The A-Banga did indeed make an exception in my favour when they shouted their defiance from the ant-hills; the Turks, they vowed, should perish, but the white man might go scot-free, because it was the first time of his coming to their land. The quietness and retirement of my daily occupation, my interested delight in studying the peculiarities of those I saw, and perhaps, too, my reputation of being a harmless "leaf-eater," all seem to have conspired to gain me a general goodwill.

Little Tikkitikki was perfectly unmoved by all the proceedings; he showed no sign of fear; he skipped about and played with the war-trophies; but chiefly he stuffed himself with sesame-pap, of which there was a lavish abundance at his disposal.

On the fourth morning the enemy had entirely vanished; the inhabitants, too, had all utterly gone. Throughout the period of warfare, the Nubians had not come out particularly strong, either in courage or in endurance. The main burden of the contest had fallen upon the "Farookh." As a matter of fact, however, the Nubian regulars and the black Farookh are equally indispensable to every commander of an expedition. The native soldiers may be the better shots, and they have the advantage of knowing the country more thoroughly and of being accustomed to the climate; moreover, on rainy days (when the Nubians would sit shivering in their huts) they will wrap their guns in their girdles and with the greatest alacrity go perfectly naked over wood and steppe to repel an advancing foe; but, at the same time, there is always the risk of their decamping at a moment's provocation,—a dilemma into which a commander would not be led by the Nubians, who would be afraid of deserting at such a distance from Khartoom. The Nubians, however, are much more often ailing; they are never perfectly tractable, having an unconquerable aversion to all restraint; they never showed themselves as remarkably valiant in our conflicts with the savages, and were in continual apprehension of being devoured. It was not so much death in itself of which they were afraid, as of being deprived of the rites of burial, which are prescribed in the Koran as indispensable for obtaining the palm of Paradise. The lack of a grave is abhorrent to the notions of every Mussulman, but the idea of being destined for the unclean stomach of a cannibal was intolerable.

Mohammed, encouraged by the favourable progress of his wound, now expressed his desire to quit our present quarters. I endeavoured to dissuade him from his purpose, and represented to him that, although the wound had closed without any suppuration, any exertion would have a tendency to open it afresh; but he persisted in his purpose, and determined upon being carried in a litter across the hostile territory. In consequence of the journey the complete healing was thrown back for a fortnight; but altogether I congratulated myself that my amateur surgery, which had hitherto been practised mainly on horses and mules, had proved so satisfactory.

By sunrise on the fifth morning after arriving at this inhospitable spot, our caravan was again in motion. The camp was burnt, and great heaps of corn, sesame, kindy, earth-nuts, and other provisions, were scattered about, and as a matter of necessity left behind upon the ground, much to the chagrin of the bearers, who had once again to face the deprivations of the wilderness.

It was not without some confusion that we crossed the Assika. The way before us seemed clear of enemies, and our crowd moved fearlessly on amongst the thickets. The white-ant hills on the outskirts of the forest continued to afford admirable stations for reconnoitring, and for enabling the advanced party to announce that all was safe.

Quitting again our previous line of march, we continued our journey towards the north, and crossed three more brooks, each of them conducting us to a fresh grass plain. Once, just as we approached the edge of a gallery, we were assailed by a shower of arrows, but the volley of bullets that we sent in reply very quickly deterred the invisible foe from any further attack. No doubt the enemy were close enough upon us to make certain of their mark, as the number of iron-headed arrows was unusually large; yet they did not succeed in inflicting a single serious wound. It happened fortunately that the bearers, who were more especially exposed to the arrows, were thrown into no disorder; they had had the careful protection of the Farookh, who had made a fresh path for themselves through the wood, on either side of the beaten track.

After passing the last of the three brooks which I have just mentioned, we came to a cultivated district, and as it was near midday we made a short halt beside the hamlets. The Bongo had now free scope for their destructive propensities; they proceeded to cut down the standing maize to their hearts' content; they not only plundered all within their reach, but laid waste the land in every direction. All the world over, war is ever war.

In ransacking the huts the plundering parties had had the luck to discover some of the missing ivory. A number of valuable tusks were recognised as being those which had been purchased from Wando, by means of some incisions that Mohammed had made upon them; the magazines in which they were concealed being revealed by the cackling of a lot of hens down amongst some unthreshed eleusine. When the hens were found a quantity of eggs was found with them, and I was in consequence treated to a very choice breakfast. Eggs are very rare throughout the district, the Niam-niam hens being as niggardly with them as the Dinka cows are with their milk.

Turning to the E.S.E. we kept now to the right of the depression of the brook, passing numerous groups of huts upon our way. Isolated dome-palms (*Hyphæne thebaica*), rare in the Niam-niam lands, reared themselves at intervals like land-marks on the route. Farther on we crossed the Diamvonoo, which flowed through a ravine precipitous and obscure, and subsequently, leaving the old road to the west, we had to ford a succession of gallery-brooks.

We had already made our way through four of these, when on approaching to the fifth we caught sight of a number of natives who, surprised at our appearance, slunk away from their huts, and tried, like beasts of prey, to find a safe lurking-place in the adjacent thickets. The capture was effected here of two Niam-niam women. They were bringing water from the brook, and being espied by the advanced guard were soon secured and conducted to the caravan, where, after the failure of the previous days, their arrival was hailed with a shout of glee. The women themselves were perfectly composed, and apparently quite indifferent, making themselves at once thoroughly at home with such of their countrywomen as they found already in our train.

It was later than usual before we halted for the night, and our men were more than ordinarily fatigued. In consequence of this our camp was pitched with haste and carelessness. The weather turned out cold and very rainy; the ground became so soft and sodden that it would afford no hold for the tent-pegs; and so all prospect of rest had to be abandoned. Every moment the pole that upheld the frail shelter above me threatened to give way. I held tightly on, and shouted through the commotion of the storm for my servants to make haste, and they only came in time to save me from a thorough drenching. This scene had to be repeated more than once.

It was touching, through the moaning of the wind, to catch the lamentations of the Niam-niam men bewailing the loss of their captured wives; cannibals though they were, they were evidently capable of true conjugal affection. The Nubians remained quite unaffected by any of their cries, and never for a moment swerved from their purpose of recovering the ivory before they surrendered the women.

Anxious next day to continue our course to the east we had to cross so many streams that they seemed to make a labyrinth of waters. The windings of the interlacing brooks and the network of entangled streams apparently corresponded almost precisely with what Livingstone describes as the hydrographical character of the country on the west of Lake Tanganyika, and which he has compared to frosted window-panes in winter. This great explorer noticed a similar source-territory through which flowed the Lualaba,* at that time quite an enigmatical stream. Its course, indeed, was

---

* In one of his letters, Livingstone describes the Lualaba as " a lacustrine river."

towards the north, but Livingstone was manifestly in error when he took it for a true source of the Nile; a supposition that might have some semblance of foundation, originating in the inexplicable volume of the water of Lake Mwootan (Albert Nyanza), but which was negatived completely as soon as more ample investigation had been made as to the comparative level, direction, and connection of other rivers, especially of the Welle.

We now found ourselves in a locality with which our own Niam-niam were by no means acquainted, and there was no facility for getting any proper guides; just, therefore, as might be expected, we missed our way, and proceeded (without knowing whither we should come) for a couple of leagues along a splendid gallery, where numbers of silver-white colobus-apes were merrily taking their pleasure.

I had my suspicions that we were going wrong, and by referring to the journal in which I had entered the details of our former route, I ascertained that we were now taking the same direction as we had followed then. Further inquiry soon convinced us that we were proceeding straight towards the spot where we had last met Wando, and that in fact we were not more than three miles distant from his residence. We were quite aware that he was not just then at his Mbanga, but still there was no doubt that if we would ensure reaching Mohammed's Seriba unmolested, it would be politic to make a wider circuit round the hostile district, and accordingly, without delay, we retraced our steps for a considerable distance.

On the confines of the gallery, the land had just been cleared for a crop of sweet potatoes, and a number of women was occupied in the work. They had a lot of dogs scampering about, and the sight of these caused quite an excitement amongst our Mittoo-bearers, who darted at them with their spears, and slaughtered them in the most remorseless fashion. Pitiable and heartrending in the extreme it was to see the poor brutes writhing upon the lances. I must confess to have felt more sympathy for the dogs in this country than for all the men.

We had now turned due east along a road that led us across the Dyagbe, the brook that ran past Wando's residence; and, after marching for three hours over a desert steppe, we finally encamped upon the left bank of a large gallery-wood, where the vegetation was so luxuriant, that, forgetting all my fatigue, I botanized until night stopped my further researches. Game was abundant, and we had a savoury supper of roast-antelope.

Next morning was wet and gloomy. In forcing our way through the dripping thickets, in order to reach the river, we got thoroughly drenched to the skin. We had also to endure incessant torture from the barbs of the calamus (the generic name of the rotang), which like so many little pike-hooks insinuated themselves through our clothes to our flesh: attached to the twigs and universally diffused among the bushes, they were a perpetual annoyance to the traveller. After we had accomplished this irritating passage, we proceeded northwards, crossed two more brooks of a similar character, and arrived at a cultivated and populous district on the banks of the Mbrwole.

The Farookh, who had been sent on for a league in advance, had effectually scoured the district, and had been rewarded by the capture of a young lady of rank: she had been taken by surprise, and in the wonted manner of the country endeavoured to save herself by taking refuge in the forest, but she was tracked like a deer, and captured after a short chase. She was attired in a magnificent apron of skins, and was elaborately as well as fantastically adorned with strings of teeth; and to judge from the numerous trophies of the chase with which she was decorated, she might be suspected of having a mighty Nimrod amongst her circle of admirers. Full-grown men are never seized on these occasions, and that for two reasons; in the first place because considering capture as identical with death, they defend themselves with the fury of desperation; and secondly, because they are of no value as slaves. In these expeditions, it is an understood thing that the sheyba, or yoke, is never employed to fetter strong men; it would be far too much trouble to look after them and to drive them along when all one's energies are required for the protection of the baggage.

The Mbrwole, which, ten miles lower down, after receiving a number of rivulets from the south, becomes a considerable stream, had here the appearance of being nothing more than an ordinary gallery-brook; and if I had not heard the name from the Niam-niam, who are always accurate in the nomenclature of their waters, I should have never imagined that it was the main-stream. The Bahr-el-Wando, as it is called by the Khartoomers, flowed due west; and though doubtless it was fed by various minor brooks, it was here little more than a ditch of a few feet in breadth; yet the entire depression, clothed with its woody heights, was scarcely less than 1500 paces broad.

The abject terror which the Niam-niam men displayed, lest they should be devoured, formed a very remarkable contrast to the quiet composure of the young woman who had just been captured, and who, without any sign of fear, entered into conversation and was ready to furnish us with whatever geographical information she could. Her calm demeanour led me to the conclusion that the Niam-niam forego eating their female prisoners of war, for the advantage of reserving them as slaves.

Under the guidance of our captive, we crossed the Mbrwole, and, taking possession of the huts on the opposite bank, we found ourselves towards midday well installed in a comfortable camp.

The proximity of our position to the thickets made a nocturnal attack more than probable. I resolved, therefore, to pitch my own tent in the middle of the huts and to keep a lamp burning throughout the night. The tent consequently became (as it was in a measure transparent) a great lantern in the darkness and formed a target for the aim of the missiles from the woods, a number of arrows being found on the following morning sticking in the top; these I have preserved as memorials of our bivouac on the Mbrwole. All night long the natives were skirmishing with our outposts, thus necessitating a continual fire in reply; but although I slept alone in my tent, the experience of the last few days had so accustomed me to the perpetual shots that my night's rest was perfectly undisturbed. I was well aware that before the enemy could get to my position in the centre of the camp, they must alarm the groups of bearers who were crouching round their fires, and must afterwards penetrate the quarters of the soldiers and of my own servants.

To get into the right road we had again to cross the Mbrwole. Another two leagues to the west along the left bank, and the river was recrossed once more. Over cultivated tracts of rising ground we proceeded to the north and came to some extensive flats of gneiss, the first we observed in the course of our return. This gneiss, being on the hither side of the river, and to the east of the furrowed soil which we noticed on our outward way between the Mbrwole and the Lindukoo, acquired an increased significance as apparently belonging to the line of elevation that traverses the watershed of the Nile.

Leaving this interesting locality, we made a palpable descent, and had next to pass over the meadow-waters that, flowing in a northerly direction, formed affluents of the Lindukoo. No regular path conducted to the farther side; pell-mell the caravan plunged into the long grass and clumps of Phrynia that made a half-floating surface to the swampy depths. Experience makes a traveller wary in getting across these marshy spots; he learns by practice how to avoid a ducking; he gets the knack of kicking down a clump of weeds without lifting his feet, and can tell to a nicety whether it will bear his weight; by caution such as this he surmounts the difficulty of "the lacustrine streams." After passing the last of these, we made our next encampment near some Niam-niam hamlets, which, in this direction, were the last before we should arrive at Aboo Sammat's territory. Our arrival here was unexpected, yet before the bulk of the caravan had come up the inhabitants had all made off, so that we found the place entirely deserted. Although the late outbreak of hostilities had put the whole district upon the alert, there were various things to prevent the foe from reckoning with any certainty upon our movements; unevenness of soil, extent of wilderness, prospect of supplies, all influenced our plans, which might be changed at any hour; and thus it happened that, in spite of all the spies that might be set to watch us, the adversary was never safe from being taken by surprise.

Ten leagues still remained between our present quarters and Aboo Sammat's hospitable Seriba, which it was our wish to reach by the shortest route.

An early hour of the following day found us at the Lindukoo, that branch of the Yubbo which I have already described as the last tributary of the Nile system, and which is distinguishable from the other rivers of the district by the eastward flow of its waters. It was here considerably enlarged by receiving the meadow-waters from the watershed. Bounded by banks some 20 feet in height, it meandered along a deep bed that was 30 feet in breadth, through low-lying steppes, which at no great distance were replaced by woods.

The bank-forests that give the flora of the southern Niam-niam lands its singular resemblance to the West African type of vegetation here came to an end. In arriving at the gneiss-hills, we had entered upon the limits of the dense bush-forest which covers Mohammed's entire territory, an area of nearly 500 square miles. Whilst, in the region of the gallery-forests, all the trees and bushes are confined to the river-banks, the intermediate spaces being occupied by uniform grass-plains, *here*, on the contrary, in the region of continuous woods, all watercourses of every kind, whether they are rivers or mere brooks are (just as in Bongoland) bounded by low open plains, which extend, without being wooded at all, to the very shores. The hydrographical system is better developed, and imparts a well-defined aspect to the scenery, the strips of open grassy steppe along the margins of the watercourses winding like streams of verdure through the dense masses of the foliage.

I swam across the narrow though copious river, while the bearers conveyed the baggage over along the trunks of trees that were thrown from side to side. Turning to the north-east we passed over two more meadow-waters and reached the Yubbo, which was now 50 feet wide, and too deep to wade; as no trees could be found of a length sufficient to serve as bridges, some grass rafts had to be extemporised.

We were now once more in our former route. Another half league brought us to the Uzze, of which, at this season, the stream was so extremely sluggish that by my usual test of a gourd-flask tied to a string I could detect no apparent current at all. The river we found was 5 feet deep and 25 feet wide.

Early on the 1st of May we were joined by some Niam-niam who were under Mohammed's jurisdiction, and who, having been stationed as outposts on the borders of the hostile territory, had been attracted into the frontier forest by the shots of the previous evening.

The last stage of our march before reaching the Seriba was soon accomplished. The road led through a charming park-like wood, through which, by subterranean channels, the meadow-waters of the Yabo and Yabongo rolled off their verdure-hidden streams. In this latitude (4° 5′ N.) the rain had had very little effect upon the lesser rivulets of the district, and the only signs of the advancing season were to be found in the increased variety of newly-sprouting plants and flowers.

At this season a lovely adornment is given to the meadows by the great red blossoms of the *Clappertonia*. To a travelling botanist in Central Africa it is very pleasant to be so frequently reminded of the name of a great predecessor.

We had a general rendezvous two leagues west of the Seriba, on the spot where we had made our first bivouac when we were starting to the south. It was here that Mohammed was desirous of erecting a new Seriba, as the buildings of the old one were becoming somewhat ruined, and this appeared a better site for defending himself against aggressors. Besides Wando on the south, he had another enemy on the west, viz. Wando's brother Mbeeoh, who, as an independent chieftain, ruled the district on the lower Yubbo, before its union with the Sway; and the combined attacks of these two placed his possessions at times in considerable jeopardy. To escape this difficulty Mohammed now resolved to undertake a campaign against Mbeeoh first, and, as soon as this was accomplished, to proceed with his measures of reprisal against Wando.

Until the enterprise against Mbeeoh was over, I was left to take up my abode with the invalided soldiers, and my own little retinue upon the banks of the Nabambisso.

CHAPTER XIII.

Solitude and hunger—Productive ant-hill—Diversion in the woods—Excursion to the east—A papyrus-swamp—Disgusting food of the Niam-niam—Merdyan's Seriba—Losing the way—Kind reception in Tuhamy's Seriba—Scenery of Mondoo—Mount Baginze—Source of the Dyoor — Mountain vegetation — Cyanite gneiss—Mohammed's campaign—Three Bongo missing—History of three skulls—Indifference of Nubians to cannibalism—Building a grass-hut—Crossing the Sway—Evil tidings — Successful chase — Bendo — Badry's recital — With Nganye—Suspension-bridge over the Tondy—Division of the caravan—Détour to the east—Elands—Bamboo-jungles—The Seriba Mbomo—Abundance of corn—The Babuckur—Crossing the Lehssy—Wild buffaloes—Return to Sabby—Home news—Hunger on the march—Passage of the Tondy.

AFTER the fatigue and excitement of our previous journey we were glad to recruit ourselves by a comfortable camp-life in the dense bush-forest on the Nabambisso. Spacious grass-huts had been erected for our accommodation until the new Seriba should be completed, and these, nestling amongst the massive foliage of the abundant vegetation, gave the spot an aspect that was almost home-like. A refreshing rain had moderated the temperature; and the air, mild and laden with the fragrant odours of the wood, gave animation both to mind and body.

Three years previously all the land had been under cultivation; but nature had soon effaced well-nigh every trace of human labour, and the roots of the trees and shrubs that had only been partially destroyed by the tillage had sprouted forth with redoubled vigour and still more gigantic development of leaf; thus attesting the unfailing power of vitality in the wilderness and the impotency of man against the persistency of nature.

In this charming locality I passed the early days of May, a month which in these latitudes may truly be called a month of rapture, when the commencement of the rains has renewed the life and growth of all around. From morning to night I strolled leisurely

DAILY LIFE IN CAMP.

To face p 120.

about amongst the bushes, but without neglecting a chance of enriching my stores of botanical treasure by every novelty that presented itself.

Meanwhile, Mohammed was occupied in the formation of his new Seriba. Hundreds of natives were employed in conveying the trunks of trees from the neighbouring forest, and these were erected side by side and close together in a deep trench; the trench was afterwards filled in with earth, and the palisaded Seriba, a hundred feet square, was all complete. So quickly was the work accomplished that on the fifth day after our arrival the invalided soldiers, by whom it was to be occupied, were removed into their new quarters. The other soldiers in the interval had vacated the old Seriba. Everything being ready, Mohammed, accompanied by his entire marching force, started off on his campaign against Mbeeoh and Wando; during his absence it had been arranged that I should make this quiet, lonely spot my temporary home.

Confined thus to a narrow area, I had now to look forward to a period of inactivity, in addition to which I had the prospect, by no means pleasant, of submitting to a scale of diet that was straitly limited. Our provisions were all but exhausted. Under the most favourable circumstances, Mohammed could not be expected back in less than twenty days, and the slender supply left for the maintenance of the few men who remained behind as my body-guard would have to be carefully doled out in daily rations to last out the time. All our cattle had long since been slaughtered; goats were nowhere to be had; nor could any hunting-booty reasonably be expected. For myself the only animal food on which I could rely consisted of some tiny fowls of the diminutive Niam-niam breed.

The season was very unfavourable for hunting, but even if it had been otherwise I should have felt it undesirable, under the circumstances, to have wandered far from my quarters: the ruined condition of our palisade left us especially exposed to an attack, and with our small supply of firearms it was advisable to be constantly on the spot. It is to this day a mystery to me how the Bongo bearers who remained with us supported life during this period of privation; but somehow or other they had a wonderful knack of discovering all kinds of edibles in the forest, and stirred up by their example I eagerly grasped at anything the wilderness afforded to supply the deficiency of my meagre *cuisine*.

In the middle of the open space of the old Seriba there happened to be a huge white-ant hill of long standing, and this rendered some timely assistance in our need; every night after there had been heavy rain, myriads of white ants appeared on the red clods and might be gathered by the bushel; they belonged to the fat-bodied, winged class, and were what are known as "sexual males." Immediately upon issuing from their dark retreat, and after a short swarming, they assemble in masses at the foot of their hill and proceed to divest themselves of their wings, leaving their heavy bodies helpless on the ground. This removal of their wings does not seem a matter of difficulty; the instinct of the insects seems to prompt them to throw the wings quite forward till they can be so mutilated by the front feet that they completely drop off. Any insects that remained upon the wing were soon brought to the ground by bundles of lighted straw being placed under them, so that it might literally be said to rain white ants. Baskets full were then readily collected for our table. Partly fried and partly boiled they helped to compensate for our lack of any kind of grease. If the day only chanced to be rainy, the night was sure to be provided with a feast; there was not one of us who had not cause to be thankful for the strange abundance of the ant-hill.

Many a time I wished myself back again in the days when we were fighting the A-Banga; for though they were days of peril, they were days of plenty, and the old Spanish proverb would ever and again force itself upon my recollection, "No misfortune comes amiss to a full stomach." At night my dream was akin to Baker's dream of pale ale and beef-steak. Nothing could elevate the vision of the mind for long; tied down to material things, it was impotent to soar; and food and drink became the single and prevailing theme which we were capable of handling by day or dreaming of by night.

Reduced to this low and depressed condition were the feelings which I experienced during the later portion of those lonely weeks that I spent in the great shed, now half-ruined, that had formed the assembly hall of the old Seriba.

As the discomforts of our situation increased and became more and more trying, I was thrown upon my own resources to seek enjoyment of a more ideal nature, and in the neighbouring woods I found the best of compensation for all my bodily privations. Whenever I was beginning to feel more than ordinarily disconsolate I would hurry off to the thickets, and there amongst the splendid and luxuriant vegetation I was sure to find an engagement which would, at least for a time, draw away my thoughts even from the appeal of hunger. In hardly any portion of the world ought an enthusiastic botanist to suffer *ennui;* wherever there exists a germ of life, there is also a stimulant to his spirit; but hardly a scene can be imagined calculated to enlist his whole interests more and to divert him better than the exuberance of bountiful nature such as was revealed upon the Nabambisso.

The stipulated time of solitude was drawing rapidly to a close, but still nothing was heard from Mohammed. Our necessities became more and more urgent: to remain where we were became more and more impracticable; and to escape from the disasters that were threatening us I proposed to set off on an excursion to the nearest settlement of any Khartoomers. Forty miles to the west of our present quarters was a Seriba belonging to Tuhamy, and a lofty mountain situated in its vicinity offered special attractions for a visit; the journey would be safe, as the route led across Mohammed's own territory, and on our way we should pass another Seriba upon the eastern frontiers of his district. Ten bearers would suffice to carry my baggage for this little trip, and I need hardly say how glad they were to accompany me under the prospect of ending, or at least gaining a respite from, their season of privation.

We started off on our march upon the 21st, and after crossing the Boddoh brook and two smaller rivulets we arrived at the Hoo. This little stream meandered through a wood remarkable for its diversity of trees, amongst which I was surprised to see the Sparmannia of Southern Africa. The banks themselves were enclosed by dense bushes of a new species of Stipularia, of which the numerous blossoms, half-hidden in their purple sheaths, gave a singular appearance to the plant. It belongs to the characteristic stream-vegetation of the spot.

Beyond the Hoo we came to a ravine of a hundred feet in depth with a charming hedge of zawa-trees; and then crossing two more brooks, copiously supplied with water and both running to the north, we terminated our twelve miles' march and found a hospitable reception in the huts of Ghitta, an overseer of some of the Niam-niam subject to my friend Mohammed. After our recent privations we seemed quite overpowered by the liberality of the entertainment offered us by Ghitta; he procured corn for the bearers, he brought out several flasks of eleusine-beer, and more than satisfied all reasonable claims upon his hospitality.

The soil of this region was once more broken by deep clefts, and was alternately a series of gentle undulations and of deep-cut ravines. Beyond Ghitta's village the road turned towards the south-east and crossed a brook; further on it passed through a district enlivened by numerous farmsteads where some sorghum-fields testified to the influence of their neighbours on the east upon the industry of the inhabitants. The district was named Madikamm, being called so after the second brook to the east of Ghitta's hamlets. The majority of men capable of bearing arms had accompanied Mohammed on his campaign; consequently the huts had hardly any other occupants but women and children, who retreated shyly as we advanced, and shut themselves up in their pretty dwellings.

The votive pillars adorned with many a variety of skulls demonstrated that at certain seasons the hunting-booty must be very large.

Leaving the villages of Madikamm in our rear, we found ourselves on the edge of a great swamp a thousand feet wide, which moved its insidious course northwards in the direction of the adjacent territory of the Babuckur. It was covered in its entire width by a huge, half-floating mass of papyrus, which, called "Bodumoh" by the Niam-niam, gives its name to the marshy waters. This was the first specimen of the papyrus that I had seen in the depth of the interior at so great a distance from the two main affluents of the Upper Nile, and it gave a new character to the locality; it is, however, a characteristic of the swampy region on the upper course of the Sway, where the reduced and meagre remnant of Babuckur, sorely pressed on every side, drag out their miserable lives; their frontiers were only a league to the north of the spot where we crossed.

After leaving the Bodumoh, our road took an E.S E. direction, which it retained as far as Tuhamy's Seriba. At the first hamlets we reached, the inhabitants viewed us with considerable distrust, as the soldiers from the nearest Khartoom settlements, and those who intended to pass through Mohammed's territory, had most arbitrarily levied some heavy taxes upon them.

Beyond the huts were open steppes covered with towering grass which shadowed many shrubs that were entirely new to me, and excited my liveliest interest. Not a few of them were in full bloom, and I walked along carrying a bouquet that it was no exaggeration to call magnificent. The natives might seem fully justified in reviving amongst themselves my name of "Mbarik-pah."

I may mention that careful as was the method which I have described of our wading over the marshy swamps it was not uniformly attended with success. More than once in attempting to cross without assistance at the head of my little troop I had come to grief;

and now once again, at the very next swamp we came to, it was my fate to have an involuntary bath. The dilemma caused us some delay. I was proceeding leisurely along, but coming to a deep hole completely concealed by the long swamp-grass I suddenly fell in, and was fished out again by my people thoroughly drenched and plastered over with an envelope of mud. It took an hour while I changed my clothes and had the filth cleansed from the articles I was carrying.

Although the temperature was really as high as that of a July day in our northern clime, the sky nevertheless was overcast and the weather windy, so that it was with chattering teeth and an inward chill that I continued my march along the steppe. All prospect of the surrounding country was obstructed by the towering grass. There was no distant vision to fill the eye, and there was little to relieve the monotony but the radiant blossoms, red and blue, of the flowering shrubs.

After a while our course was interrupted by a brook fifteen feet in width, called the Kishy. This was too deep to ford; the method therefore was adopted of bending down the boughs of the largest shrubs upon the banks, thus forming a fragile bridge, over which, by dint of caution, we contrived to make our tottering way without the misadventure, only too probable, of losing our balance. The Kishy speeds swiftly along over the level steppe in the Babuckur country, and, after receiving the Bodumoh, contributes materially to the volume of the Sway, which in that region has already assumed the dimensions of a considerable river.

The country beyond the Kishy retained the same character as that along which we had been passing. By the side of a little spring called Nambia, that went rippling between the bare gneiss flats, we made a halt for the purpose of following up some guinea-fowl, of which the notes could be heard at no great distance; the whole district teemed with these birds, and I could now again anticipate a daily meal such as I had not had for months.

Whilst we were making our halt, I was surprised by a visit from Merdyan, the local chief; he had heard of my arrival, and, accompanied by several natives, he had now come to give me welcome. Merdyan was one of Mohammed's black body-guard, and had been entrusted with the supervision of the eastern frontier of his territory; with three guns at his disposal, he had been appointed to the command of a little Seriba surrounded with fine fields of maize, which were bounded by a ravine watered by a copious brook. To reach this settlement we had to retrace our steps for a full league along a road that gradually descended through a cultivated country. A fine prospect lay open before us; upon the south-eastern horizon rose the imposing mass of Mount Baginze, and a little to the north a pointed hill called Damvo. On this day's march we accomplished a distance of about eight leagues; towards the close of it we came to one of the groves of Encephalartus, which are scattered about the district, and known amongst the Niam-niam as Mvoochpiah.

We enjoyed very comfortable accommodation in Merdyan's Seriba; the huts were clean and well-built, and I had an opportunity of renewing my observations on the domestic arrangements of the Niam-niam. A delicacy to which I had long been unaccustomed was provided for me in some fresh ears of maize, and corn was not wanting for all my people. There were two things, however, which could not be obtained. We had neither salt nor any kind of oil or grease. Riharn, my cook, having lost his proficiency, seemed to be now losing his memory; he had quite forgotten to bring the salt that would be required on our way, and what little grease could be procured had far too much the suspicion of being mixed with human fat to make it in any way a desirable adjunct to my dishes. Whatever food the natives offered to my people, even to my negroes, only filled them with horror and disgust. Amongst many others who came to the Seriba to satisfy their curiosity about me, there was one fat old man who had his wallet full of victuals hanging to his side, without which no Niam-niam ever quits his home. My little Bongo, Allagabo, spying out two tempting little brown paws, like those of a roast sucking-pig, projecting from the bag, was inquisitive enough to peep in to make a closer investigation of the contents. He got a sharp cuffing for his pains, but he was not likely to have been much tempted, as the delicacy in question turned out to be a roast-dog! At another time, my Niam-niam interpreter, Gyabir, who was here in the full enjoyment of his native food, offered Allagabo a dish of lugma (corn-pap), in which were some fragments of flesh that looked like the limbs of a little bird; but Allagabo's disgust can be better imagined than described when he discovered he was eating the legs of a frog!

I spent one day with Merdyan for the purpose of inspecting the neighbourhood, and in the course of my rambles I bagged enough guinea-fowl to supply my whole retinue. For the first time, too, I killed a black rhinoceros-bird (*Tetmoceras abyssinicus*). I had previously seen these birds in the Seribas in Bongoland, where they are so far tamed that they strut about fearlessly amongst the other denizens of the poultry-yard.

The route from Merdyan's Seriba to Tuhamy's was through an uninhabited district, and was crossed by so many streams that it was quite a matter of difficulty to determine it. Merdyan undertook to provide me with guides, if I desired it; but as any intercourse between the two Seribas was exceedingly rare, and as I heard a long and loud discussion, before we started, as to which was the right direction, I could not place much reliance upon my conductors. The country through which we had to pass was perfectly flat; the trees, too, were frequently so high and the paths so narrow that we were unable to get a glimpse of either of the two mountains which we had previously observed from the high ground on the west. Neither of these mountains could be much more than seven leagues distant. The ignorance of our guides caused us considerable embarrassment. We were in continual dread of encroaching upon the adjacent territory of the hostile Babuckur, where we should be entirely at the mercy of the cannibal tribe.

On leaving the Seriba we followed the eastward course of a little brook named the Nakemaka. We kept beside it until it reached the spot where it joined the larger stream called the Mahbodey, which we crossed by our previous method of bending down the pendent branches of the overhanging bushes, and then hopping like birds from branch to branch. All these affluents of the Upper Sway inclined to the north; all of them, moreover, had a marked descent. The next of them was known as the Meiwah, and about a league beyond we came to the actual main-stream of the Sway, which was here thirty feet in width, and really wider than the united measurements of the two streams above; such of them as we did not cross by our improvised bridges we had to pass by swimming.

After a while we came to a large forest of butter-trees, the first and last that I saw in the country of the Niam-niam. The underwood was so dense, and its foliage so fully developed, that we could not see more than ten paces in any direction; our guides completely lost their way, and, without a clue to our proper path, we wandered on. To add to our perplexity the sky became overcast with the tokens of an approaching storm, and we thus lost whatever aid we might have got from the direction of the shadows. With a vista contracted as ours the compass was of little service, and in a country like this it was very unadvisable to leave the beaten paths or to penetrate into any untried thickets. We were glad enough when we at last caught sight of two deserted huts in the middle of the wilderness. The floods of rain were beginning to descend, and we were thankful for any shelter. The storm that had burst upon us continued with such unremitting violence that we were compelled to resign ourselves to the necessity of passing the night in this wild spot. The interior of the huts swarmed with creeping things of the most revolting character, in comparison with which the most obnoxious vermin that are ever found in houses within the range of civilization would appear mild and insignificant domestic nuisances. By heaping up a pile of fresh leaves and grass, I contrived a sort of covering that protected me from actual contact with the crawling things, but the lullaby that buzzed and hummed around me was none of the pleasantest. There were swarms of white ants that were incessantly gnawing and scratching at my leafy coverlet; there were snakes and lizards rustling in the cobwebbed thatch above: there were mice scampering and squeaking on the ground below. However, for this condition of things there was no help: the best must be made of it; so I shut my ears to the commotion, and resigned myself successfully to the blissful unconsciousness of slumber.

When I awoke at dawn the rain was still falling, the heavy drops pattering down like lead upon the leathery leaves of the butter-trees. Hungry and shivering, I sat upon my grass-couch and peered out through the narrow doorway into the obscurity of the thickets, where I could see the broad backs of my negroes as they grubbed away with all their might, defiant of the storm, in the hope of getting something from among the roots to appease their craving. Hunger at last compelled us to brave the weather, and to take our chance at proceeding. At starting we directed our movements towards some mounds of gneiss, that at a little distance we could see picturesquely rising above the trees. Our intention at first was to ascend these elevations, that we might make a better survey of the land around us; but we were spared the necessity of climbing them, as on reaching their base we fell into a well-defined path which we did not hesitate to follow. It led us to the brook Shöby, and shortly afterwards to some human habitations.

Our arrival made no little stir among the natives, who had received no intelligence of the presence of a white man in that part of the country, and at first they were inclined to suspect that we must have come with hostile intentions. My Niam-niam, however, soon reassured them, and induced them to provide us with guides for our route. They led us out in an easterly direction, passing through a country that was fairly cultivated, and along which the numbers of guinea-fowl were so large that they kept me fully employed during the march. We had now only one more brook to pass, which was called the Mossulongoo, and this we accomplished in such good time that it was still daylight when we reached the Seriba of Tuhamy. Amongst the inmates of the Seriba my servants recognised several of their former acquaintances at Khartoom, and very enthusiastic were the greetings that were mutually exchanged. The controller of the Seriba received me with the most cordial hospitality, and cleared out his best hut for my accommodation. The hut was enclosed with a high palisade, which gave it an additional protection. The controller's superior and principal in Khartoom was a personage no less important than the chief writer of the *Hokkumdarieh;* and this influential authority had in the previous year given instructions to his subordinate that he was to show me every possible attention if I should chance to pay him a visit.

The Seriba was a halting-place for Tuhamy's ivory-expeditions from the Rohl to the Monbuttoo country. Situated as it was on the extreme eastern limit of the Niam-niam territory, it formed an outpost towards the Babuckur land, which Tuhamy's companies were accustomed to consider as their corn magazines, and on which they relied for their supplies to carry them onwards to the south. But the Babuckur were already wearied by the depredations to which they were thus continually exposed: their impatience made them desperate and exasperated; and a very few days after my departure they made an attack upon the Seriba, burnt it to the ground, and compelled the inhabitants to evacuate the place. Many Nubians as well as many Niam-niam lost their lives in the engagement, and the few that escaped had to make their way to the nearest Seriba, which was that established in Mondoo, at the distance of a long day's journey, situated amongst the Zileï mountains, of which the spurs and projecting terraces were visible on the eastern horizon. Subsequently to this, all Tuhamy's settlements passed by a special contract into the hands of Ghattas's son.

The brook upon which the Seriba was situated was called the Annighei. The chieftain in command of the Niam-niam in the district had formerly been independent, but had been deprived of his authority by Tuhamy's companies. His name was Indimma, and he was one of the numerous sons of Renje, but not to be confounded with the powerful chief of the same name, who was a son of Keefa. He came now to offer me his welcome, and communicated to me many interesting details about the surrounding country.

I made a little excursion to an elevation of gneiss a few miles to the east of the Seriba, so as to gain a point from which I might survey the surrounding mountains and make some observations to verify the position of the various peaks. The detached ranges for the most part were situated from ten to fifteen leagues from the site I had chosen for my survey, and I should imagine their height to vary from 4000 to 5000 feet above the level of the sea. All those who were capable of giving me any information at all upon the subject agreed in representing that the entire district was distinguished as Mundo or Mondoo, and that the principal chain of hills was called Mbia Zileï; also that at the foot of the mountains was the village of Bedelly, the native local overseer, close to which was another Seriba belonging to Tuhamy. Between me and the mountains flowed the river Issoo, a stream which I was assured was at this season fifty feet broad, and so deep that whoever attempted to ford it would be immersed up to the neck. The entire region was rich in corn, especially in sorghum. Several hundred bearers laden with it arrived during my stay at the Seriba, and I took the opportunity of laying in a stock for myself; it is difficult to obtain sorghum in the Niam-niam countries, and it was long since I had had grain of such a superior quality.

All the Niam-niam of whom I was able to make inquiries assured me that the natives of Mundo are a distinct people, differing from themselves both in habits and in dialect; their precise ethnographical position I could never determine, but I should presume that they approximate most nearly to their Mittoo neighbours on the north, and more especially to the Loobah and Abakah.

This Mundo or Mondoo is not to be confounded with the Mundo to the south of the Bongo, which Petherick reports that he visited in February 1858; it is the name of the western enclave of the scattered Babuckur. But the Mundo of which I am speaking is marked upon the map by Peney, who in 1861 penetrated westwards from Gondokoro as far as the Ayi or Yei; Petherick too has inserted the district upon his map,* under the name of the Makarakka mountains, and has assigned it to exactly the same locality as I have myself done. In spite of Petherick's protestation, many geographers have made the two Mundos identical, and have

* 'Journal of the Royal Geographical Society,' vol. xxxv.

thus fallen into the not unnatural conjecture that the Yei is the upper course of the Dyoor, a conjecture of which my journey has fully demonstrated the fallacy.

The Issoo,* as the upper course of the Tondy is here called, forms the western boundary of this mountainous district; along the south and far to the east (probably as far as the source-regions of the Yei) there stretches an offshoot of the Niam-niam terrritory. This section of the Niam-niam is called Idderoh, and is subject to an independent chieftain, a brother of Indimma's, named Ringio, who had formerly been an interpreter in Petherick's station in Neangara. The river that waters his district is called the Nzoro. On all maps, this territory of the Idderoh figures as Makarakka; but, as I have observed, this is merely a collective name given to the Niam-niam by their neighbours on the east.

We had a day's rest in the hospitable Seriba, and were well entertained with meat and vegetables. The neighbourhood was interesting, and yielded several novelties for my collection. One very brilliant ornament of the woods at this season, which I had never seen in greater abundance, was the Abyssinian Protea, a shrub about four or five feet high, with great rosy heads like our garden peony. Another plant, one of the Araliaceæ, the Cussonia, which is usually only a low shrub, here attained quite the dimensions of a tree, and its fan-shaped foliage crowned a stem little less than thirty feet in height. In the damp grass near the brooks flourished a number of ground-orchids with remarkably fine blossoms.

A yet richer booty, however, was in store for me. A few miles to the south of the Seriba, jutting up like an island from the surrounding plain, and visible from afar, rose the massy heights of Mount Baginze. There I did not doubt I should realize the fruition of many expectations.

We started upon the 27th, under the escort of a small body of native soldiers, from the Seriba.

We marched for about two leagues in a west and south-west direction, and once again crossed the little brooks that the Sway receives on its right-hand bank; at length we reached the pointed gneiss mound called Damvo, which rises about 200 feet above the level of the plain. I mounted the eminence, so as to employ its summit as the second station for my observations of the mountain

---

* According to Miani, however, the river in that district was called the Ibba, the same name by which the Tondy is known on the northern frontier of the Niam-niam.

chains. The rugged rocks were clothed with Sanseviera, and to the very top charming shrubs made good their way from between their clefts. The view was magnificent. It was the first mountainous landscape that I had seen during my journey that exhibited the true characteristics of African orography. All round were elevations, more or less conspicuous, rising like bastions isolated on the plain; whilst high over all reared the crest of Mount Baginze. The western side of the mountain was precipitous, and might almost be described as perpendicular; towards the north, on the other hand, it sloped downwards in gradual ridges: in form it reminded me of many of the isolated mountains of Southern Nubia, and more especially of those in the province of Taka.

Mount Baginze is only four miles to the S.S.E. of Damvo, but this short distance had to be accomplished by a circuitous and troublesome route leading across deep fissures and masses of loose rock, and often through grass of enormous height; half-way we came to a rapid brook hastening along through a deep cleft, which we were able to leap across. This was *the source of the Dyoor*. It was the first actual source of any of the more important affluents of the White Nile to which any European traveller had ever penetrated. My Niam-niam escort, who were natives of the district, positively asserted that this brooklet was the Sway, and thus plainly demonstrated that, however insignificant this little vein of running water might appear, they were accustomed to consider it as the highest section of the waters that contributed to the formation of the Dyoor. The Sway, they said, was the largest and longest river of their land; Baginze was their loftiest mountain; and this was the most important stream that issued from its clefts.

Before actually setting foot upon Baginze we had still to make an ascent through a fine forest, but in due time we reached the mountain and made our encampment close beneath the perpendicular wall of the western flank. The halting-place was upon the edge of a deep ravine, where a bright thread of water rippled merrily along over rocks covered with moss and graceful ferns. It was too late in the day to attempt to ascend farther than to the summit of a sloping spur projecting towards the north-west from the southern side of the mountain, and which was about half the height of the mountain itself.

The first few steps that I took were quite enough to convince me of the entire accordance of the flora with that of the Abyssinian highlands. Masses of brilliant aloes, with their scarlet and yellow blossoms, grew luxuriantly upon the slopes of gneiss; the intervals between them were overspread with a mossy carpet of *Selaginella rupestris*, whilst clusters of blue lobelia reared themselves like violets, only of a brighter hue, from the surface of the soil. Here and there, in singular contrast to the tender foliage of the shady hollows, lending moreover a new and striking character to the vegetation, I found, cropping up from amidst the rocks, the thick fleshy leaves of that remarkable orchid, the Eulophia; and on the still higher declivities I met with yet another true representative of the Abyssinian flora in a new species of Hymenodictyon, a dwarf tree of the class of the Rubiaceæ, which in some form or other appear to embrace at least a tenth of all the plants of Africa in these regions.

Wherever one of the bright bubbling streams was seen, like a shining thread upon the grey monotony of the rocks, there I was pretty sure to find the Ensete, or wild African plantain. This is a plant which is never seen below an altitude of 3000 feet above the sea. It was now to be observed in every stage of its growth, sometimes being small like the head of a cabbage, and sometimes running out to a length of twenty feet with its fruit attached to a short thick stem in the form of an onion. Not unfrequently the Ensete of the mountains bore a striking resemblance to young specimens of the *Musa sapientium*, though it exceeded it in the number of the leaves it bore, there being occasionally as many as forty on a single plant. Although I never observed any side-sprouts from the wild Ensete, it by no means follows that they are never to be seen: a single authenticated instance of the kind would demonstrate almost beyond a doubt what is already in so many respects probable, namely, that the Ensete is the original stock of the cultivated African plantain.

We had quickly improvised some huts from the long grass at the foot of the mountain, and they afforded us secure and sufficiently comfortable shelter from the downpour of rain that lasted throughout the night. On the following morning I was disappointed to find that the sky was still burdened with storm-clouds, whilst a fine, drizzling mist obscured the greater part of the view that we had proved to be so lovely.

My sojourn in the neighbourhood was limited to a single day, since the Seriba was suffering from the general dearth of provisions, and could ill afford to entertain us: there was consequently no help for it, and if the ascent of the mountain were made at all it must be made in defiance of the heavy rain. I was quite aware that the adverse weather would make the task altogether uncongenial to my guides, and I was not very much surprised to find that they had made off during the night. I had thus to start off on my own responsibility. My Nubian servants remained behind to warm their shivering limbs over the camp-fires, so that, followed only by my two Niam-niam, carrying the portfolios for my plants, I set out upon my enterprise.

I turned towards the northern declivity, which slanted in almost an unbroken line from the summit to the base. At first my view was necessarily circumscribed, and it was only after a good deal of clambering and by a very circuitous route along rugged places overhung with bushes, and across fissures full of water, that I succeeded in finding the correct path. The highest point of the ridge I found to be at the south of the summit, and thence I had a magnificent prospect, being able to see for fifty or sixty miles in an east and north-east direction.

The upper course of the Tondy was plainly visible, and beyond it were caught the terraced ridges of the country to the east. The northern and eastern spurs of Baginze were especially picturesque; the elevated level of the ground at the base was not apparent from above, so that they stood out like isolated eminences from a uniform plain: three more spurs a few miles to the south-east also appeared completely detached: they were in a straight line one behind another, the names of the two most northerly being Bonduppa and Nagongoh.

The barometrical observations made at the base, which would have determined the exact altitude of Baginze above the level of the sea, have unfortunately been lost; I believe, however, that I am not far wrong in estimating the entire height to be about 3900 feet.

The bulk of the rock of which the mountain was composed consisted of a gneiss that was so abundant in mica that in many places it had the appearance of being actual mica-schist; a speciality in its formation being the immense number of cyanite crystals that pervaded it in all directions. Wherever the springs issued at the foot of the mountain there were wide boulder-flats of broken stones, and here the sheets of mica and the prisms of cyanite, an inch or two in length, lay cleanly washed and strewn one upon another in such thick confusion that I had to wade through them as through a pile of rubbish.

Massive in its grandeur, isolated, and worn by time, Mount

Baginze thus stood before me as a witness of a former era in the world's history and as a remnant of the lofty mountain-chain which must have once formed the southern boundary of the Nile district.

It had taken me four hours to make the ascent of the mountain, but being now aware of the correct path, a single hour was all I spent in getting back to our encampment. In spite of the unpropitious weather I felt that I could have enjoyed myself for some days in exploring this enticing neighbourhood: the mountain air was even fresher and more invigorating than what I had been breathing in the Niam-niam country—and this is saying not a little; for, in spite of their meagre diet, the Nubian soldiers who came thither sickly and weakened by their idle Scriba-life always returned from their Niam-niam campaigns fat and healthy, and with renewed strength and vigour. My attendants unfortunately did not sympathise with my ideal enjoyments, but made such loud and bitter complaints at the increasing inclemency of the weather that I should not have dared to prolong my stay, even if I could.

On the third morning, then, after our arrival we began to return. Although continually in doubt as to our path, we were fortunate in hitting upon the route that was shortest, and, crossing the Shöby at a spot where it was contracted by gneiss walls and made a bend to the north, we reached the rocks in the forest of butter-trees at which so recently we had passed such a wretched night. Before it was dark we once more entered Merdyan's Scriba. The long march of nine hours, made doubly arduous by the many watercourses that had intercepted it, had been one of the most fatiguing that I had experienced. I took a day's rest, and amused myself by shooting guinea-fowl, the sport being so successful that I supplied my people with as many of the birds as they could eat in two days. We performed the rest of our journey through incessant rain, and on the evening of the 1st of June found ourselves reinstated in the old Scriba on the Nabambisso.

Here I received satisfactory intelligence from Mohammed. The condition of things had decidedly improved. Still the store of corn was small; but the gourds had ripened during our absence, fresh maize had been brought to the Scriba, and, best of all, the guinea-fowl had effected a lodgment in the neighbourhood, so that we had a constant supply of animal food ready at hand.

A circumstance soon occurred that naturally excited some consternation. The bearers who had been left with me in the old Scriba were in the habit of scouring the neighbouring fields and forests every day in search of victuals for themselves. One evening three of the party who had gone out did not return, and their companions had no hesitation in avowing their belief that they had been captured, and that they would most certainly be killed and eaten by the inhabitants of the adjacent district. Early on the following morning all the Bongo and most of the Nubians who were with me started off in a body to explore the neighbourhood. According to the statements of the Bongo, the crime had been committed in the district under the control of Maddah, to the north of the Seriba. In that direction the party bent their steps. Their supposition was apparently correct, for after following the tracks into a wood they found that they terminated in a ghastly pool of blood. Maddah was forthwith seized and hurried to the Seriba, where he was charged with being answerable for the disappearance of the men. He declared that the blood was that of an animal which had been slaughtered on the previous day; but this explanation was deemed unsatisfactory, and he was consequently placed in confinement to await Mohammed's judgment.

But when Mohammed returned he professed to be occupied by more pressing and important business. The truth was, he was anxious, if he could, to keep on good terms with the Niam-niam, knowing that their services were indispensable to him for the usual raid against the Babuckur that had to be undertaken for the purpose of getting a supply of corn to avert the prospect of his caravan being starved. Had the disaster befallen any of the Nubians or Mussulmans, there can be no doubt that Mohammed would not have suffered considerations of policy to deter him from making an example of the delinquents.

Before many days had elapsed the main body of Mohammed's corps returned from their campaign. Only a portion of the missing ivory had been recovered, for Wando, under a superstitious dread of the intimations of his augury, had persistently remained concealed in the most inaccessible places, and consequently the hostilities had been mainly directed against his brother Mbeeoh. Contrary to the general practice of the Niam-niam princes, Mbeeoh had been personally engaged in the conflict and had exhibited remarkable bravery. On one occasion it had been with the greatest difficulty that Mohammed had held his own against the hordes of his opponent, and in a raging storm had been obliged to erect a kind of rampart, made of straw, to afford a shelter from which anything like a steady fire might be opened upon the assailants.

The chances were dead against Mohammed's side, but it is notorious that the natives hardly ever follow up any advantages offered to them either by a downpour of rain or by the obscurity of night; and very frequently they lost the most promising of opportunities for crushing their Nubian oppressors.

The raid upon the Babuckur was an expedition that Mohammed did not accompany in person. He entrusted it entirely to Surroor, who took the charge of as many of the subordinate Niam-niam as could be gathered. Just as might be expected, the most savage brutalities were practised on either side. Besides securing the store of corn, which was the main object of the incursion, the Nubians were on the look-out for a capture of female slaves, which they claimed as their special perquisite. The Niam-niam on their part followed the example and did some private kidnapping on their own account; the females that they entrapped they disposed of in the following way: the youngest were destined for their houses, the middle-aged for their agriculture, and the oldest for their caldrons!

The skulls in the Anatomical Museum of Berlin that are numbered 36, 37, and 38 might be supposed capable of unfolding a deplorable tale of these depredations. Some natives brought them to me fresh boiled, only a few days after the raid had been perpetrated; they had heard from the Monbuttoo that I was accustomed to give rings of copper in exchange for skulls, and as I was not able to bring the poor fellows to life again I saw no reason why I should not purchase their remains in the interests of science. Often I reproached the Nubians of my retinue with allowing such abuses to go on before their eyes, and under the sanction of the flag bearing the insignia of the Holy Prophet; but just as often I received the answer that the Faithful were incompetent to change anything, but must submit to the will of God; it was impressed upon me that the Niam-niam were heathen, and that if the heathen liked to eat each other up, it was no concern of theirs; they had no right to be lawgivers or teachers to cannibals.

I had repeated opportunities of observing that the ivory-expeditions of the Khartoomers, although actuated by a certain spirit of enterprise, did not at all contribute to any propagation of Islamism. Negro nations once converted to Mohammedanism are no longer considered as slaves, but are esteemed as brothers. For this reason it was inexplicable to me how Islamism had spread so far in other parts of Central Africa.

Some days after the raid on the Babuckur I was witness of a scene that can never be erased from my memory. During one of my rambles I found myself in one of the native farmsteads; before the door of the first hut I came to, an old woman was sitting surrounded by a group of boys and girls, all busily employed in cutting up gourds and preparing them for eating; at the door of the opposite hut a man was sitting composedly playing upon his mandolin. Midway between the two huts a mat was outspread; upon this mat, exposed to the full glare of the noon-day sun, feebly gasping, lay a new-born infant: I doubt whether it was more than a day old. In answer to my inquiries I learnt that the child was the offspring of one of the slaves who had been captured in the late raid, and who had now been driven off to a distant quarter, compelled to leave her infant behind, because its nurture would interfere with her properly fulfilling her domestic duties. The ill-fated little creature, doomed to so transient an existence, was destined to form a dainty dish; and the savage group was calmly engaged in ordinary occupations until the poor little thing should have breathed its last and be ready to be consigned to the seething caldron! I confess that for a moment I was furious. I felt ready to shoot the old hag who sat by without displaying a particle of pity or concern. I was prompted to do something rash to give vent to my sensation of abhorrence; but I was stayed by the protestations of the Nubians ringing in my ears that they were powerless in the matter, and that they had not come to be lawgivers to the Niam-niam. I felt that I was as helpless as they were, and that it would be folly for me to forget how dependent I was upon them. What influence, I was constrained to ask, could my interference have exercised, what could any exhibition of my disgust and indignation avail to check the bias of an entire nation? Missionaries, in their enthusiasm, might find a fruitful field for their labours, but they must be very self-denying and very courageous.

The departure of the caravan for the north was delayed for several days in expectation of the return of the corps that had been sent to the west with Ghattas's company, but as no tidings of it were forthcoming we determined, without further procrastination, to proceed upon our way.

Shut out from all prospect of this year making any farther progress to the south, and debarred from the hope of accomplishing any fresh explorations, I own that I began to long for the flesh-pots of Egypt; I confess that the stores that were on their way from Khartoom to await me in my old quarters at the Scriba in Bongoland had a wondrous fascination to my eager imagination. I was also now looking forward to making several excursions during the return journey, from which I was sanguine that I might not only make fresh botanical discoveries, but also enlarge my general knowledge of the country.

Our first night-camp was made on the northern frontier of Aboo Sammat's territory, on the banks of a brook near the hamlets of Kulenjo. Until we reached the Hoo we observed no alteration in the condition of the brooks; but the galleries which I was now traversing for the last time seemed in bidding me farewell to have donned their most festal covering, being resplendent with the luxuriant blooms of the Spathodeæ, one of the most imposing representatives of the African flora. The waters of the Hoo had risen to no inconsiderable degree, and they had so much increased in breadth that they filled the whole of the level bed, which was 35 feet in width. The current flowed at the rate of 150 feet a minute, the water being nowhere more than 3½ feet deep. Our second night-camp was pitched half-way between the Hoo and the Sway, at a spot where the bush-forest was densest and most luxuriant.

The advancing season brought several changes in our mode of living. I had become so far initiated into African habits, that I now very much preferred a grass-hut to a tent. I was moreover getting somewhat out of patience with the ever-recurring necessity of holding up the tent-pole with all my strength during the storms of night, whilst I roused half the camp with my shouts for assistance. At the height of the rainy season, the weather, by a beneficent arrangement of Nature, fortunately follows certain rules from which it deviates very exceptionally; the first few hours of the morning always decided the programme for the day; when once the sky had cleared, we knew that we might resume our march in perfect confidence, and I had the satisfaction of feeling that my papers and herbarium were in no danger of being spoilt by damp, and my companions had the same security for the preservation of their powder and provisions. Towards five in the afternoon, when the sun began to sink, and the distant thunder gave warning of the renewing of the storm, we made a halt, and directed our best efforts to prepare our nightly lodging in the wilderness. The baggage was first piled together and protected by the waterproofs, and as soon as this was effected, a number of knives and hatchets were produced and distributed among the "builders." Off they were sent with all despatch. "Now, you fellows, quick to your work. Four of you," I should order my servants, "must be brisk, and get together the grass. *You* two must hack me down the branches, long and strong, and be sharp about it. No shirking now. And *you* have to get the bast. Quick, away! and quick back!" And with this hurrying and driving the work was soon done. Ten minutes, or a little more, brought the men back with the requisite materials. The framework was first erected, the forked boughs being driven into the ground and firmly fastened at the top with ligatures of bast; meanwhile the grass was being bandaged into a huge hollow sheaf, and this, when all was ready, was raised above the structure and fitted like a cap. Thus, in about half an hour, with alacrity, one of these grass-huts could be reared, small indeed, and snug as a nest, but nevertheless perfectly waterproof; and thus a sufficient shelter against the nightly rains. The storm might rage and the thunder roll without, but here the weary traveller, in safe and reliable retreat, might enjoy his well-earned repose without misgiving.

By the glimmer of a little oil-lamp of my own contrivance, in which I burnt some questionable-looking grease, of which the smell could not fail to rouse up one's worse suspicions against the natives, I would sit and beguile the hours of the evening by writing down the experiences of the day. The negroes had no such protection: they would crouch round the camp-fire, which would make their faces glow again with its fitful light, while the rain would pelt pitilessly down upon their backs.

Such was the arrangement of our camp night after night throughout our return journey.

The rain on the following morning did not cease so soon as usual, and our departure was somewhat delayed.

Meanwhile a large portion of our caravan had gone on in advance to make the necessary preparations for crossing the Sway. I did not reach the banks myself until nearly noon, and by that time the people were busily employed in conveying the baggage across. The aspect of the Sway was entirely different to what it had been on the 18th of February. The water had risen to the very top of the banks, and was twenty feet deep, with a velocity of two hundred feet a minute. Although the stream was only thirty-five feet wide, the passage over it, in consequence of the entire absence of tree-stems and the small number of bushes on the banks, offered unusual difficulties. The men who had had experience in these Niam-niam expeditions had a method of effecting a transit over the river that I think was peculiar to themselves: they set all the bearers to work to gather as many different kinds of bark as they could, and to extract all the bast out of it, and then to twist it into long stout ropes, a handicraft in which the negroes are very skilful, as in Bongoland there is an unfailing demand for cordage for hunting-snares and fishing-nets. Having fabricated their ropes, the next thing was to get them stretched across the river. This was effected by practised swimmers, who attached one end firmly into the ground by means of pegs, and swam over with the other. The arrangement of the ropes was such that they were suspended in double rows, one precisely underneath the other, the upper rope being above the stream, the lower being some feet below its surface. Ten expert swimmers then took their stand upon the lower rope, and allowed the stream to force their weight against the upper rope, which supported their chests, but permitted them to have their arms perfectly free for action. Thus supported, in a half-standing, half-floating position, they contrived to keep their hands at liberty, and to pass the packages from one to another.

I confess that it was with a beating heart that I stood and watched my precious baggage thus handed along over the perilous flood; but the lank, lean arms of the Nubians were competent to their work, and everything was conveyed across in safety. This business of crossing occupied several hours of real exertion. The difficulties of the transit may be conceived, when it is remembered that three-fourths of the negroes are entirely ignorant of the art of swimming, and that there were elephants' tusks being transported which weighed no less than 180 lbs., and consequently required two men to lift them.

We passed the night near Marra's villages, and though it was only a league from the river, it was quite dark before we entered our quarters. The residents had all vacated the district, leaving their fields of half-ripe maize to the mercy of the new-comers; although plunder was ostensibly forbidden, it was surreptitiously carried on by our bearers to a very gross extent under cover of the darkness.

The whole of the next day we halted to recruit our strength. I found my amusement in scouring the neighbourhood in search of game. Huts were dotted about here and there, but the country generally was covered with such a wonderful grass vegetation, that any deviation from the beaten paths would have involved the wanderer in great perplexity, and only too probably he would have rambled about for hours before he could recover his way.

As the caravan was on the point of starting on the succeeding morning, and I had just set out at the head of the procession, we were brought to a standstill by the arrival of some messengers bearing a letter to Mohammed from the commander of his corps that had been sent towards the west. To judge from the date of the letter, the Niam-niam who brought it must have travelled at least forty miles, and perhaps considerably more, in a day.

The letter contained evil tidings. Ghattas's agent and Badry, Aboo Sammat's captain, wrote in the utmost despair. Three chieftains had combined to attack them as they were crossing a gallery on Malingde's territory; three of their number had been slain, and out of their ninety-five soldiers, thirty-two had been so severely wounded as to be *hors de combat*. They had now been closely besieged for six days, and were with extreme difficulty defending themselves behind their abattis; provisions were fast failing; and even water could only be obtained at the risk of losing their lives. Ahmed, the other captain, had fallen at the first outset of the engagement, and his body had not been recovered for interment, but had fallen into the hands of the cannibals. The only means of rescuing the wounded soldiers would be to carry them away in litters, and this could only be effected at the cost of abandoning seventy loads of ivory that had been buried in a swamp. The letter concluded with an urgent appeal for speedy succour, and Mohammed determined to send it without delay; two-thirds of his armed men should be despatched to the relief of the sufferers.

The selection of this relieving-force had to be made at once, and it may be imagined that it was no easy matter for Mohammed to overcome the repugnance of those who had no relative or personal friend in jeopardy. It was naturally a bitter disappointment to those men who were thus marked off for this unexpected service to have to renounce the pleasant prospect of their expedition being so near its termination, and to be compelled to expose themselves anew to the dubious fortune of war. However, in spite of remonstrances and murmurings, the conscription was completed in a very summary fashion, and it was still early when the remnant of our party, with its undue proportion of bearers, continued its northward march.

It was a bright and lovely forenoon; the steppe was adorned with its summer verdure; what had before been bare red rock, was now covered with tender grass, which reminded one of our own fields of sprouting corn. Africa seemed like a universal playground, exciting our people to sport and merriment.

The lovely park-like country, with its numerous scattered bushes, offered unusual facilities for the chase, and small herds of antelopes, a long unwonted sight, appeared and as rapidly disappeared in the surrounding landscape. Once, however, five hartebeests, at a little distance from our road, made a stand, and eyed the caravan as intently as if they were rooted to the spot. I took deliberate aim at the breast of one of them, and although the whole five wheeled round and galloped off into the thickets, I felt sure that my shot had taken effect. Notwithstanding the want of sporting dogs, and in spite of the confusion caused by the multiplicity of tracks, we managed, by following the spots of blood, to make out the proper traces of the wounded hartebeest. As I was approaching one of the smaller thickets, I observed a couple of kites making their circling flight just above the trees; this was a manifest token that the wounded animal was not far off.

After a considerable search we came upon the creature lying lifeless in the grass.

It may be readily understood from these details, that without dogs, and over so bewildering a country, the capture of game, even after it has been shot, is very often a matter of no trifling difficulty. Moreover, time and distance have to be taken into consideration. Our caravan was often half a league in length, and it was important not to leave any gaps in the procession, as nothing would be easier than for the rear division to mistake the narrow path they had to follow. However fleet the huntsman may be, the antelope is fleeter still, and the impatience and excitement exhibited by the sportsman, hurried because he is travelling, have a tendency to increase the alarm of the animal of which he is in chase, and which is already terrified by the unwonted sight of man. On the level steppe, where the grass grows to a height of five or six feet, the pursuer can only get momentary glances of the creature's horns, and all along in his chase he is conscious of making hardly any more advance than if he were buffeting with the waves of the sea.

The animal I had killed was soon cut up, and I made a meal off its roasted liver. Leaving some of my people in charge of the carcass, I set out, intending to return at once to the caravan to despatch some bearers to bring in the spoil to the encampment; but I missed my road, and, notwithstanding the help of my compass, I lost an hour or more in wandering over the rugged paths of an extended elephant haunt. Coming to a depression that was partially under water I saw several leucotis antelopes turn off in front of me, and as the water obstructed my farther progress I made a venture and fired my last shot at a solitary buck that was standing at a distance of not much less than five hundred paces. The animal instantaneously disappeared, and the noise of the report caused several others, in a state of affright, to scamper across the swamp. My Niam-niam were soon at the place where the antelope seemed to have fallen into the earth; to my surprise they soon began to make signs of triumph, and I could hardly believe my eyes when I saw them dragging the victim along the ground. It was quite dead and the bullet was in its neck.

Wonderful good fortune had thus, at very slight cost to myself, thrown into my hands an ample supply of meat, which after their recent deprivations gave unbounded satisfaction to my people.

Carrying with us the piece of meat that was designed for our supper, we entered the camp just as darkness was coming on. I found the people quartered on the slope of a ridge of hills near the frontier of Bendo's district, a league and a half to the south of the residence of the behnky himself.

Towards the south-east I had a view of the hills of Babunga, about ten miles off on the frontier of the Babuckur territory.

All the huts in Bendo's mbanga had been lately rebuilt in a style that displayed considerable taste, the tops of the straw-roofs being so much decorated that they looked like various specimens of ornamental basket-work. We were able to procure a good stock of maize, which made a welcome change from the uniformly bad bread which we had been eating previously for so long. Bendo himself was quite a character; his singularities amused me; he was a kind of fine gentleman, extremely particular about his *toilette*, and would never allow himself to be seen unless he had been carefully painted and adorned with his high-plumed hat.

I did some botanizing on the hill of Gumango and found it full of interest. We next crossed the Rye, and proceeded to the adjacent villages of Gumba. Our camp was scarcely pitched there when a message was received from Mohammed instructing us to wait for him. On returning to his Seriba he had found that all the soldiers for whose fate he had been concerned, and whom he was hurrying off to rescue, had already arrived there safe and sound, having succeeded in breaking through the enemy and in carrying off their wounded. He was now returning to us with his full force. Pending his arrival we remained in Gumba's villages for the two succeeding days.

He came back at the appointed time, and the recovery of the

parted friends caused great joy and excitement in the caravan; innumerable were the questions asked, and no accumulation of answers seemed to allay the curiosity.

My own attention was very much engaged by the accounts given by Badry, the captain who had been appointed to the command of the corps in the place of Ahmed; I knew that his word was to be relied on, and his information was of great value to me as throwing light upon the geography of the country about the lower portions of rivers, some of which I had crossed only in their upper course and sometimes quite close to their fountain-heads.

I heard many details of the conflict between Mohammed's party and the Niam-niam, the leading incidents of which I will now proceed briefly to relate.

It was while they were crossing one of the brooks overhung with the dense forests which now for so long I have designated as galleries, that the fatal attack took place; the consternation of the defenceless bearers, and consequently the confusion of the whole party, would seem to have been very terrible. The first discharge of Niam-niam lances had strewn the ground with dead and wounded, the column of the unfortunate bearers furnishing the larger proportion of the victims. Previous to the attack not a native had been seen. Nothing could be more crafty than their ambush. Some of them had taken up their position behind the larger trees; some had concealed themselves in the middle of the bushes; whilst others, in order to get an aim from above, had ensconced themselves high up, contriving to lie full length upon the overhanging boughs where the network of creepers concealed them from the keenest vision. Badry's recital brought vividly to my mind the battles with the Indians in the primeval forests of America, where similar stratagems have been continually resorted to.

The soldiers kept up their fire with energetic vigour; they are accustomed to carry a number of cartridges arranged like a girdle right round their waist, and having their ammunition thus conveniently at hand they kept up their discharges unintermittingly until they had collected their wounded; but the bodies of those who had been actually killed all fell into the hands of the assailants and were carried off without delay, all attempts at recovering them being utterly unavailing, because the irregularity of the ground prevented any organised plan of attack.

The bearers, meanwhile, had flung away the heavy loads, and in wild flight had retreated to an adjacent hill that rose above the steppe; here they were in a short time joined by the Nubians, who sought the eminence as commanding a view whence they might survey their position and concert measures for their future protection. Most of the deserted ivory, of course, had become the prey of the foe, but some of the Nubians had taken the precaution of burying the burdens in a swamp within the gallery, under the hope that they might recover it in the following year. Thus deprived of their proper occupation, the bearers were at liberty to carry the wounded, and a treaty was concluded with the enemy so that the party ventured to quit their quarters. The natives, however, were utterly treacherous; they were bent upon the annihilation of the intruders, and so, reinforced from the neighbouring district, they made a fresh and savage attack. In consequence of this the Nubians were compelled to come to a stand in the open plain, and lost no time in collecting whatever faggots they could get to make an abattis.

Behind this abattis they had to hold out for three entire days. The excited Niam-niam persevered in harassing them with unwearied assaults; and as three independent chieftains had summoned their entire forces for the attack, the combined action was unusually formidable; not until the store of lances and arrows was all used up were the furious sallies brought to an end and the Nubians permitted to go upon their way. The enemy, it was said, displayed such unabated energy that when all their ordinary lances had been spent they procured a supply of pointed sticks, which they proceeded to hurl with all their might against the Nubian band; it was, moreover, asserted that the quantity of shields and lances was so large that the besieged used no other fuel for their camp-fires during the entire period of their detention. Besides the weapons that were burnt, the negroes attached to the caravan brought away a considerable number of lance-heads, which they had tied up in bundles of nearly a hundred and designed for trophies to decorate their own huts.

I now return to the narrative of our own proceedings.

Our old friend the "minnesinger" paid us another visit in our camp, and entertained us once again with the droll elaboration of his poetic faculty; as the theme on this occasion upon which to exercise his epic muse, he chose the heroic deeds of Mohammed, which he chanted out with characteristic energy.

As our train proceeded along the hilly region between Gumba and Nganye, it was easy to make the observation that there was no appreciable difference in its magnitude compared with what it had been when we traversed the same district more than four months

SUSPENSION-BRIDGE OVER THE TONDY.

previously. A considerable number of the wounded were still carried on litters, and formed a new feature in the procession. One poor fellow had had the entire sole of his foot literally peeled off by a lance. Ali, the leader of Ghattas's company, had also two severe wounds, one on the neck, the other on the thigh; but although both of them were still open, the sturdy negro made light of his trouble, marched on merrily enough, chattering to his companions every now and then according to the current phraseology of the Nubians, enforcing his assertions by the ejaculation, "Wollahi! wollahi!" ("by Allah! by Allah!"). These people are far greater heroes in enduring pain than would be expected from their pusillanimity in battle.

With Nganye the Nubians spent a day of riot and revelry in honour of the African Gambrinus. The chieftain had already prepared for their entertainment, and had sent to Mohammed's hut an enormous vase of beer, the vessel being a fine specimen of native pottery, a masterpiece in its way, and so heavy when it was full that it required two men to lift it. I spent a day in a hunting excursion. I started towards the west, and succeeded in killing two small antelopes and in bagging a large number of guinea-fowl that, in a liberal mood, I distributed amongst my companions; the chieftain himself, when he visited me on the following day, enjoyed a meal off the tender flesh of the birds, which during the rainy season is particularly rich and savoury.

Before leaving his Seriba, Mohammed had sent a message to Nganye to warn him of the advance of the caravan, so that he might have sufficient time for the preparation of the bridge by which it could cross the Tondy. This work was executed without delay, and a suspension-bridge of a very curious and original construction had been thrown across the rushing waters.

The march from Nganye's residence to the river led through the marvellous grass-thickets which I have already described. The grass was now shooting up afresh in all its wild luxuriance. The season for the great elephant-hunts was at an end, and Mohammed was well satisfied with the quantity of ivory his friend had secured. He told me that Nganye, although he ruled over a district that was smaller in extent (though it contained nearly as many hunting-grounds as that of Munza), had furnished him with a much larger supply of ivory than the powerful Monbuttoo king.

It was near the river, in some huts newly-built in Penceo's district, that we passed our last night in the Niam-niam country. A wide tract of wilderness had been lately rooted up in order to acquire fresh arable land against the time when the soil already in cultivation should be exhausted. In these places it is wonderful to see how the masses of shrubs that have been oppressed by the exuberant growth of the trees, sprout out with renewed vigour: free, as it were, from a long restraint, and reanimated by an open sky, these step-children of the sylvan flora seem to overwhelm the wanderer with their beauteous bounty.

On the 24th of June we reached the Tondy and its hanging bridge. To convey the baggage across this tottering erection was the work of nearly an entire day. The place of our present transit was four miles to the east of the spot at which we had crossed on our outward journey; it had been chosen higher up the river for several reasons, not only because the stream was narrower and the banks were higher, but principally because the trees were of a larger, more substantial growth, better adapted for the purpose of being converted into piers for the suspended ropes which formed the bridge. The river was here sixty feet wide, but near the banks it was so full of fallen trees and bushes, of which the boughs projected as though growing in the water, that the width of the stream was practically diminished one-half. The velocity of the current was about 115 feet a minute, the depth nowhere being less than 10 feet.

The materials of the suspension-bridge consisted exclusively of branches of the wild vine intertwined with thick elastic ropes of unusual strength. The French traveller d'Abbadie noticed a similar stratagem for crossing rivers on his tour to Enarea, and bridges improvised very much in the same manner are constructed from creeping plants in South America. In order to get the ropes raised to a sufficient height, a regular scaffolding of fallen stems has to be erected on either side of the river, by means of which the festoons of cords are raised to a proper altitude. The clambering from cross-piece to cross-piece upon this unstable structure, poised in mid-air, seemed to require little less than the agility of an orang-outang; while the very consciousness of the insecurity of the support was enough to make the passenger lose his composure, even though he were free from giddiness and already an adept in the gymnastic art.

The day was far advanced when, after crossing the Tondy, we turned towards the left, and quitted the thickets in order that we might find an open grass-plot sufficiently extensive to accommodate our caravan. The separate detachments were all gathered together, and then divided into two parties, as before returning to Sabby Mohammed had resolved to make an excursion eastwards as far as the borders of his

Mittoo territory, so that he might fetch away what ivory he had in store there. The greater part of the bearers and soldiers were sent on direct to Sabby, and I arranged for my own bearers, under the conduct of my servant Osman Aboo Bekr, to accompany them, whilst for myself I reserved just as much baggage as was necessary, and joined the party that was proceeding to the east. It chanced that Ghattas's corps was taking the same route, and as it led through districts which were well supplied with corn, we all marched in company.

After subduing the Mittoo who were resident close to Nganye's territory, Mohammed Aboo Sammat, in the previous February, had founded a Seriba on the Upper Lehssy, at no great distance from the villages of Uringama, one of Nganye's behnkys. On account of its singular fertility the district was a very favourite station for the various Rohl-companies on their way to and from the Niam-niam lands, and the sagacious Kenoosian, well aware of the advantages afforded by their frequent visits, and knowing, moreover, how numerous elephants were in the surrounding regions, had lost no time in making a settlement in the locality. The name of the local overseer of the Mittoo people was Mbomo. As the owners of the land were mutually satisfied with each other and on the best of terms, the soldiers of the Seriba lived on the most amicable footing with the neighbouring Niam-niam. The Seriba Mbomo was about twenty-one miles to the E.S.E. of the spot where we crossed the Tondy, the road by which we travelled lying almost in a straight line in that direction.

Soon after starting, just as we re-entered the obscurity of the forest, the men in the van of the procession made signs that there was something stirring among the bushes. We came to a halt, and hurrying to the front as stealthily as I could, I made out the forms of some light-coloured animals that were lurking in the shadows of the underwood. They turned out to be five splendid elands. They appeared not to have noticed our approach, and grazed on, as peacefully as oxen, under a large tree just in front of us. Simultaneously one of the blacks and myself fired at the foremost buck that chanced to be standing full broadside in our face. The startled animals made a bound, and put their running powers to the test, their short weak legs carrying their ponderous bodies at full gallop across our path. All at once a crashing noise and a heavy fall; the wounded victim was ours: a good supper was provided for our caravan.

In external appearance this African elk exhibits varieties as great

150 THE HEART OF AFRICA.

as the hartebeest and other common species of antelopes, and on this account it seems to claim some detailed notice. In zoological gardens it is very rare to find two individual examples exactly alike, and the greatest diversity is observable in the shape of the horns; as instances of this, I may refer to the representation here introduced of two pairs of horns which I have selected from my

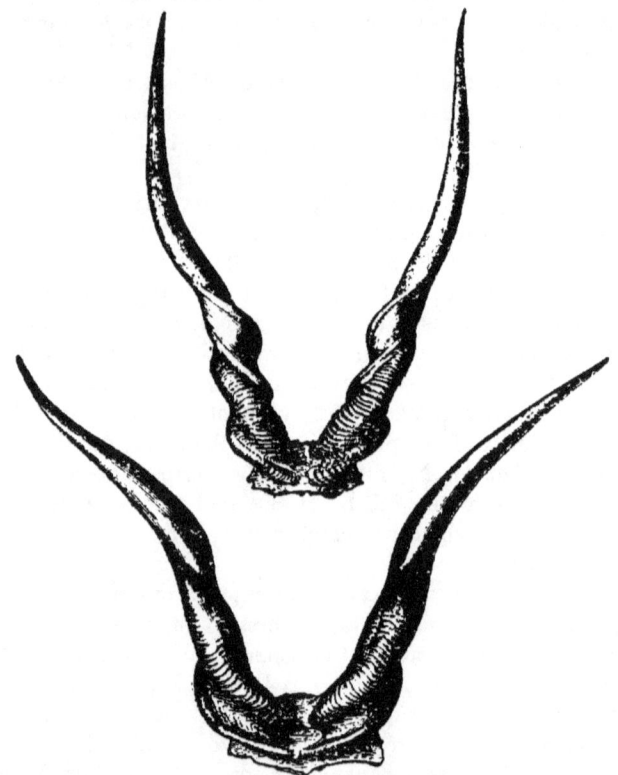

HORNS OF CENTRAL AFRICAN ELAND.

collection, and which may be taken as examples of the two most extreme forms that came under my notice. They are about a yard in length, the pair that is more divergent making only one spiral turn, while the other makes a turn and a half; both are more than three feet long. All the elands that I saw had extremely short sleek hair of a bright yellow tan colour verging on the flanks to a light bay; the mane was black and erect, being about three inches long.

In every district through which I travelled I observed their skin to be always marked in well-defined stripes, which are not, as some travellers have supposed, to be taken as indications of the youth of the animal: I have seen full-grown specimens that were marked on each side of the body with no less than fifteen parallel stripes, about as wide as one's finger, of a pure white running from the black line of the back transversely down to the middle of the belly, which is often marked with a large black spot. The flesh of the eland ranks amongst the better kinds of antelope-meat, and it is quite as palatable as that of the hartebeest.

We encamped about a league from our suspension-bridge, in the midst of a splendid wilderness, where, in spite of the torrents of rain, I passed a night of entire comfort in my warm nest of grass. A little way to the north of our encampment there was a small gneiss hill called Manga. Before halting for the night we had crossed two brooks, which with a supply of water alike copious and rapid hastened on to join the river at no great distance away; the first of these, the Mokungudduly, rippled along over smooth blocks of gneiss, and was bordered by flower-bespangled meadows that, stretching onwards in a forest glade, were watered besides by countless springs.

The march of eight leagues that lay before us would pass through an unbroken forest, and required us to make an early start upon the following morning; accordingly when we set out we found the whole wood veiled in mist and the ground still reeking with the heavy dew. The forest flora continually tempted me to deviate to either side of the pathway. My interest was especially attracted by the splendid Encephalartus, which seemed abundant throughout the district. Amongst other new types of plants which met my notice was the *Tithymalus*, one of the cabbage-like euphorbiæ, the first that I had seen throughout the entire region. A large variety of conspicuous shrubs, many of them covered with fine blossoms, gave the forest almost the aspect of an artificial park.

No less than eight running streams had to be crossed during this march: the first three joined the Tondy, the rest being tributary to the Lehssy. The third brook was called the Baziah, the fifth the Ulidyatibba; succeeding this, and enclosed by walls of gneiss, came the Lehssindah.

About a league to the right of our path, and to the south of the place where we forded the Lehssindah, rose several gneiss hills, of which the two highest peaks were called Ndimoh and Bondoh.

Our route had hitherto been quite level, and apparently at a considerable height above the valley of the Tondy; but it now began to descend for a couple of leagues to the Morokoh. This wide and rapid stream flowed through a tray-like valley surrounded by open grass-plains that sloped downwards on either side to the meanderings of the water. In front of us, to the east, the whole country had a gentle but regular elevation, for looking over the right bank of the Lehssy we could make out the locality in which the union would have to be sought of the chain of the Zilei mountains in Mondoo with those that extend between the Tondy and the Roah.

The scenery of the steep declivity towards the south-west which we now reached assumed a character very different to the park-like landscape through which we had been passing. For many miles the eye rested upon treeless steppes broken by bamboo-jungles that seemed almost impenetrable, standing in detached groups, their dark olive-green contrasting admirably with the bright hue of the grass, and giving a novelty to the general aspect. Immediately beyond the Morokoh our path began to rise, and led us into the semi-obscurity of one of these jungles.

A short time before reaching it, we had left on our right a series of hamlets inhabited by the Niam-niam belonging to Dippodo's district: a league further on lay the villages of Uringama, on the extreme eastern frontier of Nganye's territory, the Lehssy forming the boundary between the Niam-niam and the Mittoo; and a few more leagues still in the same direction would have brought us to the north eastern limits of the Babuckur.

We reached the Lehssy shortly before sunset. The Seriba was built close upon the opposite bank, but it was so enclosed by the tall bamboos that towered high above the palisade that it was completely hidden from our view. The actual source of the Lehssy was at no great distance; the river here was about fifteen feet wide, and four feet deep, and flowed in a N.N.W. direction: the water was as clear as crystal, a peculiarity that appertains to all streams that are enclosed by bamboos, which delight in a soil that is intersected by springs. The stems of the bamboos rose to the height of forty feet; slender and graceful they bent themselves into an arch which stretched far across the stream; and as hardly anywhere could a more inviting spot be found for a siesta, so hardly anywhere could water be met with more tempting for a bath than that which flowed limpidly over its gravel bed.

On my arrival at the Seriba, I soon became convinced that I was in a land where corn was abundant; the very liberality of the messes of sorghum-kissere that were served up to my people was an ample proof that there was no scarcity here. In times gone by I had myself had an utter disdain for this food of the Soudan, but now, after so long a deprivation, I relished it heartily. It was no doubt heavy and indigestible enough; still I could make a good meal of it; only on rare occasions during the Niam-niam journey had I tasted any sorghum at all, and when I had, it had been doled out in infinitesimal quantities, but with the fresh enjoyment of this luxury now, and with the returning opportunity of getting some real roast-mutton, our previous privations were soon forgotten.

The Seriba Mbomo was ten leagues to the south of Kuddoo, on the Roah. Mohammed, with a thoughtful consideration of my tastes, had taken means to enable me to fill up some missing links in the chain of our route. During his march in February he had made one of his men who could write take down all the information he could get from the Mittoo guides; and from the same authority I obtained verbal confirmation of the reports which I had previously gathered, so that I was able to map out the entire district with what I believe is tolerable accuracy.

In the sketch of the route there were enumerated as many as twelve brooks that had to be crossed in the interval between Kuddoo and Mbomo, all supplied more or less copiously with water, even in the dry winter season. Reckoning from north to south, the series came in the following order: the Tee, the Burri, the Malikoo, the Marikohli, the Mangawa, and the Wary; then came the watershed between the Lehssy and the Roah, marked by the Gherey hills, which I afterwards visited; then followed six more brooks, the Kooluma, the Magbogba, the Makaï, the Patioh, the Manyinyee, and the Malooka. Although all these streams have their origin quite close to the left bank of the Roah, yet they take a very devious course before they actually join it; the last five, indeed, do not directly meet the river, but join another stream to the west of the route called the Dongodduloo, which unites itself with the Tee or Tay; the brook that flows past Ngoly's village, and which is known to the west of Sabby as the Koddoh, being an affluent of the Roah.

On the watershed, bamboo-jungles extend over an area of many square miles. The species which is thus found in such immense masses is the same which is so prolific in the lower terraces of the Abyssinian highlands.

The well-tilled soil of Mbomo's district reminded me very much of the country about Kuraggera; the land appeared well populated and covered with extensive fields of maize and sorghum. The extent to which maize was cultivated was quite surprising; whole acres were planted with it, and I obtained a large supply of fresh ears. I had these all dried and ground, and thus provided myself with a considerable quantity of flour, enough to meet the requirements of several weeks to come. The maize is here liable to the same drawback as it is elsewhere. It is very easily spoiled. This happens from two causes; it has a tendency to turn mouldy, and it is very subject to the gnawings of worms; the meal also ferments sooner than any other species of grain. The means adopted by the natives to keep it during the winter is simply to tie the ears in great sheaves and to hang them up on some detached trees, where they can have plenty of air, and yet be out of the reach of the noxious vermin.

One of the best productions of the country is the bean (*Phaseolus lunatas*), the same that is so much cultivated by the Mittoo; it is one of the most palatable species with which I am acquainted; its pods, which are short, broad, and crescent-shaped, never contain more than two large beans.

Although the settlement had been so recently established, Mohammed was very pleased with the store of ivory that had been secured.

For three whole days I rambled about on the banks of the Lehssy, meeting with excellent sport.

On my previous wanderings I had skirted about three-fourths of the frontier of the Babuckur territory. As this territory lay but a short distance to the south-west of Mbomo, being bounded by the Tondy, I was able to obtain from the soldiers of the Seriba some particulars of the country of which I had seen the natives largely represented among the slaves of the various settlements at which I had sojourned.

The Babuckur must either have migrated to their present quarters from the south, or they must be the remnant of a nation that has been constrained to make its way to the north and to the east by the advance of the Niam-niam. It is said that their dialect is found amongst some of the tribes to the south of the Monbuttoo; this is not at all unlikely, as, like those tribes, they have an established system of agriculture and give great attention to the breeding of goats. Limited to an area of not more than 350 square miles, the eastern portion of this people is very much exposed to the raids of the Khartoom traders and to the depredations of the Niam-niam chieftains, who for years have considered their land as a sort of outlying storehouse, from which they could at pleasure replenish their stock of corn and cattle. By reason of the perpetual persecutions to which they have been subject, their population has gradually become more and more compressed, and their crowded condition itself probably accounts for the vigorous intensity with which they now ward off any acts of hostility; they are equally warlike and resolute; they will fight till they have shed their last drop of blood; and as cannibalism is commonly reported to be practised among them, their assailants are generally content to carry off whatever plunder is to be secured, as hastily as possible, without waiting to pursue or trying to subjugate them. Their eastern neighbours, the Loobah, though themselves harassed by the oppressors from the north, are continually at war with the Babuckur.

The other portion of the Babuckur has withdrawn to the frontiers of the Bongo and Niam-niam that lie between the Sway and the Tondy, about sixty miles to the north-west of the portion to which I have been referring; the complete identity of the race, thus severed only in situation, is verified not only by the one term "Babuckur" being applied indiscriminately to the two sections, but still more by the complete similarity of the dialects, as I afterwards proved by comparing the vocabularies that I compiled. The Bongo call the western division of the Babuckur "Mundo."*

The Babuckur are a typical negro race. Their complexion is very dark. As slaves they are very useful, being of a docile and enduring temperament, handy in the house, and expert at almost any ordinary work. They are short in stature, and have a vacant, not to say a repulsive, expression. The women, when they have once passed their youth are, as a rule, the very incarnation of ugliness, for besides having extremely irregular features, they mutilate their faces in a most frightful way. All married women pierce the rims of their ears and both their lips, and insert bits of grass-stalk about an inch long in the holes, some of them having as many as twenty of these grass-slips about their mouth and ears. The sides of the nostrils are treated in the same way as amongst the women of the Bongo, as I noticed in its proper place.

As Mohammed was anxious to inspect his Mittoo Seribas again

* This is the Mundo of Petherick.

before returning to his chief settlement, I did not wait for him, but, accompanied by a small retinue, I started off on the 29th of June, taking the nearest route to Sabby. For the first four miles we followed the same path by which we had come to Mbomo, and although the rain fell incessantly, the bamboo-forest was so unbroken that it afforded us an effectual shelter, and we reached the descent to the Morokoh with dry skins. After crossing the brook we

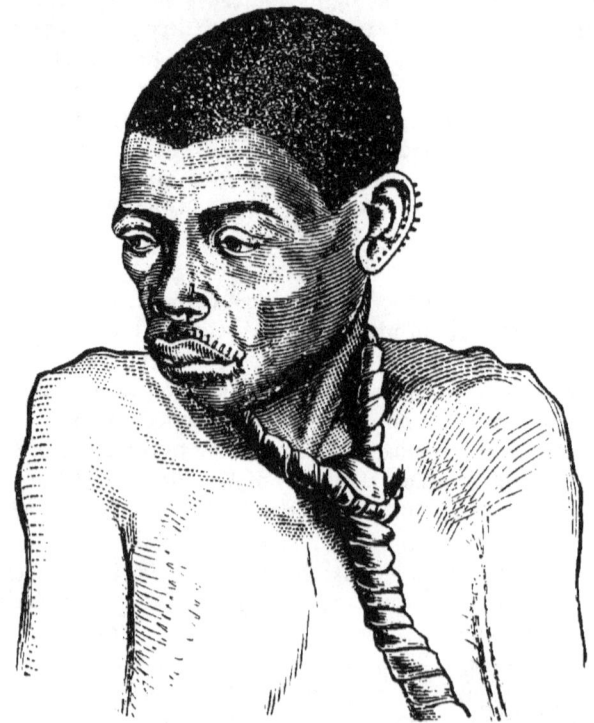

BABUCKUR SLAVE.

turned off in a north-westerly direction, at an acute angle to our previous path.

An immense tract of forest, utterly barren and uninhabited, was now before us. The nearest cultivated spot would be the villages of the Bongo, near Ngoly, which could not be less than forty miles away, and certainly could not be reached within three days. After crossing four little meadow-waters, and fording the Lehssindah where it flowed between its gneiss banks, we encamped for the night about a league further on, near another of these meadow-waters, which are very numerous, and which, spreading themselves out in open glades, sometimes 500 paces wide, break the monotony of the wooded scene.

The whole region was enlivened by herds of hartebeests, and choosing my position at the head of the procession, I was ever on the *qui vive* to pursue them. My exertions in this way made the distance that I actually travelled three times as much as it need have been; but I had no other reward for my pains than the amusement I derived from the grotesque movements of the agile creatures.

After I had comfortably settled myself for the night in my grass nest, a circumstance occurred of a kind which more than once had happened to us before. I was roused by a dull heavy sound that seemed to shake the ground like an approaching earthquake. Our camp was tolerably extensive, for, besides my own retinue, a considerable number of Mohammed's bearers, conveying a large quantity of his ivory, had been sent in our party; but large as our numbers were, the whole camp was thrown into commotion, and shouts and gun-shots were heard from every quarter. The explanation of the uproar was that an enormous herd of buffaloes in their nightly wanderings had come scampering down upon our position, and exposed us to the manifest risk of being trampled to death.

Early on the second morning we reached the banks of the Lehssy. The deep river-bed was now quite full, the stream being forty feet wide and flowing in a westerly direction at the rate of sixty feet a minute. The bearers performed the passage by the ordinary manœuvre of bridging over the water. For my own part I thought to adopt a scheme which would give some variety to the monotony of these proceedings, and became the victim of a little episode of by no means an agreeable nature. There would be a difficulty, I felt, in wearing my boots to cross the tangled branches of which the extemporised bridges are formed; they would permit no sure hold to the feet, and to walk over bare-footed would not have been a prudent experiment, as I might become footsore and prevented from marching; I therefore abandoned all idea of clambering over, but undressed myself and proceeded to swim across the flood. When I was just within a few strokes of the opposite shore, all at once I experienced a painful shock that throbbed through every limb; I had come into contact with one of the prickly mimosa-bushes, which I have already described as frequently hedging in the various streams.

The river-bed being now full to its entire capacity, the water had completely risen above the dangerous shrubs, so that they had quite escaped my notice. I knew the nature of these thorny barriers by experience, and when I mention that I never found the stoutest boots able to withstand the penetrating power of the spikes, it may be imagined to a degree what agony I now suffered. It was like stranding on a reef of thorns. The utmost refinement of cruelty could hardly devise an instrument of torture much more effectual than these mimosæ. However, swim I must. With a desperate effort I got myself free from the entanglement of the shrubs, and bleeding from a hundred lacerations, I contrived to reach the land. I felt as if my whole body had been scarified. But there was no time to lose; so, in spite of the nervous shock, the angry wounds, and the smarting skin, I set out at once in continuation of our march.

We travelled five leagues that day and crossed six separate meadow-waters and glades of the same character as those already mentioned.

After proceeding for a considerable distance over bare red rocks, we were overtaken by a sudden storm of rain, and had to take hasty measures for protecting the baggage. But the interruption did not prevent me from doing a little interesting botanizing during the interval of delay. I found two of the prettiest plants that the land produces here, showing themselves in great abundance: a little orchid (*Habenaria crocea*) with saffron-coloured blossoms, and a sky-blue Monbretia, not unlike a squill. In many places the barren rocks were overspread with patches of these plants, and they looked as though a carpet had been laid out upon them, the colours blending into patterns that would not disgrace the flower-beds of our modern gardening.

Early in the morning of the third day we entered the splendid forest of Humboldtiæ, through which, only ten miles to the west, we had passed at the commencement of our Niam-niam campaign. After the forest came an open steppe, with a distant view of the hills in front, which we should again have to cross, though more to the east than before. The passage of the Mah being accomplished, the ascent began, and led through a wood, where the foliage was so dense that it was quite impossible to see many steps ahead. In an instant a herd of twenty buffaloes, snorting and bellowing, with tails erect, came galloping past in mad career. Dizzy with confusion I discharged my double-barrelled rifle amongst the brutes;

another moment and I could see nothing more than the massive foliage: the buffaloes had vanished, and I heard no more of them than the distant thunder of their heavy tramp.

The hills before us were called Mashirr; they were a continuation of the steep declivity of Mbala-Ngeea in the west, to which I have already alluded, extending onwards towards the south-east and forming a portion of the ridge that had been on our right during the whole of our march. On the summit, as far as the eye can reach, there is an extensive plateau, broken by detached groves and handsome trees, and sloping down towards the north, to the depression of the Tee. For the first time, after long missing them, we found some tamarinds, under the ample shade of which we made a short noonday halt, and then started off through some deep defiles that led to arid plains. Before reaching the Tee we counted four little brooks that flowed in an easterly direction to join it; the first of these, to the north of the hills, was the upper course of the Nungolongboh, and was full of water in a deep bed enclosed by an avenue of trees. A ridge of hills ran parallel to our path upon the left, and after we had crossed the second brook we observed a mass of red rock rising to about 300 feet upon our right. Many small herds of hartebeests came in sight. I lamed one of the animals with a rifle-shot, and was grieved to see how cruelly it was afterwards butchered by the Bongo, the poor brute being so unmercifully mangled by their lances that I had no little difficulty in getting a piece of solid flesh large enough to carry off and roast.

So much time was lost in our chase of the antelope that the evening came on whilst we had still some leagues to travel, and we soon found ourselves marching on in complete darkness. I was amongst the stragglers of our party, and we lost our way several times before we were finally collected by the clanging roll of the kettle-drums on the southern outposts of the Bongo. It was quite midnight when, weary with our exertions and drenched by passing through so many swamps, we arrived, after a circuitous route, at the village of Ngoly.

At this place we remained a day to recruit our strength. In the environs of the village I found the Encephalartus (here in its most northerly position), the seeds, as large as hazel-nuts, strewing the ground in all directions.

At this season, too, the fruit of the wild date-palm was ripe, and I collected a large quantity of it, with which I made an unsuccessful attempt to concoct some African palm-wine. The fruit possesses the same pleasant aroma as the common date, but it is only a third of the size, and is very unpalatable, being harsh, dry, and woody.

On the 3rd of July we marched, without a single halt, for nine consecutive hours, until we found ourselves once again in Sabby. The last few leagues were accomplished in a drizzling rain. Large herds of antelopes frequented the district; but it was vexatious to find myself continually foiled in chasing them by the over-eagerness of my own dogs, which I was quite unable to restrain.

Our entry into Sabby made a wonderful impression upon Tikki-tikki. He caught sight of a number of cattle quietly grazing before the gate of the Seriba, and, jumping to the conclusion that they must be a herd of wild antelopes that had accidentally strayed there, could not comprehend why no one endeavoured to avail himself of so splendid a chance to secure a prize. Subsequently, when he witnessed the process of milking, his delight knew no bounds; he laughed aloud, and declared that so comical a sight he had never seen before.

This journey had been one of the most pleasant and the most successful that had ever been undertaken in so remote a part of the continent. Its pleasantness was owing to my state of health and to the fine air of the Niam-niam countries; its success was due to the favourable circumstances under which I had travelled. In Europe the general idea of such a journey is that it must be a sort of martyrdom, made up of indescribable fatigue, exertion, and deprivation; but, without hesitation, I may affirm that, to a traveller who can only maintain his strength and activity, it is far otherwise; though he may find his enterprise laborious, he will not find it wearisome; it will be what a German would describe as *mühsam* rather than *mühselig*. Fatigue and hardships are estimated comparatively, not so much to themselves, as to the ordinary comfort of domestic life. In fact, our days' marches were often so short that I became quite impatient. Our Niam-niam campaign from Sabby occupied 150 days, and in that time, apart from a few unimportant deviations, we had only travelled 560 miles in all; according to the calculations registered in my journal at the time the whole distance accomplished was about 248 leagues.

After the forced marches, however, that we had recently been making, I was heartily glad of the five days' rest which I was now enabled to enjoy in Sabby. A large packet of letters was awaiting my arrival, and to read through a correspondence which had been accumulating for a year and a half was an agreeable engagement for the period of unwonted repose. It was now for the first time that I heard of Sir Samuel Baker's adventurous expedition, and now that I got my earliest intimation of the Egyptian Government having undertaken to establish a footing in the Gazelle district. Kurshook Ali, a born Osmanli and one of the chief ivory merchants of Khartoom, who possessed a Seriba there, had been invested by the Governor-General with the title of Sandjak, and been placed at the head of two companies of Government troops, one company being regular Turks (Bashibazouks), the other composed of negroes (Nizzam). The arrival of these troops had excited a great amount of consternation through all the Seribas, for, apart from the fact that it too probably seemed to jeopardise the very foundation of the rights of the holders to the territory, it certainly presaged the levying of those taxes and imposts which the presence of Government soldiers always entails.*

After I had re-arranged and re-packed my collection, and seen that it was properly enveloped in waterproof cases, I provided myself with a fresh relay of bearers, and, on the 8th of July, proceeded again towards the north, eager to get the provisions which, having been forwarded from Khartoom, were now delayed beside the sluggish waters of the Gazelle. Mohammed, however, had not yet appeared, but was still making his requisitions of corn in his territories amongst the Mittoo. In consequence of his not returning with the anticipated contributions there was an increased dearth in Sabby, and my poor bearers were becoming absolutely destitute. Their sufferings during their arduous five days' toil were little short of incredible. The Seribas of Shereefee, which were passed upon the way, were as "hard up" for sustenance as Sabby itself; and besides this, the Bongo that were settled thereabouts were all in avowed hostility to my own Bongo, so that no spirit of hospitality was to be expected along our route.

Throughout this portion of our trying journey, the bearers, incredible as it may appear, subsisted solely upon the wild roots which they could grub up; they had positively nothing else to support them, and only digestions such as theirs could have endured

---

* It was in fact the commencement of a new, and by no means auspicious era for the land and its inhabitants. A year later all the Seribas were declared to be Government property, and the trade in the Upper Nile districts was entirely monopolized. Military, instead of mercantile governors were appointed, and the bands of soldiers were incorporated into the army of the Soudan.

the strain. The pressure under which we laboured of accomplishing the journey without loss of time was so urgent that there was not leisure to avail ourselves of any temptation to the chase, and, however much we might feast our eyes, we were under the stern necessity of keeping back our feet from pursuing the elands and waterbocks which had ventured from the wilderness and were grazing peacefully in almost close proximity to our line of march.

It was on the 10th that we reached Shereefee's chief Seriba, but we did not enter it. I had openly declared myself to belong to Mohammed's party, and indeed could not do otherwise than foresee the bitterness of those contentions which so soon afterwards broke out and led to such serious issues.

Most fortunately we were free from rain all the day. The groups of sycamores, which on our former visit had furnished such a commodious encampment under the shelter of their splendid foliage, invited us once again to take up our quarters beneath them; but we had hardly settled ourselves under their shade before we were surprised by the sudden outbreak of a storm, which continued with much violence. The woody landscape around was pleasant enough, and I was compensated in a way by the beauty of the scenery for the lack of provisions; but I looked forward with eager hope for a period of refreshment when there would be an end to chilly baths and clothes perpetually wet.

The passage over the Doggoroo was not made without considerable trouble, as we had to fell some trees and lay down a lot of brushwood so as to construct one of our improvised bridges. The last night-camp between the Doggoroo and the Tondy was deplorably wretched; our provisions were positively exhausted; all we could do was to send some messengers to the nearest Seriba to insure that we should have a supply of some kind in readiness for us on the following morning. It was also necessary to have extra bearers, as comparatively few of the Bongo of Sabby had any knowledge of the art of swimming.

After arriving at the height, from whence, for some miles round, we could survey the expanse of the submerged lowlands, we had still several hours before we could decipher in the distance the forms of the swimmers bringing the burdens of which we were in such urgent need. My bearers could not control their impatience; greedily they pounced upon the first bags of corn that were brought to land, and without waiting for the grain to be cooked, they thrust it by handfuls into their mouths. Their strong teeth easily crunched it up, the hard dry corn being as readily devoured by them as if they had been accustomed to it all their lives. Horses, or ruminants of any kind, could not more readily have disposed of a feed of oats.

I had thoroughly to undress myself in order to pass over the flooded depression, and even upon the banks of the stream I stood knee-deep in water. The passage over the river was tedious, mainly in consequence of the sharp edges of the marsh-grass and the numerous pit-holes in the bottom making any rapid progress very dangerous. No less than two hours had I to dawdle away my time in this cheerless position before the caravan could be brought entirely over. A small raft, constructed of bundles of grass tied together, was used for the purpose of ferrying the baggage across; and, thanks to the excessive care that was used, not a single article failed to be transported in safety.

At this date (July 12, 1870) the Tondy was flowing with a velocity of eighty feet a minute; the depth of the channel, now over-full, proved to be no less than twenty-four feet, and the entire width of the stream, as it reached from the reedy border on one side to that on the other, extended to something more than 120 feet. The river had now risen more than four feet beyond the ordinary limits of its inundation, and our train had repeatedly to make wide deviations from its proper route in order to keep where the bottom was tolerably level and free from dangerous holes. The day was well-nigh spent in contending with rain and flood, and it was quite dusk before we hailed the welcome sight of the hospitable huts of Koolongo.

CHAPTER XIV.

Flourishing condition of Ghattas's establishments—Arrival of stores—Trip to Kurkur—Hyena dogs—Dislike of the Nubians to pure water—Present of a young elephant—Cattle-plagues—Meteorology—Trip to the Dyoor—Bad news of Mohammed—Preparations for a Niam-niam campaign—A disastrous day—Loss of my property—Burnt Seriba by night—A wintry scene—Rebuilding the Seriba—Cause of the fire—Bad news of the Niam-niam expedition—Start to the Dyoor—Counting steps—Kind reception by Khalil—My new wardrobe—Low temperature—Maintenance of Egyptian troops—The army and the slave-trade—Suggestions for means of transport—Defeat of Khartoomers by Ndoruma—Hippopotamus-hunt—Birds on the Dyoor—Hippopotamus-lard—Khalil—Character of the Nubians—Strife in the Egyptian camp—Commencement of a new tour—Crocodiles in the Ghetty—Memorials of Miss Tinné—Dirt and disorder—The Baggara—The Pongo—Frontiers of the Bongo and Golo—Idrees Wod Defter's Seriba—Corn-magazines of the Golo—The Kooroo—The goats' brook—Arrival at Seebehr's Seriba.

THUS it was that after an absence of eight months I found myself happily back again at my old quarters. The place itself was little altered, except that the Seriba seemed to be in a more flourishing condition than in the previous year. The Bongo deserters, who had caused the failure of the Niam-niam expedition, had in consequence of a campaign against the Dinka tribes, on whose territory they had taken up their quarters, not only themselves returned to their former abode, but had induced three times as many Bongo as there were before to come and settle upon Ghattas's property. These people, who were now present in such superfluous numbers, had ten years ago all taken themselves off at the first appearance of strangers settling in their land. I saw that numerous tracts of woodlands had been cleared and brought under cultivation, and that various clusters of houses and farmsteads had grown up around. Altogether I should say that there could not have been many less than 600 fresh huts, which would represent at least 2500 souls. Since my departure, too, Ghattas senior had bidden his last farewell to earthly property, and his Seribas on the Upper Nile had all become the inheritance of his eldest son.*

After being away so long I felt that it was almost like coming home, and realized something of the sensation of treading again the soil of my fatherland when I gazed afresh upon this country, so rich in its woodland charms, so abundant in its smiling sunny cultivation, so contrasted in its character to the gloomy and inhospitable forests of the Niam-niam, which I had just quitted. I could not be otherwise than conscious that I had taken a step which brought me nearer Europe. The large establishment with its diversified population of full many a hue, the mere sight of clothes and linen that had known what it is to be washed, the unaccustomed diversity of victuals of which we could partake, all seemed so different to the contracted resources and meagre fare to which of late I had been subject, that I could hardly resist the impression that I must be living in a city, and could almost fancy myself already back at Khartoom. But before that could happen there were many obstacles to be overcome, and I must submit for various reasons to stay where I was. The journey to the Meshera, at this season of the year, presented nothing but countless marshes, the very birthplace of the miasma which in its turn begets fever. Fresh deprivations for months to come would be the penalty of attempting at once to proceed up the river, and I had, moreover, reason to mistrust the capability of my constitution to withstand disease if I put it to too stern a test. I resolved, therefore, to tarry as patiently as I could, and to console myself with the pleasure of anticipation. In addition to this I had several important tasks which had never been satisfactorily finished, although I felt that the main object of my mission had been generally accomplished.

The temptation to a second Niam-niam tour was too strong to be resisted. I felt that it was my business to strike while the iron was hot, because future travellers only too probably would find that opportunities so good as my own were closed against them, and such undoubtedly has proved to be the case.

Exactly a month after our arrival a party was despatched to the Meshera for the purpose of fetching the supplies which were on their way to me. Not only my own effects, but Ghattas's too, were all lying crammed up in the meagre and not over-safe accommodation of the hold of the boats.

* The Egyptian Government, however, left him but a very short time in possession of his heritage.

One occupation which continuously engaged my attention consisted in my supervision of the arrangement of my miscellaneous collection, which had increased very largely. It was necessary that everything should be put into a condition ready for its long transport.

Another demand upon my time arose from my having my correspondence for the ensuing year to complete and my journal to transcribe. My industry at this period had its full reward. The documents that I then copied and the outline maps that I dotted down were all preserved, and were the only compensation I had to make good the subsequent melancholy loss of all my other papers.

It will easily be understood how delighted I was, on the 23rd of August, to receive my new consignment of supplies. Although a good many articles had either been damaged by damp or devoured by insects, yet a sufficient proportion of them remained so uninjured that I was perfectly satisfied, and could venture with the utmost confidence to make my preparation for another journey. I was able to distribute a good number of presents of garments, pistols, and guns amongst the controllers of the various Seribas, whose acquaintance I had made, while the replenishing of my store of beads and stuffs gave me an opportunity of making certain acknowledgements of the good offices of my attendants. But the services which Mohammed Aboo Sammat had rendered me were far larger than all, and for these I had no return in my power to make.

Furnished thus afresh with a number of conveniences and luxuries which the interior did not supply, I found myself enjoying an amount of comfort that reminded me of Europe, and in the improvement of the quality of my daily food I almost forgot the hardships I had suffered.

I was desirous of devoting the remainder of 1870 to the further and more complete investigation of the Dyoor and Bongo lands. With this intention I betook myself next to the Seriba of Doomookoo, and spent the first half of September in an interesting excursion to Kurkur, a district which, if ever the history of this land should be properly written, will have a claim to one of its most prominent chapters.

Kurkur, just at present a Seriba of Aboo Guroon's, twenty-eight miles to the W.S.W. of the chief Seriba of Ghattas, is a name already known, having been mentioned by Petherick, who, as the first explorer of the district, in 1856, had established a mart somewhere in the neighbourhood, making it the extreme point to which he advanced in his search for the ivory of the productive region.

Upon my route I crossed and re-crossed a number of small affluents which, coming westwards from Bongoland, joined the Dyoor. I gave, however, a particular attention to the course of the Molmul, which hitherto had been regarded merely as an arm of the Dyoor, but which I ascertained beyond a question to be an entirely independent stream. I crossed it close to Doomookoo, and again on my return at another place eight miles further to the north. It bears among the Bongo the name of Maï.

Between Doomookoo and Kurkur the scenery was pretty and undulated, wooded eminences alternating with extensive tracts of cultivated plain. The rises in the ground are made by low ridges of hills that run in a north-west direction on either side of the Nyedokoo, an affluent of the Dyoor that is always full of water. I looked in upon two little Seribas belonging to Agahd, called Kehre and Neshirr, and just before reaching Kurkur I called at Nguddoo, one of Kurshook Ali's settlements. The various territories of the different traders are quite confusing, as they lie scattered about in the more extensive territories.

The Seriba of Kurkur was situated in a flat bushy region, rich in every variety of game. I was told that the former Seriba, visited by Petherick, stood eight miles to the south-west, on the Legbe, an important affluent of the Dyoor. Twelve miles further to the south, and parallel to the Legbe, is the Lako, which is another tributary of the Dyoor.

I remained at Kurkur for three days. Whilst I was there the natives killed a couple of giraffes. The controller had in his possession several of these animals alive, which had been caught in the neighbourhood, and for which he hoped to find a sale at Khartoom.

The spotted hyena dogs (*Canis pictus*) are very common in this region. I saw one specimen in the Seriba that was perfectly tame, requiring no other restraint than a cord, and yielding to its master with all the docility of an ordinary dog. This fact appears to corroborate the assertion of Livingstone (which, however, he makes with some reserve, not having personally witnessed the circumstance), that the natives of the Kalahari Desert are accustomed to break in this animal and train it for the chase.

Twelve miles to the north of Kurkur was another subsidiary Seriba, belonging to Aboo Guroon, and called Dangah, after a Bongo chief who lived there at the time when Petherick was in the country; another surviviving chief named Dyow, also mentioned by Petherick, had his abode five miles further to the west; he came to pay me a visit, and retaining the recollection of the condition of the country under an earlier aspect now passed away, he made the usual lamentations over the destitution of the land and its present deficiency of game.

The Nyedokoo, enclosed by dense jungles of bamboo, passes close to Dangah, and in the rainy season is about thirty feet wide and ten feet deep. The inmates of the Seriba were supplied by its bright and sparkling waters, and I rejoiced at having an opportunity to send my stock of linen to be properly washed. Of the forty Seribas that I visited I saw scarcely more than three that were situated in immediate proximity to running water, the supply from the wells being generally impure, besides being obtained in quantities too limited to be of much service for washing clothes.

The Khartoomers seem to have a very wonderful faculty for picking out the worst possible places for the formation of their settlements. Although they are excellent swimmers, they are so much accustomed to the dust and dirt of their own home and to the turbid floods of their beloved Nile, that even here, where streams are so abundant, they have a morbid prejudice against all pure water whatsoever. They forget that the waters of the Nile are wholesome in spite of being turbid, and make no distinction between them and the waters of the noisome swamps of Central Africa; while they heap imprecations upon the insalubrity of the climate, which, they say, gives them pestilence, guinea-worm, fever, skin-disease, syphilis, and small-pox, they take no pains to avoid the very spots which are the primary cause of all their suffering.

After leaving Dangah I turned back towards the east, and, having called at Agahd's subsidiary Seriba Dubor on the way, I soon re-entered my own headquarters. The circuit I had thus completed was about sixty-five miles.

On the 15th of September Mohammed Aboo Sammat passed through the Seriba on his way to the river, with his store of ivory. It was a good opportunity for me to send intelligence of myself to Europe; and, under his care, my letters were despatched by the speediest route, so that in the course of five months they were in the hands of my friends. A fortnight sufficed for the indefatigable Mohammed to reach the Meshera, start off his boats on their way to Khartoom, and return to our Seriba.

Mohammed upon his return made me a present of a somewhat uncommon description. On his way through the forest of Alwady he had fallen in with a troop of elephants, two of which had been killed by his people, one of them being a female that was accompanied by her still sucking calf. The little elephant had been secured and attached to the caravan, and on arriving at the Seriba was introduced to my quarters as a gift to myself. I was in possession of a milch cow, and took the greatest pains to cherish my new *protégé* by supplying it with large quantities of milk; but all my attention was in vain, the young animal had been so weakened by improper or insufficient diet, and so exhausted by the forced marches, that no subsequent care could save it, and in a few days it expired.

The proceeds of this year's cattle-raids upon the Dinka had been exceedingly large; and as Ghattas's company had been prevented from carrying out a Niam-niam campaign, they had been able to concentrate all their forces for plunder. The captured cattle, under the charge of a number of Dinka herdsmen, had been installed in a large yard set apart for the purpose close to the Seriba. There was consequently no lack of meat, and, at a very reduced price, I was allowed to purchase whatever cattle I required to be slaughtered for myself and for my people.

My milch-cow was an almost invaluable possession. In spite of its yield of milk being somewhat meagre, it supplied me for eight months with a morning draught, and in the subsequent season of necessity its contribution to my daily diet was still more precious. Half the cattle sickened with all sorts of internal disorders, and the greater proportion of the animals that were slaughtered would not have endured the climate much longer. I am sure, however, that notwithstanding the fact that these breeds have been entirely unaccustomed to salt, its admixture with their food would infuse new life and vigour into them; nothing but this, I feel convinced, kept up my own supply of milk and prevented my cow from becoming emaciated.

During the rainy season of 1870 the Dinka cattle were decimated by various plagues, and the district of the Lao was especially ravaged, old Shol losing some thousand of her stock. The most common of these cattle-plagues was called Atyeng by the Dinka, showing itself by open wounds like lance-cuts in the hoofs; sometimes the wounds would make their appearance on the tongue, rendering the animal incapable of grazing, so that it could get no nourishment, and sank through exhaustion. Another malady called Abwott, to which only the cows are subject, consists of a swelling which affects the uterus, and carries them off in a night. A third, known as the Odwangdwang, appears just as contagious, though not so generally fatal as the two former; the animals refuse their food for forty-eight hours, but under favourable circumstances, on the third day commence grazing again.

The Khareef of 1870 terminated on the 21st of September, no rain falling after that date. A heavy fall of hail occurred on the 25th of August, when the hailstones were as large as cherries; this was the only time that I remember seeing hail within the tropics, although in May 1864, when I was on the Egyptian coast of the Red Sea, just to the north of the tropic of Cancer, I witnessed one of the severest hailstorms that could be imagined.

This year's rainy season was remarkable for the violence of the separate storms, but also for the small number of decidedly wet days; of these I counted ten in July, twelve in August, and ten in September, the number altogether corresponding very nearly to what I had recorded in the previous year. Nevertheless, the rainfall was so great that the sorghum in all the low-lying fields rotted in the ground; the condition of the crops, however, was equally bad in all places where the soil, although rocky, was sloping and threw off the water too rapidly, for between the intervals of rain the heat of the sun was so overpowering that the corn was parched up through lack of moisture.

By reference to a few notes that I saved I find that the 4th of October, in a meteorological point of view, was an important day, as being the date on which the wind first veered round to the north-east. I cannot speak positively as to the date when the south wind had first set in, as I was absent amongst the Niam-niam and Monbuttoo at the time; but my impression is that it was not far from the same time as in the year before, viz., the 16th of March; thus the entire period during which the south-west winds had been prevalent was seven months. But although the north-east wind had thus commenced on the 4th of October, there was no perceptible fall in the temperature until the 20th of November; after that the thermometer at sunrise stood at about 70° Fahr.

As the flora at this season presented little with which I was not already familiar, my time was spent very much under the same routine as in the previous autumn; I continued my occupations of measuring the natives, studying their dialects, collecting insects, preparing skulls, and joining the people in chase of small birds. But, all along, I did not lose sight of my projected journey, and applied all the experience I had gained so that I might equip myself for renewing my wanderings with the best advantage. My health was by no means impaired, but, on the contrary, I had gained fresh vigour in the pure air of the southern highlands, where I had undergone more fatigue than I could have previously trusted myself to encounter; I came to the resolution, therefore, that I need not fear to accompany Ghattas's next expedition, and visit the central portions of the Niam-niam countries that were still unknown to me. The journey was specially attractive to me as promising to enable me to complete my exploration of the hydrographical system of the Gazelle, taking me as it would to the middle sections of those rivers, which, indeed, I had already crossed, but only in their upper and their lower courses.

Being desirous of making some exchanges and effecting some purchases to complete my supplies, I set out on a tour to Kurshook Ali's head Seriba, with which I was already well acquainted. This excursion occupied from the 24th of October until the 4th of November. The owner, as already mentioned, had been sent out by the Egyptian Government at the head of a body of troops; but before reaching the interior he had succumbed to the pestilential climate of the Dinka, and had been succeeded in command by a Turkish Aga, who had accompanied him as lieutenant, and who, having broken up his camp in the Dinka country, had turned farther to the west.

Credit had been opened for me in all the establishments of the Khartoomers, and not only were the magazines of Kurshook Ali's Seriba amply supplied with stores, but Khalil, the controller, received me hospitably and rendered me all possible service, so that I accomplished my business most satisfactorily.

The little trip gave me another opportunity of twice crossing the Dyoor, and thus, by taking fresh measurements, of adding to the information I had already gained about this important river. At ten o'clock in the morning, when the atmosphere was at a temperature just under 80° Fahr., the temperature of the water was just over 90°.

The passage was effected in a ferry-boat of the most wretched description; it was composed of nothing more than a couple of hollow stems bound together by ropes and caulked with common clay, the miserable craft demanding perpetual vigilance to keep it afloat at all. It is a striking proof of the unconquerable indolence of the Nubians that during their fifteen years' residence in the land, although they are beyond a question acquainted with the art of ship-building, they have never attempted to construct an ordinary boat for the daily passage of such an important river as this.

Whilst here I received sad news of my friend Mohammed. On his way back from the Meshera to Sabby he had hoped by taking a short cut through the wilderness to avoid all conflict with the marauding parties of his enemy Shereefee; but, in spite of all his precautions, his antagonist had gained information of his movements, and, setting an ambush in the forest, made a murderous attack upon him. The assault was far more sanguinary in its results than that of the previous year. As usual the Khartoomers refused to fire upon their compatriots, and Mohammed was thus entirely dependent for his protection upon his black spearmen, of whom several were killed. Mohammed's cousin, who had brought the stores from Khartoom, fell a victim to a gun-shot quite at the beginning of the fray, and Mohammed himself received so many sabre cuts about his face and head that, deluged in blood, he was left on the ground for dead. Shereefee's Bongo pursued Mohammed's Bongo in all directions, and Mohammed's stores all became the spoil of Shereefee, who did not as before scatter the beads and valuables about the ground, but had everything conveyed to his own Seriba. The booty amounted in all to at least two hundred packages. The shameless marauder made an avowed boast of his achievements, ostentatiously displayed his ill-gotten wealth to all around him, and even strutted about arrayed in Mohammed's new clothes.

In the course of the night Mohammed was picked up, apparently lifeless, by his faithful blacks and carried to Sabby, where he received every attention, but it was some weeks before he was sufficiently recovered to write an account of his misfortunes, which he despatched to the friendly Seribas, sending it by witnesses who could explain the true condition of affairs.

These events naturally excited the utmost indignation in the Seribas, all the controllers of which were friendly and well-disposed towards Mohammed. The slave-traders, on the contrary, who had settled in the country, and all their adherents, took the part of Shereefee. That a Mussulman, on a peaceful journey, should be the subject of a premeditated attack by one of his own faith, was a circumstance without a precedent even in this land of violence and club-law; but, what most provoked my own anger and disgust was the cool indifference with which the commander of the Egyptian troops (the lieutenant who had succeeded Kurshook Ali) viewed the whole affair. When Mohammed appeared in camp and demanded that retributive justice should be exacted for the ill-treatment and loss that he had sustained, the commander endeavoured to throw doubts upon all his statements, and did not hesitate, in spite of the testimony of all the witnesses, to shield Shereefee, by whom, no doubt, he had been previously bribed. Who shall say what order or justice is to be expected in this land of license, when even the Government official, sent out as the first representative of the State to protect and administer its laws, could proceed to such a degree of avaricious partiality? And yet the people in Khartoom have the audacity to descant upon "the suppression of the slave-trade"!

Aboo Guroon, with whom I spent several pleasant days, was busy from morning to night in his preparations for the forthcoming Niam-niam campaign, and it afforded me much amusement to watch him as he sorted out and packed his varied store of ammunition. Several companies had combined for the expedition, and he invited me to remain and start with him, as Ghattas's party, to which I was attached, would not follow for some weeks later.

In this common enterprise Aboo Guroon had a special interest of his own, having but a short time since lost one of his Seribas in the Niam-niam land. The garrison had been massacred, and all the arms and ammunition had fallen into the hands of the sons of Ezo, who having got possession of the weapons turned them to such good account that they inspired the Nubians with great respect for their military skill.

Although I should have much preferred to travel in company with Aboo Guroon rather than with Ghattas's agent, there was one insuperable impediment: my baggage was not ready, and it would require some little time to select the articles that would be of most practical use to me as well as what would involve me in the smallest outlay for bearers. I was obliged, therefore, to forego Aboo Guroon's offer. If I had joined him I should have escaped the calamity of fire from which I soon afterwards suffered so severe a loss, but perhaps only to share a worse fate, for Aboo Guroon was one of the first victims of an engagement with the Niam-niam, a very few days after he set out.

Just at this time all the controllers of the different Seribas were actively engaged in preparing for their combined and extensive ivory-expedition. With their aggregated forces they hoped to subdue the refractory chieftains in the north, who had been guilty of much treachery towards the Nubians: their primary proceedings were to be taken against Ndoruma, the daring son of Ezo.

It had been the rapid diminution of the ivory in these districts that had caused the Khartoomers of late to direct their expeditions to the territories of the powerful kings of the south, leaving the smaller chieftains with a comparatively insignificant interest in the traffic. These chieftains, therefore, did all in their power to obstruct the progress of the Nubians, and endeavoured by foul means, instead of by fair, to obtain a share of the copper which they coveted. They commenced a system of hostility in order to get possession of the store of metal which, as long as they had ivory to dispose of, had come to them in the peaceful way of commerce. To the dismay of the Khartoomers, the natives soon showed that they were quite capable of putting whatever firearms they captured to a formidable use, and I shall very soon have to relate how completely all the Niam-niam expeditions came to grief in consequence of the vigorous opposition of the natives.

Meanwhile I was fully occupied by my preparation for the long journey before me. My anticipations were not to be realized. Just at the time when I was rejoicing that my health had braved all the perils of the climate and my good fortune seemed to be at its height, I was doomed to drink of that bitter cup of disappointment from which none of my predecessors in Central Africa have been exempt.

The description which has already been given of the large establishment owned by the firm of Ghattas, where, with all my provisions, I was now awaiting the start of the caravan, must have made the place in a large degree familiar to the reader. For the clearer apprehension of the event I have now to relate it may be advisable to repeat the following particulars. The colony consisted of about six hundred huts and sheds, which were built almost entirely of straw and bamboo. In the intervals between the huts were erected the large sun-screens known as "rokooba," which were made of the same materials; and, to separate allotment from allotment, there were long lines of fences, which were likewise composed of straw, and these were arranged so close to each other that they scarcely admitted the narrowest of passages, perhaps but a few feet across, to run between them. Everything that human ingenuity could contrive seemed to have been done to insure that, with the cessation of the rainy season there should commence a period of the extremest peril, and, for myself, I can avow that fear of fire became my bugbear by day and my terror by night. In spite of my remonstrances I saw the crowding together of the huts continually become more and more dense, and the enclosure packed full to the utmost limits of its capacity. It became a manifest impossibility in the case of the occurrence of fire, on however small a scale, to prevent it spreading into such a conflagration that the safety of the whole establishment must be imperilled. The material of the structures, dried in the tropical heat, would accelerate and insure the devastation that must necessarily ensue.

The catastrophe, which I had dreaded with such ominous apprehension, befell us at midday on the 1st of December.

This most disastrous day of my life had opened with its accustomed routine. I had been engaged all the morning with my correspondence and in arranging the notes of the various occurrences that had transpired since the despatch of my previous budget. I had partaken of my frugal midday meal, and was just on the point of resuming my writing, when all at once I heard the excited Bongo shrieking "poddu, poddu" (fire, fire!) Long, how long none can tell, will the memory of this burst of alarm haunt my ear. It makes me shudder even now. Eager to know the truth, and to ascertain how far the ill-omened apparition of misfortune had already spread, I rushed to the doorway of my hut, and beheld the devouring element doing its work at a distance of only three huts from my own; the flame was rising fiercely from the top of a hut; there was no room for hope; just at that time of day the north-east wind always blew with its greatest violence, and it was only too plain that the direction of the gale was bringing the fire straight towards my residence. The space of a few minutes was all that remained for me to rescue what I could.

Without an instant's delay, my people flocked to the scene of the alarm. Without stopping to discuss what was most prudent or to consider what was most valuable, they laid hold upon anything that came to hand. The negro-boys took particular care of all the stuffs and of their own clothes, as being in their estimation of the greatest consequence, and by their means all my bedding and two of my leathern portmanteaus were carried safely out of the Seriba. I myself flung my manuscript into a great chest which had already been provided against any accident of the sort, but my care was of no avail. My servants succeeded in hastily conveying five of my largest boxes and two cases to the open space of the Seriba where the direction of the wind made us presume they would be out of danger; but we only too soon learnt our mistake; the wind chopped and veered about, the hot blasts fanned the flames in every direction till there was hardly a place to stand, and it was hopeless to reckon upon any more salvage. A prompt retreat became absolutely necessary; great masses of burning straw began to fall in every quarter, and the high straw-fences left but narrow avenues by which we could escape. The flames sometimes seemed to rise to a height of a hundred feet above the combustible structures of dry grass, then all at once they would descend, but only to lick with destructive fury some adjacent spot, while a perpetual shower of hot sparks glared again in the roaring air. The crowds, as they rushed away before the advancing flames, were like a swarm of flies buzzing around a lighted torch. I cast a look towards the remnant of my property which we had thought we had rescued, and to my horror I perceived that the chests were enveloped in smoke, and immediately afterwards were encircled by the flames. It was a moment of despair. How my heart sank at the sight none can imagine, for those chests contained all my manuscripts, journals, and records, in comparison with which the loss of all the effects in my hut appeared utterly insignificant, though they were the burdens of a hundred bearers. Regardless of the shower of sparks, which singed my very hair, I made a frantic rush forwards, the dogs, with their feet all scorched, howling at my side, and stopped breathless under a tree, where I found a shelter alike from the raging of the ardent flame and from the noonday glare. In the confusion of the flight I had been unable to get my hat, and was thus fully exposed to the midday heat.

Below us from amidst the crackling waves of fire came the crashing noise of the roofs as they collapsed, and ever and again there broke forth the louder report caused by the explosion of our ammunition, and many a loaded gun that had been left behind discharged itself and exposed the fugitives to a new and random danger. The Nubians behaved themselves with a strange composure, not to say indifference; the majority had little or nothing to lose, yet many an account-book must have perished in the flames, so that not a few of them hoped to turn the disaster to a profitable account. The priests, however, were not quite so unmoved; they stood before their doors and howled out the shrieking formulæ of their incantations, by which they pretended to control the course of the raging fire. It was very remarkable that the spot

DEVASTATION.

where a Faki had been buried, and which was marked with a white banner to distinguish it as a place for prayer, was spared from the general conflagration, although it was within a few yards of where my burnt chests had been laid. The departed Faki was now as good as a canonised saint, and had proved himself a genuine sheikh.

The entire Seriba by this time was wrapped in flames, which seemed still to spread in every quarter. The wind, as it rose, carried away with it whole bundles of smouldering straw, which it soon fanned into fire amidst the huts that were scattered on the exterior of the palisade.

Very dry at this season, the steppe had hitherto been preserved, because the harvest was not yet complete, and it was not very long before this too was caught by the raging fire; even the old trees around did not escape, so that it seemed as if the whole district were being submerged in a sea of flame. Half an hour completed the great work of devastation. After that period it was possible to make a dash between the charred posts of the huts, but only for a few moments, so intense was the heat of the ground and so overpowering the glowing atmosphere that pervaded the scene of destruction. A crowd of people kept on bringing vessels of water to try and extinguish the flames before they had totally destroyed the clay "googahs" which held the sole supply of corn.

After a while I succeeded in getting to my garden, which, bereft of the greater part of its recently-constructed hedge of bamboo, presented a truly melancholy aspect. As the sun sank we began to make a search for anything that might have been spared amidst the still glowing embers of the huts. I had saved little beyond my life. I had lost all my clothes, my guns, and the best part of my instruments. I was without tea and without quinine. As I stood gazing upon the piles of ashes I could not help reckoning up the accumulation of my labours which had there, beneath them all, been buried in this hapless destiny. All my preparations for the projected expedition to the Niam-niam; all the produce of my recent journey; all the entomological collection that I had made with such constant interest; all the examples of native industry which I had procured by so much care; all my registers of meteorological events which had been kept day by day and without interruption ever since my first departure from Suakin, and in which I had inscribed some 7000 barometrical observations; all my journals, with their detailed narrative of the transactions of 825 days; all my elaborate measurements of the bodies of the natives, which I had been at so much pains and expense to induce them to permit; all my vocabularies, which it had been so tedious a business to compile; everything, in the course of a single hour, everything was gone, the plunder of the flames. It had been for the sake of better protection, as I thought, that I had resolved not to part with my journals, and had kept my collection of insects in my own possession; I had been afraid of any misadventure befalling them; but now they might just as well have been at the bottom of the Nile.

There I sat amongst my tobacco-shrubs upon my stock of bedding that had been rescued from the flames; but I fear that I could not boast of overmuch of the spirit of resignation. The remnant of my property was soon reckoned up; it consisted of a couple of chests, my three barometers, an azimuth compass, and the ironwork which survived from the different productions of the Niamniam and Monbuttoo.

Evening drew on: just as usual, the cow with her calf came and provided me with two glasses of milk; I had a yam or two, a picking from the inside of a half-burnt tuber, a morsel from a similarly half-burnt lump of pickled meat, and I had come to the end of my slender stock of provisions. My dogs kept up a continual howling; their sufferings from their burnt feet must have been excessive, and they whined in concert with the general desolation. The servants, however, were as calm and undisturbed as usual. Neither the Nubians nor the negroes seemed to be much concerned; and why should they? They had just nothing to lose.

I looked around and counted up my party. It consisted of seven bipeds and seven quadrupeds; the same number of each, and each of about the same sensibility.

When the darkness of night had really set in, the region of the Seriba had all the aspect of an active colliery. The venerable figtree in front of the main entrance was still flaring away, and the palisade was yet burning, apparently shutting in the scene of ruin with a garland of light. It was a ghastly illumination. To the Nubians the spectacle was not altogether a novelty. The sight of a negro village in flames was to them familiar enough; but now the tables were turned, and they had to learn for themselves what it is to be hungry and destitute of every prospect of supply. Such were the conditions under which we had that night to seek our rest.

Hardly anything could be more impressive than the scene that revealed itself on the following morning. Not merely the places where the fire had raged, but the regions around were strewn with a thick layer of ashes; the steppes and sorghum-fields were whitened with them. It would have been easy to imagine that the rich green of the tropics had for a time retreated, and allowed itself to be replaced by a gloomy and wintry vegetation transported from the arctic zone. Almost as white as snow were the layers of ashes that had settled on the sorghum-fields, only broken by the heaps of half-burnt clods that rose like hillocks of turf upon a moor. The smoke still lingered on the ground, and veiled the general scene; the trees seemed to stretch out their dry bare arms to heaven, and helped to complete the resemblance to the winterly aspect of the frozen world.

It was a pitiful sight to watch the brown and swarthy figures of the negroes, wrapped in their brown and swarthy rags, run hither and thither amongst the still smouldering ruins; and the wretchedness of the view was not a little aggravated by the bloated carcasses of half-roasted donkeys and sheep that lay scattered about in various parts. Troops of women were bustling about and carrying water-vessels of every sort, eager in their endeavours to put out the lurking fire that was threatening the corn-magazines that hitherto had escaped. These clay-built reservoirs of corn were the only memorials that seemed to survive the devastation. Blackened indeed by the smoke, the "googahs" were still erect. Varying in height from five feet to seven, they were hardly ever wanting in the homes either of the Dyoor or Dinka: and now as they stood surmounting the otherwise universal *débris*, their very numbers made them conspicuous, and, forming a fantastic feature in the scene, gave their testimony as to what had been the close proximity of hut to hut.

Hurrying up from the surrounding country, the natives flocked to search for beads amidst the ruins, although every bead must necessarily have been spoilt. Others of them, with a better purpose, set to work to construct sheds of straw for the shelter of the houseless.

The next day was opened with a general effort to restore the buildings of the Seriba. Hundreds of Bongo, Dyoor, and Dinka brought the necessary wood, straw, and bamboos, and proceeded to construct their new huts with much dexterity: on an average, six men would completely finish a hut twenty feet in diameter in a couple of days.

No common sense had been learnt through the late calamity, for not only was the Seriba erected on the selfsame spot, but in the selfsame manner as before. The fear of being assassinated by the Dinka was assigned as the reason for refusing to follow the example of Khalil, the controller of Kurshook Ali's Seriba, who, in rebuilding his establishment, had insisted upon placing the Vokeel's residence and the magazines alone within the palisade, leaving the soldiers' huts in detached groups outside. In vain, day after day, did I repeat my warning of the danger they were inviting of the repetition of a similar misfortune; but all my exhortations to care and prudence were utterly wasted; the people were obstinate, and I could not help passing many a sleepless night in continual dread of a second catastrophe that I was aware I was powerless to avert.

The cause of the fire, when subsequently discovered, did not give me the least surprise. One of Ghattas's soldiers had been quarrelling with his slave, having accused her of unfaithfulness; and in order to frighten her, and extort a confession of her guilt, he had discharged a gun into the interior of his hut. I afterwards remembered hearing the report; as gunshots, however, were far from uncommon, I paid no particular attention to the circumstance: but the smouldering paper-cartridge had lodged in the straw-roof, and ten minutes later the hut was in flames. Although the origin of the fire was thus easily explained, the Mohammedan fatalists never swerved from their belief that the misfortune was unavoidable, and was ordained by the decree of destiny.

All my reproaches failed to reach the real offender, who immediately after the fire quitted the scene of the disaster he had brought about. But, in my opinion, Idrees, the controller, was himself primarily responsible for all the trouble. He allowed a senseless firing to be carried on inside the Seriba, not only at every new moon, but on a hundred other occasions, and I was in a perpetual state of vexation and anger whenever I saw the lighted wads flying about amongst the dry straw-roofs: then, again, he allowed each person to increase the number of his huts, rokoobas, and hedges, just as he liked, until the appearance of the Seriba was that of an inexplicable maze. In his capacity of Vokeel it was undoubtedly his place to allot a proper space to each individual; but so far from seeing that this was done, he himself did his utmost to increase the complication of buildings, and had erected a huge rokooba for his horse just in front of my hut; it was this very rokooba that had been the means of communicating the flames to the chests containing my manuscripts, as they stood on a portion of what, previously to its erection, had been a wide open space.

By the 11th of December some newly-built huts were at my disposal, a place of security on that day proving doubly welcome, as a heavy storm of rain came on about four o'clock in the morning, lasting for quite half an hour. This exceptional storm rose from the south-east, veered round to the south, and finally passed away towards the south-west. The entire day remained cold and dull, with slight showers falling at intervals. For the first time the temperature fell to 65° Fahr., having previously varied between 75° and 80°. The coldest season of the year now set in, and lasted for a couple of months; during this time the thermometer in the early morning was comparatively low, and the barometer varied much more than in the height of the rainy season.

Bad news flies apace, and following close upon the destruction of the Seriba came the intelligence of the total defeat of that first detachment of the Niam-niam expedition that had been despatched to the south; besides a number of native bearers, 150 Mohammedans were reported to have lost their lives.

The immediate effect of these disastrous tidings was to make me know that all hope of extending my wanderings in that direction must finally be abandoned. Bitter as had been the misfortune that had befallen me, it would not of itself have deterred me from my project of a second Niam-niam journey, but, now that Aboo Guroon was killed, there was no one who could provide me afresh with such articles as I had lost. I possessed neither boots nor shoes, guns nor ammunition, paper nor instruments, and even my watches, which were so essential to me, were gone; what use then to think any further of a journey to unknown countries under such circumstances as these? Convinced of the vanity of any attempt to proceed, I was therefore obliged, with a heavy heart, to turn my thoughts towards Europe; no succours could reach me for more than a year, and even then my great distance from Egypt made their safe arrival more than doubtful.

Still more than six months remained before the trading-boats would start on their return journey down the Nile; I felt bound to employ this time to the best of my powers, and I was not long left to make up my mind as to what I would do. Amongst the few of my effects that were snatched from the flames I discovered ink, together with materials for writing and drawing: and the sight of some sketches that had accidentally been rescued with my bedding first roused me from my feelings of total despair, and told me that I must once again begin to collect and investigate, and preserve my observations by means of pen and pencil. Necessarily depressed in spirits, I once again turned to as many of my former pursuits as I could, although I felt the increasing pressure of poverty and hardship, and was as dependent as a beggar upon the hospitality of the Nubians, many of whom viewed my presence in the country with suspicion and distrust. My present discomfort was still further aggravated by its contrast with the comparative ease and abundance which the arrival of my European stores had latterly afforded me.

I came to the resolution of quitting the scene of my disaster, and, accompanied by my servants, determined to withdraw to Kurshook Ali's* Seriba beyond the Dyoor, where I knew that Khalil, the kind-hearted controller, would render me what relief he could under my present urgent necessities, although the amenities of life to which the Nubians had any pretension were very few. Accordingly on the 16th of December, followed by a small herd of cows, I turned my back upon the Seriba that had arisen from the ashes of its predecessor, and started by a new and more southerly route for my intended quarters.

For nearly three years my watches had gone with remarkable accuracy; their loss was quite irreparable, for the Nubians have no other means of computing time than upon the great dial of the firmament,† and they tell the hour of the day by simply observing the position of the sun in the heavens. The only resource left to me for estimating the distance that I travelled was to count my steps, and in my despondency over my losses I found a kind of melancholy satisfaction in the performance of this monotonous task, which probably had never fallen before to the lot of any other African traveller. My patience, however, was, as it were, an anchor of safety that I threw out after my calamity: I seemed to myself like a ship which, though seaworthy in itself, has thrown overboard its cargo as the only hope of getting into port. An enthusiast I set out, enraptured with Nature in her wildest aspect, and an enthusiast should I have remained, had not the fire clipped my wings; but now, helpless on the inhospitable soil of Africa, I could not but be conscious how powerless I was to contend with the many obstacles, both physical and material, that beset my path; but in the place of

* The Turkish name is properly pronounced Kutshook Aly, but I give the words as I believe they are more generally written.

† The negro races of Central Africa also, without any notion of hours as a division of time, are able to indicate the time of day by the same method, which for the equinoctial regions may be considered quite practical.

enthusiasm, patience, which overcomes all misfortune, came to my aid, did me good service, and kept me from sinking.

I must confess that the first few days' journey threatened to exhaust what spirit still remained to me, but by degrees my equanimity was restored, and persevering in my design I soon became accustomed to a practice to which I owe some of the most reliable results of the survey of my route. As a consequence of this method of counting my steps I succeeded in attaining very considerable accuracy in the relative distances noted on the map, although very probably I may have been unable to avoid an error of from 5 to 8 per cent. in the absolute distances themselves; of course my steps were not so perfectly uniform in length as the divisions of a measuring rod; but, after all, the footsteps of a man are a much more accurate standard of measurement than those of a beast; the camel, for instance, as is well known, when it is urged to greater speed does not increase the number of its steps, but only increases their length; whilst the paces of a man, at whatever rate he may walk, do not vary much from an average length. Anyone may easily put this matter to the test for himself by measuring the distance between his footprints on the moist side of a river, and he will find that no increase nor diminution in his rate of progress will make a very material difference in their successive distances. My own paces varied, according to the nature of the roads, from two feet to two feet four inches in length, and my method of computation is readily described. I first counted hundreds, telling off each separate hundred on my fingers; when I had reached five hundred I made a stroke in my note-book, and on reaching another five hundred I made a reverse stroke upon the one already made, thus forming a cross, so that every registry of a cross betokened a thousand paces; all beyond five hundred were carried on towards the next stroke, and between the various strokes and crosses I inserted abbreviated symbols, as notes about the condition and direction of the road; thus I was prevented from either over or under estimating the number of my steps, and at the close of each day's march was able at my leisure to sum up all the entries and duly record the result in my diary. In the six months that elapsed before my embarkation at the Meshera I had in this way taken account of a million and a quarter of my footsteps.

The route which I had taken towards the Dyoor led through Dubor and Dangah. On the 16th of December the Molmull was still full of water, but had no longer any perceptible current; the brook passed along a considerable, though gradual depression, the rising ground about Dubor being visible for a long distance to the west. All the pools and ponds by the wayside were now completely dry; a couple of swamps was all that remained of the affluent to which the copious brook near Okale, with its surrounding groves of wine-palms, owes its existence. The Nyedokoo was reduced to half its former dimensions, and was now but fifteen feet wide and three deep, although the current was still strong.

Before its union with the Dyoor, the Nyedokoo receives a considerable increase in its waters from the left, and on our way northwest from Dangah we had to cross two small brooks, both flowing into the Dyoor; the larger of these was called the Kullukungoo. We made a short halt in a little Scriba belonging to Agahd's company, and then began to descend the eastern side of the valley of the Dyoor, which might be described as a steep wall of rock eighty feet in height. We marched for a distance of four miles through a lovely wood on the right bank of the river, and were greatly diverted by the extraordinary numbers of hippotamuses that frequented this part of the stream.

I had the kindest of receptions from my old friend Khalil, who did all that lay in his power to make my visit enjoyable, and showed great sympathy with me in my misfortunes. His magazines were plentifully stored with stuffs and ammunition, and, as I had unlimited credit with him, he was able to supply me with some of the articles that were more immediately necessary. In the Scriba I found some people who understood something of the art of tailoring, and with their help I set to work, to the best of my ability, to make good the defects of my wardrobe. By taking to pieces the few garments that remained to me and using the fragments for patterns, I managed to procure some new clothes, all of which I cut out myself. In none of the Scribas was there a single piece of linen or of any durable material, and I could obtain nothing stronger than their thin calico. But a still more serious inconvenience was the want of any proper protection for my feet, and I could not at all get accustomed to wearing the light slippers of the Turks. The loss, too, of my hat was irreparable, but I contrived a sort of substitute by pasting together some thick cartridge-paper and sewing some white stuff over the whole; this hat possessed considerable durability, and in lightness was all that I could desire. In spite of the poverty of my wardrobe I was rejoiced to find that in cleanliness at least it was a match for that of the Khartoomers, who attach great importance to their washing-garments being of a spotless whiteness. The superiors amongst them, such as the Vokeels and the agents of the trading firms, even in these remote districts, not unfrequently appear in Oriental costume as gorgeous as though they were parading the streets of Khartoom; they all possess cloth clothes made in the Egyptian Mamelook fashion, and these are donned on special occasions, as, for instance, whenever they pay formal visits to their neighbours. For my own part I could never consent to array myself in an Oriental costume, knowing that the most meagre garb of European cut commands far higher respect throughout the domains of the Egyptian Viceroy than the most brilliant and elaborate uniforms of the East. The adoption of the European style of dress in Egypt itself has been remarkably rapid, and between the years 1863 and 1871 I noticed a very conspicuous alteration in this respect.

The 25th of December was the coldest day that I experienced during my residence in the interior. Half an hour before sunrise the thermometer registered 60° Fahrenheit, whilst on the two preceding mornings at the same hour it had stood at about 62° Fahrenheit; but it never afterwards fell so low again, and notwithstanding the coldness of the mornings the temperature at midday rose regularly above 85° Fahrenheit, and on the 28th the thermometer out of doors and exposed to a north wind registered 96° Fahrenheit in the shade, whilst inside the huts it rose no higher than 88° Fahrenheit. The uniformity of the temperature throughout the year is a remarkable peculiarity of these far inland districts, which in winter-time are neither subject to the great heat in the middle of the day nor to the cold by night, which are experienced in the steppes and deserts of Nubia. The temperature of 60° Fahrenheit was the lowest that was registered during a residence of two years and a half, and was quite exceptional, only lasting for a couple of hours just before sunrise. As a comparison between this and the relatively cool climate of Tropical America I may mention that observations in Guatemala gave the average temperature for a period of twelve years as the same as this one exceptional minimum registered throughout my two and a half years' residence in Central Africa.

The camp of the Egyptian Government troops had been removed to the west, and was now a good seven days' march beyond the Dyóor. For the maintenance of the troops, contributions were levied on all the Scribas: the Government, it is true, paid two Maria Theresa dollars for each ardeb (1½ cwt.) of corn; but as the bearers from the more remote places were obliged either to consume more than half of their own loads upon their journey, or else to obtain extra provisions from the Seribas through which they passed, this payment was necessarily very inadequate. Some of the controllers managed to raise their portion of the compulsory tribute by sending herds of cattle to those Seribas that were nearest to the camp, and there getting them exchanged for the required corn; but as some of the settlements were as much as twenty days' journey from the encampment, it was perfectly impossible to provide means of transport to such a distance, and besides this difficulty, there was a constant occurrence of scarcity of corn in all the Seribas; the unreasonable Turkish commander, however, took not the smallest heed of these inconveniences, but, by insisting upon the full satisfaction of his demands, went far towards hurrying the settlements into bankruptcy and ruin.

Instead of introducing order and regularity into the country, the first measures of the Government official tended only to engender odium and discontent, and completely crippled all the more promising tendencies of the mercantile intercourse of the Seribas. For the suppression of the slave-trade they did absolutely nothing. Along the Nile, it is true, where the route was open and everything obliged to be above-board, the Governor-General had commenced proceedings for the suppression of the slave-trade by a series of bombastic and pompous proclamations; but here, in the deep interior, there was every facility for the carrying on of the avowedly prohibited traffic.

Nowhere in the world can more inveterate slave-dealers be found than the commanders of the small detachments of Egyptian troops; as they move about from Seriba to Seriba, they may be seen followed by a train of their swarthy property, which grows longer and longer after every halt.*

In the course of my narrative I have repeatedly shown that the inadequacy of the means of transport throws great difficulties in the way of the maintenance of a large and concentrated body of men. Fifty pounds is the standard weight of a bearer's burden on the longer journeys, and it does not require much calculation to make it evident that in comparatively a few days this burden will be materially encroached upon by the bearer himself; he must necessarily exhaust it by his own requirements. Thus, for marches

* Eye-witnesses tell me that in 1877 the same abuses went on in the Upper Nile districts.

of many days' duration, man becomes the most unsuitable of all instruments for transporting provisions. It was, therefore, not unnaturally a matter of constant consideration with me as to whether this difficulty might be obviated in any way, and whether longer expeditions might be undertaken into the interior without that continual risk of the failure of their means of subsistence, which was now so perpetually threatening them as often as they had to make their way either across uninhabited wildernesses or through hostile territory.

The introduction into these lands of carts drawn by oxen, such as are in use in South Africa, could only be done with very great caution, as it would involve much outlay both of time and money; in the first place, the transport of the heavy waggons themselves into the country would be far from easy, and then drivers who could train the beasts to their work would have to be obtained from remote districts; and even if these preliminary obstacles were overcome, it remains somewhat doubtful whether the breed of Dinka cattle could produce animals of sufficient strength and powers of endurance for such a purpose. In addition to all this I have already shown, in my account of my Niam-niam journey, that it would be impossible to penetrate with bullock-waggons of any sort beyond latitude 5° N.

It has been proved by experience that all donkeys, mules, horses, and camels succumb sooner or later to the effects of the climate; thus oxen would remain the only animals available as beasts of burden; but as those of the Dinka would be as incapable of carrying loads as of drawing waggons, it would be necessary to import suitable cattle from the Baggara Arabs, thus following the example of the slave-traders from Kordofan and Darfoor, who thence obtain all the animals that they use for riding.

Any sort of hand-truck in these countries must necessarily be limited to a single wheel, for, as I have often said, the paths are everywhere quite narrow, being in fact no wider than ordinary wheel-ruts; in most cases they barely allow any one whilst he is walking to put one foot before the other, as the tall grass closely hems in the avenue on either hand.

After giving much attention to the subject, I am convinced that the most suitable form for any hand-trucks would be something like that used by the Chinese, running upon a single large wheel, which the framework that contains the goods spans like a bridge; a construction which, it is well known, permits loads of considerable weight to be moved by one man. In Central Africa, however, these trucks would have to be made chiefly of steel and iron, and ought to be constructed so that they should be propelled by a couple of men, one pushing behind and one pulling in front, by means of two poles run longitudinally through the barrows. They would then, I think, be applicable to every variety of soil, and would be equally adapted for the swamps and for the flooded depressions of the rivers, for the rocky ground of the mountainous regions, for the densest forest and for what to broader waggons would present hardly inferior difficulties —the open steppes. I should estimate that, at a very moderate computation, trucks of this build could bear upwards of five hundredweight; and thus the traveller would find the number of men he wanted reduced to one-fifth, and still be in a position to convey everything that was really necessary.

I spent the remainder of the year in Kurshook Ali's Seriba. Whilst I was there, some Nubian soldiers arrived, who, having been eye-witnesses of the late engagement with the Niam-niam, brought us more circumstantial evidence of the defeat that the united forces of the several trading companies had suffered. The caravan had been composed from the three companies of Aboo Guroon, Hassaballa, and Kurshook Ali, and included a larger number of bearers than it was customary to take into the Niam-niam lands; thus the entire party numbered close upon 2250, of which not less than 300 were provided with firearms. The assault had been made at a spot about a day's journey to the north of the residence of Ndoruma, the son of Ezo, just as the caravan with all the baggage was entering the obscure gallery of a bank-forest, and after the two leaders, Aboo Guroon and Ahmed Awat, on their mules at the head of the procession, had already emerged from the farther end. To the consternation of the Nubians, the attack was rendered doubly formidable by the skilful use of the firearms which the Niam-niam employed against them from behind the massive tree-stems. Cut off from their people, the two leaders were killed at the outset of the conflict, the one by a lance and the other by a bullet.

During the whole course of the battle, Aboo Guroon's people alone displayed any shadow of bravery. A detachment forced their way through the gallery, and rescued the body of their leader from the hands of the enemy, so that this old servant of Petherick, one of the earliest and most experienced of the traders with the Niam-niam, was consigned to an honourable grave, whilst the dead bodies of all his fellow-sufferers fell into the hands of the Niam-niam. Ndoruma, who led on the attack in person, had some months previously captured large quantities of guns and ammunition, and as he was in possession of several fugitive slaves from the Seribas who had been familiarised with the use of firearms, he had lost little time in compelling them to impart their knowledge to their fellow-countrymen. The Nubians have the most pusillanimous dread of bullets, and any savage nation that enjoys the reputation of having guns in its possession may be tolerably sure of being spared any visits from them. It may therefore be imagined with what success the Niam-niam pursued their victory, and with what disgrace the intruders retreated in hasty flight. All the baggage, including a hundred loads of powder and ammunition, fell into the hands of Ndoruma.

From what I could gather from some Niam-niam with whom I had communication, Ndoruma's enmity towards the Khartoomers was not entirely founded upon the exhaustion of the ivory-produce of his country. The Nubians, too shortsighted to foresee the consequences of their folly, are accustomed, whenever they can do so without injury to themselves, to commence an unjustifiable system of depredations upon any land from which they have no longer anything to gain by an amicable trade. In this way they have acted with impunity towards the Bongo, Mittoo, and others; but with the Niam-niam, a people whose strength consists in their constitutional unity, they have exposed themselves to a severe retribution. In their repeated razzias against the surrounding nations they have been addicted to the practice of carrying off the women and girls, and this has roused the Niam-niam, who ever exhibit unbounded affection for their wives, to the last degree of exasperation. It is this diabolical traffic in human beings that acts as the leading incentive to these indiscriminating Nubians, and has caused so much detriment, by the decimation of the Bongo, to their possessions. In one part, as amongst the Bongo, it has resulted in bringing about an insufficiency of labour, and in another, as amongst the Niam-niam, it has thrown a barricade of hostility across their further progress.

Of the three companies that had met with this serious repulse, Kurshook Ali's company had suffered the smallest loss; its column of bearers, who were bringing up the rear of the procession, had retreated in time; but of the soldiers of the company, who had naturally hastened to the assistance of their fellow-countrymen, ten were killed and four more were carried away severely wounded. According to the protocol that Khalil received, all of these had been pierced by bullets. Apart from the grievous loss of life and property that this occurrence entailed, it foreboded nothing but discouragement for the future of the ivory-trade; the controllers of the Seribas felt absolutely powerless before the overwhelming fact that the Niam-niam had used firearms, and, under the circumstances, they were entirely at a loss to know how to induce their disheartened troops to re-enter the formidable country. The soldiers openly declared that they had been hired to fight against savages on the Upper Nile, and by savages they meant people who used lances and arrows; but to do battle with people who were armed with genuine bullets was going beyond their contract, and this they positively refused to do.

All the bearers who had escaped from the conflict with their lives, hurried back in crowds to their settlements, and circulated in the environs of the Seribas the most horrible accounts of the heart-rending massacre they had witnessed. As the demands of the expedition had nearly emptied several of the Seribas of their fighting force, those settlements that were on the Dinka frontiers were consequently for the time considerably exposed to the danger of attack from their neighbours. Accordingly, in the course of a few days, it happened that we were solicited by the inhabitants of a neighbouring Seriba of the deceased Aboo Guroon to send them an armed succour, as the Dinka around them were assuming a most threatening attitude. Khalil complied with their request by sending a small detachment of soldiers to co-operate with the remnant of armed men who had been left in charge of the garrison.

All these events combined to give my life in the Seriba much more excitement than before, and my intercourse with strangers was far from unfrequent. Many of the Gellahbas, mounted upon their donkeys or Baggara oxen, passed through the place to do business in the purchase of living ebony, and their rivals, the Turkish soldiers, ever and anon paid us a visit whilst on their way to make their requisitions of corn at the adjacent Seribas.

On the 25th I made an excursion to the banks of the Dyoor, for the purpose of hunting hippopotamuses, as well as of verifying the condition of the river by taking measurements in two fresh places. Six miles to the S.S.E. of the Seriba, I reached the left bank of the river at a place where it was overgrown with tall reeds, and on our return we crossed again four miles farther down. Between these two positions was a deep basin, in which a number of hippopotamuses throughout the year found sufficient water in which to perform their evolutions. A couple of miles lower down were the two crossing-places of earlier date. Between the most northerly and the most southerly of the four spots I have mentioned, the general direction of the Dyoor is due north, varied by gentle windings to the N.N.E. and N.N.W.

I sat for hours upon the rocky slopes of the right bank of the river watching the hippopotamuses as they plunged about in the water, and occasionally firing at them as opportunities occurred for an aim; but a light rifle was all that I had saved from the fire, and the small shot that it carried did not have much effect upon the unwieldy beasts. The range of my rifle was rarely more than 150 feet, and of the hundred shots that I discharged very few did any serious damage, and only two animals appeared to be mortally wounded. Early on the following morning the natives of the surrounding districts found the body of one of the creatures that I had killed by a bullet behind the ear lying amongst the reeds in the river-bed, and they spent several hours in cutting up the ponderous carcass.

To the same degree as its waters were enlivened by fish and hippopotamuses, were the banks of the Dyoor animated by birds and many varieties of animals. The forests were denizened by several species of the monkey family, that during the winter months found there an abundant harvest of ripened fruit. The grotesque form of the red-billed rhinoceros-bird rocked to and fro on the half-bare branches, and one of the most splendid of African birds, the sky-blue Elminia, was especially frequent. The bare sand-flats in the half dry river-bed were the favourite resorts of the water-birds. The quaint-looking umbers (*Scopus umbretta*), which are generally seen sitting solitary by the shady swamps in the woods, were here marshalled along the banks in flocks of twelve or fifteen ; these birds, with their ponderous crested heads pensively drooping in the noontide heat, seemed in their "sombre weeds" rather to belong to the dreary wastes of the chilly north than to the smiling grass-plains of the Upper Nile. Then there were the great herons (*Mycteria senegalensis*) gravely strutting about, or skimming the dark blue surface of the water on their silvery pinions. The Khartoomers call this bird Aboo Mich, or father of hundreds, in commemoration of the munificence of a traveller who is said to have given a hundred piastres (five dollars) for the first specimens of this noble bird. In other places the sacred ibises had congregated into groups, and with their bills turned towards the water, stood or squatted motionless under the vertical beams of the midday sun. The return of the dry and cool winter months regularly brings these birds, like their compatriots the Khartoomers, into the more southerly negro-countries. Ever and again the sharp cry of the osprey from some invisible quarter would rouse the traveller from his reveries, as though by its yelling laughter it were mocking at his meditations. Storks, which are so prominent a feature in the Central Soudan, and are so highly reverenced in Adamawa, did not appear in these regions, and throughout my journey to the Niamniam I never saw them.

We were hard at work on the following day in turning the huge carcass of the hippopotamus to account for our domestic use. My people boiled down great flasks of the fat which they took from the layers between the ribs, but what the entire produce of grease would have been I was unable to determine, as hundreds of natives had already cut off and appropriated pieces of the flesh. When boiled, hippopotamus-fat is very similar to pork-lard, though in the warm climate of Central Africa it never attains a consistency firmer than that of oil. Of all animal fats it appears to be the purest, and at any rate never becomes rancid, and will keep for many years without requiring any special process of clarifying; it has, however, a slight flavour of train-oil, to which it is difficult for a European to become accustomed. It is stated in some books that hippopotamus-bacon is quite a delicacy, but I can by no means concur in the opinion; I always found it unfit for eating, and when cut into narrow strips and roasted, it was as hard and tough as so much rope; the same may be said of the tongue, which I often had smoked and salted. The meat is remarkably fibrous, and is one continuous tissue of sinews.

My old friend Khalil commanded greater respect from his subordinates, and maintained more order and discipline in his Seriba, than any other controller belonging to a Khartoom mercantile firm with whom I ever became acquainted. With him, the settler who had been longest in the country, I spent many a pleasant hour, and from his confidential gossip I gained many a hint that enabled me to form an accurate judgment upon the state of affairs. He complained very much about the undisciplined troops of his countrymen that were sent to him from Khartoom; he emphatically denounced the slave-trade, and although he could not enter much into the humanity of the attempts for its suppression, yet he was fully alive to the disadvantages that it exercised upon the internal administration of the

Seribas. He was extremely anxious that the natives under his jurisdiction should suffer no diminution in their numbers, and would often dispute with the itinerant slave-dealers their right to carry off property that they had obtained from his territory; he even endeavoured to exercise control over his subordinates in the subsidiary Seribas, although they generally contrived to elude his watchfulness. Whenever it happened that any orphan Dyoor or Bongo children had been sold to the Gellahbas, he would use all sorts of remonstrances, and would spare no argument to induce the traders to surrender their booty.

"This boy," he would say, "you can't have him: in the course of three or four years he will be old enough to be a bearer, and will be able to carry his 70 lbs. of ivory to the Meshera; and this girl, you musn't take her: she will soon be of an age to be married and have children. Where do you suppose I am to get my bearers in future, if you run off with all the boys? and where do you expect that I shall find wives for my Bongo and Dyoor, if you carry all the girls out of the country?"

However reserved might be my behaviour towards the Nubians, yet my long period of daily intercourse with them gave me a tolerably deep insight into their character. It may perhaps appear incomprehensible how, with any equanimity, I could have endured for two years and a half the exclusive society of what was, for the most part, a mere rough rabble; but it must be remembered that the social position that I was able to maintain amongst them was very different to what it would have been amongst a party of rude and unpolished Europeans, and their religious fanaticism, as well as the entire difference of their habits, raised a strong barrier of defence against any sort of intimacy. Amongst the thousands of Nubian colonists with whom I was thrown in contact, I never met with a single individual who offered me any insult either in word or deed; I never had occasion to enter into anything like domestic relations with them, and never did otherwise than eat and sleep perfectly alone and in the seclusion of my own hut. But in spite of all my reserve I was a constant witness of the scenes in their daily life, and I believe that very few of their habits escaped my notice; it may not, therefore, be altogether uninteresting to insert here some results of my observations upon the character of my old travelling-companions.

Throughout this account of my wanderings I have, for the sake of simplicity, always used the term "Nubians" to denote the present inhabitants of the Nile Valley, in contradistinction to the Egyptians and true Arabs (Syro-Arabians) on the one hand, and to the Ethiopian Bedouins and true Negroes on the other. I do not for a moment deny that the present Nubians (meaning by this term only the people who dwell on the banks of the river) must have sprung from various races. Independently of the three dialects of the Nubian language, which are those of Dongola, of Kenoos, and of Mahass (in which it is supposed that the still undeciphered ancient Ethiopian inscriptions are written), and independently of Arabic being the actual mother-language of the natives, who have, in fact, immigrated from Asia, and some of whom, as for instance the Sheigich, have hitherto remained ignorant of the Nubian language altogether; they are yet all so united by one common bond alike of general habits and physical character, that they no longer exhibit any perceptible distinctions. It must also be remembered that these Nubian natives of the Nile district have for centuries not only intermarried, but have also mixed so indiscriminately with slaves of every origin, that they have lost all traces of being other than a single race. Accordingly the use of the term "Nubian," under the restriction named, may be justified in more than one respect, and may be fairly employed in geographical, ethnographical, or historical relations.

Whoever has become acquainted with the passive natives of Berber or Dongola* in Egypt only, or more especially in Alexandria, where they are trusted with the charge of house and home, and whoever has witnessed the patience with which they endure the antipathy of the residents, will be at a loss how to reconcile his own impression with the unfavourable one given by a traveller so faithful as Burckhardt,† who knew them before they were subjected to Egyptian domination, and has left on record his version of their national character.

As far as my own experience went, with regard to morality, I decidedly preferred the people of Berber to the Egyptians, and I believed that the change for the better that had taken place since Burckhardt's visit to Berber and Shendy in 1822, had been owing to the more rigid government of the Turks on the one hand, and to the increasing physical luxury of the people of Berber on the other; for in their own homes I never found them to be otherwise than quiet and harmless.

My impressions, however, were at that time very imperfect; but

---

* The Egyptians call them simply "Barábra."

† 'Travels in Nubia,' by the late John Lewis Burckhardt. London, 1822.

when I saw the people on the territory of the Bahr-el-Ghazal, that pasture-land for their hungry spirits, where they are beyond the jurisdiction of the Government and are no longer in dread of bastinadoes, extortions, taxation, or summonses to the divans of the satraps, and where there are no Egyptians to mock them with the insulting cry of "Barabra,"—then I discovered the true side of their nature, and all their leading traits came fully to light. Their character, a curious mixture of exemplary virtues and most repulsive vices, was not like a mechanical medley of antagonistic qualities, but was a composition in which each single quality seemed to partake of mingled good and evil, though unfortunately the evil decidedly preponderated.

The camp of the Government troops was situated close to the chief settlement of the most powerful of all the Khartoom Seriba owners, Seebehr Rahama, who himself resided there. His territory included the western portion of the district occupied by the Khartoomers, and was immediately adjacent to the most southerly outposts of the Sultan of Darfoor. A few days before I started on this little journey to the west, a circumstance had occurred that had thrown all the inhabitants of this Seriba into a great commotion, and which did not augur altogether well for my projected tour. A conflict had broken out between the black Government troops and Seebehr's Nubian soldiers, and twenty Nubians as well as many of the negroes had lost their lives in the fray. The Turkish Bashibazouks, instead of remaining neutral, had joined in the affair and taken part against the blacks. The reason of this coalition between the Egyptian Turks and the Nubian settlers was, that the Turkish commander had given orders that their common enemy, Hellali, should be seized and imprisoned. This Hellali, it will be remembered, was the man who had been appointed to the special command of the black troops of the Government, and who had represented himself as the owner of the copper-mines in the south of Darfoor, stating that they had to pay him 4000 dollars annually. He was really the cause of the present quarrel, and the events that led to his imprisonment will not take long to describe.

Hellali had drawn upon himself the odium of all the Khartoomers, because, by alleging himself to be the owner of the land in the south of Darfoor, he threw doubt upon their legal right to the soil on which they had founded their Seribas; he was consequently summoned to Khartoom to give an account of his conduct. All the representations by which he had induced the Viceroy to undertake the expedition to the Gazelle had turned out to be nothing but the fraudulent devices of a swindler; Hellali had never possessed land in this district at all, and much less had received any grant of territory from the Sultan of Darfoor. For months it had been rumoured that he intended to retire with his black troops to that part of the country, and in spite of his appeal to the seal and signature of his Highness, by virtue of which he claimed possession of the lands, the suspicion against him increased to such an extent that the Turkish commander appeared to be justified in proceeding to violent measures against the alleged favourite of the Viceroy.

The immediate cause of the disagreement may now be related. Hellali had ordered his soldiers to make requisitions of corn upon the natives under Seebehr's jurisdiction, who had hitherto been accustomed to furnish contributions to none but their own master. The strange troops were proceeding by violence to appropriate the contents of the granaries, when the Nubian soldiers, with Seebehr himself at their head, sallied out from the Seriba, and attempted to drive off the intruders. Hellali's people immediately opened fire upon the Nubians, and the very first shot wounded Seebehr in the ankle. This was the signal for a general battle, and many lives were lost on either side. For the first few days the Egyptian camp, so near the Seriba as it was, was in imminent danger, and could with difficulty hold its own against the ever-increasing numbers of antagonists, for of course all the neighbours hastened to the assistance of Seebehr, whose fighting force already amounted to more than a thousand. In this dilemma the Turkish commander was obliged to resort to the diplomatic measure to which I have referred, so as to avert the serious consequences that threatened himself and his troops.

The third New Year's Day that I passed on African soil now dawned, and it was precisely on the 1st of January, 1871, that I found myself starting off upon my long-projected tour to the west. I left my little Tikkitikki to the temporary guardianship of Khalil, and set out accompanied by two of my servants, the negro lads, and the few bearers that were necessary to carry the little remnant of my property.

My scheme was first of all to pay a visit to Bizolly's Seriba, thirty-two miles to the north-west, the same that had been Miss Tinné's headquarters seven years previously.

We crossed the Wow at the same wooded spot as we had done in April 1869. This river, the Nyenahm of the Dyoor, the Herey of the Bongo, during the rainy season has a depth of fourteen to sixteen feet without ever overflowing its banks: even at this date the bed of the noble forest-stream was still quite covered with water, the depth of which near the banks was three or four feet, decreasing in the middle of the current to less than two feet. The varying depth, however, did not affect the velocity, which was uniform throughout and about ninety-eight feet a minute. The width of the Wow I found by careful measurement to be 132 feet.

Beyond the river we passed through cultivated lands, leaving Agahd's chief Seriba on our left; we then crossed a low range of hills stretching towards the north-east, and brought our day's march to an end in the hamlet of a Dyoor chief named Dimmoh, where we encamped for the night.

Our night-camp afforded me an opportunity of renewing my familiarity with the idyllic village life of the Dyoor. The sorghum harvest had long been gathered in, and the dokhn had been safely stored in the great urn-like bins that were so essential a fixture in every hut; a second crop was now in course of being housed, consisting of the kindy (*Hyptis*) that springs up between the stubble, many of the women being engaged in the task, which is very tedious, of cleansing the poppy-like seeds. About the fields were lying many of those strange cylinder-shaped melons, which appear to be peculiar to the Dyoor, with their rind like that of the bottle-gourd and as hard as wood. There were also large numbers of the fleshy variegated calices of the Sabdariffa dried all ready for storing, a condition in which they retain their pungency, and serve the purpose of giving the soups of the natives an acid flavour almost as sharp as vinegar.

After going awhile uphill over some rocky ground we came to a declivity of nearly a hundred feet; at the bottom of this we had to cross a wide swampy depression covered with the Terminalia forests that so often characterise such localities. The holes and hollows, although they were now completely dry, gave ample testimony as to what must be the number of the pools that would obstruct the path during the height of the rainy season. In a short time we reached the hamlets of a Dyoor chief named Woll, that were scattered about an open plain covered with cultivated fields; this was the frontier of Bizelly's territory. A tree something like an acacia, the *Entada sudanica*, remarkable for its pods, a foot long and thin as paper, and breaking into numbers of pieces when ripe, was the chief feature in the bush-forests of the environs, although it is a tree which is generally rare in the country.

Over rocky soil and through tracts of dense bushwood we marched on, until in front of us we saw a kind of valley-plateau, bare of trees, apparently shut in on the farther side by an eminence extending towards the north-east, which is the general direction of the territory of the Dyoor in this district. Here we entered a little Seriba of Bizelly's, known by the name of Kurnuk,* where we were well entertained during the midday hours.

In the afternoon we set off again, and mounted the wooded height covered with great tracts of the Göll tree (*Prosopis*), which is noticeable for producing a fruit very like the St. John's bread. Then again descending, we came to the dried-up bed of a watercourse that was closely overhung with bushes. Beyond this were various cultivated plots, dotted here and there with huts; and we next entered a splendid forest of lofty Humboldtiæ, which by its extent and denseness reminded me of our own European woods. Our path was shaded by these noble trees until we reached the Ghetty, or "Little Wow," six miles above the spot where Dr. Steudner lies buried on its bank.

This tributary of the Dyoor was about as large as the Molmull near Aboo Guroon's Seriba; its bed was between fifty and sixty feet wide; its banks were ten feet high. At present it was little more than a narrow ditch, with no perceptible motion in its waters, but I was told that lower down it widened out into pools that were always full of water. But insignificant as the Ghetty looked, it was large enough to be the resort of crocodiles so daring and voracious that they were the terror of the neighbourhood, the rapacity of the creatures very probably arising from a prevalent scarcity of fish. A few weeks previously, when the stream was full to the top of its banks, a Dyoor boy as he was swimming across had been snapped at by one of these ravenous Saurians and had never been seen again. It is surprising in the dry season, into what tiny pools and puddles the crocodile will make its way, and where, buried in the miry clay, it will find a sufficiently commodious home.

The Ghetty is bordered by bushes nearly identical with those which are found on the banks of all the streamlets of this land; the *Morelia senegalensis*, the *Zizygium*, and the *Trichilia retusa* may be noted as amongst the most common.

* "Kurnuk" is the term used by the Nubians and Foorians for a shed; the corresponding expression in the Soudan Arabic being "Daher-el-Tor," literally, the back of an ox; thus "kurnuk" means generally any roof with a horizontal ridge.

I was told that Bizelly's head Seriba, known amongst the Bongo as Doggaya Onduppo, was situated upon the right bank, about eight leagues to the north-west of the spot where we crossed the stream, which here forms the boundary between the Wow tribe of the Dyoor and the district populated by the Bongo. We continued to advance for another league and a half, going up a densely-wooded acclivity until at length, fairly tired out with our exertions, we entered, quite late in the evening, Bizelly's subsidiary Seriba, called by the Bongo Doggaya-morr.

Here, for the first time, I found myself on what, to my mind, my scientific predecessors had made nothing less than a classic soil. Here it was that Theodor von Heuglin had resided from the 17th of April, 1863, to the 4th of January, 1864; here, or at least in an adjacent village of the Wow tribe, had Dr. Steudner * expired; and close in the vicinity had Miss Tinné passed through a period of wretchedness which all her wealth was powerless to prevent. Never could I leave the Seriba without being conscious that every shrub and every plant was a memorial of those who had been before me, for all were representatives of that hitherto unknown flora of which Heuglin had collected the first botanical data, and which Dr. Kotschy has depicted in his noble work 'Plantæ Tinnianæ,' partly from the drawings of Miss Tinné herself.

Within the Seriba, too, I was constantly reminded of the miserable condition to which this expedition, so comprehensive in its original design, had been reduced. The region bore every token of having an unhealthy climate. The stagnant meadow-waters and foul streams all around had all the appearance of being veritable and prolific breeding-places for fever and malaria. A great ruined tenement, now a mere lodgment for sheep and goats, marked the spot where the remains of Miss Tinné's mother, who fell a victim to the pernicious climate, were temporarily deposited until the opportunity came for them to be removed to her distant home. A dejected fate indeed, and a miserable resting-place for one who had been reared amidst the comforts and luxuries of the highest refinement.

Before leaving Bizelly's Seriba we received intelligence of the

* Dr. Steudner died on the 10th of April, 1863, from an attack of fever, a few days after he had commenced, in company with Heuglin, his first journey into the interior; his object had been to reconnoitre the country to the west of the Meshera, and to find a suitable place for the accommodation of Miss Tinné's party during the rainy season.

murder of our old friend Shol, the wealthy Dinka princess, into the details of whose personal charms and associations I have, in an earlier page, entered with some minuteness. The natives, it seems, had accused her of inviting the "Turks" into the country; and as many of the tribes in the neighbourhood had been exposed to attacks from Kurshook Ali's troops, they determined to avenge themselves on Shol, as being a long-standing ally of the Khartoomers. Knowing that she slept alone in her hut, a troop of men belonging to the Wady (a tribe settled to the east of the Meshera) set out by night, and under pretext of having business with Kurdyook, her husband, knocked at her door. She had no sooner appeared in answer to their summons than they attacked her with deadly blows; and setting fire to all the huts drove off nearly all the cattle that was to be found in the place.

A lovely march of about six miles to the north-west, through an almost unbroken and in many places very dense bush-forest, brought us to Ali Amoory's † chief Seriba, distinguished by the natives by the name of Longo. The Parkia-trees were just beginning to bloom. The wonderful spectacle that these presented was quite unique; their great trusses of bright red blossoms, large as the fist and smooth as velvet, made a display that was truly gorgeous, as they depended from the long stalks which broke forth from the feathery foliage of the spreading crowns.

In spite of the constant traffic between the different Scribas there seemed to be no lack of game; traces of hartebeests were everywhere visible, whilst the little madoqua antelopes bounded like apparitions from bush to bush. Guinea-fowls were just as prolific as in the wildest deserts of the Niam-niam. Heuglin, no inexperienced sportsman, had certainly here chosen a remunerative ground for his zoological researches.

Our path was crossed by three watercourses, which were now for the most part dry. By their confluence these three streams formed an important tributary of the Dyoor, called the Okuloh, their separate names before their junction, reckoning from the southernmost, being respectively the Dangyah, the Matshoo, and the Minnikinyee or "fish-water;" their uniformly north-eastern direction attested the material fall in the level of the ground at the boundary between the rocky soil and the alluvial plains of the Dyoor.

* The real name of the firm is Ali-Aboo-Amoory, and it has acquired an undesirable notoriety for its fraudulent dealings with Miss Tinné's expedition.

Longo ranked as a first-class establishment. It contained a larger number of huts than even Ghattas's Seriba, which it surpassed also in dirt and disorder. Every hedge was crooked, every hut stood awry, and the farmsteads were as ruined as though they had for years been abandoned to the ravages of rats and white ants. Disgusting heaps of ashes and scraps of food, piles of rotten straw, hundreds of old baskets and gourd-shells stood as high as one's head all along the narrow alleys that parted hut from hut; whilst outside the Seriba, just at its very entrances, there were masses of mouldy rubbish, overgrown with the most noxious of fungus, that rose as high as the houses; at every step there was sure to be an accumulation of some abominable filthiness or other, such as nowhere else, I should think, even in the Mohammedan world, could be found in immediate proximity to human habitations; altogether the place presented such a dismal scene of dirt, decay, and disorder that it was enough to induce a fit of nightmare upon every one with the smallest sense of either neatness or decorum. Truly it was a wonderful specimen of domestic economy which this horde of undisciplined Nubians had thus elaborated.

The level country for a mile or more round the Seriba was occupied by the arable lands belonging to the settlement. Longo was one of the oldest establishments in the country, and the adjacent soil was no less productive than that around the Seriba of Ghattas. The Bongo villages were all situated at some distance to the west.

All the year round a considerable number of slave-traders resided in the place, and were always attended by those wild sons of the steppes, the Baggara of the Rizegat, who, with their lean, fly-bitten cattle, had to camp out as well as they could in the environs of the Seriba. They had never before set eyes upon a Christian, and full of eager wonder they flocked together to survey me, keeping, however, at a distance of several yards from personal contact, probably dreading the malign influence of the "evil eye" of a Frank. Their curiosity was still further roused when they saw me drawing pictures of their cattle, and when I offered them my various sketches for their own inspection they appeared to lose much of the alarm which they had exhibited, and so effectually did I succeed in gaining their confidence that some of them were induced to sit for their own portraits. All those that I drew had fine light brown complexions, slim muscular frames, and perfectly regular features; the expression of the face might fairly be pronounced open and honest, and exhibited the strong resolution that might be expected of a warlike nation whose occupations, when not in the battle-field, were in hunting and cattle-breeding. Their profiles all formed quite a right angle; their noses failed to be aquiline, but were rounded and well-formed; the faces of the younger men were good-tempered looking, having a somewhat effeminate expression, which was still further increased by the high round forehead. All of them seemed to wear their hair in long slender braids running in rows along the top of the head and drooping over the neck behind.

On the 6th of January I resumed my progress. Taking a south-westerly direction I accomplished a good day's march of eighteen miles and reached Damoory, Amoory's subsidiary Seriba on the river Pongo. A rocky soil covered with bush had predominated for the greater portion of the distance, the route having been perfectly level and unbroken by the smallest depression. We had crossed the beds of five brooks which were nearly dry. Taking them in order they were, the Okilleah, a mere line of stagnant puddles; the Kulloo,* a larger brook overhung with sizygium-bushes, and containing water as high as one's knees; the Horroah, a dry hollow bed; the Daboddoo, with a few pools; and the Ghendoo, with holes from which the water had either dried up or drained away. All these, when supplied with water, were tributary to the Pongo, and flowed towards the north-west.

Midday between the Kulloo and the Horroah, we had come upon a gigantic fig-tree (*Ficus lutea*), one of those memorials of the past that are so often seen in Bongoland, marking, as they do, the site of an earlier native village. The name of the place was Ngukkoo. The enormous tree had a short stem enveloped in a perfect network of aërial roots, struck downwards from the branches, whilst at the summit it spread out into a crown of foliage that under the vertical midday sun formed a shadow on the ground of which the circumference, as I proved by actual measurement, was not less than 230 feet.

During the latter portion of the march we had seen a considerable number of candelabra Euphorbiæ and Calotropis. The appearance of the Calotropis (called in Arabic "el Usher") was indicative of a more northerly type of vegetation, as the plant is characteristic of the steppes of Nubia, Arabia, and the frontiers of India: this was the first time I had seen it in the territory of the Scribas; it had

---

* "Kulloo" is in this neighbourhood the generic name for brooks of this character.

evidently been introduced into this part of the country by traders from the north, and the solid stems of the plants, which elsewhere are little more than shrubs, bore ample witness to the long-established traffic on this commercial highway.

Damoory was situated close to the right-hand bank of the Pongo, as the Bongo call this affluent of the Bahr-el-Arab. On earlier maps the river was marked as the Kozanga, but this I found to be merely the designation of a small mountainous ridge that extended for several leagues along the left bank of the river to the south-west of the Seriba. On the 17th of July, 1863, Theodor von Heuglin * had visited the spot for the purpose of selecting a dry and rocky eminence in the woods where a camp might be erected for the headquarters of Miss Tinné's expedition. If this scheme had been carried into practice the melancholy sacrifice of life that resulted from the unwholesome atmosphere of Bizelly's Seriba might happily have been spared; but the difficulties of properly organising so large a party of travellers were insuperable, and the project of removal to that healthier resort fell to the ground.

In its upper course through the district inhabited by the Sehre, the Pongo, as already noted, bears the name of the Djee; it flows towards the north-east, and after leaving the Bongo territory beyond Damoory passes through that of the Dembo, a tribe of Shillook origin related to the Dyoor: on this account the Khartoomers call it the Bahr-el-Dembo.

The Dembo are under the jurisdiction of Ali Amoory, whose territories extend far beyond the river to the north-west, and join the country of the Baggara-el-Homr, his most remote Seribas being on the Gebbel Marra, in the locality of a negro tribe called the Bambirry, probably also a branch of the great Shillook family; but it should be stated that, according to some accounts, these Bambirry are true Zandey Niam-niam who have immigrated from the south and settled in their present quarters.

The scenery about Damoory was extremely like that around Awoory in the Mittoo country; in fact it altogether reminded me of what I had seen on my trip to the Rohl, especially as the Pongo exhibits not a few points of resemblance to that river. Damoory is built on rising rocky ground, thickly covered with wood, and close to the eastern or right-hand bank of the river. The slopes that enclosed the river-bed were about fifteen feet in depth, and between

* This was the most westerly point that Heuglin reached in Central Africa.

them and the actual stream there was, on either side, a strip of soil subject to inundation during the rainy season and now broken up with numerous pools and backwaters. At this date (January 7, 1871) the water was moving sluggishly along between clay banks, some 10 feet down and 70 feet apart; but it did not cover a breadth of more than fifty feet and was nowhere more than four feet in depth. Its velocity was the same as that of the Wow; but whilst both the Wow and the Dyoor rolled along, even at this season, in considerable volume, the Pongo was comparatively empty, and, as I saw, it must have offered a very striking contrast to its appearance during the Khareef, when no doubt it could make good its pretensions to be a river of the second class. On the other side of the Pongo there was a low tract of steppe, at least 3000 paces wide, which, of course, represented the territory subject to inundation on the left bank. I subsequently found that the entire length of the river, from its source to Damoory, could not at the most exceed 200 miles, and I thus became able more completely to realize the very remarkable periodic changes which occur in the condition of the stream.

In various parts of the depression the vegetation of the open steppe is replaced by close masses of *Stephegyne*: these form marshy clumps, and from their general habit very strongly resemble our alder-beds of the north.

Close to the Seriba a deep chasm, called Gumango, opens out into the valley of the river; it is one of the landslips, so common in this region, caused by springs washing away the ferruginous swamp-ore from below, and an inexperienced traveller might easily be led to mistake it for the bed of a periodical watercourse of considerable magnitude. It is thickly overgrown with brambles and creepers. The shrub Tinnea plays a prominent part in the underwoods all around Damoory.

Just above the Seriba the course of the river was due east for a distance of four miles, and in pursuing our westward journey we marched along the left bank in the direction contrary to the stream until we arrived at the spot where it made its bend away from the south. Here we crossed. The sandy bed was not more than 100 feet wide, a grassy depression beyond was about 400 paces across. On the borders of this we came upon some ruined huts projecting above the grass, evidently the remains of a forsaken Scriba of Bizelly's, which had likewise been called Damoory, after the name of the Bongo community that had had their homes in the district.

The Bongo had now withdrawn beyond the right bank of the river, and thus the Pongo had been left as the boundary between the populated country and the actual wilderness.* With very slight deviations the remainder of our journey to Seebehr's great Seriba was in a direction due west. The ground rose considerably, and on our left was a tall eminence of gneiss, called Ida, a northern spur of the Kozanga ridge and (with regard to our present position) about 500 feet high. A deep brook, the Ooruporr, rising somewhere on the slopes of this Mount Ida, here crossed our path, the line of its banks being distinctly marked out by some specimens of the wild date-palm. A little farther on we came to a dry, deep chasm, that formed the bed of a periodic stream known as the Andimoh, which likewise descended from the hill of Ida; its banks were marked by crags of gneiss and studded with bamboos.

We passed onwards over masses of gneiss almost spherical in form, overgrown with moss-like clusters of selaginella, and reached the bed of the brook Karra, lying in its deep hollow. To this little stream the Nubians gave the name of Khor-el-Gauna, on account of the jungles of bamboo that enclose its rocky banks, which descend in successive steps so as to produce a series of cascades. The Bongo reckon the Karra as the boundary between their country and the country of the Golo; it is also considered to be the line which separates the domain of the landowner Ali Amoory from that of Idrees Wod Defter, whose Seriba is about thirty-five miles from Damoory and, as nearly as possible, half-way along our route thence to Seebehr's chief settlement.

Beyond the Karra the path led over very undulated country; and we had twice to cross a brook called Ya, which, formed mainly of a series of deep basins, worked its devious way along a contracted defile. Having at length mounted a steepish eminence of red rock we appeared to bring our long ascent to an end, and commencing a gradual descent we proceeded till we reached the brook Attidoh, beside which we encamped for the night.

Large herds of buffaloes thronged the chief pools of the swampy bed, and before it became quite dark I managed to creep within range of a group of cows with their calves. The only result of my exertions was that one calf fell dead upon the spot where it was struck, all my other shots apparently taking no effect. Half the night was spent in roasting, broiling, and drying the flesh of the young buffalo, and all my party were in great good humour.

* In the dialect of the Soudan these distinctions are respectively rendered by the terms "Dar" (cultivated land) and "Akabah" (wilderness).

The forests for long distances were composed exclusively of lofty Humboldtiæ, and increased in magnitude and denseness as we advanced farther amongst them; they were so fine that they might well bear comparison with any of the best wooded districts of the Niam-niam. We crossed a half-dry khor (or stream-channel) called the Ngoory, and shortly afterwards a marshy brook, with a considerable supply of water, called the Akumunah; both of these joined the Mongono, of which the bed at the place where we crossed it was so dry that it appeared only like a tract of sand, seventy feet wide; but by turning up the loose sand to the depth of six inches, a copious stream of clear water was discovered to be running on its subterranean way over a gravelly bottom. In the rainy season the Mongono assumes quite a river-like appearance, for I discovered traces of important backwaters that had been left by its inundation, and the banks that bounded its sandy bed were not much less than eight feet high.

The frequent appearance of the Abyssinian Protea convinced me that the elevation of the ground was greater than what we had left behind us: as matter of fact we were at an average height of 2100 feet above the level of the sea.

The Yow-Yow, a narrow sort of trench, made up of a series of deep pools, next intersected our path. On the other side of this I mounted a crag of gneiss, whence I obtained an extensive view towards the west, and observed an elevated line of woods stretched out with the precision of a wall from S.S.W. to N.N.E. The elevation was beyond the Atena, a brook that we reached after first crossing two other minor streams. The bed of the Atena was formed of sand and gravel; although it was dry, with the exception of some occasional water-pools that had not failed, it was fifty feet in width. The steepness of the banks demonstrated that in the rainy season they enclosed what would be allowed to be a considerable river. Two more brooks with deep beds had still to be crossed, and then we entered upon the cultivated land adjacent to Idrees Wod Defter's Seriba. Two miles more, along a continuous ascent, brought us to the Seriba itself.

Idrees Wod Defter was a partner in Agahd's firm. His Seriba had been built about three years previously, and was composed of large farmsteads, shut in almost with the seclusion of monasteries by tall hedges of straw-work; they were occupied by the various great slave-traders who had settled in the country. Four huts and a large rokooba had recently been erected for the accommodation of the numerous travellers who passed through, chiefly second-class

THE GOLO.

traders, who, like itinerant Jews, wandered about from place to place, hawking their goods. Idrees himself resided in his Niamniam Seribas, which, I was told, were near Mofio's residence, seven or eight days' journey distant. Besides this chief settlement there were two subsidiary Seribas, one about four leagues to the southeast, on the western declivity of the Kozanga hills, and another at the same distance to the south-west, the controller of which was named Abd-el-Seed. The farmsteads of the chief Seriba stood in their separate enclosures, and were not surrounded by the ordinary

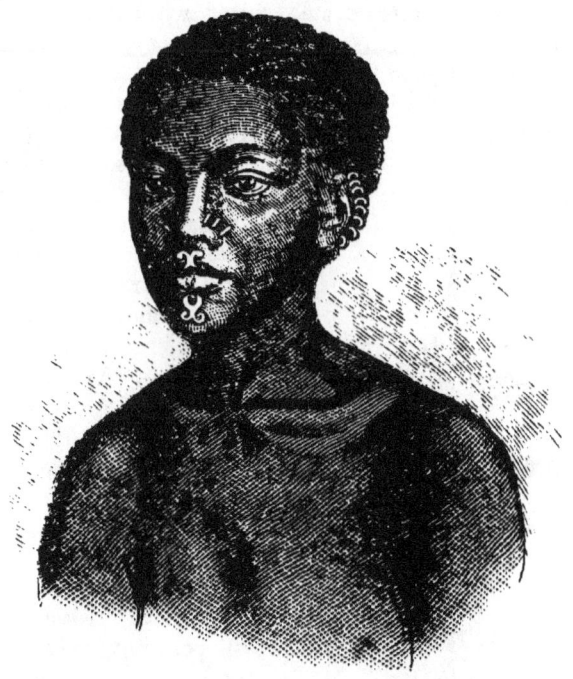

GOLO WOMAN.

palisade. Close by, on the south, a little spring trickling forth from a cleft in the ground suddenly expanded into a clear rippling brook that ran merrily to the west.

The natives that served the necessary demands of the Seriba belonged to the tribe of the Golo. In manners and in general appearance they very much resemble their eastern neighbours the Bongo, although the dialects of the two tribes have very little in common. More than any other negro tongue with which I gained much familiarity, the Golo dialect seems to abound in sounds resembling the German vowels *ö* and *ü*, and, like some of the South African dialects, it contains some peculiar nasal tones, which may be described as sharp and snapping, and which are quite unknown to the neighbouring nations.

Just as I was on the point of leaving the Seriba of Idrees Wod Defter, my old friend Mohammed Aboo Sammat arrived. He came in the train of a large party of Bongo who were conveying corn to the place, and as, like myself, he was on his way to the Egyptian camp, we joined company and started without further delay to the west.

Half a league beyond the Seriba we left the cultivated land and re-entered the forest wilderness near the village of the Golo chief Kaza. Far and wide the fields were sown with sweet potatoes, and dokhn corn was extensively cultivated. In the village of Kaza we noticed several of the peculiar corn-magazines upon the construction of which the Golo spend so much care. They are at once bold and graceful in design. The actual receptacle for the corn is made of clay and is in the form of a goblet; it is covered with a conical roof of straw, which serves as a movable lid; to protect it from the ravages of rats it is mounted on a short substantial pedestal, that is supported at the base by stakes arranged as a series of flying buttresses. Altogether the structure is very symmetrical; and the clay is worked into tasteful graduated mouldings that add considerably to the general finish of the whole. The dwelling huts of the Golo also display peculiarities in their style of building, and bear evident marks of being erected with unusual care and labour.

CORN-MAGAZINE OF THE GOLO.

The Seriba we had just quitted was situated on the watershed between the Kooroo and the Pongo. We crossed the last stream in

SLAVE-TRADERS FROM KORDOFAN.

To face p. 209.

the Pongo system just beyond Kaza's hamlets; it was called the Abbuloh, and was now thirty-five feet wide and two feet deep. Farther on, the path gradually rose through a shady wood until we reached an eminence strewn with blocks of gneiss; then descending, still through woods, we came to a copious brook of about the same dimension as the Abbuloh. This was the Bombatta, which flowed in a north-western direction and joined the Kooroo. The next brook, the Abeela, moved in the same direction, and was composed of a connected series of deep basins. Two more rivulets of the same character followed, the second of which, named the Ngoddoo, flowed past a flat bare elevation of gneiss and joined the Kooroo only a short distance to the west. Amongst the autumn flora of this region the Hydrolia was very conspicuous, its brilliant sky-blue blossoms blending with the grass so as to form a charming carpet over the depressions of the brooks.

An hour after crossing the Ngoddoo we arrived at the bank of the Bahr-el-Kooroo, as this important affluent of the Bahr-el-Arab is called by the Mohammedan settlers; the name is probably borrowed from the Baggara Arabs, as amongst the Golo (whose territory it divides from that of the Kredy on the west) it is sometimes called the Mony, and sometimes the Worry; by the Sehre it is called the Wee. At the place of our transit it was flowing towards the N.N.W., and the current was rather rapid. The entire breadth of the bed was between ninety and a hundred feet, but of this only sixty feet was covered with water, the depth of which nowhere exceeded two feet. At one spot the river flowed over blocks and layers of gneiss that were overgrown with mossy Tristichæ. The banks stood fifteen feet high, and although there were woods on either side that grew right down to the water, many indications remained of their being subject to a periodical inundation: a canoe left high up on the dry ground was an evidence how full of water the river must be during the rainy season.

We kept continually meeting small companies of slave-traders, mounted on oxen or on donkeys, and having their living merchandise in their train.

The long tracts of one species of forest-tree reminded me very much of the masses of the alder-like Vatica on the Tondy. Beyond the west bank of the river the path led up the steep side of a valley, and the level of the soil rapidly increased. Then we came to a series of ruts like deep ditches, some quite dry and some still filled with running water. We counted six of these before reaching the Beesh, or Khor-el-Rennem, which is an affluent of the Beery and the largest of the three tributaries of the Bahr-el-Arab which I had the opportunity of seeing.

The Khor-el-Rennem, or goats' brook, received its name from the circumstance that once, during the period of the annual rains, a whole herd of goats had made an attempt to cross the stream and had all been drowned in the rushing flood. It was shut in by trees and bushes of many kinds, and these cast a gloomy shade over the chasm which was worn by the waters; it was now only a foot deep and fifteen feet wide.

Here, again, the land on the western shore rose suddenly like a wall, a peculiarity in the topography of the country that testified to the continual increase of its level above the sea.

Two easy leagues forward, generally over cultivated country and past several hamlets belonging to the Kredy tribe, the Nduggo, and I reached what I designed should be my resting-place for a while at Seebehr's Seriba, which was also the Egyptian camp. The distance of seventy miles from the Pongo had been accomplished in four days. By this time I had become quite accustomed to the habit of counting my steps. I had become my own "perambulator," and could not help thinking, as I marched along, of Xenophon and his *parasangs* in the expedition of the Greeks. One day of our ordinary marching would accomplish about four or five parasangs.

CHAPTER XV.

Increasing level of country—Seebehr's Seriba—Dehm Nduggo—Helplessness of the Turks—A loathsome scene—Seebehr's court—Ibrahim Effendi—Establishment of Dehms—Ivory-trade and slave-trade—Population of Dar Ferteet—The Kredy—Overland route to Kordofan—Raw copper—Rough mining—Underwood of Cycadeæ—Kredy huts and mills—The Beery—Inhospitality at Mangoor—Numerous brooks—Dehm Gudyoo—Scorbutic attack—A dream and its fulfilment— Remnants of mountain-ridges—Upper course of the Pongo—Information about the far west—The Bahr-Aboo-Dinga—Barth's investigations—Primogeniture of the Bahr-el-Arab—First break in the weather—Elephant-hunters from Darfoor—The Sehre—Abundance of game—A magic tuber—Deficiency of water—A comfortless night—Cheerfulness of the Sehre—Lower level of land—A miniature mountain-chain—Norway rats—A giant fig-tree—An evil eye—Return to Khalil's quarters.

SEEBEHR's Seriba was 2145 feet above the level of the sea, 435 feet higher than Bizelly's Seriba on the Ghetty, and 691 feet higher than Ghattas's chief settlement. There was but little observable change in the character of the vegetation, yet the hydrographical condition of the country very plainly attested a complete alteration in the nature of the soil. Although our present latitude was 8° N., the general aspect that came under the observation of a traveller was almost identical with what he would see between latitude 6° and latitude 5° in passing southwards from Bongoland to the Niam-niam.

Immediately after crossing the Pongo we quitted the soft absorbent soil, and entered upon a region so prolific in springs that all the year round, every rivulet, brook, and trench, and even the smallest fissure in the earth, is full of water, and that of the brightest and purest quality. Between the Pongo and Seebehr's Seriba we had crossed no less than twenty brooks and two rivers of considerable magnitude. Just as had been the case in the Niam-niam lands, water trickled from every crevice and found an outlet on every slope, whilst in the low-lying country of the Dyoor and Bongo, on the edge of the red swamp-ore, where chasms and watercourses are quite as abundant, no springs ever break forth during the winter months, and the half-dry beds are supplied by no other water than what has been left from the previous Khareef.

This circumstance seems in a certain degree to illustrate the conformation of the south-western side of the Bahr-el-Ghazal basin; for the general direction of all the streams that contribute to its volume would be at right angles to the lines of the terraces that rise one above the other at various levels above the sea.

The Seriba was enclosed by a palisade 200 feet square; hundreds of farmsteads and groups of huts were scattered round, extending far away along the eastern slope of a deep depression which was traversed in the direction of the north-west by a brook that was fed by numerous springs. The whole place, in all its leading features, had the aspect of a town in the Soudan, and vividly reminded me of Matamma, the great market town in Gallabat, where all the inland trade with Abyssinia is transacted. To establishments of this magnitude the natives give the name of "Dehm,"* which is, in fact, an equivalent for "a town." The heights to the east of the place were more important than those immediately bordering on the depression, and in the N.N.E. very high ground was visible in the distance. Towards the west the country sloped downwards for a couple of leagues to the river Beery, which, it has been mentioned, is an important tributary of the Bahr-el-Arab.

The Egyptian troops were encamped at the southern extremity of the settlement, and were under the command of the Vokeel-el-urda, Ahmed Aga, who had been the lieutenant of the late Sandjak. The black swindler, Hellali, was still kept in confinement, his company of soldiers being treated as prisoners of war and placed under the surveillance of the other troops in a section of the camp allotted to the purpose. Great scarcity of provisions prevailed, for, in addition to the troops, the population had been augmented by the arrival of many hundreds of slave-dealers from Kordofan. Immediately on receiving information of the schemes that were being plotted against his copper-mines by the Egyptian Government, Hussein, the Sultan of Darfoor, had prohibited all intercourse between his own frontiers and the Seribas of the Khartoomers; consequently the traders from Aboo Harras, in Kordofan, found themselves obliged

---

* The Khartoomers have given the word Dehm an Arabic plural, "Dwehm;" and by this term they distinguish the great slave-marts of the west.

to take a longer and more dangerous route across the steppes of the predatory Baggara; but, in spite of every difficulty, the presence of the Government troops offered such an attraction that the number of the traders was just doubled. They were enticed by the hope of carrying on a lucrative business with the avaricious Turkish soldiers, whose influential position gave them opportunities that were specially advantageous for making high profits; but besides this, the attempt, however abortive, of the Government authorities in Khartoom to suppress the slave-trade along the Nile had had the effect of driving up the traffic in the upper countries to such a premium that the dealers were spurred on to fresh energy. Since the last rainy season upwards of 2000 small slave-dealers had arrived at the Seriba, and others were still expected.* All these people, like the troops, lived upon Seebehr's corn-stores, and thus provisions became so scarce that they could hardly be purchased for their own weight in copper, which, with the exception of slaves, was the sole medium of exchange.

It might not unnaturally have been expected that the Egyptian troops would have taken up their position in the richest and most prolific of the corn-lands; but, instead of this, they had quartered themselves on the extreme limit of the Seribas in the Bahr-el-Ghazal district. Their avowed reason was that they might be better able to overlook the approaches to the copper-mines of Darfoor, but their real motive was in order that they might be nearer the fountain-head of the slave-trade and in direct communication with the northern territories, from which the main supply of living merchandise was obtained. I have already drawn attention to the impossibility of raising the contributions of corn required by the Egyptian commander, and I now became a personal witness of the unreasonableness of his demands; he appeared to have no other object than to exhaust the land already impoverished by the slave-trade, and in true Turkish fashion he set to work to involve all that remained in utter ruin.

In point of fact, however, it must be owned that it was a matter of considerable difficulty (after the bloody conflict that had resulted from Hellali's compulsory levies) for Ahmed Aga to raise the necessary supplies for the coming Khareef; but he made his requisitions in the most unfair way; his partiality was extreme, for while he exempted some Seribas from any contribution at all, he imposed upon others a demand for a double supply. My friend Mohammed was one of the

* The entire number that year rose to 2700.

oppressed. He had been called upon to furnish fifty ardebs of corn, a quantity corresponding to the burdens of 150 to 170 bearers, and not only was his Seriba at Sabby at a distance of seventeen days' journey from this spot, but his corn-magazines were still another four days' journey farther on, so that the mere maintenance of the bearers for three weeks would take thirty ardebs more. Mohammed, in truth, had not sufficient corn of his own to meet the demand of the Divan, and, in order to make up what was deficient, would be reduced to the necessity of purchasing at famine prices from other Seribas which already were well-nigh exhausted.

I took upon myself to intercede with the Aga, but to no purpose; he was utterly inflexible, and, not content with insisting upon his original demand, inflicted a heavy fine for the delay in the payment of the tribute, by exacting a contribution of 100 ardebs instead of fifty. But what irritated me more than anything else was the barefaced iniquity with which he backed up Shereefee in his refusal to make any compensation to Mohammed for the outrage, no better than a highway robbery, which he had perpetrated upon him, whilst at the same time he pretended to upbraid Mohammed for what he called his implacability. The solution of the matter was very easy. Shereefee had bribed Ahmed Aga with a lavish present of slaves, and that was a gift as acceptable as cash, just because they were a recognised medium of currency.

Notwithstanding the crowd of human beings thus aggregated, the bill of health, as far as it was influenced by the climate, was perfectly satisfactory. There were, of course, occasional cases of hereditary or insidious disease; but even amongst the slaves, closely packed as they were, the mortality was inconsiderable, and the human bones that lay scattered about were comparatively fewer than what I had grown accustomed to notice in other places. The effeminate Turkish soldiers, however, grumbled excessively at their position; they besieged me with petitions that I would not only represent their misery to the Governor-General in the strongest terms, but that I would do my utmost to convince the authorities that neither profit nor glory could be gained from an enterprise which was exposing their lives to so much peril. "Do this," they said, "and you will be doing us one of the greatest favours that it is in the power of mortal man to confer, and the blessing of Allah be with you!"

Certain it is that these Turks, fit for nothing better than to lounge about on a divan, were the most unsuitable beings imaginable ever to have been sent on an expedition into the wilds of Central Africa. A year of their ordeal had scarcely passed, and already their complaints were piteous enough to melt a heart of stone; they seemed helpless as babes, and I verily believe that had it not been for the Nubians they would have been cheated and trampled on and reduced to the direst necessities in this land of solitude and starvation. They were all indifferent walkers; they could not endure the food of the country; they sorely missed their "schnaps;" they were aggrieved at the loss of their wheat-flour and their rice, and did not understand going without their habitual luxuries. It was indeed a kind of set-off against all this that they could be as indolent as they pleased. There was nothing to do, and nothing they did; they did not plant out a single plot of maize, they did not lay out a kitchen-garden of the simplest kind; but, loitering about from morning till night, they kept up their unfailing growls of discontent, dealing out their invectives against the "wretched" land and its "wretched" people. No wonder they complained of *ennui*. Divest a Turk of his fine clothes, his formal etiquette, his measured speech, and his little bit of honour which may be described as "l'extérieur de la vertu et l'élégance du vice," and little remains to elevate him above a Nubian of the worst class; nevertheless the mutual antipathy that existed between the Turks and the Nubians was very marked, and verified the proverb that "Arabs' blood and Turks' blood will never boil together."

The remarkably large contingent of Gellahbas that chanced to be within the place gave the dirty crowds of men, such as are more or less to be invariably found in every Seriba, a more motley aspect than usual, and altogether the Dehm offered a deplorable contrast to the freshness of the wilderness that we had so long and so recently been traversing. The hawkers of living human flesh and blood, unwashed and ragged, squatted in the open places, keeping their eye upon their plunder, eager as vultures in the desert around the carcass of a camel. Their harsh voices as they shouted out their blasphemous prayers; the drunken indolence and torpor of the loafing Turks; the idle, vicious crowds of men infested with loathsome scabs and syphilitic sores; the reeking filthy exhalations that rose from every quarter—all combined to make the place supremely disgusting. Turn where I would, it was ever the same: there was the recurrence of sights, sounds, and smells so revolting that they could not do otherwise than fill the senses with the most sickening abhorrence.

Such were my impressions as I made my entry into the Dehm Nduggo, as the settlement is called from the Khredy tribe with which the neighbourhood is populated. My first consideration was whether I would become the guest of the Turks or of the Nubians; I had to choose whether I would sue for hospitality at the hands of Seebehr or of the Turkish Aga. After due deliberation, I made up my mind to apply to Seebehr, for, as the Turks had taken the smaller share in the affair with Hellali, I concluded that they constituted the less powerful element, and, in truth, they were themselves dependent upon Seebehr's liberality. But what perhaps influenced me still more was that my firman from the Government had been lost in the fire, and that consequently I was lacking in credentials to make any formal and authoritative demands; and I did not wish to be at the mercy of the commander. As it was, Ahmed Aga did not even fulfil the stipulations that had been made in my favour by the Government in Khartoom, and all that I could get out of him was a supply of good writing-paper to enable me to go on with my sketching.

Amongst the effects of Kurshook Ali, on which I had set my hopes, I could discover nothing that would be of the least service to me: his successor had long since, in true Ottoman fashion, disposed of everything that could be turned to account, a proceeding that subsequently involved him in a lawsuit with the son of the deceased Sandjak.

Meanwhile I was most kindly received by Seebehr, and as long as I remained in the Seriba I had not the faintest cause of complaint. He was himself in a debilitated state of health; the wound that he had received in the late fray had proved very dangerous, the bullet having completely penetrated the ankle-bone. The only means employed for healing the wound was repeated syringing with pure olive-oil, a remedy which, though slow, had been efficacious; for when I saw him, after some weeks had elapsed since the casualty, the injury was all but cured.

Seebehr* had surrounded himself with a court that was little less than princely in its details. A group of large well-built square huts, enclosed by tall hedges, composed the private residence; within these were various state apartments, before which armed sentries kept guard by day and night. Special rooms, provided with carpeted divans, were reserved as ante-chambers, and into these all visitors were conducted by richly-dressed slaves, who served them

---

* Seebehr's name at full length was Seebehr-Rahama-Gyimme-Abee.

with coffee, sherbet, and tchibouks. The regal aspect of these halls of state was increased by the introduction of some lions, secured, as may be supposed, by sufficiently strong and massive chains. Behind a large curtain in the innermost hut was placed the invalid couch of Seebehr. Attendants were close at hand to attend to his wants, and a company of Fakis sat on the divan outside the curtain and murmured their never-ending prayers. In spite of his weakness and his suffering, he was ever receiving a stream of visitors, who had something to say to " the Sheikh," as he was commonly called. I often paid him a visit, and, to my surprise at first, was accommodated with a chair by the side of his bed. He repeatedly bewailed the helplessness of his condition, saying how vexed he was at being unable personally to provide for my requirements, adding that if he had been well, he should have had the greatest pleasure in escorting me over his lands. It was a great relief to my mind that he did not apply to me for surgical advice. I was glad to encourage him by my approbation of the remedy he was using, which, if it possessed no particular virtue, had at least the recommendation of being perfectly harmless.

A draft that I made on my account at Khartoom was duly honoured, and I obtained a hundredweight of copper from Seebehr's stores; this I employed without delay as cash, and purchased soap, coffee, and a variety of small articles from the hawking hangers-on of the slave-traders, as well as a large supply of cartridge-paper for the preservation of my botanical specimens.

The greatest service, however, that Seebehr afforded me was in providing me with boots and shoes of European make; no acquisition was to be appreciated more highly than this; and in finding myself once more well-shod I felt myself renovated to start again upon my wanderings with redoubled vigour. None but those who have been in my condition can comprehend the pleasure with which I hailed the sight of the most trivial and ordinary articles. Once again I was in possession of a comb, some pipe-bowls, and lucifers. As I was not in the least inclined to forego my smoking while on the march, I had been obliged, in order to get a light for my tobacco, to make one of my people carry a blazing firebrand throughout the recent journey.

No sooner was I installed in the huts allotted to me than I received a succession of visitors; some of them crossed my threshold from mere idle curiosity, whilst others came either with some vague hope of profit or from some innate love of intrigue. I was honoured by a call from the great Zelim, Ali Aboo Amoory's chief controller, who came to express his hope that I had been satisfied with my reception in his Seriba, which I had visited during his absence. Then I made the acquaintance of some of the more important slave-traders, who had long been settled in the place and who came burning with curiosity to know the real object of my journey. But the most remarkable of all my visitors was a certain Ibrahim Effendi, who held the office of head clerk and accountant in the Egyptian camp. His life had been one unbroken series of criminal proceedings, and he had been guilty of frauds and swindling transactions to an extent that was absolutely incredible. Originally a subordinate in one of the departments of the Egyptian Ministry, he had, during Said Pasha's Government, forged the Viceregal seal and attached it to a document professing to appoint him to the command of a regiment that was to be formed in Upper Egypt, and prescribing that the local government there should defray all the expenses of levying and equipping the troops. This document he had the audacity to present first with his own hands to the governor of the province, and then he proceeded to present himself in the Upper Egyptian town as the colonel of the new regiment. Only those who are acquainted with the disorder and despotism that prevailed in every branch of the Administration during the lifetime of that Viceroy could believe that such a deception would be practicable; but I am in a position positively to assert that the fraudulent artifice did really for a while succeed. Two months afterwards, the troops having meanwhile been embodied, the Viceroy happened to make an excursion up the Nile, and seeing a great many soldiers on its banks, inquired the number of their regiment and why they were there. His astonishment was unbounded when he was told of a regiment of whose existence he had never previously heard. Ibrahim was summoned at once. Throwing himself at the Viceroy's feet, the culprit colonel confessed his guilt and begged for mercy. The good-natured Said, who never suffered himself to lose his temper, far less to go into a rage, merely sentenced him to a few years' banishment and imprisonment in Khartoom. As soon as Effendi had completed his term of punishment and regained his liberty, he started afresh as clerk to some of the Soudan authorities; but his habits of fraud and embezzlement were as strong as ever, and he was caught in the act of decamping with the cash-box, and was this time banished to Fashoda on the White Nile, as being the safest place for dangerous characters of his stamp. After he had been here for several years, our friend managed to excite the compassion of Kurshook Ali, who was passing through the place, and he was induced to give him his present post of head clerk to his division of the Government troops. This appointment brought Effendi to the district of the Gazelle.

Well versed as he was in the ways of the world, Effendi, by his wit and versatility, seemed to have the power of winning every heart. His position here in the Egyptian camp offered only too wide a scope for his love of intrigue. He had played an important part in the affair with Hellali, having doubtless been at the bottom of the stroke of policy that had reconciled Seebehr to the Turkish soldiers by bringing the hated Hellali to chains and to the yoke of the sheba. Probably he was again bidding for the command of some troops, and I am bound to confess that he seemed in a fair way of being able before long to gratify his old predilection for military organisation.

The uninhabited wilderness stretching to the west of the Pongo, a district long known to the inhabitants of Darfoor and Kordofan under the name of Dar Ferteet,* represents one of the oldest domains of the slave-trade, and at the present day, as far as regards its aboriginal population, presents to the eye of a traveller the aspect of what may be described as "a sold-out land." Only within the last fifteen years have the Khartoom trading-companies penetrated into the district watered by the Gazelle, but long before that numbers of slave-dealers had already formed settlements in Dar Ferteet, then, as now, streaming into the country from Darfoor and Kordofan accompanied by hundreds of armed men, and coming, year after year, in the winter months so as to accomplish their business and get back to their homes before the rainy season again set in. Some of them, however, did not return, but remained permanently in the land, and, under the sanction of the more influential chieftains, founded large establishments (Dehms) to serve as marts or depots for their black merchandise. As soon as the ivory-traders, with their enormous armed bands, made their appearance in the country, the Gellahbas received them with open arms; and the Nubians, in order to provide for the storing of their ivory and ammunition, forthwith combined their Scribas with the

* Ferteet is the term by which the Foorians and Baggara distinguish the Kredy tribes as a nation from the Niam-niam. In a wider sense the term is applied to all the heathen nations to the south of Darfoor. In the Soudan the guinea-worm is also called Ferteet, probably because the heathen negroes are especially liable to its attacks.

Dehms already established, so that in the course of time these places assumed the appearance of the market-towns of the Soudan. The Gellahbas by remaining in their old quarters reaped a twofold advantage: in the first place, the large contingents of armed men that were now introduced into the country relieved them from the necessity of maintaining troops of their own; and, secondly, they were exonerated from the heavy imposts that they had been compelled to pay to the native Kredy chieftains, as these were very speedily reduced by the Nubians to the subordinate position of mere sheikhs or local overseers of the natives. In the course of my tour through Dar Ferteet I became acquainted with five of these towns, which represented so many centres of the slave-trade in this part of the country.

But although the various Khartoom companies who had thus taken up their quarters in the Dehms sent out expeditions every year to the remotest of the Kredy tribes in the west, and even penetrated beyond them to the Niam-niam in the south-west, it did not take them very long to discover that the annual produce of ivory was altogether inadequate to defray the expenses of equipping and maintaining their armed force. Finding, however, that the region offered every facility for the sale of slaves, they began gradually to introduce this unrighteous traffic into their commercial dealings, until at length it became, if not absolutely the prime, certainly one of the leading objects of their expeditions; thus the people whom the professional Gellahbas had at first hailed as friends grew up, ere long, to be their most formidable rivals. For example, Seebehr Rahama himself, who had to maintain a fighting force of a thousand men on his territories, had, as the result of his ivory-expedition in the previous year, gained no more than 300 loads or 120 cwt., a quantity which realised but little over 2300*l.* at Khartoom; but at the same time he sent probably as many as 1800 slaves direct to Kordofan, there to be disposed of on his own account.

Ethnographically considered, Dar Ferteet presented a wondrous medley. Perhaps nowhere else, in an area so limited, could there be found such a conglomeration of the representatives of different races as upon the cultivated tracts in the environs of the Dehms: they were evidently the miserable remnants of an unceasing work of destruction. As we have already observed, the neighbours of the Bongo upon the west were the Golo and the Sebre, who combine together and have their homes in common. Beyond them, still farther to the west, are the Kredy. These Kredy do not seem to be limited to any particular district, but, like blades of any one particular species of grass, crop up every now and then, in detached groups, amongst the other species. The tribes which predominate, or at any rate those which I had the most frequent opportunities of observing, were the Nduggo, who were settled around Seebehr's Dehm; the Bia, who were settled all about Dehm Gudyoo; and the Yongbongo, who occupied the region between the two.

Of all the people of the Bahr-el-Ghazal district with whom I made acquaintance, the Kredy, I think, were the ugliest; and whether it was in consequence of their longer period of subjection, or that they were depressed by their straitened circumstances, I cannot say, but certainly they were, to my mind, very inferior in intelligence to the Golo, the Sehre, and the Bongo. In form the Kredy are thick and unwieldy, and entirely wanting in that symmetry of limb which we admire in the slim figures of those who inhabit the swampy depressions of the Gazelle; but, although their limbs are strong and compact, they must not be supposed to be like the muscular and well-developed limbs of Europeans. They are like the true Niam-niam in being below an average height, and resemble them more particularly in the broad brachycephalic form of their skulls; there is, however, a very marked difference between the two races in the growth of the hair and in the shape of the eyes. Their lips are thicker and more protruding and their mouths wider than those of any other negroes that I saw throughout the whole of my travels. Their upper incisor teeth were either filed to a point or cut away, so as to leave intervening gaps between tooth and tooth; in the lower jaw there is no mutilation, and the teeth being left intact may perhaps account for their language being more articulate than any other in this part of Africa, although, at the same time, it bears but the slightest resemblance to any of them. Their complexion is coppery-red, the same hue that is to be noticed among the fairer individuals of the Bongo; but, like the majority of the Niam-niam, they are generally coated with such encrusted layers of dirt that they appear several shades darker than they really are: as a rule I should say that they are decidedly fairer than either the Bongo or the Niam-niam.

The Kredy are bounded on the north by the Baggara-el-Homr; on the north-west, three and a half days' journey from Dehm Nduggo, reside the tribe of the Manga, who are said to be quite distinct from the Kredy; on the west, five or six days' journey from Dehm Gudyoo, on the Upper Bahr-el-Arab, are the abodes of the Benda, whose land has long been known to the Foorians under the name of Dar Benda, and used to be the limit of their venturesome slave-raids; still farther to the west are the settlements of the Aboo Dinga, who are said to have no affinity either with Kredy or Niam-niam. The most important of the western Kredy tribes are the Adya, Bia, and March, and towards the south-west their territory is approximate to the frontier wilderness of Mofio, the Niam-niam king. Finally, in the south, there is a mingled population of Golo and Sehre, the Sehre decidedly very much predominating in numbers.

Before I had learnt the true state of things with respect to the caravan-roads that started from Dehm Nduggo, I had indulged the hope of making my homeward journey by the overland route through Kordofan: but when the difficulties and drawbacks came to be reckoned up, I was compelled, however reluctantly, to relinquish a project so perilous as marching across the steppes of the Baggara, and to reconcile myself to retracing my course by the more secure and habitual highway of the Nile. I could willingly have borne the exposure to fatigue, and it might be to hunger: I could have risked the peril of being attacked, and could have stood my chance of procuring the necessary provisions and means of transport; but the extreme uncertainty as to the length of time which the slave-dealers' caravans would take upon their northward return was of itself sufficient to deter me from my scheme.

Taking seven leagues as an average day's march, the journey from Dehm Nduggo to Aboo Harras on the southern frontier of Kordofan is estimated to take thirty days. This statement was confirmed by various independent testimonies, and I found moreover that it corresponded with the distance of the two places as indicated by my map, a distance which, according to the position that I assigned to Dehm Nduggo, would be a trifle under 380 miles. The route first of all leads in a N.N.E. direction to Seebehr's most northerly Scriba, Serraggo, a distance which it takes three days to accomplish. Another day's march and the traveller reaches Dalgowna, a depot much frequented by the slave-dealers and situated on the isolated mountain of the same name as itself, from which there is said to be an extensive view across the northern steppes. The Beery flows quite close to this Gebel Dalgowna, on its way to join the Bahr-el-Arab farther to the north-east. Three days' journey more and the Bahr-el-Arab is attained, just at a spot where it marks off the frontiers of the Baggara-el-Homr. On account of the so-called Bedouins (known as "Arabs" in the common parlance of the Soudan) residing upon its banks, the river has received, from the traders of Kordofan and Darfoor, the designations both of the Bahr-el-Arab and the Bahr-el-Homr: that these two appellations belong to different rivers is quite a fallacy, and the mistake, which has found its way into many maps, very probably originated in travellers sometimes calling the river by one name and sometimes by the other. There is really but the *one* river. After another three days' march Shekka is reached, the great rendezvous in the territory of the Baggara-Rizegat. It may thus be seen that the journey from Dehm Nduggo to Shekka may be accomplished in ten or twelve days, according to the length of the day's march.

According to the statements that I gathered and have now recorded, Shekka, I should suppose, corresponds with a position described by Escayrac de Lauture in his valuable accounts of these regions, and which he distinguishes by the name of Sook-Deleyba (*i.e.*, the market near the Deleb-palms). Shekka, in fact, appears to be an important market-place and rendezvous for the itinerant slave-dealers, as well as for the Baggara Bedouins, many of whom have permanent homes there; it is the site also of the residence of Munzel, the Sheikh of the Rizegat. But it is most notorious of all as being the principal resort of all the great Kordofan slave-traders: being beyond the jurisdiction of Egypt and its arbitrary officials, who are in the habit of extorting a specific sum per head for hush-money on every slave that is conveyed into the country, it is a spot that enables them to transact their nefarious business free from the burdensome imposts, and to transmit their living merchandise in whatever direction may suit them, all over the provinces of the Soudan.

The journey from Shekka to Aboo Harras, I was given to understand, would require eighteen days, and even with very long days' marches could not be accomplished in less than fifteen days. All my informants agreed most positively in asserting that there were no streams of any magnitude to be crossed, and that even in the height of the rainy season there were no brooks nor swamps to offer any serious obstacle to travellers. There was, however, no time of the year, not even in the middle of winter, when the Bahr-el-Arab could be crossed by any other means than swimming, or by rafts constructed of grass.

The caravan-roads from Dehm Nduggo to Darfoor were closed at the time of my visit. They nearly all started in a N.N.W. direction.

Almost immediately after leaving the Seriba, the traveller would have to cross the Beery, and proceed for three or four leagues until he arrived at the subsidiary Seriba Deleyb; another day's march to the north-west would bring him to one of the minor Seribas, of which the controller's name was Soliman; and two days more would find him at a Seriba on the Gebel Mangyat, as the natives call that district. The notorious copper-mines Hofrat-el-Nahahs are said to be situated six days' journey to the south of this region of the Manga, and to lie on the southern frontier of Darfoor. The copper is brought into the market either in the shape of clumsily-formed rings, full of angles, varying in weight from five pounds to fifty, or in long oval cakes of very imperfect casting. The price that I had to pay for the hundred rottoli (about 80 lbs.) that I obtained from Seebehr was 1500 piastres, or 75 Maria Theresa dollars, which would be represented by about £15 of English money.

Seebehr had a Seriba on the frontiers of Darfoor that was in constant intercourse with this important place, and through his interest I obtained a sample of the ore of these far-famed mines It weighed about five pounds. One half of it I handed to the Khedive of Egypt at an audience with which he honoured me; the other half I deposited in the Mineralogical Museum at Berlin. The specimen consisted of copper-pyrite and quartz, with an earthy touch of malachite, commonly called green carbonite of copper, but containing a very small quantity of the real metal.

No systematic mining seems to be carried on in the "Hofrat-el-Nahahs," and the man who brought me the sample carefully concealed in his clothes, informed me that the ore was found lying like loose rubble in the dry bed of a khor. It may be presumed that by boring galleries, or even by hewing out quarries, a large supply of the metal might be obtained without any vast expenditure of time or money, for even in the present condition of things, while the solid rock still remains intact, the yield of copper for years past has been very considerable. The Foorian copper even now takes a prominent part in the commerce of the entire Soudan; it is conveyed across Wadai to Kano in Haussa, and, according to Barth, it holds its own in the market even against that imported from Tripoli.

It was on the 22nd of January that I prepared to resume my wanderings. In the evening I took my leave of Sheikh Seebehr, and attended by six bearers, with which he had provided me, I departed from the Seriba.

My first destination was the settlement of one of the companies associated with Kurshook Ali, which was situated on the Beery, about twenty miles from Dehm Nduggo. The route for the most part was in a south-westerly direction, over elevated ground that was channelled by no less than ten running streams and khor-beds, and along country that was splendidly adorned with goodly forests. The defiles extended from the south-east to the north-west, and stretched away towards the valley of the Beery, which ran parallel to our course at a few miles' distance to the right.

The first irregularity in the soil which crossed our way consisted of a deep river-course, which was now quite dry and shaded by thick foliage; the second was made by the stream of the Uyeely, which, flowing out from a narrow streak of thicket that corresponded very much in its vegetation with the galleries of the Niam-niam, with deliberate current passed onwards to the west. Midway between the Uyeely and the next stream, called the Uyissobba (the native word for "a buffalo"), which consisted of a series of pools that ranged themselves in a continuous series along an open swamp-steppe, there stood a grove of tall trees. I was much surprised to find the frequent occurrence of the same species of Cycadea which I had observed in the Niam-niam lands, but which here, through the absence of any underwood, made a majestic upward growth, and expanded their noble fans at the summit of a stately stem.

The Kredy-Nduggo call the Encephalartus "kotto," and my attendants acquainted me with the fact that they could manufacture a sort of beer out of the central portion of the stem, which was marrowy and full of meal. Some of the specimens that I saw had great cylindrical stems two feet high, a very decided contrast to those that I had previously seen, which were all quite low upon the ground. The male flowering heads were often as many as eight or ten upon a single stem. In the shadowy light admitted by the tall Humboldtiæ that towered above, their stiff crowns had all the appearance of being alien to the scene and a decoration imported from some foreign soil.

After crossing a rippling brook we came to a village belonging to the Kredy chief, Ganyong, on Seebehr's territory. The fishing-nets, forty feet long and eight feet broad, with their great meshes and floating rims made of the stalks of the borassus, bore ample testimony, as they hung outside the huts, to the productiveness of the Beery.

The style of building amongst the Kredy appeared to me extremely slovenly and inartistic. Most of the huts were entirely wanting in substructure, and consisted merely of a conical roof of grass raised

KREDY HUT.

upon a framework of hoops. They recalled to my mind the huts of the Kaffirs. Ganyong had some corn-magazines of a very remarkable construction. They were made very much upon the principle of the "gollotoh" of the Bongo, having a kind of basket supported on posts and covered with a large conical lid; but underneath the main

KREDY CORN-MAGAZINE.

receptacle and between the posts there was a space left large enough for four female slaves to do all the necessary work for converting the corn into meal. A deep trench was cut, and, being firmly cemented over with clay, formed a common reservoir into which the corn fell after it had passed from the murhagas or grindstones. The stones were arranged so as to form a cross. The women who were employed sang merrily as they worked, and in the course of a day the quantity of corn they ground was very considerable.

At the next hollow, which appeared to have been a marsh that was now dry, was a kind of defile rather thickly sprinkled over with huts, where we found the native women busily engaged in gathering the Lophira-nuts that they call "kozo," and use for making oil. The succeeding brook was named the Uyuttoo, and was lined on either side by avenues of trees; it was not much more than a trench, but it was full of water. Farther on, right in the heart of the wood, we made a passage over a khor, and having for a while mistaken our way, we made a halt at a rivulet that was but eight feet wide, but abundantly supplied with running water. It was already quite dusk, and we were obliged to abandon all hope of getting as far as the Scriba that day. I sent my bearers, therefore, to make the best investigation they could of the surrounding country, and to find out some settlement where we could encamp for the night, as it appeared to be quite impossible for us to bivouac with any degree of comfort in the midst of the still vigorous growth of grass.

Just in time a village belonging to Kurshook Ali was discovered, and, after making a circuitous route to the south-east, we fixed upon a convenient resting-place for the night. Next morning we proceeded down to the river over very irregular ground, up hill and down hill, and repeatedly broken by deep fissures. The dimensions of the Beery in this district were anything but important: it flowed towards the west, making a good many bends and curves, and after a while turning short off to the north. At this date it extended over about two-thirds of the width of its channel, the depth of the stream varying from one to two feet, and the water flowing at the rate of about one hundred feet a minute. The banks were about eight feet high, and were crowned on either hand by trees that, rising some fifty feet, threw out their boughs and overhung the stream to a considerable distance with a leafy canopy. I found a place in the most shadowed portion of the wood where the river had formed a deep basin, and I took a bath, which I found something more than refreshing, and, with the temperature at 68° Fahr., I was obliged to take a good run to get warm again.

A mile to the south of the river there was an extensive tract of land covered by farmsteads, merely separated from each other by hedges, and inhabited principally by some Gellahbas who had settled there and by some of the black soldiers. Just beyond these, in a deep depression, the rivulet of the Rende made its way towards the north-west. Facing the settlement and towards the south, the valley sank very low, whilst towards the west and south-west, the country rose considerably in prominent wall-like ridges.

The controller of the place was named Mangoor, but he was unwell and out of temper, and consequently had no hospitality to show me, nd allowed me and my people to start next day with empty stomachs and without any contribution of supplies. Nor was much to be got out of the native local overseer, Gassigombo, who had the supervision of such of the Kredy tribe of the Jongbongo who had settled there; the country was so impoverished that he had neither goats nor poultry to part with.

On the following morning I found myself thoroughly unwell, and so weak that I hardly knew how I should hold out during the next stage of our progress. I had now double cause to regret the loss of all my stock of tea, for although I tried to compensate for the want of it by taking an extra quantity of coffee, it did me but little good, and was comparatively useless in bracing up my nervous system. I made it, however, as strong as I could, and took it with me to sustain my flagging energies and keep up my elasticity as I went along.

The Dehm Gudyoo, to which I was directing my steps, was about twenty-two miles distant, and was one of the chief establishments of the slave-traders who had settled in the country. There were no less than ten brooks to be crossed, of some of which the channels were partially dried up; every one of them without exception flowed from west to east towards the Beery, which lay from this point onwards upon our left hand, apparently following a southerly direction. The altitude above the sea, which hitherto upon the route from Dehm Nduggo had been tolerably uniform, began to increase considerably. The region was less thickly covered with trees, but light brushwood took their place, whilst the monotony of the steppes was broken by dwindling watercourses. These seemed to flow from north to south, and were described to me under the following names: the first was the Rende, and had a tolerably strong current; the next was the Buloo, flowing along in a deep rift between walls of red rock; then came the Zembey, a mere meadow-brook; to this succeeded the Kungbai, flowing in its channel along the open steppe; next in order was the Ramadda, a swamp-khor, that had but little current, on the banks of which a number of little springs were constantly yielding their fresh supply.

After this, the way began to ascend, blocks of hornblende and schist occurring every now and then to vary the uniformity of the general configuration of the soil. As we again descended we came to another series of brooks. The first was named the Bidulch, and ran rapidly along, its banks being clearly indicated by rows of Raphia-palms; the next was of similar character, called the Gatwee, its borders again lined by the Raphia: then came the Gobo, a much smaller stream that murmured along its red granite channel; and then the Kadditch, shut in by a kind of gallery-vegetation. The last of the series, by which we passed the night, was a stream fifteen feet wide with a rapid current, the water of which was up to our krees; it was the Gresse, a feeder of the Beery, and here it had an aspect that very much resembled the Beery as we observed it at the unfriendly Dehm. It was now full 30 feet wide, and made its way amongst blocks and over flats of gneiss between lofty banks that slanted down abruptly to the stream. The declivity, amidst the openings of the thickets, revealed the red rock of the swamp-ore in many places, whilst down below, the flats of the gneiss were everywhere apparent.

From the Gresse we had still eight miles to march along very rising ground before we reached Dehm Gudyoo. As well as being one of the oldest halting-places of the slave-dealers of Dar Ferteet, and in number of huts quite equal to Dehm Nduggo, this town contained a Seriba of Agahd's company, and served as the headquarters of a division of Khartoom soldiers, who made annual expeditions to the territory of the Niam-niam king Mofio, in the west. Gudyoo himself, formerly a Kredy chief and a great patron of the slave-dealers, had now settled down to the east on the banks of the Beery as an ordinary sheikh of Agahd's possessions. Dehm Gudyoo formed the most westerly and, with the exception of Mount Baginze, the highest point that I visited in all my travels in Central Africa. The altitude of the Dehm was about 2775 feet, and not much less than 500 feet higher than Dehm Nduggo. From various indications in the character of the soil I seemed to have no alternative than to conclude that these elevations continue to rise still more decidedly beyond Dehm Gudyoo, and that most probably a considerable watershed would be found in the region in that direction.

The character of the vegetation reminded me in more than one respect of the flora of the Niam-niam lands. Dehm Gudyoo stretches itself out on the northern declivity of a valley, and consists of huts and farmsteads, which, rising one above another in a kind of amphitheatre, gave an imposing aspect to the scene. Probably the number of huts exceeded 2000. From a spring close to the lowest tier of houses issued a considerable brook, named the Kobbokoio, which was shadowed over with tall trees and thick bushwood that gave the borders very much the appearance of the Niam-niam galleries. In the farther environs of this Dehm there were a good many instances of plants that were very nearly allied to those of the Niam-niam, and the dualism which characterised the vegetation was very marked, and ever and again recalled what I had observed before. On the higher parts of the hill-slopes I found the *Albizzia anthelmintica* in considerable quantities, the bark of which is the most effectual remedy that the Abyssinians are acquainted with for the tapeworm.

Although I had cause to congratulate myself upon the hospitable reception that I found at Agahd's Seriba, and appreciated the hospitality that was extended to me, my condition altogether was so wretched that I might almost as well have been left in the wilderness. A kind of scorbutic affection that had for some little time been lurking in my system, probably in consequence of my having been deprived for so many months of proper vegetable diet, now broke out with some violence, my gums becoming so sore and the inside of my mouth so inflamed that I could not take anything but water without experiencing the greatest pain. The restricted supply of provisions in the place naturally aggravated my condition. As it happily fell out, Faki Ismael, the superintendent of the establishment, made me a present of some sweet potatoes, which he had just received from Dar Benda: at this season they were very scarce, and proved very acceptable, being the only food of which I could venture to partake. In spite of my ailments, however, I did not suffer my three days' residence in Dehm Gudyoo to pass away without employing them as profitably as I could : I made a collection of words in the Kredy dialect, and carefully inspected all the most interesting plants in the district.

In this important centre of the slave-trade I had also ample opportunity of investigating many of the details of that disgraceful traffic. Nowhere could I walk, either in the narrow streets and lanes, or in the adjacent fields, without coming in contact with herds of unfortunate slaves, both male and female, of various nationality and destined for various branches of the market.

The rude and primitive manner of grinding corn employed throughout the Mohammedan Soudan contributes very much to perpetuate the immense demand for female slave-labour. The laborious process is performed by pounding the grain upon a large stone, called "murhaga," by means of a smaller stone held in the hand; it is the only method of grinding corn known to the majority of African nations, and is so slow, that by the hardest day's work, a woman is able to prepare a quantity of corn only sufficient for five or six men.

The accompanying illustration represents one of the daily scenes in my travelling life, and may serve to give an idea how slavery degrades a woman almost to a level with the brutes. A newly-captured slave, with the heavy yoke of the sheyba fastened to her

SLAVE AT WORK.

neck, has been set to work at the murhaga, whilst a boy holds up the yoke in order that it should not interfere with the freedom of her movements. Until this lavish waste of human labour is suppressed, no hope is to be entertained of any diminution in the demand for female slaves.

At Dehm Gudyoo I learnt a great many details about the aspect of the land still farther west that had been traversed by the various companies of Agahd, Bizelly, Idrees Wod Defter, and Seebehr Adlan. When we took our departure I found that our road had a decline. In order to reach the Bongo territory again I proposed to proceed in a kind of arc towards the south-east down to the Dehm Bekeer, where the extensive establishments of the Gellahbas, stretching away for miles, were collected. In a straight line the distance between Dehm Gudyoo and Dehm Bekeer would not exceed five-and-thirty miles, but our deviations were so frequent and so long that it took us two days of exceedingly hard marching to reach our destination. The entire district, a thoroughly unbroken wilderness, was the true source-land of the Beery and the Kooroo, both of these rivers at the points where we crossed them being in the incipient condition of mere brooks; nor did they seem to surpass the other streamlets, thirteen in number, which we had to cross, in their supply of water.

The universal direction which the streams took was from south to north. Reckoning them in their order after leaving Dehm Gudyoo, the first was the Domwee, quite a little channel filled with a flowing current: after a considerable rise in the land, we came to the Ghessy Beery (*i. e.*, the Little or Upper Beery) with its broad water almost stagnant and shadowed by an extensive gallery-wood; then came a dried-up channel at the bottom of a broad and outspread valley, of which the western slopes were marked by crests of hills some 400 or 500 feet in height; to this succeeded an uphill march, which led to a soil so elevated that it opened an ample prospect into the far distant east, embracing at least the chief landmarks for some eighty miles round; next succeeded a brook called the Yagpak, of which the waters, still deep, where hemmed in by thick shrubberies; next came a little watercourse with languid stream; and then a rivulet twenty feet wide, full of water, and named the Gulanda, the direction of which was indicated by the bushes on the banks, where we spent the night. The level of the soil was here about 380 feet lower than it had been at Dehm Gudyoo. Farther on, close following upon each other, came two dried-up khors; after which the land once more began to rise again in alternate flats of gneiss and lofty eminences of swamp-ore, hills named Bakeffa and Yaffa lifting themselves up conspicuously on the east; next we reached a small dried-up course that intersected a valley made up of gneiss flats, bounded on the west by the elevation of a hill, called the Fee-ee; then, at about equal distances from one another, were crossed four khors, now dry, that gave an undulated character to the ground; proceeding onwards we came to the half-dry, half-swampy depression known as the Ohro; and last of all we arrived at an inconsiderable water-channel of which the stream was deep, but apparently stationary, and was described by the Kredy as being the upper course of the Kooroo, distinguished here by the name of the Mony.

The district over which we thus had travelled very much resembled the northern regions of the Kredy lands in its wooded character and in the absence of meadow-lands and steppes; only it was utterly wanting in that distinctive abundance of springs which is so marked in latitudes below lat. 8° N. The deficiency of water, in comparison to what we had before experienced, was very obvious. The flora offered some few novelties.

In the dried-up watercourses I frequently saw one of the rodentia which had hitherto been little known to me: this was the reed-rat, (*Aulacodes*) called by the Foorians the "Far-el-boos." I had the good fortune to bring down three of them, and, after having been limited for three days to a diet of soaked sweet potatoes, I very much appreciated a meal from their delicate and tender flesh.

Never shall I forget the hospitable reception which Yumma, Kurshook Ali's Vokeel, showed me at this Seriba, nor the circumstances under which it transpired. My gratitude was all the more keen because the discourtesy and inhospitality which I had experienced from Mangoor were still fresh upon my memory. I was really worn-out by the fatigue of marching, and very much debilitated by my compulsory abstinence in consequence of my scorbutic attack, when in the early evening we reached the Dehm. We wandered about for a considerable time amongst the scattered homesteads, and had some difficulty in discovering the palings of the Seriba. After we succeeded in getting inside, we found all the huts perfectly quiet, and it appeared almost as if invisible hands had prepared the coffee which was handed me as soon as I had taken my seat upon the "angareb" in the reception-hall. The ruler of the Seriba happened that evening to be absent somewhere in the environs, and it was not known for certain whether he would return that night. Feeling that it was quite a matter of speculation what kind of entertainment I should have on the following day, I threw myself down without taking any supper, and composed myself for my night's rest.

Whoever has wandered as a lonely traveller in the untrodden solitudes of a desert likes to tell his dreams: in them the true situation of a man often mirrors itself; for, unrestrained by any control of reason, images arise from the obscurity of the past, so that, at times, it seems as if a painful vividness was being stamped upon recollections, which, as reproduced, are really very contradictory to the actual facts. It happened to me very much in this way at Dehm Bekeer, only I had the compensation that the visions that I saw were not disproved, but confirmed, by my experience.

Weary and worn-out as I was, and no longer master of my faculties, I seem very soon to have fallen asleep. Memory, unshackled from the guardianship of reality, began to revel in the ideal delights of a material world. I fancied that I was in a spacious tent that was glittering with the radiancy of countless lamps, that the tables were groaning under the most tempting viands, and that troops of servants in gorgeous livery were in attendance upon the guests, to whom they brought the mellowest and rarest of wines. And then it was race-time at Cairo, and the entertainment was sumptuous with all the splendour of the fairest imagery of ' The Arabian Nights,' the host no less than the Governor of Egypt himself. And then I seemed all at once to wake, and was quite bewildered in trying to decide whether I was in the smoke-clouds that envelope the interior of an African grass-hut or whether in truth I was reclining under the shelter of a royal marquee. My frame of mind enhanced the force of my fancy: but soon the delusion took a more distinct phase, and I seemed to divine that there was really about me a group of well-dressed servants, and that whilst some were bringing in various dishes and sparkling goblets which they placed beside my lowly couch, others were running about with tapers and lamps, and others with embroidered napkins under their arms were conveying the choicest dainties in lordly dishes or offering lemonade and sherbet from the brightest crystal. I rubbed my eyes. I took a draught of what was offered me. I surveyed the scene deliberately, and came to the surprised conviction that what I had been dreaming was a reality!

Yumma, the controller of the Seriba, had returned home late in the evening. No sooner was he informed of my arrival than he had had all his retinue of cooks aroused from their night's rest to give me an entertainment worthy of his rank. He was more than half a Turk, and acquainted far beyond the other superintendents of the Seribas with the elegancies and comforts of a Khartoomer's household. Everything he possessed in the way of valuable vases or tasteful table ornaments was brought out and exhibited in my honour. He set before me bread of pure white flour, maccaroni, rice, chickens served with tomatoes, and innumerable other delicacies which I could hardly have supposed had ever found their way to this distant land. It was quite midnight before the preparations for the impromptu banquet were complete, and then, whether I wanted or not, I was bound to partake. My tortures were the tortures of Tantalus; however eagerly I might covet the food, the inflammation in my gums put an emphatic veto upon my enjoyment, and it was only with the acutest suffering that I could get a morsel of meat or a drop of fluid between my lips. As soon, however, as I was somewhat better, the improved diet told favourably upon my constitution, and after a few days I was ready to start afresh upon my travels with renovated energy and recruited strength.

The environs of the Dehm are inhabited partly by the Golo and partly by the Sehre. Amongst the natives the town itself is known by the name of Dehm Dooroo, called so after a deceased chieftain of the Golo. The present native overseer of the Golo population is called Mashi Doko. To the south and south-west of the town, the ground gradually rises, and in the main might be called hilly in all directions, as right away to the horizon there are continued series of hill-crests and ridges. Above the general undulation of the land these rise high enough to form conspicuous landmarks, and afford the wayfarer considerable assistance in the direction of his journey; many of them present an appearance that is quite analogous to that of the hill-caps which have been mentioned as characteristic of southern Bongoland; generally they consist of bright masses of gneiss. The shape of these hills is defined in the Arabic of the Soudan as "Gala;" the Bongo call it "Kilebee." They are quite isolated, and are always rounded elevations of grey gneiss projecting, sometimes like flat plateaux, and sometimes like raised eminences, from the swamp-ore around, and they give the landscape the aspect so characteristic of Central Africa.

They may readily be supposed to be associated in character with those gneiss flats which are scattered all over the land in every variety of shape and size, and any one must involuntarily become subject to the impression that they indicate a spot where in bygone ages there were the summits of mountains that have long since been worn down by the tooth of time, and that these elevations were the ridges that had separated the channels of the very rivers that I had discovered, which by various agencies, chemical and mechanical, were now conspiring to carry off the *débris* of the mountain mass and convey it to the distant ocean.

On leaving Dehm Bekeer, a mile south from the Scriba, we reached a small stream called the Ngudduroo, and on the farther side of it, after traversing a hilly tract for about two miles, we came to another stream which in winter could boast only of a very weak current, although even then the breadth of its bed was fifteen feet, thoroughly covered with water. The banks were about eight or ten feet in height, and stood out dry above the stream. Yumma, who accompanied me, declared that it was the upper course of the river of Damoory and Dembo, consequently that it was the Pongo, and he affirmed that, in his frequent marches along its banks, he had distinctly followed it right into that district. Both the Golo and the Sehre throughout the environs called it the Djee, and as I proceeded along my way I derived fresh confirmation for Yumma's statement about the river from the circumstance that it is also called the Djee by those Sehre who reside on the farther side, at Dehm Adlan. All along my route back, moreover, towards the east, I did not come across any river large or small which could possibly be identified as the upper portion of what is the Pongo to Damoory.

Some four or five leagues to the north-west of Dehm Bekeer there is stationed one of Kurshook Ali's subsidiary Scribas. The natives of the district are Golo, and the Seriba has been established upon the banks of the Hahoo, a little stream that subsequently joins the Kooroo. Two leagues to the south-west of the Dehm rises a hill, steep in every aspect; it is designated the Kokkuloo, and commands a wide view of the country around. I found a number of intelligent people in this locality, whose information about the neighbouring Niam-niam was of considerable service to me in ascertaining various facts, and by comparing and combining their separate accounts I was able to gain a fairly accurate idea of the country. The particulars that I gathered were for the most part appertaining to the territories of the two Niam-niam chieftains Mofio and Solongoh. Mofio's residence was described as being situated to the W.N.W. of our present position, and in consequence of the number of streams that had to be crossed and the deserts that had to be traversed, it could not be reached in less than twelve days, even if the march were urged on with all possible speed, whilst at an ordinary pace it would take fifteen days at least; there was, however, a way from Dehm Nduggo which was less circuitous, and did not offer the same difficulties in furnishing the bearers with supplies: this could be accomplished in about eight days. The home of Solongoh, who was a son of Bongohrongboh, was not distant more than a five days' march to the S.S.E., and only separated from the domain of Kurshook Ali in the lands of the Golo and Sehre by one of the desolate frontier wildernesses. There was a third independent Niam-niam chief, whose territory, however, was of insignificant extent. He was called indifferently Yapaty or Yaffaty, and was the son of Mofio's brother Zaboora: he had his mbanga three days' journey to the south-west of Dehm Bekeer.

At the period of my visit Yumma was on terms of open enmity with Solongoh, his territory being constantly threatened by that powerful prince, whose sway extended as far as the Bellandah, who are bordering upon the land of Aboo Shatter. Just before this, in fact only a few days previous to my arrival, Solongoh had been repulsed in an attack which he had made, although he had summoned his full force and had advanced within a couple of days' march of Dehm Bekeer. As Yumma foresaw that another engagement was imminent, he would not permit me to remain any longer in his Seriba, because he knew that he could not be responsible for the issue, and it was in vain that I begged him not to have any apprehension on my account. But the audacity of the Niam-niam was so gross that it was intolerable, and must be suppressed at all hazards. To such a pitch had this shameless daring grown, that even the arms of the soldiers had been stolen by people sent by Solongoh into Dehm Bekeer for the purpose. Under cover of night they had contrived to get into the Seriba, and had managed to purloin several guns whilst the unsuspecting owners were sound asleep.

My researches in Dehm Gudyoo enabled me to gather certain information which is of some consequence as affecting the proper hydrographical delineation of the countries through which I was travelling. Six days' journey south-west by west from the spot at which we were sojourning stood a Seriba, which was Idrees Wod Defter's principal repository of arms and ammunition; it was situated, as I was informed, upon the banks of a river that flowed to the north-east, and afterwards joined another river that was so much larger that the passage over it could at all seasons only be effected in boats. To this river the Khartoomers give the name of Bahr Aboo Dinga; it is said to be about two and a half days' journey beyond Dar Benda, where Idrees maintains another Seriba. It is a river that is likewise well known to the company of Seebehr Rahama, which makes a yearly visit to the country that is inhabited by the Aboo Dinga, a distinct negro people, quite different alike to the Kredy and to the Niam-niam. The direction of the stream Aboo Dinga was reported to be E.N.E. or due east, and all the statements concurred in making it identical with the Bahr-el-Arab, which intersects the country of the Baggara-el-Homr.

No one seemed able to decide the question where the Bahr Aboo Dinga came from. I suspect its source is somewhere amongst the mountains of Runga, to the south of Wadai, a spot of which various travellers have given such reports as they have been able to gather. Barth,* in the itinerary which he gives of his eastward route from Massena in Baghirmy to Runga, makes an entry which may contribute something in the way of elucidating the question. He says that he came "on the forty-second day (*i. e.*, one day's journey to the south of the residence of the prince of Runga) to Dar Sheela,† a mountainous district with a river flowing to the east, beyond which lies Dar Dinga." No one is more conscious than I am myself how little stress is to be laid upon a mere resemblance in the sound of names. Hundreds of times, and in every diversity of place, I have found that any conjecture based upon the apparent similarity is utterly worthless; but in this case the resemblance was not a chance coincidence, for the assigned bearings and distances (as reckoned from the two starting-points of Barth and myself) so thoroughly correspond as to suggest the sense of a mutual agreement between the scenes that we explored; it seems also very probable that Barth's river Kubanda is identical with my river Welle.

Various reasons, into which it is unnecessary to enter with more minuteness here, might be alleged to show that it is in the highest degree probable that the river in question is likewise identical with a river which is affirmed by the two entirely independent witnesses, Teïma ‡ and Fresnel,§ to exist in this district, and to which the name of Bahr-el-Ezuhm, or Azzoum, is assigned.

Although these statements are only given in their main and essential features, and not in detail, they will suffice to cast some degree of clearness upon the source of the Bahr-el-Arab, that river which appears hitherto to have been very much underrated in all

---

* Barth, vol. iii., p. 578.

† Some geographers fall into error with respect to this place by making Dar Sheela identical with the well-known Dar Sileh or Dar Silah, which is a different negro Mohammedan country, many of the people of which I have seen

‡ *Vide* De Cadalvene et de Breuvery, 'L'Egypte,' vol. ii. p. 237. where the Orientalist König has given his interpretation of a map, which Teïma-Walad-el-Sultan-Messabani (Governor of Kordofan, subject to the control of Darfoor) had himself projected.

§ Fresnel pursued his researches in Djidda in the years 1848 and 1849.

the maps of the country. The evidence which demonstrates that the river is entitled to the rank of primogeniture amongst all the tributaries of the Gazelle system, has already been collected in a previous page. We have only to take account of the extraordinary length, as may be gathered from the foregoing data, to which the Bahr-el-Arab extends, and we shall be at once bound to concede that in all discussions connected with that endless question of the sources of the Nile, the Bahr-el-Arab takes at least an equal rank with the Bahr-el-Gebel.

Leaving the Djee at some little distance to our right, we continued our return journey to the Wow and the Dyoor, starting in a N.N.E. direction, and persevering for twenty-five miles until we reached Dehm Adlan, just as it had been described to me by the same reliable authorities to whom I was indebted for such detailed particulars about the districts of Mofio and Solongoh. Nearly throughout the march the country was quite destitute of inhabitants, and we crossed eleven little streams all running from west to east and flowing into the Djee. We had first to cross a half-dry khor, surrounded on all sides by open steppes, and then proceeded to the farms of the Sehre sheik, Bereeah, which were situated just beyond a considerable brook, of which the water was nearly at a standstill and which bore the name of Langeh.

Our pathway now led us through bushwoods and over soil that was generally rocky, till, after accomplishing about two leagues, we came in sight of Bakeffa, a hill of which I had previously taken the bearings; it reared itself so much above the flat table-land that it could be seen from afar. All round the west, far as the horizon embraced the view, the whole country was apparently one elevated plateau. For a long time we had a river named the Gumende on our left, and at intervals passed through the galleries of forest-wood that enclosed its banks; after a while we had to cross the stream at a spot where it was thirty feet wide and ten feet in depth. As surveyed from this place, the horizon upon the north-east was shut out by the rising of some steepish ground. The next brook that we reached was named the Nyusseta; its water was nearly stationary, and beyond it were still standing the dejected ruins of a previous Seriba of Bizelly's. Having traversed a rocky tract broken by repeated bushwoods, we next arrived at the large brook Gopwee, of which the channel was deep, but the waters nearly still, its banks being shrouded with very thick foliage. Then we reached the Dibanga, of which we found that the bed was of considerable depth; but at this season it was divided into a number of separate pools. Farther on we passed a gallery-brook, in which the water had no movement, and finally we came to a much larger stream, of which the surface of the water was ten feet in breadth, the height of the woody banks which shut in the channel varying from twenty-five feet in some places to forty in others. Its name was the Ndopah. The woods, which almost completely overshadowed it, were composed in a large measure of great Sterculiæ, which the Niam-niam call kokkorukkoo, and to which I have already called attention as being so conspicuous in the gallery forests of the south.

Upon the banks of a little stream, by the sides of which the trees were arranged as it were in avenues, and where a kind of glen was formed amongst them, we came to an establishment of slave-dealers, who, in company with some elephant-hunters from Darfoor, had taken up their quarters at the place which the Khartoomers simply designate by the name of Bet-el-Gellahba, or "the abode of the slave-dealers." As we were unable to reach the Dehm to which our steps were bent, we were compelled to take up our quarters here for the night.

On the following morning, which was the 5th of February, I was very much surprised at the singularly clouded aspect of the sky. After a long interval the night had been warm, the atmosphere being oppressively close, an indication that, just as might be anticipated at the beginning of February, a change of weather was impending, and there was about to ensue a transition from the coolness of winter to the heat of summer without any interruption in the dryness of the air.

Before we arrived at the Dehm of Seebehr Adlan, who was a Seriba owner associated with Agahd's company, we had to journey over lands that were under vigorous cultivation and to pass by numerous farmsteads of the Sehre. On our way it was necessary to cross two considerable brooks that flowed in the hollow of some deep depressions, and were closely shut in by lofty trees. Beyond the second of these, which was called Ngokkoo, on the steep side of a valley slope, lay the aforesaid Seriba, in the immediate environs of which were clustered many groups of Gellahbas' farmsteads, numerous enough to constitute a Dehm, which, however, was far smaller than any that we had previously visited. The resident dealers in slaves were partly Foorians and partly Baggara, and had an interest in the ivory-traffic as well as in their living merchandise. They conducted their business in the regular Bedouin fashion, with sword and lance, disposing of their spoil at the nearest Scribas, where their activity was much appreciated. The Baggara, who come into the country in the train of the slave-dealers (whether for the purpose of tending the oxen which are wanted as beasts of burden or of superintending the transport of the slaves), are all of the tribe of the Rizegat, the Homr being the most irreconcilable enemies of all the Gellahbas, no matter whether these come from Kordofan or Darfoor, or whether they be natives of Khartoom or other Nubians.

At the distance of a mile from the Seriba, towards the east, the Djee had already expanded into a river some forty feet broad; its bed was full of water, which, however, did not exceed two feet in depth; it flowed deliberately towards the north, between lofty walls of swamp-ore and over moss-grown clumps of gneiss that half-obstructed its flow along its bed. The embankments on either side seemed to be equally inclined to the base of the valley, which they overtopped by an altitude of nearly 600 feet; so prolonged was the depression, spreading outwards for several miles, that the aspect of the locality was quite remarkable. The affluents of the river joined the main-stream by gorges in the soil, which sank perpendicularly to the bottom; and the land had the singular appearance of having been regularly parcelled out into distinct allotments.

The contented little community of the Sehre had established itself in well-packed quarters, which were ranged for some distance around the Seriba. The prospect all around was very diversified, the landscape presenting pleasing alternations of light and shade, the dense woods being relieved by the recurrence of the culture-lands and homesteads of the natives.

In general appearance the Sehre may be said to bear a striking resemblance to the Niam-Niam, except that they are not tattooed. Originally they were a tribe of slaves subject to the Niam-niam chieftains, but recently they have migrated farther north, very probably encouraged to that movement by the depopulation of the land in consequence of the large and perpetual capture of the people for slaves. However, many of the Sehre still remain subject to the dominion of the Niam-niam prince, Solongoh. The prolonged intercourse that has existed between the two people has done a great deal towards obliterating the nationality and peculiar cutsoms of the Sehre and to assimilate them to the Niam-niam; but to a large extent they retain their own dialect, which, as might be expected, has many points of resemblance with the

Zandey. Many of the Sehre are quite accustomed to the Zandey tongue and speak it fluently. The long hair is precisely like what is found among the Niam-niam, and the mode of arranging it in tufts and twists is identical. Their complexion is a dark chocolate colour.

The Sehre are a robust and well-built race, and in this respect they more resemble the Golo and the Bongo. Their ethnographical independence, however, does not admit of a question. Their huts attest the interest which their owners take in them, and the amount of care that is bestowed upon the management of their households is larger than what is anywhere to be observed amongst the Golo, not to mention those of the poor degenerate Kredy. The peculiar huts appropriated to boys, which I have mentioned as being adopted by the Niam-niam and called "bamogee," are found here, and are always built in a style that is most symmetrical. But their most remarkable structures are their corn-bins, which are of a shape that I never saw elsewhere. They are made in the form of a drinking-goblet, and are nearly always artistically decorated with mouldings and with a series of rings almost as perfect as though they had been produced with the aid of a lathe. They are always built on a pedestal, which must be climbed in order to push aside the projecting lid.

Among the Sehre I never saw either goats or dogs, and, as far as I could judge, their residences had no other live stock about them but a few cocks and hens.

There is nothing very remarkable about the arms of the Sehre; their lances resemble those of the Bongo, and are very rare and quaint-looking weapons. The bows and arrows are considerably smaller than those of the Bongo, the arrows in particular being of that short and stumpy make that I had noticed amongst the Bellanda.

The women's attire consists of bunches of grass or leaves, fastened to their girdle before and behind, and very like what is worn by the Bongo; it is also generally adopted by the women of the Golo and Kredy. There is the same partiality for inserting bits of straw in the sides of the nostrils that is so common amongst the Bongo women, but the example here is to a certain extent followed even by the men. Many of the women have the circular plate let into their upper lip like the Mittoo women. At the Dehm Adlan I observed several women who had an appendage hanging from the lower lip in the shape of a piece of lead several inches long. The teeth, both of men and women, are left unmutilated, the only disfigurement being an artificial separation made between the two central incisors. According to the ordinary fashion of Central Africa, infants at the breast are carried in a girth, similar to a saddle-girth, worn over the shoulders just in the same way as amongst the Monbuttoo women.

Hunting in the neighbouring wildernesses, which cannot extend much less than twenty miles in every direction, and which appear to be entirely void of inhabitants, must be a very productive pursuit. In all my travels I never came across such numerous and abundant hunting-trophies as here amongst the homesteads of the Sehre; they were contrived out of branches of trees resting one against another and self-supported like the guns of soldiers in camp, and were crowded with the skulls and horns of animals that the natives had secured. Hundreds of buffalo-horns, including a surprising number of those of the females, were attached to the structures which stood in front of well-nigh every hut, and were as numerous as though hunter vied with hunter in his separate display. Every variety of horn was represented: intermingled with the buffalo-horns were those of the eland-antelope, the water-bock, the harte-beest, and the bastard-gemsbock, whilst skulls of wart-hogs, and occasionally even skulls of lions, were not wanting to help adorn the trophy.

The proprietor of the Seriba happened to be absent on an excursion to the western districts of the Niam-niam, but his Vokeel did his utmost to provide me with a hospitable reception; and, taking into account the impoverishment of the land and the general deficiency of provisions that prevailed, I am bound to award him my best thanks for his courtesy and attention.

Beyond the Kooroo, and just half-way between Dehm Adlan and Dehm Gudyoo, there stands a hill of considerable altitude, named Taya. The whole distance required two days' hard marching to get over, the road being straight through uninterrupted wilderness until it reached the farmsteads of the Kredy sheikh, Gudyoo, on the banks of the Beery.

Shortly after midnight on the 8th of February there arose such a violent storm that I was roused from my sleep, although I was sheltered by one of the best protected of the huts. A complete change of wind ensued, and for the first time this season the south-west wind set in afresh and for some time maintained its position for the greater part of the day. The nights in consequence became so much warmer that any covering for the bed could easily be dispensed with. We tarried here three days, and then started for another three days' march on our return to Bongoland, over a country all but destitute of water, for the Pongo may be described as a river that separates a district full of springs from one that is just as barren of them, although the change in the level of the country comes on so gradually that it can hardly be said to be observable. In the course of our journey we had to cross the three running brooks known as the Ngokurah, the Simmere, and Ngonguli, and to pass by several villages of the Sehre, of which the sheikhs were respectively called Kombo, Villeke, Badja, and Barraga. The last huts and the last water were left behind about four miles after quitting the Pongo, and henceforth water for drinking had to be sought for with considerable trouble, as all the pools and marshes that supplied any were only to be found scattered at wide intervals one from another.

We spent our first night close to the farms of Barraga, a spot which seemed especially remarkable for the clusters of trophies, all covered with the skulls of baboons. Everywhere there seemed to be an extensive cultivation of cassava, a product of the soil that seems hardly known at all to the Bongo. Many things that I saw in their cultivation bore evidence to their comparatively recent

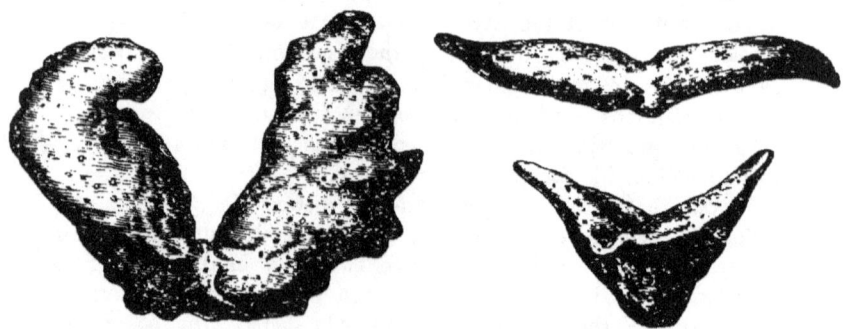

"KARRA," THE MAGIC TUBER.

migration from the country of the Niam-niam. Sweet potatoes were as common as cassava, and in addition to this were the ricinus, the edible solanum of the Niam-niam, here called "dyooyo," and the horse-bean (*Canavalia*), which here bears the name of "nzerahno." I also found a very peculiar creeper, with a double horny or finger-shaped tuber attached to the axils of the leaves, like the edible helmia, to which genus of plants it doubtless belongs. It is transplanted by the natives from the woods and trained in the neighbourhood of the huts, and is known under the name of "karra." I had already noticed this plant in the Kredy villages on the Beery, where I was told that the tubers were very much used as a purgative medicine; but amongst the Niam-niam, who likewise occasionally cultivate it, I heard a different account. There it was said that the tubers are looked upon as a sort of charm, and it is believed that a good show of them upon the leaves is an infallible prediction of a prolific hunting-season. It was, moreover, affirmed that if a huntsman wants to render his bow unerring in its capabilities, he has only to hold it in his hand while he "slaughters" one of the tubers over it, that is, takes a knife and cuts off the end and chops it in pieces.

The first tract that we passed in our still eastward return route was a uniformly thick wood, without any declivity at all in the ground, or anything to indicate that it was ever broken by a watercourse or standing pool of rain. About midday we made a halt at a marshy brook named Kanda, now dry, and set to work to explore the neighbourhood in the hope of discovering some water, for, after a march of eleven miles in the heat, we began to suffer from thirst. After a long search my people succeeded in meeting with a puddly slough, from which the dirty superficies had to be carefully removed in order to get at a little clear water. It was a disgusting swamp, the haunt of buffaloes and wild boars, full of excrements and reeking with filth, a compound of mould and ammonia. It was not until it had been strained through handkerchiefs and well-boiled that the water was purified of its odious smell. Only three miles farther on we had the good luck to find the watercourse of the Telle, overshadowed by thick foliage and running in a tolerably bright stream: a sufficient inducement to make the spot our resting-place for the night.

On the third day of our march we again passed several dry khors that had little pools of water in them, but very inadequate to our needs. In one of these there was lurking a herd of hartebeests, which by the greyish fawn-colour of their winter coats had quite an exceptional appearance. Hundreds of maraboo-storks were congregated around a marshy pond, where they were fishing for snails and worms.

At dinner we were again obliged to put up with the most abominable and revolting of water; our stock of provisions was miserably short, and although I had knocked over a few guinea-fowl, I had neither water in which to boil them, nor grease in which to fry them. In the afternoon we were startled by a storm, which, coming up from the north-east, rolled away towards the south. We endeavoured to get shelter in the wood beneath the thick foliage of the numerous great Lopbira-trees, but it was all in vain; for, after having waited till daylight was waning, we were obliged to proceed in the darkness, and, thoroughly drenched to the skin, marched for a couple of hours till we came to the banks of a rivulet, where we were again overtaken by the rain.

A tedious trying night, spent without a roof over my head, seemed to fill up the cup of bitterness which I was destined to drink upon this tour of privation. In the darkness no grass could be discovered, and on account of the dampness of the atmosphere no fire could be kindled, so that it was entirely without protection from the wet and cold that I had wearily to await the following morning, when, half-perished by exposure, in spite of the continued storm, I resumed my way, now become more arduous than ever, because, as a result of the rain, it had become exceedingly slippery. The rain of this night had been quite an exception, and was very transient; it passed away, and the prevalence of the north wind, during the last three days overpowered by a current from the south-west, was for a time restored.

Never do I recollect having seen a more cheerful little people than the Sehre, if I may judge them by those who acted as my bearers. No mischance, no fatigue, no hunger nor thirst, seemed ever to take the smallest effect upon the happy temperament of these poor negroes. As soon as we halted they began their jokes and pranks. There was not a woe-begone countenance to be seen; groans and sighs were utterly alien to their disposition, and no sooner was their work over, toilsome as it was, than they began to play, like a lot of boys fresh out of school. Sometimes one would pretend to be a wild animal, and was chased by the others; or sometimes they would contrive and carry out some practical joke. Nothing seemed to entertain them more than to act the part of a great clumsy tortoise, and to waddle about on all-fours, accompanying their movements by all kinds of grunting and clacking noises. And all this jocoseness went on while their stomachs were empty. "If we are hungry," they would say, "we sing, and forget it."

We proceeded thirteen miles still eastward from the Telle, and then the wooded country, which had continued in an unbroken succession of thick trees of every variety all the way from the

Pongo, came to an end. It was succeeded by extensive steppes and marshy lowlands, which every here and there were relieved by clusters of Terminaliæ. The lowland was bounded towards the east by a range of hills, the base of which we reached about four miles farther on. The direction of the elevated land lay from the south-east to the north-west.

Deviating now from the east a little more to the north, our route conducted us towards Ngulfala, a Seriba in Bongoland, about fourteen miles away. We had to make our way through a complicated system of rounded caps of gneiss, and to wind round flat-topped hills that gave the district the aspect of being a miniature mountain-chain, the source-land probably of the Ghetty and the watershed between that stream and the Pongo. The rise in the ground was very obvious. The highest of the rounded eminences, named Atyumm, was about 200 feet above our path, and at least 500 feet above the adjacent steppe below; it had a hemispherical form, very like that of Gumango, near Bendo's village, in the Niam-niam country.

Before reaching Ngulfala we had to cross the Ghetty, here a meagre stream, corresponding to the absorbing nature of the soil through which it flows. The distance between the spot and where we had crossed it at Bizelly's Seriba is about forty miles, but the river presented just the same aspect—a broad, deep rift in the earth, with its water almost stationary in its pools. A considerable number of maraboo-storks were seen, either standing upon the banks or dipping into the water-holes for fish and mollusks (*Anodontæ*).

The altitude of the Seriba above the level of the sea was 1905 feet, about 500 lower than Dehm Adlan; but it should be observed that an accidental rise in the ground is made simply by the hill-system of Atyumm, itself nearly 500 feet, so that (without allowing anything for the cutting of the stream) the gradual descent of the land during the thirty or thirty-five miles that it extends eastwards from the Pongo must amount altogether to just about 1000 feet.

The lower level of the soil becomes more obvious still over the next stretch of country. The nearest Seriba in Bongoland, called Moody, belonged, like the one before it, to the possessions of Agahd; and the thirteen or fourteen miles that led us there brought us over a tract of perpetual marshes, the flat steppes that divided them being traversed by five khors that we found perfectly dry. The names of these khors were reported to me as the Mingangah, the

248 THE HEART OF AFRICA.

Bolongoh, the Boddoowee, the Doggolomah, and the Kodda-hirara, of which, if the testimony of my Bongo bearers is to be trusted, the two former take their course northwards to the Ghetty, and the three latter make their way southwards to the Wow.

In Moody I took a day's rest, as I had done in Ngulfala. I required it very much, as I had taken a violent cold, and felt altogether weak and out of sorts. Throughout the time we halted there was a strong north wind blowing, very keen and chilly.

Feeling somewhat better towards evening, I took a short ramble amongst the homesteads of the place. It was here that I came across

A BONGO CONCERT.

the grave of the departed Bongo chief Yanga, with its monumental erection, of which I have already given an illustration, vol. i. p. 129.

The Bongo here seemed to show a remarkable originality in their contrivances. In their huts I was continually finding some furniture or implements which in other parts of the country had long become obsolete. The variety of their musical instruments, as I have described them in the chapter devoted to their manners and customs, is very great, and to exemplify the use of them, I may here introduce a sketch which represents four young men whom I saw in Moody, and who had met together to while away the evening by performing quartets.

The controller at Moody was in possession of a couple of caracal-lynxes, which he had caught when they were quite young, and which he was training, intending to send them when full-grown to Khartoom. One of the Bongo men was employed in attending to them, and in order to keep them supplied with food he was obliged to spend the greater portion of his time in catching rats. He used to bring them home, tied up in dozens, from the banks of the neighbouring river-course. These rats were of a reddish-brown colour, with white bellies, and were called "luny" by the Bongo; except that they are smaller in size, they are very like what we know as "Norway rats." They are never found except in the proximity of water, and in every respect but in colour appear to be undistinguishable from those which infest the huts and granaries. Whether the Norway rats in their dispersion have ever reached as far as these remote districts is a question that I cannot answer, as the investigation of the specimens I brought with me was not completed.

Two leagues to the south-east of Moody lies a subsidiary Seriba of Kurshook Ali's, named Moddu-Mahah; and three leagues farther on in the same direction is the chief Seriba of Hassaballa, known amongst the Bongo as Gellow. This is situated on the hither side of the Wow, and at no great distance from it. The narrow strip of land between the Wow and the Dyoor contains at least half-a-dozen smaller Seribas, which lie along the route to the Bellanda, and which belong partly to Kurshook Ali and partly to Hassaballa.

The little Seriba Moody, together with all its huts, was overshadowed by a single fig-tree, of such enormous growth that it was quite a magnificent example of the development to which that tree may attain. It belonged to the species named the *Ficus lutea*, the mbehry of the Bongo. It was not that the height of the stem of this giant of Moody was very excessive; the remarkable growth displayed itself rather in the prodigious thickness and spreading habits of the powerful arms, every one of which was so massive that it might stand a comparison with the stoutest of our pines and firs. The peculiar bark only appears on parts of the stem; its colour is light grey, and, like that of the plane, it is scored with diagonal lines. All the boughs, right up to the highest, are furnished with external pendent roots, that hang in the air like a huge beard; they encompass the trunk of the tree with a regular network, like rope and string.

A singular story was associated with this noble tree at Moody, and I found the entire population of the Seriba still under the influence of the astonishment and alarm that had only recently been excited. It appeared that one of the great branches, having become worm-eaten and decayed, had fallen to the ground, and as it fell would inevitably have utterly smashed a contiguous hut if it had tumbled in any other direction than it did. This fall of the huge bough was attributed by the Nubians to the direct agency of an "evil eye," which it was alleged had been directed against the tree by a soldier who had happened to be passing through the place the day before my arrival. Just as usual the people had been collected in front of their huts under shade of the tree, when the man in question, pointing significantly to the bough, said, "That bough up there is quite rotten; it would be a bad business if it were to come tumbling down upon your heads." No sooner said than done. The words were hardly out of the fellow's mouth before there was a prodigious cracking and creaking, and down came the huge branch with a crash to the ground. There lay the fragments. I heard the testimony from the very lips of eye-witnesses, and what could I say?

It took us two days more to accomplish our return journey to Wow. The chief Seriba of Agahd's company lay to the north-east of Moody, and, allowing for a slight deviation from the direct route, was about thirty-five miles distant. The country was clothed with light bushwood, but in no part did it exhibit anything like the same richness of foliage as the western lands that we had left behind. We had to pass over two low-lying marsh-districts, Katyirr and Dumburre, where, hidden amongst the tall, half-withered grass, we found several cavities filled by springs of water. At Dumburre we came across traces of a deserted settlement, which, according to the statements of the Bongo of my party, were the remains of the very earliest Seriba that had been established in the land. Our night was spent upon the borders of a marshy stream called the Moll, and was very uncomfortable on account of a heavy north-east gale which blew from ten o'clock.

The dogs that were with me were kept in a constant state of excitement by the perpetual rushing that went on in the bushwood, and it was impossible to restrain them from scampering off into the darkness, and carrying on a hunting game on their own account.

All through the night they kept running in and out of the camp, very often returning bespattered with blood. A farther indication of the abundance of wild animals that existed in the neighbourhood was afforded by the continual howling of hyenas, which, in a manner that was quite unusual, kept us disturbed all through the night.

For our supper that evening we had had a couple of fine reed-rats, measuring just twenty-one inches from their snouts to the root of the tail. Before leaving Dumburre I had had a small steppe-burning of my own. By the help of my bearers, who were set to the work of beating the bush, I had quite an interesting hunt, the produce of which had been two zebra-ichneumons and the two far-el-boos (reed-rats), which had been carried with us in triumph to the camp.

Beyond the Moll we entered upon a hilly region, the ground being much broken by scattered shrubs. On both sides of the pathway lines of red rocky hills emerged in the distance, varied occasionally by flats and rounded projections of the ever-abundant gneiss. The next watercourse to which we came was the Dabohlo, a marshy spot, but now nearly dry, upon which we could discern the traces of a large number of buffaloes. Here, also, we had a very prolific *battue* of guinea-fowl; for the early morning hours had tempted them to collect by hundreds around the little puddles which were left standing every here and there within the limits of the marsh.

Far as the eye could reach there was nothing to be seen but a gently-sloping steppe, entirely void of trees, which it took the bearers 3000 paces to get over; but this accomplished, we reached a depression in the same marsh-lands (now, however, perfectly dry) that were relieved in various places by groups of Terminaliæ. Beyond this the ground began to take a considerable ascent, the valley upon the far east being bounded by a range of hills that ran from south-east to north-west; and the rise continued through the four remaining miles that brought us to the Seriba.

Thus, after forty-nine days' absence, and numbering 876,000 paces in the interval, I again returned to the quarters of my good friend Khalil. While I had been away he had, for my special accommodation, most considerately erected some new and pretty huts in which I was very pleased to spend the remainder of my sojourn.

CHAPTER XVI.

Tidings of war—Hunting on the Dyoor—Reed-rats—Transport of corn—Dyoor fishing—River-oysters—Ignorance of the Soudanese—Change of weather—An execution—Return to Ghattas's Seriba—Allagabo—Start to the Meshera—Strange evolutions of antelopes—Cattle-raids—Traitors among the natives—Needless alarm—Remains of old Shol—Lepers on board—Ambiguous slave-dealing—Down the Gazelle—A horrible night—A false alarm—Taken in tow—The Mudir's camp—Crowded boats—Confiscation of slaves—A pleasant surprise—Slave-caravans on the bank—Arrival in Khartoom—Telegram to Berlin—Seizure of my servants—Remonstrance with the Governor-General—Mortality in the fever season—Tikkitikki's death—Θάλαττα, θάλαττα.

THE first boats had reached the Meshera early in the year, and the number of soldiers in the Seriba kept continually increasing by the arrival of fresh contingents from Khartoom. Their arrival gave new life to the Seribas; friends and relatives who had not met for years exchanged greetings and recounted mutual experiences, whilst news from Khartoom was eagerly circulated and as eagerly received.

For myself there was a collection of little notes sent by a friend at Khartoom that could not do otherwise than excite my keenest interest. They were six months old, but not the less on that account did they stimulate my curiosity: in them I read, in sentences that were almost as brief as telegrams, of the startling events of the previous autumn. Naturally I turned to my letters from home, hoping to gather further particulars of the strange occurrences that had thus been partially unfolded, but I found that these letters had all been written a year ago, whilst peace still prevailed throughout Europe, and that they only referred to ordinary and commonplace topics. So incomplete, therefore, were the intimations that I received of all that had transpired since November 1869, that the events all remained an enigma to me which I could very imperfectly comprehend. It is true that I had come across slave-traders in the west who had recently arrived overland from Khartoom, and who had plenty to tell of what was going on in the Soudan, but not a syllable fell from their lips about the great war of the Franks, for who besides myself was interested in the least in the fall of the Emperor of the French, or who cared either to hear or to relate the victories of the Germans? Although when I visited Khartoom many months had elapsed since the fall of Magdala, yet near as it was to the seat of war, the intelligence of the Abyssinian campaign even then had scarcely reached the town.

Meagre as were the details of my latest intelligence, it may be imagined that they roused me to the greatest excitement, so that it was with the most feverish expectation that I awaited the arrival of a son of Kurshook Ali, who would bring definite tidings as to whether there was peace or war in Europe.

As it had been my intention to return home immediately after my Niam-niam tour, I had given no orders in the previous year for any quantity of fresh stores to be sent me from Khartoom; consequently the boats that now arrived had brought me nothing beyond the few articles that I knew would be necessary on my passage down the river; these inconsiderable things, meanwhile, had been left at the Meshera; but after the hardships of the last few months, I felt that the possession of the merest trifles would be an incalculable boon to me.

The two months that I spent in Khalil's huts were passed almost entirely in hunting. Not only was the abundance of game about the valley of the Dyoor a great inducement to sport, but such was my nervous condition that continual exertion was the only thing that made my life endurable. I found walking to be the best antidote to depression and the most effectual remedy for headache and languor: and it was only during the hours that I passed in the wilderness that any of my former energy returned. Whenever I found myself within the walls of my hut I was conscious of nothing but weariness and dejection and was only fit for lounging on my bed; it was but rarely that my love of sketching from nature in any degree diverted me or gave me its wonted amusement.

Khalil had lent me a capital gun, a weapon specially suited for antelope-shooting, that did me good service. During the months of March and April I brought down as many as five-and-twenty head of the larger kinds of game, including amongst them specimens of nearly all the different species of antelopes that the fauna of the country could boast. The number of caama and leucotis antelopes appeared little short of inexhaustible. The flesh of the leucotis served as a substitute for beef and mutton, both of which at that time were exceedingly scarce in all the Seribas. I had no butter or lard of any description, but the meat was very palatable when simply boiled in water. The lean goats' meat, with its soapy flavour, was the only alternative, and that after a while became utterly loathsome to me. For a long time I had had no vegetables at my meals, and indeed for months I had lived without any vegetable diet at all with the exception of some sorghum cakes.

I was informed that the end of February was the best time of the year for hunting reed-rats (*Aulacodus Swinderianus*). Accordingly

HUNTING REED-RATS.

one day I arranged an excursion to the Dyoor, and, engaging a number of natives who were used to the sport to bring their lances and to beat up the game, I set off under their guidance to the spot that they considered the most promising. At that season of the year, when all the grass was so thoroughly dry, it did not seem as though it could be a matter of much difficulty to kill almost unlimited numbers of these reed-rats, if only they could be got at; and so in fact it proved.

As soon as a spot is discovered frequented by the animals, a ring of the tall grass is set alight, so that escape is rendered impossible, and every one of the poor brutes within the circle of flame is compelled to show itself. The reed-rats invariably keep in concealment until the very last moment, and when finally they make an attempt to escape they get their feet so scorched and their coats so singed that it is very difficult to secure a perfect specimen; they are in this respect like the wild hares of the deserts, which are subject to the delusion that however close at hand their pursuers may be, they may still be safe by remaining quiet in their hiding-places; as soon as they are obliged to quit them they get killed by stones and clubs. In many parts where the grass that had survived the steppe-burning was unusually thick, the Dyoor had only to thrust in their spears at random and they had every chance of spearing one of the reed-rats. The case is pretty much the same in the various pools full of fish left by the subsidence of the river.

The Aulacodus finds a habitat in all the tropical regions of the continent; it is ordinarily found in the neighbourhood of brooks and rivers, burying itself in deep holes amidst the reeds; when, however, it is in search of its food it will wander away to a considerable distance from its place of concealment, and thus allow the hunters a chance of killing it. The larger rivers are the natural channels for the wanderings of the creature, its movements in the water being assisted by its hind feet being furnished with webs.

A full-grown reed-rat is never less than twenty inches in length, but a third of this must be assigned to the rat-like tail, which is coated over with thin hair, nearly black on the top and light grey underneath. The snout, throat, breast, and belly are covered with hair almost as prickly as the bristles of a young hedgehog, light grey in colour; on the back and sides the colour is shaded down to a brownish hue, that is to say, the grey hairs are tipped with a lightish tan-brown. In February the half-grown animals shed their bristles and acquire an entirely new coat. The skin is about an eighth of an inch thick, but is quite soft, and may easily be torn; it is lined with a uniform layer of fat. The meat is excellent when roasted; it is rich, and without being sweet and, insipid like that of the rock rabbit, it is free from any unpleasant flavour; in quality it is about equal to poultry, whilst in taste it may be described as being intermediate between veal and pork. As a cloven-footed animal, without horns and non-ruminant, the Nubians of course consider it to be unclean; but the Mohammedans of the steppes and deserts are not so scrupulous; to the Baggara and the Foorians a roast reed-rat is as great a delicacy as a hare is to the Bishareen and Hadendoa.

Tikkitikki, armed with his bow and arrows, was an eager participator in our sport. He declared that reed-rats are never found in the land of the Monbuttoo, but are perfectly well known to all the

FAR-EL-BOOS. (*Aulacodus Swinderianus.*)

Niam-niam, who call them "remooh," or "alimooh." In common with many other Africans, the Niam-niam often adopt the practice of burying their stores of ivory (either as a protection from the disasters of war or from the chance of fire) in the damp soil of the swamps, which are the haunts of the Aulacodus; the ivory forms just the substance that meets the requirements of the animal for sharpening and grinding down its front teeth, and consequently gets gnawed in every direction.

Khalil required 300 bearers to convey his stores from the Meshera, but as these could not be collected in a day, and as the prevailing scarcity made it impossible to maintain any others beyond the soldiers that were already in the Seribas, the new-comers were turned out to pick up what they could for themselves from amongst the neighbouring Dinka until the entire troop could be got together. A good many days elapsed before the great caravan was complete; and, in the meantime, the soldiers who had already started were having continual conflicts with the Dinka, who were resolved not to part with their corn without a struggle.

On the 4th of March, 200 of Ghattas's Bongo bearers arrived at the Seriba on their way to carry corn to the Turkish camp. All their loads put together would hardly have amounted to twenty ardebs. Hopelessly stupid are the people; it roused my indignation to think how, in spite of the hard and level roads that were established during the dry seasons, they had never introduced a single vehicle of any description into the country. Thirty hand-barrows or three bullock-waggons would have amply sufficed to convey the whole of the corn, and yet they employed these 200 bearers, who during the twenty-four days that they would be on their journey to their destination and back, would, at the very lowest computation, consume as much as forty ardebs of durra, just double the quantity they had to deliver. The extortions of the Government are thus, in the course of the year, three or four times as great as they need be; the troops may require some 600 ardebs of corn, but in procuring this, at least another 600 ardebs would be wasted, to say nothing about the reckless and lavish expenditure of time and strength which is thrown away upon the proceedings. I cannot help repeating these details, in order to show to what a senseless system of robbery these negro-countries are exposed as soon as ever they come within the grasp of Mohammedan rule.

In March the natives employ themselves in fishing. Towards the middle of the month the numerous backwaters and swamp-channels that have been left by the Dyoor are separated into independent basins by means of dams; they may be seen thrown up in all directions across the intricate ramifications of the water; when these basins have been thoroughly drained, the fish are left lying above, or just embedded in the mud and slime, and may easily be taken with the hand. All the inhabitants of the district were in some measure concerned in the fishing of the Dyoor, and it afforded me a pleasant diversion, when I was out on my hunting-excursions, to stop awhile and watch the artifices by which they contrive to entrap the fish.

At the part of the river which, being deep, was frequented by hippopotamuses, the right-hand bank was more than fifteen feet high, and rose perpendicularly from the water; the upper section of the soil of the bank was a ferruginous clay which went down to a depth of eight feet, below which was a broad white stripe some four feet thick, resting upon the gneiss that apparently was the substratum of the entire alluvium of the river-valley. The white stripe of the soil had a chalky look, and contained fragments of quartz; it consisted of a crumbling product of felspar, such as may frequently be seen, under similar circumstances, in the hollows of other river-courses and brooks throughout the country.

In all parts of the dry sandy bed may be found the shells of the river-oyster (*Etheria Cailliaudii*), which is wanting in none of the affluents of the Upper Nile, and is known to the Niam-niam as the "mohperre." In the deeper parts of the bed of the Dyoor these oysters exist in groups, adhering firmly to blocks of swamp-ore that, having become detached from the top of the banks, have fallen into the river, and so are permanently under water. The flavour of this mollusk is rather sweet and mawkish, and to me particularly unpleasant.

On the 20th, my temporary abode was very considerably enlivened by the arrival of Soliman, the owner of the Seriba, the eldest son of the late Kurshook Ali. He was quite a young man, and entirely inexperienced in the management of the extensive property that he had recently inherited from his father.

With much pleasure I still remember my first meeting with Soliman, and can yet recall the eager curiosity with which I turned the conversation to the position of the European Powers. As he was the chief of a great mercantile firm, and consequently associated with the more educated class of Khartoomers, I quite hoped that he would be able to give me some decisive political intelligence; but all the information that I could obtain from him was that when he left Khartoom in January, no announcement of peace had reached that town.

Old Khalil, who had never been out of the negro-countries for fifteen years, was just as ignorant of political matters as the lowest of his countrymen; not only had he to ask what was the name of the Governor-General of Khartoom, but he seemed to be quite unconscious that Egypt was in any degree an independent country. Most of the people were quite unacquainted with the name of the Khedive in power, and I heard some of them ask what was the name of the Pasha in Cairo; of one thing, however, they said they were perfectly sure, namely, that Abdul Aziz was the sovereign who ruled over all the believers, and that all the kings of the Franks were his vassals; it was true, they confessed, that the Emperor of Moscow, some years ago, had the audacity to pretend that he was independent; but now, thanks to the fidelity of the great Sultan's vassals, he was very glad to eat humble-pie, just as it had happened before with Buonaparte, the "Sultan-el-Kebir."

Such was the ignorance of the Soudanese; and the few sentences that I have recorded will serve for an epitome of their political knowledge. When they heard me talking to Soliman about peace and war in the land of the Franks, they wanted to learn what sort of people the Prussians (the "Borusli") were. Soliman answered them with the greatest *naïveté*. He described Prussia as a "country with very few people," meaning to imply that it was about the smallest of the great Powers. "And have these few people," they went on to inquire, "made the great Emperor of the Franks a prisoner? Do you mean that they have taken the Emperor, whose likeness is stamped on all the gold money?" "Oh, yes," answered Soliman, "he was a big rascal; and Heaven has rewarded him according to his deserts."

It was on the 30th of March that the people arrived from the Meshera, and no one can tell how delighted I was to get the few stores that had been sent me from Khartoom. Provided as I was with a new stock of paper, I again set about my botanical work, which had so long been suspended, and renewed my investigations with redoubled ardour; it was the opening of the third spring-tide in which it had been my singular happiness to gather the tribute of Central Africa to lay upon the altar of science. The period of my return to Europe was getting near, and I was eager to make a collection of all the bulbs and tubers that I could; I was careful to dig them up before they had thrown out any of their fresh shoots, and was very successful in procuring a large number, which I deposited in Berlin in a state of perfect vitality; amongst them were many are plants, and particularly some specimens of the *Cycadeæ* from the country of the Niam-niam. In consequence, however, either of the defective construction of the plant-houses, or of the inexperience of the gardeners, many of these subsequently died.

The meteorological events of 1871 deviated in some degree from their normal rule. The seasons were not at all sharply defined, as they had been in the two preceding years. Through March there was a perpetual struggle between directly contrary winds; first the north-east wind contended violently with the south-east wind, and only desisted to commence a conflict just as furious with the south-west. About the middle of the month the days were extremely hot, and the dominant north-east wind raged with almost the intensity of a simoom, that threatened to convert the land into a desert. On two separate days there were some slight showers, but the first heavy rain was that which fell on the 31st. In April there were six slight falls, and four very heavy falls, of rain, the south-west wind being generally prevalent, although there were several days when the rude, rough Boreas still struggled vehemently for the mastery. In May there were five showery days and three that were thoroughly wet.

The reappearance, for the first time, of various plants and animals marked, as it were, the separate stages of the advancing season, and prompted me to make a sort of farmer's calendar of the different events. It was on the 16th that the wind suddenly veered to the south-east and some drops of rain fell, the first that had occurred since the passing shower on the 11th of February. The direction of the wind seemed now to be settled, and in the course of the night I heard a cricket chirping on the grass. Before many days had past the cicadas put in an appearance, and in the middle of the day the air resounded with their shrill tones, clear almost as the ring of metal. At the beginning of April the humidity of the atmosphere rapidly increased, whilst the heat remained intense, the average temperature being not less than 81° Fahr. This unhealthy concurrence of hot atmosphere with damp had the effect of bringing out an angry eruption all over my body, causing an irritation so violent that my rest at night was completely destroyed.

The 3rd of April, three days after the first decidedly heavy rain, is noted in my register as being the first day upon which the floor of my hut was covered with those uncomfortable visitors which never wait for a welcome; I mean particularly those strange *Arachnidæ*, the Galeodes (or scorpion-spiders), with their great venomous mandibles, and the whole family of scorpions proper. My poor negroes were terribly punished by them, and from head to foot there was not a portion of their body that enjoyed immunity from their attacks. It was after a very heavy rainfall that, on the evening of the 18th, I saw the first winged white ants (sexual males) issue from the clay pyramid of their "gontoor."

AN EXECUTION.

Towards the middle of the month the stores of corn were so nearly exhausted that Khalil was obliged to decline showing any hospitality to the Gellahbas that passed through the Seriba. Soliman himself was compelled to quit the place, and his old Vokeel took a trip to his Bongo Seribas to gather together what additional supplies he could. For myself, I was suffering privation almost as severe as I had endured in the previous May upon the shores of the Nabambisso, on some days being unable to obtain a single handful of durra-corn; still, distressing as my condition was, I could not at once make up my mind to retrace my steps to Ghattas's head Seriba. I was quite aware that I should be better off there for provisions than anywhere else, but the disaster of the 2nd of December had left such an impression upon my mind that the very name of the place was hateful to me; and I felt that I should for my own part much prefer to drag out four months in a starving Seriba and a barren wilderness, rather than enjoy meat and milk at the cost of residing amidst the scenes of my disappointment and misfortune.

One day, just about this time, a former Bongo chief, who had escaped to the mountains on the southern frontier, was captured after a long pursuit, and brought back by Kurshook Ali's people to the Scriba. He had clandestinely murdered many of the Nubians, and had instigated the natives to revolt against their conquerors. His condemnation and execution now followed forthwith. I heard nothing of the matter until it was all over, but my negroes, who had been witnesses of the whole proceeding, gave it as their opinion that the punishment was well-deserved. They described to me the mode of carrying out the sentence. The delinquent, they said, had been taken out a considerable distance into the forest, dragging after him a long sheyba that was fastened to his neck; all at once he had been felled to the ground by a tremendous blow, directed just below the knees, from one of those huge swords four feet long that have been made for centuries at Solingen near Düsseldorf, and are still manufactured for the especial use of the African Bedouins and Arabs; two more heavy blows had then cut off his arms; and last of all, the attack had been levelled at his head, which was hacked, rather than cleanly severed, from his body.

There are always to be found in this country those who are singularly dexterous in the use of the swords that I have mentioned. They use them for performing amputations in their own barbarous way. If mortification from an ulcer or any other cause seems to be setting in, so that a hand or a foot is deemed incurable, the limb is fastened to a block of wood, and with one blow of the sword the part affected is severed almost within a hair's breadth of the part that is sound. Instances far from unfrequent have been known where the sufferers have had the fortitude to perform the operation, hazardous as it is, upon themselves. The custom is of great antiquity amongst the Arabs, and probably is not to be disassociated from the ancient Gospel precept, "If thy right hand offend thee, cut it off, and cast it from thee."

Reluctant as I was, I found myself compelled at last to yield to the urgent solicitations of my hungry Bongo and to set off for Ghattas's Seriba. We started on the 21st. We found the Dyoor, which had risen during the last few days, somewhat subsiding again, but the whole breadth of the bed was still covered with water, although only two and a half feet deep; in the two previous years it had not begun to rise until a fortnight later. Aboo Guroon's Seriba was just in the same miserable condition of want as the district we had left, and we found the natives eagerly engaged in collecting the bitter berries of certain kinds of the Capparideæ, of which, after soaking them repeatedly in boiling water, they manage to make a sort of pap. The berry of *Boxia octandra* is likewise used for a similar purpose, having being first dried in the sun to remove the astringent cotyledons, and then pounded in a mortar.

As we continued our journey, we could not be otherwise than surprised at the large flocks of maraboo-storks that we saw congregated amidst the burnt grass in the low steppes adjacent to the bed of the Molmul: most probably they were searching for the bodies of the snakes, lizards, and mice that had been killed in the recent conflagration.

With the 4th of May came the commencement of the general sowing of crops; men's hearts revived, and they began to anticipate happier times.

Ghattas's granaries still contained some corn; and a small number of cattle, the residue of his once enormous herds, was yet to be seen in his farmyard. But, in spite of my sense of these material comforts, the crowded Seriba was most repulsive to me: changed indeed it was in a way; but in its essential character it had remained true to its old composition. Certain it was that the swarms of rats that had infested the huts and undermined the soil had been all but exterminated by the fire; the crowds of red-headed lizards (*Agamas*) that used to frisk up and down the old rotten palisade were no longer to be seen; the horned beetles (*Scarabæus nasicornus*) and their grubs, that had once covered every dung-heap, were totally annihilated; it was man alone who was unchanged, and the same revolting forms, infected with syphilis, scabs and boils, were spreading their putrid miasma around. Tottering along betwixt the crooked, tumble-down straw-hedges and amidst the heaps of garbage and of refuse might still be seen the wretched fever-stricken beings, with shorn heads covered with scabs and every limb a mass of festering matter; everywhere prevailed the moaning and groaning of a lingering death; the people were not so much what they were accustomed to call themselves and each other in their curses, " dogs and the sons of dogs," they were rather sons of *dirt*, born and bred in an atmosphere of abscess and corruption.

I found my former garden ragged and barren as a wilderness; the only surviving memorials of what it had been were the tomatoes flourishing persistently upon the fertile soil, and the sunflowers that gloried in the tropical sun. Some of the sunflowers rose in great pyramids of foliage to a height of over ten feet, and with their huge disks of blossom ever turned towards the full glare of light, presented an appearance that was very striking. In this strange world their splendour could not but irresistibly attract me, and I often sat down on the ground before them, and, while gazing on their brightness recalled the fading memories of the past and conjured up anew the recollections of my distant travels, looking back upon the scenes I had passed, as a traveller looking through the back window of his carriage might take a retrospect of the country he had left behind.

In order to obtain a short reprieve from my melancholy and unpleasant surroundings and to finish up with a few days' quiet enjoyment of nature, I resolved, towards the end of May, to take a farewell trip to Geer, and so to pay a parting visit to the Bongo. I had become quite attached to this people, and had determined to take a Bongo boy back with me to Europe. My young *protégé* was named Allagabo.* He seemed to me to be sharper and quicker in ability than many of his race, even of those who were considerably older than himself; and I intended him accordingly to be properly educated; his family lived in Geer, and whilst I was there I received various visits from his father, uncle, and aunt, to all of whom I

---

* Allagabo is the Arabic rendering of the Greek Theodore (gift of God); by the Dinka the lad was called "Teem," *i.e.* "a tree," because his native name was "Lebbe," which is the Bongo word for a species of mimosa.

made what presents I could, and immortalised them in my portfolio. They no longer exercised any right over Allagabo, as he had been stolen from his home a long time before by the Dinka, and disposed of by them to the controller of the Seriba in exchange for some cattle. The boy's good fortune was quite a matter of congratulation to his relatives, as they were fully convinced he would lead a much happier life with me than he could possibly expect in his own savage home. His mother, some years previously, after one of the regular cattle-exchanges, had been carried off as a slave to Khartoom; she was the only one of his relations for whom Allagabo had any yearning, and later, when he had grown accustomed to his European life and begun to confide in me, he used to tell me that the image of his mother haunted him in his dreams and hovered over him with tears in her eyes. I made many inquiries for her in Khartoom, but never succeeded in learning anything about her. For his father Allagabo had little affection or respect. When I was making presents I had noticed that he was always urging me to hand my gifts by preference to his uncle, saying that his father did not deserve them, and upon my asking him the reason, he told me that once during the time when he was suffering from one of the diseases of childhood, his father had been utterly indifferent to his condition, but that his uncle had helped to nurse him with the greatest tenderness.

The appearance of the first new moon after my return from my pleasant little trip was saluted with the usual nonsensical firing of guns, which threatened to cause a disaster similar to that over which I have already poured out my Jeremiad. It was the same old story; bullets were whizzing and whirring in all directions, when one of the straw-roofs took fire; the flames were extinguished with much difficulty, and before any very serious damage had been done, but my powers of endurance were exhausted; I would not abide the chance of further repetition of the peril, and insisted upon preparations being at once taken in hand for sending off the boats to Khartoom.

An accidental circumstance favoured my design. Intelligence had casually reached me that Abdel Mesih, a son of Ghattas, was making a tour amongst the eastern Seribas of the Rohl, and intended very shortly to come on to us. To me the information was very opportune, as it gave me a handle, which I did not fail to use, to induce Idrees, our controller, to hurry on his movements in my behalf. I made him understand how much worse it would be for him if Abdel Mesih should arrive before I had taken my departure; for most certainly if I had the chance I should report upon the negligence that had caused the burning-down of the Scriba, and should demand compensation for all my losses. The consequences, I warned him, would be that his master would at once remove him from his post, and that he would have to go back to his place in Khartoom a poor beggarly slave. My threats answered their purpose admirably; they put Idrees into a frightful state of alarm; he lost no time in pushing matters forward, and on the 4th of June everything was ready for the march to the Meshera.

Our party consisted of fifty soldiers and rather more than 300 bearers. We started along our former road to the north-east, through the low-lying country of the Dinka, which I had previously traversed during the month of March; but so advanced was the season that the whole region now presented quite a new aspect. Bulbous plants of every variety shed their enlivening hues over the splendid plains, which were adorned by noble trees, park-like in their groupings. There was a descent in the land, but it was scarcely perceptible. We were only aware that we were approaching the limits of the rocky soil, when, on emerging from the bush, we saw stretching far before us the first great steppe that marked the commencement of the Dinka country. Scattered at intervals over the plain were some very remarkable groves. These were not only singularly compact, but their outline was as sharply defined as if it had been drawn by compasses, each cluster seeming to form itself around some unusually tall tree that was a common centre for the rest. The fantastic forms of the wild Phœnix and the candelabra-Euphorbia were the most conspicuous amidst these striking groups.

Our first night-camp was pitched at a deserted murah belonging to the Ayarr tribe. The deep holes that remained where wells had formerly been sunk, allowed us to make a very interesting inspection of the character of the soil; we had advanced exactly 7000 paces from the extremity of the rock, and on looking into the holes I could see that the ferruginous swamp-ore was here covered by a homogeneous layer of grey sandy soil, ten feet in thickness. These steppes are scarcely at all above the level of the Gazelle,* and, consequently, from July to the end of the rainy season they are con-

* The barometer gave an altitude of 1396 feet here, and about the same at two other points on our route to the Meshera, but as these were only single readings I cannot vouch for their accuracy. Readings at the Meshera taken in 1869, and repeated in 1871, gave 1452 feet as the height there.

stantly under water; traces of the inundation were apparent in the empty shells of the water-snail (*Ampullaria*) that were scattered about, and in the pools I found some of the little tortoises (*Pelomedusa gehafie*, Rüpp.) that have their home in the Gazelle itself.

On the following day we crossed the territory of the Dwuihr; the country retained the same character of level steppe broken by clumps of trees, but in consequence of the recent showers the roads in parts had become quite marshy. There were many detached huts scattered about.

As we advanced, our attention was attracted by a herd of hartebeests sporting together scarcely 500 paces from our path, and apparently quite unconscious of the proximity of a caravan nearly half a league in length. So regular were their evolutions as almost to suggest the idea that they were being guided by some invisible hand; they ran in couples like the horses in a circus, and kept going round and round a clump of trees, whilst the others stood in groups of three or four intently watching them; after a time these in turn took their place, and, two at a time, ran their own circuit in the same fashion. How long these movements might have continued I cannot say; but my dogs soon afterwards made a dash in amongst the antelopes and sent them flying in all directions. The circumstance that I have now related may appear somewhat incredible; but I can only say that I had ample time to witness it, and that I was as much surprised at it as my readers can possibly be. I can only imagine, in explanation, that it was pairing-time, and that the animals were blind to all external danger.

I remembered that I had witnessed something similar, three months previously upon the Dyoor. A party of three of us were rambling over a plain covered with short grass, when we saw two little Hegoleh-bocks (*A. Madoqua*) chasing each other upon one side of us; they kept up that peculiar grunting that belongs to their kind; a moment after, and they were on the other side of us; in another moment they were back again; and by watching them we found that they kept making a circle round the spot on which we were standing, and, although we shouted and tried to scare them, they persisted in twice more performing their circuit about us.

Our next task was to cross a swampy brook overgrown with the Habbas-mimosa, and the Bongo bearers made a diversion in the day's proceedings by instituting a *battue* in the long steppe-grass, in which they succeeded in killing four ichneumons.

The following section of our march was through bush-thickets abundant in pools; and to judge by the numerous traces that we noticed, it must have been a district that was much frequented by elephants.

The ever-recurring swamps seriously impeded our third morning's march, which was across the forest of the Alwady. The first villages that we reached belonged to the district of Teng Teng; here we deviated from the road that led directly towards the Meshera, and turned eastwards through more populous parts, hoping that provisions for the large troop of bearers might be foraged up with less difficulty. The natives, according to their wont, withdrew as we approached, so that, although the region was really well cultivated and thoroughly inhabited, it was now quite deserted; and the large murah belonging to a Dinka chief named Dal Kurdyook was reduced to a condition hardly better than a wilderness, except that the well-kept soil was covered with some hundreds of the great wooden pegs that are used for tethering the cattle.

Hardly was the baggage down from off the bearers' backs before the command was issued for a cattle-raid. Off and away was every one who had arms to carry. Unless meat could be had, the bearers must starve. There was no corn left; and as to grubbing in the earth for roots, the days' journeys were far too arduous to permit any extra fatigue for such a purpose. Meat must be got.

It was a strange sensation, and sufficiently unpleasant, to find myself left alone with my few helpless servants in the deserted murah; the Dinka might fall upon us at any moment; and against their thousands what chance had we? In the course, however, of little more than an hour my suspense was at an end. The marauders had made good use of their time, and now came back in triumph with fifteen cows and 200 sheep and goats. The leader of the band had the reputation of being one of the most adroit hands at cattle-stealing that the Khartoom companies had ever had in their service, seeming to put his party, almost by instinct, upon the right track for securing their prey. His experience made him quite aware that the bulk of the herds had all been cleared far away from the murahs and despatched to the most inaccessible of the swamps of the Tondy; they had had twenty-four hours' start, and it was useless for a caravan, with its own baggage to look after, to think of going in pursuit of them. Still, one thing was certain; although all the large herds were gone, yet there must have been cows with their calves that were left behind for the support of the households that were in hiding close in the neighbourhood; against these the plot was laid, and succeeded by a very simple stratagem. The marauders marched out a little way to the south, turned short off into the forest, and then, having arranged themselves in a semicircle embracing the murah, proceeded in unbroken line right through the bush, driving everything before them. The result was, that within half a league of the place of encampment the whole of the reserve of Dal Kurdyook's cows, as well as other animals, fell into the hands of Ghattas's people. A portion of the sheep and goats was spared to be driven onwards with us to the Meshera, but all the rest were slain and consumed offhand the very night on which they were captured. Such a wholesale slaughter, or such a lavish feasting, as took place in Dal Kurdyook's murah I never witnessed before or since. When we took our departure on the following morning the layer of white ashes that covered the ground was literally dyed with the blood of the victims.

On the fourth day of our march, at a spot near the residence of Kudy, we re-entered our former road. The country was alternately wood and cultivated land. It was enlivened by numerous hamlets, and altogether, although it was neither rocky nor undulated, it had a general aspect, to which the detached clumps of trees contributed, not unlike Bongoland.

Kudy was a Dinka chief, a close ally of Ghattas's marauders, and one of those characters, not uncommon in Central Africa, who have gained an inglorious notoriety for their treachery and infidelity to their own countrymen. How he managed to maintain his position in the place after his confederates had taken their departure, I cannot imagine, as his authority did not in the least extend beyond the immediate vicinity. The incidental meeting of our party with their ally of course put it into their heads to set out on another cattle-raid, and Kudy was appointed to the command. He had only to lead them out for a couple of leagues to the south-west of his residence to a region where Ghattas some years ago maintained a Seriba, and the object was effectually accomplished. Quite early in the day they came back with an immense number of sheep and goats, and nearly every bearer had a kid upon his shoulders. The quantity of corn, however, was very insignificant. Everything was done in the quietest way possible; there was not the least excitement. The people were so accustomed to these raids that the execution of them was quite a matter of routine.

On the following morning we reached the murah of Take, another Dinka chief, and while we made a halt our people effected yet another raid. Just as on the previous day, the produce in the way of corn was next to nothing, but large numbers both of goats and sheep were driven in, the whole of which were killed and cooked forthwith for the benefit of the soldiers and bearers.

In spite of the good understanding that existed between the Khartoomers and both these chieftains, every village throughout the district was utterly deserted, and, with the exception of the families of Take and Kudy themselves, we did not see a single human being.

The march of the sixth day led us through the territory of the Rek, a district remarkable for its wide sandflats. All along I had noticed that the pasture-lands were cropped so closely by the cattle that it might almost be fancied that they had been mown with a scythe.

Next day at noon we encamped beneath the sycamore by the wells of Lao. By some misunderstanding my people had come to the conclusion that we were to halt here for the night. Accordingly they unpacked all my things, and I was about settling myself in an empty hut when the tidings were told that the caravan had already renewed its march. By the time that I was again prepared to proceed the whole train was out of sight, so that under the guidance of a man who knew the proper route we had to follow in the rear as rapidly as we could. While we were on our way a violent storm came up from the west, and, bursting over our heads, soon put the whole locality under water. To add to our discomfort, our road happened to be through a wood, and it was growing dusk, so that we had to go on stumbling into the continuous puddles, that were often very deep. In getting through these places I was at a great disadvantage, my heavy boots preventing me from keeping up with the light ambling trot of the natives.

As we toiled along through the miry forest in the thick of the drenching rain, we were startled by hearing a volley of firearms in the direction of the caravan. Pitiable as had been our plight before, we felt it worse than ever now: nor did we doubt but that the party in advance had been attacked in retribution by the ill-treated Dinka. With throbbing hearts we reached the outskirts of the wood, every moment expecting to catch sight of the enemy who would cut us off at once from the main procession; but seeing the fires burning hospitably in the neighbouring villages we were soon reassured, and on rejoining our people found that the sounds that had alarmed us had been caused simply by the soldiers discharging their guns so that they might not become foul through the charges getting damp.

Early next day, the eighth of our march, long before reaching the spot, we saw the tall columns of smoke rising from the murah of our old friend Kurdyook, the husband of the murdered Shol, and on approaching had the satisfaction of surveying the scene, which had long been strange to us, of a well-filled cattle-park. The very lowing of the herds was a welcome sound. Kurdyook himself soon appeared, and expatiated in very bitter terms upon the lamentable fate of his wife. We passed close to the spot where her huts had stood, and where our caravan had been so hospitably entertained on taking leave of her. The great Kigelia alone remained undisturbed in its glory; the residence was a heap of ashes, and there was nothing else to tell of poor old Shol's former splendour than the strips and shreds of a great torn spirit-flask.

Very little rain had fallen here. The river had scarcely risen at all; we were able consequently to get down with dry feet to the edge of the Meshera, where, about noon, we were conveyed across to the little island upon which the Khartoomers pitched their camp. Between Ghattas's Seriba and this spot I had counted 216,000 paces, showing that the entire distance we had walked was about eighty miles.

Except that the island which served for the landing-place had been completely cleared of trees, the general appearance of the Meshera during the last two and a half years had undergone little alteration; the growth of the papyrus had diminished rather than otherwise, and the ambatch was still altogether wanting.

Not only attacks from the neighbouring tribes of the Afok and Alwady, but continuous outbreaks of cattle-plague had decimated the herds left by Shol, and there had been a great scarcity of corn.

Before setting sail I had a good deal of squabbling with Ghattas's people. I did not want to be brought into the close quarters with either lepers or slaves which the limits of a boat's deck necessitated, and protested that if I did not shoot the first that came on board, I would at least take good care to report them to the Government. My endeavours in this way to secure my comfort were very far from being so successful as I wished. I had previously written to Kurshook Ali to engage the same boat which had brought him into the country to carry me back to Khartoom, making it an express stipulation that the boat should not convey any slaves. We had come to terms, and everything was apparently quite settled, when it turned out that the boat was not going to return until late in the year. To defer my departure so long was out of the question. Slaves or no slaves, it was all-important to me to be at Khartoom as soon as possible; and when I found that Ghattas's people were this year going to ship only a limited number, I came to the resolution that, under the circumstances, I would take my chance with them. I knew that Sir Samuel Baker was on the Upper Nile, and did not doubt that his presence would have the effect of making the Government take the most strenuous measures against any import of slaves. I represented as strongly as I could to the people the danger they were incurring by having such property on board, but I might just as well have remonstrated with the winds. In spite of all I could say, twenty-seven slaves were shipped, not avowedly as slaves, but so nearly in that capacity as at once to bring them under suspicion of being destined for the market. Undesirable as their company was, still I was thankful to be free from contact with any lepers; making the best, therefore, of an unpleasant business, I went on board on the afternoon of the 26th of June.

I confess that I felt a little tongue-tied, through not being myself entirely free from blame. I could not deny that I had three slaves of my own; these were Tikkitikki the Pygmy, Allagabo the Bongo, and Amber the Niam-niam. The other Niam-niam youth I left behind in the Seriba, after having gained him his freedom and seen him duly admitted into the Mohammedan sect by circumcision, the only means by which his social position could be secured. With regard to these lads I profess I had not the least squeamishness in carrying them away with me, and I felt none of that misgiving which other travellers have expressed when they have been tempted to a like proceeding. I felt that I could not leave them to a doubtful fate after they had been serving me faithfully for nothing, and attending me for two whole years in the desert; and I had no kind of idea that I was reducing myself to the level of a slave-dealer by determining to retain them and to introduce them to European civilisation, for if I left them behind I was quite aware that they would be immediately consigned to the ordinary lot of slavery. Rather was I disposed to compare myself with those noble-minded Orientals who, although they look upon the regular slave-dealer's calling as the vilest and most degrading of all professions, yet do not consider the possession of slaves to be in itself illegitimate or inconsistent with the purest morality.

It may be well to transcribe here my original diary of the passage down the Gazelle. It will not, I believe, be without interest, if it be only to show that the length of the river has hitherto been much exaggerated on all previous maps:—

"*June 26th.*—Sailed for about four hours, until evening, along the Kyt. A light breeze. The Kyt channel from eight to ten feet deep; its bottom one great mass of vallisneria.

"*27th.*—Dull, cloudy day. A contrary N.N.E. wind has prevented us from getting beyond the mouth of the Dyoor.

"*28th.*—Slow progress, on account of the continued N.N.E. wind. In the afternoon a more favourable breeze. The boat's crew affirm that after passing the mouth of the Dyoor the water becomes whiter. I cannot say that I can perceive any difference; the water is clear and colourless, and free from any flavour of the swamps, as if it had been distilled. Elephants to be seen marching about the shore, considerably in front of the demarcation line made by the trees. To the west of the channel are columns of smoke from some adjacent murah. Acacia-forests (none of the trees more than forty feet high) line both sides of the land subject to inundation; nowhere do these exceed a width of two miles. We proceed through clumps of ambatch, and make a wide bend to the west round an island which the sailors call Gyerdiga. Continued sailing at night under a good west wind.

"*29th.*—Quite early at a place where the river is not 500 feet across; the contracted spot enclosed by bush-forest. Soon afterwards we pass the mouth of the Bahr-el-Arab. There is a favourable breeze from the south-east. In the afternoon we reach the first Nueir villages. Some of the great *Balæniceps rex* are standing on the white-ant hills; have they been there ever since I last saw them there, two years and more ago? At evening a negro is dying from dysentery; according to custom, the poor creature is thrown overboard before life is really extinct. I fear my own feelings of satisfaction at getting home again make me somewhat callous to this horrible proceeding.

"*30th.*—A clouded sky, and the wind contrary. We heave-to in a backwater that is overgrown with grass for seventy-five feet from either bank: a solitary doom-palm marks the spot. Again sail on throughout the night, the breeze having once more become favourable.

"*July 1st.*—At 8 o'clock A.M. pass the Nueir villages, at which we stayed for a day on our passage out. It is unsafe to land now;

a Vokeel of Kurshook Ali's was murdered not long since. The district is full of bushes; white-ant hills and low acacia-hedges are frequent. A hippopotamus is leaning against a great stem upon the bank; we approach within thirty paces of the flesh-coloured brute, but it makes no attempt to get into the water. A bullet is fired, but seems to take no effect; the great beast totters about as though it needed support. All the crew assert that it is hopelessly ill, and has gone, as usual, on the land to die; no one, however, explains why it still stands upright. Large herds of Dinka cattle graze on the northern bank. Towards evening we arrive at the lake-like opening by the mouth of the Gazelle, where the water is a mile across. A tremendous gale gets up from the N.N.E.; the boat is tossed about on the muddy bottom of the river and dashed against the floating islands of grass. The mast and sail-yards creak as though they must snap in two; the boatmen shout according to their habit, but the Reis cannot join them because he is hoarse with a cold. There is an incessant invocation of the saints of the Nile: a mingled outcry of 'ya Seyet, ya Sheikh Abd-el-kader, Aboo Seyet, ya Sheikh Ahmed-el-Nil.'

"*2nd.*—A good west wind carries us betimes past the mouth of the Gazelle. I am surprised to find the floating grass in almost the same condition as in the winter of 1869; the water, however, is higher now, and consequently the entrance to the main-stream is easier."

All the comfort of our future progress was marred by the incessant plagues of flies, and all its regularity was interrupted by the same grass-obstructions that had impeded us on our former voyage. Before we could enter the side channel known as the Maia Signora, we had to make our way by a narrow cut of water that rushed along like a wild brook, and forced itself through the masses of vegetation on either side of the river, which here, I should suppose, was about half a mile wide. The depth of the fairway varied from six to eight feet, and the boat nowhere touched the bottom.

We spent the 3rd in sailing along the channel of the Maia Signora, which was 300 feet in width. Towards evening we re-entered the main-stream. At night we continued to drift along, borne gradually onward by the slow current; but, in case of being surprised by sudden gusts of strong wind, we did not hoist a sail. The open channel was about 500 feet in width, but on the northern side it was divided from the actual shore by a growth of grass that was scarcely less than 3000 feet across. The morning brought us in sight of the huts in the Shillook district of Tooma.

A horrible association will be for ever linked to my memories of that night. Dysentery is a disorder to which the negroes, on changing their mode of living, are especially liable, and an old female slave, after long suffering, was now dying in the hold below. All at once, probably attacked by a fit of epilepsy, she began to utter the most frightful shrieks and to groan with the intensest of anguish. Such sounds I had never heard before from any human being, and I hardly know to what I may compare them, except it be to the unearthly yells of the hyenas as they prowl by night amidst the offal of the market-towns of the Soudan. Beginning with a kind of long-drawn sigh, the cries ended with the shrillest of screams, and were truly heart-rending. From my recess in the bow of the boat, that was partitioned off by a screen of matting, I could not see what was going on, and conscious that I was quite powerless to accomplish any alleviation for the sufferer, I tried to shut out the melancholy noise by wrapping myself closely round in my bed-clothes. Presently I was conscious of the sound of angry voices; then came a sudden splash in the water amidst the muttered curses upon the "marafeel" (the hyena), and all was still. The inhuman sailors had laid hold upon the miserable creature in her death-agonies, and, without waiting for her to expire, had thrown her overboard. In their own minds they were perfectly convinced that she was a witch or hyena-woman, whose existence would inevitably involve the boat in some dire calamity.

It was about five o'clock in the afternoon when we passed the mouth of the Giraffe. Nearly all next day a contrary north wind prevailed, and was so strong that we were obliged to put in upon the right-hand bank. From the spot where we lay-to I counted as many as forty villages on the opposite shore. The district was called Nelwang, and the whole of the surrounding region belonged to the once powerful Shillook chieftain Kashgar, now no longer formidable, as he had lately been reduced to subjection and his entire dominion converted into a regular Egyptian province. Of this altered condition of things we had received no intelligence, and consequently we were in no little trepidation when we saw the natives crossing the river in large numbers just above the place where we were stopping. But we need not have been under any apprehensions. It was soon manifest that the Shillook party had no hostile intentions, and were gathered together merely for a hunting-excursion in the forests beyond the right bank of the river.

On observing the crowd of Shillooks our first impulse had been to make our way into the middle of the stream. It was past noon, and we were intently watching the movements of the hunters, when our attention was suddenly attracted by four men, dressed in white, shouting and gesticulating to us from the opposite bank. We could not imagine what Mohammedans were doing in this part of the country, and without loss of time pushed across and took the men on board. They proved to be Khartoom boatmen sent by the Mudir of Fashoda to inform us that his camp was close at hand, and that it was requisite for all boats coming down the river to stop there and submit to a rigid investigation as to what freight and passengers they were carrying. Our long sail-yard had been observed from the camp, and active measures had immediately been taken to prevent us from continuing our voyage without undergoing the prescribed scrutiny.

We had not long to wait before an unaccustomed surging of the water made us aware that a steamer was quite close upon us; in a few moments more the tug-boat "No. 8," was alongside, and a rope thrown out by which we had to be towed down to the camp.

However elated I might be at the prospect of being so soon restored to intercourse with men of a higher grade than those with whom I had been long associated, I must confess that this our first greeting from the civilized world rather jarred upon my sensibilities, and in the sequel resulted in some bitter disappointment.

For nearly a couple of hours we were quietly towed down the river until, at a spot just above the mouth of the Sobat, we came to a side arm of the main-stream, called the Lollo. Turning off abruptly into this we found ourselves proceeding in a direction that was quite retrograde as compared with that in which we had just come, and in another couple of hours reached the Mudir's temporary camp in the district of Fanekama. His force consisted of 400 black soldiers, fifty mounted Baggara, and two field-guns.

The Lollo flows almost parallel to the main-stream at a distance varying from a quarter of a league to two leagues. It is said to be about eighteen leagues in length; its current is extremely weak, and its depth from ten to fifteen feet; in many places it was from 800 to 1000 feet in width, and consequently at this season as wide as the main-stream itself: during the winter, however, it dwindles down to a mere shallow khor.

The little steam-tug was an iron boat of 24 horse-power, its sides so eaten up by rust that they were like a sieve, and the decrepit old captain, almost as worn-out as his vessel, was everlastingly patching them up with a compound of chalk and oil. Besides this, there were lying off Fanekama three Government boats and two large "negger" belonging to Agahd's company, that had come from the Meshera Elliab on the Bahr-el-Gebel; these had been conveying no less than 600 slaves, all of whom had been confiscated. Notwithstanding that Sir Samuel Baker was still on the upper waters of the river, the idea was quite prevalent in all the Seribas that as soon as "the English pasha" had turned his back upon Fashoda, the Mudir would relapse into his former habits, levy a good round sum on the head of every slave, and then let the contraband stock pass without more ado. But for once the Seriba people were reckoning without their host. The Mudir had been so severely reprimanded by Baker for his former delinquencies that he thought it was his best policy, for this year at least, to be as energetic as he could in his exertions against the forbidden trade; and his measures were so summary, and executed with such methodical strictness, that unless I had known him I could scarcely have believed him to be a Turk. He was now especially anxious to show off his authority before me as the first witness who would have the power of reporting his activity and decision to the world at large.

The first thing was to get all slaves whatever carried on shore, that is to say all who were black and who were not Mohammedans; no distinction was made in favour of such as had already been in Khartoom, although they might have been reported in the list of the crews that had worked the boats up the river.

Among the 600 slaves now brought in Agahd's boats there were representatives of no less than eighteen different tribes. The smallpox, however, had raged so frightfully among them that fear of contagion alike for myself and my people deterred me from taking advantage of the unusual opportunity offered for ethnographical investigation. It must not be supposed that these 600 slaves had been the only passengers on Agahd's boats; in addition to them there had been 200 Nubians, and thus it may be imagined that the most crowded cattle-pens could hardly have been more intolerable than the vessels throughout their voyage.

Many of the black soldiers under the Mudir's command, recruited as they had been at Khartoom from slaves previously confiscated, made very fair interpreters to assist in classifying the new arrivals according to their race and nationality.* Everything about the slaves had to be registered. Their number, the number of tribes that they represented, their age, their sex, the way they had been purchased, the place where they had been captured, the circumstances under which they had fallen into the hands of the Khartoomers, and all particulars of this sort, had to be entered in a book. Then each of the Nubians was separately questioned about his own home, his name, his rank, his trade or profession, the number of his slaves, and the price he had paid for them respectively; to each of the traders there was then handed a copy of his own affidavit, to which he was obliged to affix his seal.

An inventory, to be retained for the Government, was next taken of all property; guns, ammunition, and ivory being expressly specified. The three Arab clerks entered into such minute details, and made their reports so prolix, that it was necessary for them to apply an amount of patient industry of which I could hardly have believed them capable.

Besides these notaries the Mudir kept a number of smiths and carpenters perpetually employed in the fabrication of the iron fetters and wooden sheybas to bind the Reis and all the men that were not absolutely indispensable for the navigation of the boat. Every possible precaution seemed to be taken, and even seals were made for the use of those who had none of their own with which to attest their affidavits. It took two days to complete our inspection; but when it came to an end, three soldiers were sent on board as a guard, and we were allowed to proceed. Free from the polluted air of Fanekama, I began to feel that I could breathe again.

A day and a half brought us to Fashoda, where I was equally surprised and gratified to hear of a kindness that had been intended to be shown me. Dyafer Pasha, the Governor-General, immediately on hearing of the destitute condition in which I had been left by the burning of Ghattas's Seriba, had despatched to me such a munificent

* This is a circumstance that would greatly facilitate the restoration of confiscated slaves to their own homes; but it is a matter for much regret that the principle of enfranchisement has been resolutely opposed by all authorities who have hitherto borne a hand in the suppression of the slave-trade. The Anglo-Egyptian treaty of August 4th, 1877, in its third article declares the return of slaves with their life and liberty to be a matter of impossibility. The present mode of liberation, therefore, merely conducts its subjects from one house of bondage to another, and should accordingly awaken the protest of every true philanthropist.

supply of provisions of every description as would have kept me well for months not only with the means of subsistence, but with many of the elegancies of a civilised life. Had this liberal contribution reached me before I left Bongoland, I think I should have been vastly tempted to defer my return to Europe for another year; but it was not to be: the supplies having been placed under the charge of a company of soldiers who were going up the Gazelle to reinforce the troops already stationed in Dar Ferteet, the change of wind and the condition of the water had delayed their progress till it was too late to proceed, and they had been obliged to stay at Fashoda until the commencement of the winter.

The condition of the unfortunate slaves had become far worse since their confiscation; the very measures that ought to have ameliorated their lot had been but an aggravation of their misery. The supply of corn was rapidly coming to an end; they had, in fact, hardly anything to eat, and the soldiers on guard never dreamed of making the least exertion to provide in any way for their needs, resorting to the use of the kurbatch much more freely than their former masters, who had now lost whatever interest they might have had in their welfare.

My powers of endurance were sorely tried. Incessant on the one hand were the murmurs and complaints; incessant on the other were the scoldings and cursings. If some luckless negro happened to be blessed with a tolerably good and robust constitution, so that he kept fat and healthy under all his hardships, he was continually being made a laughing-stock and jeered at for being "a tub;" if, on the contrary, a poor wretch got thin till he was the very picture of misery, he was designated a "hyena," and perpetually bantered on account of his "hyena-face." I used to have whole kettles full of rice and maccaroni boiled for the poor creatures, but it was, of course, utterly beyond the compass of my resources to do much towards supplying their wants.

On approaching the district of Wod Shellay, we perceived countless masses of black specks standing out against the bright-coloured sand. They were all slaves! The route from Kordofan to the east lay right across the land, and was quite unguarded; the spot that we now saw was where the caravans are conveyed over the river on their way to the great depot at Mussalemich.

At length towards sunset, on the 21st of July, we reached the Ras-el-Khartoom. Our entire journey from the Meshera had been accomplished in twenty-five days, six of which had been consumed in stoppages at Fauekama, Fashoda, and Kowa. With a quickened pulse I set out alone on foot for the town. Evening was drawing on, and although I met numbers of people, there was no one to recognise me; in my meagre white calico costume I might easily have passed for one of those homeless Greeks, who, without a place to rest their heads, have been forced to seek their fortune in the remotest corners of the earth. I made my way at once to a German tailor named Klein, who had been living for some years in Khartoom, and by the vigorous prosecution of his trade had contributed in no small degree towards the promotion of external culture in the town. He soon provided me with some civilised garments, and I felt myself fit to make my appearance before my old friends, at least such as remained, for some I grieved to learn were dead, and others had left the place.

I found Khartoom itself much altered. A large number of new brick buildings, a spacious quay on the banks of the Blue Nile, and some still more imposing erections on the other side of the river, had given the place the more decided aspect of an established town. The extensive gardens and rows of date-palms planted out nearly half a century back, had now attained to such a development that they could not be altogether without influence on the climate; in spite of everything, however, the sanitary condition of Khartoom was still very unsatisfactory. This was entirely owing to the defective drainage of that portion of the town that had been built below the high-water level. In July, when I was there, I saw many pools almost large enough to be called ponds that could never possibly dry up without the application of proper means for draining them off; stagnant under the tropical sun, they sent forth such an intolerable stench that it was an abomination to pass near them. When it is remembered that Khartoom is situated in the desert zone (for the grassy region does not begin for at least 150 miles farther to the south), there can appear no necessary reason why it should be more unhealthy than either Shendy or Berber; all that is wanted is that the sanitary authorities should exercise a better management and see that stagnant puddles should be prevented.

As I have already intimated, I found that during my absence, not a few of my former acquaintances had fallen victims to the fatal climate; but no loss did I personally deplore more than that of the missionary Blessing, who died just a fortnight before my arrival; Herr Duisberg had left Khartoom, and since his departure Blessing had managed all my affairs, and it was from him that I had received my last despatches in the negro-countries.

On the day of my arrival I telegraphed to Alexandria to announce my safe return. The message reached its destination in the course of two days; the charge for twenty words was four dollars. The telegraph had only been established during the last few months, and as yet was scarcely in full working order. The officials were young and inexperienced at their work, and the direct line of communication was broken in two places by the messages having to be conveyed across the river. Except for the conciseness of its forms of expression, Arabic is extremely unsuitable for telegraphy; the deficiency of vowel symbols makes proper names all but undecipherable to any one who is previously unacquainted with them. But with all its temporary short-comings, the establishment of the telegraph will ever rank as pre-eminent amongst the services rendered by the Government of Ismail Pasha.

Dyafer Pasha, to whom I was so much indebted for his liberal intentions on my behalf, received me with his unfailing cordiality, and gave me a lodging in one of the Government buildings that was at his disposal; but notwithstanding all his generosity to myself I could not feel otherwise than very much hurt at the unscrupulous manner in which he acted towards my servants. Their faithfulness to myself had made me much interested in them, and I felt intensely annoyed when I found that, without any communication with me, they had been seized, thrust into irons, and set to work in the galleys, leaving me with no one but my three negro-lads, and without the services of anybody who knew how to cook. The fact was that, although I had not been made acquainted with it, besides their wives and a child they had been in possession of some slaves on their own account, representing them as having been consigned to their care by friends in the upper district, who wanted to forward them to their homes. The whole lot were now confiscated in one common batch; no distinction was made—men, wives, and children were all included in the general fate. This was as illegal as it was unjust, for every slave who has borne any children is reckoned as a wife, although there may have been no regular marriage.

Four separate appeals did I take the trouble to make to the Pasha for the emancipation of my servants. Even at last my success was only partial, for I could not obtain the restitution of freedom either to the women or the children, although their confiscation had been specially illegal. The Pasha was on the point of starting for Egypt, but I could not permit any circumstance of the kind to prevent my doing everything in my power to assist my servants, who had shown such fidelity for a period of three years. I resolved, therefore, to take the men on with me to Cairo. I incurred a considerable extra expense by travelling with so large a retinue; but I would not be daunted, and, after a world of trouble, I succeeded ultimately in obtaining redress for their grievances.

On the 9th of August I once again took my passage on board a Nile boat, this time under more comfortable and less ambiguous circumstances. With a favourable wind and high water our voyage was very rapid. On the fourth day we reached Berber. Here I found excellent quarters in the house of my friend Vasel, and for the first time, after many months, had the enjoyment of intercourse with a well-educated fellow-countryman. Vasel had been a benefactor to the land by erecting a large portion of the telegraph lately opened between Assouan and Khartoom, and, in spite of his exertions in a climate that had been fatal to so many Europeans, had hitherto enjoyed unbroken health.

The deaths during the last fever-season had been more than usually numerous. In Khartoom, in 1870, almost all the resident Europeans had been fatally attacked, and now, on reaching Berber, I learnt that my old friend Lavargue had succumbed to fever only a short time before my arrival. He, too, had been residing for many years in the Soudan.

And now the next to go was my little Tikkitikki. He had for some time been marked by the unsparing hand of death, and here it was during my stay at Berber that I had to mourn his loss. At Khartoom he had been taken ill with a severe attack of dysentery, probably induced by change of air and very likely aggravated by his too sumptuous diet. His disorder had day by day become more deeply seated; my care in nursing seemed to bring no alleviation, and every remedy failed to take effect; he became weaker and weaker, till his case was manifestly hopeless, and, after lingering three weeks, sunk at last from sheer exhaustion.

Never before, I think, had I felt a death so acutely; my grief so weakened and unmanned me that my energies flagged entirely, so that I could scarcely walk for half an hour without extreme fatigue. Since that date some years have passed away, but still the recollection of that season of bitter disappointment is like a wound that opens afresh.

The other two negro-boys, according to my intention, were to be playmates and companions for my little Pygmy; but now that he had been taken from me I took measures to provide for them in a different way. The elder one, Amber, a true Niam-niam, I left behind in Egypt, under the care of my old friend Dr. Sachs, the celebrated physician of Cairo; my little Bongo, Allagabo Teem, was taken to Germany for the purpose of receiving a careful education.

I was delayed in Berber by the sad circumstances of my little *protégé's* death; but independently of that, my stay was prolonged by waiting for a courier who, by the orders of his Highness the Khedive, was on his way to meet me. The German Consul-General, Herr von Jasmund, with his accustomed solicitude for all who were in any way entrusted to his protection, had procured me this favour. Fearing that I should be in want, he had commissioned the courier to bring me money, medicines, arms, and clothing of all descriptions. Meanwhile I had amply provided myself at Khartoom with everything of which I stood in need, and was consequently anxious, if I could, to stop the progress of the envoy. It was, however, several days, even with the help of the telegraph, before I could find out how far he had advanced, or could succeed in countermanding his orders.

On the 10th of September I was ready to start for Suakin. The route that I took was the same, through the valleys of Etbai, by which I had journeyed on starting three years previously. My little caravan consisted now but of thirteen people. By the help of fourteen camels we accomplished the journey in a fortnight, without any misadventure. Once again I was in sight of the sea. It was with the truest interest that I regarded the faithful few that were round about me, and as I looked down from the summit of the Attaba, 3415 feet high, that enabled me to gaze beyond the intervening stretch of land to Suakin and to catch the extended deep blue line of sea, my feelings could be understood by none except by a wanderer who, like myself, had been lingering in the depths of an untraversed country. On the 26th of September I embarked at Suakin, and after a pleasant voyage of four days landed at Suez; by the 2nd of November I had reached Messina.

Thus, after an absence of three years and four months, I was once again upon the soil of Europe.

APPENDIX I.

TABLE OF HEIGHTS OF VARIOUS POINTS VISITED DURING THE JOURNEY.

(COMPUTED BY DR. WILHELM SCHUR.)

DURING my journey I made use of three aneroids, all of which I brought back safe to Europe; they were subsequently most carefully tested under various conditions of temperature and pressure by Dr. Wilhelm Schur, who undertook to estimate and reduce to standard measure the various observations I had made. I here append only the final results of his investigations, but for more complete details I would refer to the Journal of the Geographical Society of Berlin (vol. viii., p. 228), where he has described at length his method for ascertaining the proper corrections of my registries, after allowing for the variations from the mean condition of the barometer.

I very rarely failed three times in the course of a day to note the readings of the aneroids, but these numerous observations were only entered in my diary, and consequently perished with the rest of my papers in the conflagration of the 2nd of December, 1870; only those observations, therefore, that were made subsequently to that ill-fated day, and a few others that were sent home promiscuously in my correspondence, were available for Dr. Schur's deductions.

But altogether the following figures will suffice to give very approximately a true conception of the heights of the regions that I visited, and it may be of some interest to compare the results with those obtained during the geometrical survey that is requisite for the formation of the proposed railway between Suakin and Berber.*

In the approximate heights given below, Dr. Schur has reckoned 25 meters as being equivalent to about 82 English feet.

* The position of this district with regard to the points of the compass may be seen in the map of the road from Suakin to Berber, which I published in vol. xv. of Petermann's 'Geographical Communications,' Table 15. 1869.

A.—Points between the Red Sea and the Nile on the Road from Suakin to Berber.

		Height above the sea.	
		Meters.	Eng. ft.
1	Three hours W. of Suakin.	212·1	695
2	Tamarisk wood, 7½ hours W. of Suakin.	544·2	1785
3	Wady Teekhe, 11½ hours W. of Suakin.	618·9	2030
4	First Attaba (pass), 13 hours W. of Suakin.	924·5	3033
5	At the pools in the valley between the two Attabas.	913·5	2996
6	Second Attaba, highest pass.	1041·7	3415
7	Upper Wady Gabet, below the Attaba.	925·8	3037
8	Singat, summer camp in the great Valley of Okwak.	941·3	3088
9	Wady Sarroweeb, 4 hours E.S.E. of Singat.	1037·7	3404
10	Wady Harrassa in Erkoweet, 8 hours E.S.E. of Singat, near the summer camp.	1137·8	3732
11	At the base of the high hill of Erkoweet, on the N. side.	1250·2	4101
12	Summit of the hill of Erkoweet.	1676·1	5499
13	2 hours W. of Singat, 1 hour from O-Mareg, E. of the small pass.	1007·3	3304
14	3¼ hours W. of Singat, W. of the small pass.	1072·5	3518
15	O-Mareg, summer camp in the valley.	971·7	3188
16	Small Wady, 3 hours W. of the Mareg, in front of the pass.	949·5	3115
17	Near the wells in Wady Amet.	810·1	2658
18	On the S. slope of the W. end of the mountain O-Kurr, 5 hours west of the wells of Amet.	803·3	2635
19	Small Wady, an hour W. of Wady Arab.	739·9	2427
20	Grassy Wady W. of Wady Arab, an hour from the great khor-bed.	762·5	2501
21	Near the wells in Wady Kamot-Atai.	735·3	2412
22	Wady 4 hours E. of Wady Habob.	705·6	2314
23	Wady Dimehadeet.	717·5	2354
24	Wady Habob, eastern arm.	741·0	2431
25	Wady Habob, western arm.	600·2	1969
26	Wady Kokreb, camping-place, 1871.	694·5	2278
27	Wady Kokreb, camping-place S. of last.	597·6	1960
28	Great Wady, an hour W. of Wady Kokreb.	657·0	2155
29	5½ hours W. of small isolated hill near Wady Derumkad (Upper Wady Yumga).	650·0	2132
30	Wady Yumga.	587·6	1927
31	Wady Derumkad.	581·4	1907
32	Small isolated hill, an hour W. of Wady Derumkad.	578·0	1896
33	Valley near the acacias S. of the wells of Roway.	590·2	1936
34	Below the small pass above the Wady Laemeb.	580·1	1903
35	End of rising ground in the upper Wady Laemeb.	532·8	1748
36	In the middle of Wady Laemeb.	574·6	1885
37	In the middle of Wady Laemeb.	513·9	1686

APPENDIX I. 285

POINTS BETWEEN THE RED SEA AND THE NILE—*continued.*

	Height above the sea.	
	Meters.	Eng. ft.
38 In the lower Wady Laemeb, 2 hours E. of O-Feek.	458·8	1505
39 Wady at the foot of the hill O-Feek, southern side.	498·6	1635
40 2 hours E. of the bush-forest at O-Baek.	508·2	1667
41 O-Baek, bush-forest near the wells.	476·3	1562
42 Rain-pool, 2 hours W. of O-Baek.	459·0	1506
43 5½ hours W. of O-Baek.	438·8	1439
44 Wady Eremit, camping-place in 1871.	464·4	1523
45 Wady Eremit, camping-place in 1868.	446·0	1463
46 Depression in Wady Aboo Kolod.	399·8	1311
47 Wady Darrowreeb or Derreeb.	414·0	1359
48 Wady Aboo Zelem.	452·2	1483
49 Pools of Aboo Tagger, 2½ hours E. of Berber (el Mekherif).	403·6	1324
50 Town of Berber (el Mekherif) 30 feet above the highest level of the Nile.	417·0	1368

B.—POINTS ON THE NILE BETWEEN LAT. 9° AND 18° N.

	Height above the sea.	
	Meters.	Eng. ft.
1 Above Wolled Bassal (from the boat).	399·7	1319
2 Town of Matamma (from the boat).	404·4	1326
3 Town of Shendy (from the boat).	408·8	1341
4 Town of Khartoom, 20 feet above the highest level of the Blue Nile.	407·2	1336
5 Meshera, on the island on the Kyt, the extremity of the Bahr-el-Ghazal.	442·7	1452

C.—POINTS IN THE BAHR-EL-GHAZAL DISTRICT.

	Height above the sea.	
	Meters.	Eng. ft.
1 Ghattas's chief Seriba in Dyoor-land.	471·2	1545
2 Kurshook Ali's chief Seriba on the Dyoor.	542·1	1778
3 Agahd's small Seriba Dubor, in Bongoland.	565·5	1854
4 Aboo Guroon's small Seriba Danga in Bongoland.	543·7	1783
5 Bizelly's small Seriba Doggaya-mor in Bongoland.	554·5	1818
6 Idrees Wod Defter's Seriba in the Golo district.	703·6	2306
7 Seebehr Rahama's chief Seriba in the Kredy district.	696·0	2282
8 Dehm Gudyoo, Agahd's Seriba.	846·3	2775
9 On the brook Gulanda between Dehm Gudyoo and Dehm Bekeer.	729·1	2391

POINTS IN THE BAHR-EL-GHAZAL DISTRICT—*continued.*

	Height above the sea.	
	Meters.	Eng. ft.
10 Dehm Bekeer, Kurshook Ali's Seriba.	771·0	2528
11 Dehm Adlan, Seebehr Adlan's Seriba in the Sehre district.	747·1	2450
12 Agahd's small Seriba Ngulfala, in Bongoland.	581·0	1905
13 Agahd's small Seriba Moody, in Bongoland.	575·0	1886
14 Take's residence in the Dinka country.	426·5	1399

D.—POINT BEYOND THE NILE DISTRICT.

	Height above the sea.	
	Meters.	Eng. ft.
1 Munza's residence in Monbuttoo-land, Aboo Sammat's Seriba.	825·4	2707

APPENDIX II.

EIGHT ITINERARIES IN ILLUSTRATION OF THE DISTRICTS TO THE SOUTH AND WEST OF MY ROUTE.

A.—Idrees Wod Defter's Route to the W.S.W. from Deim Gudyoo.

First day.—Four hours to the village of the Kredy chief Mangirr, on Agahd's territory.

Second day.—Six or seven leagues to some Kredy hamlets still on Agahd's territory.

Third day—Long day's march of seven or eight hours to the deserted villages of a former Kredy chief, named Koiye.

Fourth day.—Eight leagues across an uninhabited district; night in the wilderness.

Fifth day.—Seven leagues to a small Seriba belonging to Idrees Wod Defter on Mount Berangah.

Sixth day.—Seven or eight leagues across an inhabited district to the chief Seriba of Idrees Wod Defter, situated on a river flowing to the north-west. The Kredy tribes of the district are called Bia and Mehre; the local chief is named Gariaongoh.

Seventh day.—Five hours' march to the west to a subsidiary Seriba belonging to Idrees, called Adya, after the Kredy tribe of the district.

Eighth day.—Long day's march of eight or nine leagues across the wilderness.

Ninth day.—Half a day's march to Idrees's most westerly Seriba in Dar Benda, of which the chieftain is named Kobbokobbo. The Benda are an independent nation, with their own dialect.

Tenth day.—Seven or eight hours to the great river, said to flow here in an easterly direction, and requiring to be crossed in boats at all seasons: the population on the banks is composed of the ivory-trading Aboo Dinga, and the land is called Dar Dinga, or Dar Aboo Dinga. A king, known to the Nubians by the name of Ayah, to whom several chieftains are tributary, resides to the north-west of Idrees Wod Defter's chief Seriba. Dar Dinga is also the resort for many slave-caravans under the management of the great dealers from Darfoor and Kordofan. The companies of Seebehr Rahama, Seebehr Adlan, and Agahd, likewise visit the country to purchase ivory from the chieftains.

B.—YUMMA'S ROUTE TO THE W.S.W. FROM DEHM BEKEER TO THE RESIDENCE OF MOFIO.

First day.—Six or eight leagues to the last villages of the Sehre: they belong to Kurshook Ali's territory, and the Sheikh is named Sahtsy. His residence is situated on a small river, named the Ville or Wille, that is said to flow in a north-western direction, and to belong to the system of the river of Dar Dinga: it is at no part of the year less than twenty feet deep.

Second day to Eighth day (inclusive).—Seven long days' marches over uninhabited wildernesses to the borders of Mofio's territory, where his behnky Boborungoo has his mbanga.

Ninth day.—A short march over cultivated land to the residence of the sub-chieftain Bakomoro.

Tenth day.—A long march mostly through wild forest to the residence of Kanso, a behnky of Mofio's.

Eleventh day.—The road turns to the north-west and leads by a long day's march to the behnky Abindee. A river flowing towards the north is crossed here; it is named the Ngango, and after joining the Welle or river of Sahtsy, flows into the great river of Dar Dinga, farther to the north-west. In its lower course the stream is known as the Mboma.

Twelfth day.—Half a day's march to the mbanga of Gazima, the sub-chieftain in command of the district and a brother of Mofio's.

Thirteenth and Fourteenth days.—Two days' march to the residence of Mofio, only a good day's journey to the south-west of Idrees Wod Defter's chief Seriba. The river on which it is situated is said to be called the Mbette, and to flow into the Mboma.

C.—ROUTE TO THE S.S.E. FROM DEHM BEKEER TO SOLONGOH'S RESIDENCE.

First day.—An ordinary day's march across the Ngudduroo and the Djee (leaving the Kokkuloo hill on the left) to the brook Biserry, which has been followed by Nubians, and found to join the Wow. Unless the rainfall has been very excessive, the brook may be waded even during the Khareef. Mount Daragumba lies about two hours to the south of the passage over the Biserry.

Second day.—A good day's march to the south-west across the wilderness to a little brook, named the Kommoh, said to flow into the Biserry.

Third day.—The Dar (or inhabited land) of Solongoh's territory is reached towards evening. Night spent at the residence of Karya, the chieftain's behnky and brother.

Fourth day.—The road bends more to the south, and leads by a long day's march to the mbanga of another sub-chieftain named Ndundo, also a brother of Solongoh.

Fifth day.—South-west to Yagganda, a third brother and behnky of the chieftain. Mount Yahre is passed on the east.

Sixth day.—Across the Nomatina or Nomatilla, a copious river, declared by the Niam-niam to be identical with the Wow, which in its lower course in Bongoland they call the Nomatilla. Half-a-day's journey to the mbanga of Solongoh.

Two days' march to the north-east from Solongoh lies Kurshook Ali's Seriba Aboo Shatter, in the land of the Bellanda, which for the most part belongs to Solongoh. About half-way there stands the residence of a behnky of the chieftain's, named Ndimma; and a day's journey north of Kurshook Ali's settlement lives another sub-chieftain, named Mamah; consequently the Seriba forms an enclave in Solongoh's territory. Solongoh's father was named Borrongboh or Bongorboh, and was the brother of Mofio and Zaboora.

YUMMA'S ROUTE TO THE SOUTH FROM DEHM BEKEER TO YAFFATY AND INGIMMA.

First and Second days.—Two days to the S.S.W., across uninhabited frontier wildernesses.

Third day.—Towards evening is reached the residence of the small chieftain Yaffaty or Yapaty, the son of Zaboora, who had shaken off his allegiance to his brother Mofio.

Fourth day.—A moderate day's march to the south to the residence of Bogwa Riffio, a behnky and brother of Yaffaty.

Fifth day.—Across the brook Mbomoo, flowing northwards, and said to empty itself into the Nomatilla, to Boggwa Yango, a sub-chieftain of Bombo.

Sixth day.—An ordinary day's march to the mbanga of the powerful chief Bombo. A day's journey to the north-west is the residence of Nembo, and about the same distance to the north-east that of Nzembe, both of these are brothers and sub-chieftains of Bombo.

Seventh and Eighth days.—Through uninhabited wildernesses.

Ninth day.—Across a great navigable river said to pass through the territory of a chieftain named Sena, whose residence lies to the east of the route; on this account the Nubians call the stream the river of Sena. By the Niam-niam it is called the Ware.

Tenth day.—To the residence of a son of Ezo (not to be confounded with the chief of the same name, who was the father of Ndoruma and Ugetto) on the river of Sena, said to be identical with the river of Wando (the Mbrwole).

Eleventh and Twelfth days.—Through inhabited country, the territory of the old decrepit chieftain Ezo. Two long marches to the south of the river is the residence of Ingimma, the most powerful of the sons of Ezo.

Thirteenth and Fourteenth days.—Half-a-day's march beyond Ingimma's territory is the great river of Kanna, known as the Welle. After crossing the river to the south of Ingimma's residence, that of Kanna is reached in two days' journey to the east.

E.—ADERAHMAN ABOO GUROON'S ROUTE TO THE S. FROM HIS CHIEF SERIBA TO THE NIAM-NIAM AND MONBUTTOO.

First day.—Eight hours to the south-west to Kurshook Ali's Seriba Nguddo.

Second day.—Six hours to the south : night in the wilderness.

Third day.—Half-a-day's march to Aboo Guroon's Seriba Mahah, on the brook Lako.

Fourth day.—Seven hours' march to the S.S.W. to Gebel Reggeb, where Aboo Guroon has his small Seriba Hibboo.

Fifth day.—Half-a-day's march to the south-east to the little Seriba Mbellembey, the joint possession of Aboo Guroon and Ghattas. The local chief of the Bongo in Mbellembey is named Ghirrah.

Sixth day.—Half-a-day's march to the south-east to Ghattas's Seriba Gebel Higgoo, on the southern frontier of the Bongo country.

Seventh day.—To the south-west, leaving the territory of Mundo (Babuckur) on the east. Eight hours across the wilderness to Aboo Guroon's Seriba on the northern frontier of the Niam-niam country. The Seriba was under the control of a Niam-niam slave, named Fomboa, and was destroyed in 1870 by Ndoruma. The name of the local chief was Ukweh.

Eighth day.—To the south, across the Sway (Dyoor). Night-camp in the wilderness on the Bikky.

Ninth day.—A long day's march of about nine hours across the wilderness to the south-west, to the residence of Dukkoo, a brother and sub-chieftain of Ndoruma.

Tenth day.—A long march to the south and west, the residence of Mbory, a behnky of Ndoruma. Half-way lies the spot where Ndoruma attacked and defeated the united companies in 1870.

Eleventh day.—A whole day's march to the residence of Ndoruma on the Barah, a brook that is said to empty itself into the Bikky. Ndoruma is the most powerful of the reigning sons of Ezo.

Twelfth day.—Half-a-day's march to the mbanga of Gettwa or Ngetto, a brother of Ndoruma and an independent chieftain; his lands lie to the south of Ndoruma's.

Thirteenth day.—An ordinary day's march to the south-east, to the village of Mashmany, a behnky of Ngetto.

Fourteenth day.—Long march to the south-east, across uninhabited country.

Fifteenth day.—Half-a-day's march to the territory of Malingde. In the middle of the day is reached the villaga of Owra, a son of the wealthy chieftain.

Sixteenth day.—A whole day's march to the south-east, to the village of a local overseer, named Bazway.

Seventeenth day.—Half-a-day's march to the residence of Malingde or Marindo, one of the numerous sons of Bazimbey.

Eighteenth day.—A whole day's march to the W.S.W., to the residence of Malingde's behnky Bahzia.

Nineteenth day.—A long day's march to the south-east, to the villages of Malingde's behnky Yaganda.

Twentieth day.—Across uninhabited country: night in the wilderness.

Twenty-first day.—Half-a-day's march to the residence of Wando's behnky Bagbatta.

Twenty-second day.—A long day's march to the river of Wando (Mbrwole): night on the banks. This stream is said to pass through the territories of Sena and Indimma: in its lower course it bears the name of the Ware.

Twenty-third day.—Through the remainder of the border wilderness on to the territory of Izingerria (in Munza's dominions), near the villages of his behnky Dedda.

Twenty-fourth day.—Southwards to the numerous villages of Izingerria's territory.

Twenty-fifth day.—In the same direction to the residence of one of Izingerria's behnkys.

Twenty-sixth day.—A short march to the residence of Izingerria himself.

F.—AHMED AWAT'S ROUTE TO THE S.W. FROM NDORUMA TO EZO.

First day.—A good day's march to the west, to the residence of Ndoruma's behnky Komunda.

Second day.—In the same direction, to the residence of Tumafee, another behnky of Ndoruma.

Third day.—To the residence of Mbanzuro, a brother and sub-chieftain of Ndoruma.

Fourth day.—To the residence of Ndoruma's behnky Byazingee.

Fifth and Sixth days.—In a south-western direction across uninhabited regions.

Seventh day.—Half-a-day's march to Baria's territory: halt at the border villages.

Eighth day.—A day's march through populous districts to Baria's residence, near which Ahmed Awat, Hassaballa's head-controller, has erected a Seriba. Baria is an old friend and ally of the company.

Ninth day.—A good day's march to the south, to the residence of Sango, a brother and sub-chieftain of Ndoruma.

Tenth and Eleventh days.—Across uninhabited country: two nights in the wilderness.

Twelfth day.—A day's march to the abode of Ndenny, a son and former behnky of the deceased Sena.

Thirteenth day.—To the residence of Baziboh, the son of Sena, now an independent chieftain.

Fourteenth day.—To the Gangara mountains, the home of the A-Madi and their kindred tribe, the Imberry.

Fifteenth and Sixteenth days.—Through populated districts to the residence of the old chieftain Ezo.

G.—ROUTE FROM KURSHOOK ALI'S CHIEF SERIBA ON THE DYOOR TO ABOO SHATTER, IN THE DISTRICT OF THE BELLANDA.

First day.—Eight hours' march to the south-west and south, through Hassaballa's small Seriba to Kurshook Ali's subsidiary Seriba Mittoo in Bongoland.

Second day.—Six hours' march to the south, to a second Seriba belonging to the same company, and called Longo. A small Seriba of Agahd's lies to the east of the route: it is called Mbor, and is not far from the left bank of the Dyoor.

Third day.—Seven or eight leagues to the site of a former Seriba of Kurshook Ali, named Murr.

Fourth day.—Across the frontier wilderness on the south of the Bongo territory: night in the wilderness.

Fifth day.—A short march to the border villages of the Bellanda, under the control of a behnky of the Niam-niam chieftain Solongoh.

Sixth day.—Half-a-day's march to Aboo Shatter, a lofty isolated mountain, from the summit of which all the detached hills of southern Bongoland and the mountains of Mundo (Babuckur) are said to be visible. The local chief of the Bellanda, under Kurshook Ali's jurisdiction, is named Akoo, whilst the chief of the Niam-niam, tributary to Solongoh, is said to be Bongurr. Six hours to the north-east of Aboo Shatter is a second Bellanda Seriba, belonging to Kurshook Ali, called Dongoh: it is said to be near the left bank of the Dyoor. Six hours farther to the east, and beyond the river, is a third Seriba belonging to this company, named Asalla. A few hours to the north of Asalla are Aboo Guroon's Bongo Seribas, called Gebel Regheb and Abooleghee by the Nubians, after the Bongo Sheikh of the district. The native name for Abooleghee is Karey, that of Gebel Reggeb being Hibboo.

H.—ROUTE TO THE SOUTH FROM KULONGO TO GEBEL HIGGOO AND MUNDO.

First day.—Five hours to the S.S.W. to Kurshook Ali's small Seriba Kileby. Four hours to the west of Kileby lies the small Seriba Ngorr, belonging to the same company.

Second day.—Seven hours' march to Ghattas's subsidiary Seriba Mboh, of which the local chief of the Bongo is named Doliba. A deserted Seriba of Kurshook Ali's, of which the local chief was named Abrass, is passed on the road. Two considerable brooks (the Molmul and the Nyedokoo?) are crossed between Kileby and Mboh.

Third day.—Six or seven hours to Ghattas's Seriba Doggaia, of which the local chief is named Bonyira.

Fourth day.—Four hours' march to Ghattas's Seriba on Gebel Higgoo. The Bongo district is called Longo, the local chief Higgoo. Three hours to the east is a much frequented Seriba belonging to Ghattas; it is situated on the so-called Gebel Shiteta (cayenne-pepper hill), and called Roome by the Bongo. The local overseer of the district is named Bomadioh. Sabby lies two days' march east of Gebel Shiteta; after crossing the Tondy the road leads on the first day through the village of the Bongo sheikh Guiya, who is in Aboo Sammat's territory. Mundo lies only two leagues to the south of Gebel Higgoo; the route to the Niam-niam lands across this mountainous region of the Babuckur leads through a dangerous defile, where travellers are often attacked by the natives. This is the Mundo visited by J. Petherick in February 1858, the names of the places which he passed are given by him in the Bongo dialect, and several of them, such as Yow, Dangah, Mahah, Murr, and Lungo, are retained to the present time.

APPENDIX III.

LIST OF MAMMALIA OBSERVED DURING MY TRAVELS FROM THE GAZELLE.

(WITH THEIR NATIVE NAMES.*)

1. *Troglodytes niger.* Geoff. (Variety: *Schweinfurthii* Gigl.)
   Bongo: Dadda.
   Niam-niam: Irangba or Manjarooma.
   Monbuttoo: Nohzo.
   Sehre: Sango.

2. *Colobus guereza.* Rüpp.
   Bongo: Ndollo.
   Niam-niam: Mbeggeh.

3. *Cercopithecus griseoviridis.* Desm.
   Dyoor: Ngero or Angehro.
   Bongo: Manga.
   Niam-niam: Ngalangala.
   Kredy: Ohlo.

4. *Cercopithecus pyrrhonotus.* Ehrb.
   Dinka: Agohk.
   Dyoor: Abworro.
   Bongo: Gumbi.
   Niam-niam: Gungbeh.
   Golo: Toggwa.
   Kredy: Nyagga.

5. *Cercopithecus pygerythrus.* F. Cuv.
   Niam-niam: Ndumm.

6. *Cynocephalus Babuin.* Desm.
   Dyoor: Bimm.
   Bongo: Kungah.
   Niam-niam: Bokkoo.

7. *Cynocephalus sp.*
   Sehre: Mbeeri.
   Golo: Filli.
   Kredy: Booroo.

8. *Otolicnus Teng.* Geoffr. (*Galago senegalensis.* F. Cuvier.)
   Dinka: Londorr or Nehngby.
   Dyoor: Anyoi or Anynai.
   Bongo: Ndohr.
   Niam-niam: Bakumbosso.

9. *Otolicnus Pelei.* Temm. (*Galago Demidoffii.* Fisch.)
   Niam-niam: Mbottoo.

10. *Megaderma frons.* Geoffr.

11. *Vesperugo sp.*
    Bongo: Beeroo.
    Niam-niam: Tooreh.

12. *Scotophilus leucogaster.* Geoffr.

13. *Nycteris hispida.* Geoffr.

14. *Phyllorrhina caffra.* Lund.

* The native names will also show the geographical distribution of the various animals. I am indebted to Professor R. Hartmann for the names of all but the doubtful species.

APPENDIX III.   295

15. *Erinaceus sp.*
    Dyoor: Ohkoddo.
    Bongo: Ndudoopirakpeh.
    Niam-niam: Dundulch.
    Golo: Iddoo.
    Kredy: Ohko.
    Sehre: Mbarra.
16. *Sorex sp.*
    Dyoor: Ushull.
    Bongo: Tondo, or Shondo.
    Niam-niam: Ndelly.
    Golo: Diffee.
    Kredy: Djanje-kreie.
17. *Ratelus capensis.* G. Cuv.
    Dyoor: Ogang.
    Bongo: Nyirr.
    Niam-niam: Torubale.
18. *Lutra inunguis.* F. Cuv.?
    Niam-niam: Limmu.
19. *Canis familiaris.* L.
    Dinka: Dyong.
    Dyoor: Grook.
    Bongo: Bihee.
    Niam-niam: Ango.
    Mittoo: Weehy.
    Golo: Ovio.
    Kredy: Kohno.
    Sehre: Borro.
    Monbuttoo: Nessy.
20. *Canis variegatus.* Cretschm.
    (*C. aureus auctorum.*)
    Dinka: Awaun.
    Dyoor: Toh.
    Bongo: Galah.
    Niam-niam: Hoah.
    Kredy: Glommu.
    Golo: Ndaggeh.
    Sehre: Ndeh.
21. *Canis pictus.* Desm.
    Dinka: Kwaty.
    Bongo: Well.
    Niam-niam: Tiah.
    Sehre: Sahr.
22. *Octocyon Lalandii.* H. Sm.?
    Dinka: Paudey.

23. *Hyæna crocata.* Zimm.
    Dinka: Angwee.
    Dyoor: Utwomm.
    Bongo: Heeloo.
    Niam-niam: Wegge.
    Mittoo: Moddaoo.
    Golo: Mboo.
    Sehre: Mboh.
24. *Viverra civetta.* Schreb.
    Dyoor: Yuoll.
    Bongo: Kurrukkoo.
    Niam-niam: Teeya.
25. *Viverra genetta.* L.
    Dinka: Augonn.
    Dyoor: Anyara.
    Bongo: Dongoh.
    Niam-niam: Mbellee.
    Golo: Nifah.
    Kredy: Ndilly.
    Sehre: Mehre.
26. *Herpestes fasciatus.* Desm.
    Dinka: Agorr.
    Dyoor: Gorr.
    Bongo: Ngorr, or Dai.
    Niam-niam: Nduttwah.
27. *Felis leo.* L.
    Dinka: Kohr.
    Dyoor: Moo.
    Bongo: Pull.
    Niam-niam: Mbongonoo.
    Golo: Singilee.
    Kredy: Ganye-kaza.
    Sehre: Sirringinny.
28. *Felis leopardus.* Schreb.
    Dyoor: Kwaty.
    Bongo: Koggo.
    Niam-niam: Mamah.
    Kredy: Sellembey.
29. *Felis caracal.* L.
    Dyoor: Nwoi.
    Bongo: Mudyokpollah.
    Niam-niam: Mobboroo.

30. *Felis serval.* Schreb.
   Dinka: Dohk.
   Bongo: Gregge.
   Niam-niam: Ngaffoo.

31. *Felis maniculata.* Temm: Rüpp.
   Dinka: Angow.
   Dyoor: Bang, or Gwang.
   Bongo: Mbira-oo.
   Niam-niam: Dandalah.
   Golo: Dahre.
   Kredy: Lehje.
   Sehre: Sahte.
   Mittoo: Ngorroh.

32. *Sciurus leucumbrinus.* Rüpp.
   Dyoor: Aiyeda.
   Bongo: Remme.
   Niam-niam: Bederry.

33. *Sciurus superciliaris.* A. Wagn.
   Dinka: Allohl.
   Dyoor: Anynai.
   Bongo: Urenge.
   Niam-niam: Bamumba, or Bakumbah.
   Golo: Angah.
   Sehre: Serenna.

34. *Mus decumanus.* Pall.
   Bongo: Luny.
   Niam-niam: Gwah.

35. *Mus alexandrinus.* Geoffr.
   Dinka: Lohk.
   Bongo: Higgeh-roo, or Rohpattah.
   Niam-niam: Babilly.
   Kredy: Ohtoh.
   Sehre: Dyoo.

36. *Golunda pulchella.* Gray.
   Dinka: Manyang.
   Dyoor: Weeo.
   Bongo: Yangah.
   Niam-niam: Sikka.
   Golo: Ngadze.
   Mittoo: Gaggah.

37. *Meriones Burtonii.* A. Wagn.
   Dinka: Maval kondo.
   Dyoor: Omadda.
   Bongo: Mokokoh, or Higgehnyakkah.
   Niam-niam: Zakadda.
   Golo: Fyako.
   Kredy: Iltee.
   Sehre: Dyoo.

38. *Mus gentilis.* Brants.
   Bongo: Mangbelle.
   Niam-niam: Ndekkitelly.

39. *Aulacodus Swinderianus.* Temm.
   Bongo: Bohko.
   Dinka: Lony.
   Dyoor: Nyanyahr.
   Niam-niam: Remvo or Alimvoh.
   Golo: Elle.
   Sehre: Abattara.
   Kredy: Mbadja.
   Mittoo: Wohko.

40. *Lepus æthiopicus.* Ehrbg.
   Dinka: Anyorr.
   Dyoor: Ap-woio.
   Bongo: Battah.
   Niam-niam: Ndekutteh.
   Kredy: Ohzo.

41. *Hystrix cristata.* L.
   Dyoor: Shyow.
   Bongo: Kehoa.
   Niam-niam: Nzingeneh.

42. *Oryctcropus æthiopicus.* Sundev
   Dyoor: Mohk.
   Niam-niam: Kahre.

43. *Manis Temminckii.* Sund.
   Dyoor: Kong.
   Bongo: Konn.
   Niam-niam: Bashishee.

44. *Elephas africanus.* Blum.
   Dinka: Akonn.
   Dyoor: Lyady.
   Bongo: Kiddy.
   Niam-niam: Mbarah.

APPENDIX III.

Mittoo: Kiddy.
Golo: Offio.
Kredy: Morrongoh.
Sehre: Shah.

45. *Rhinoceros bicornis.* L.
Dyoor: Umwoh.
Bongo: Basha.
Niam-niam: Kangah.
Kredy: Gruruppo.

46. *Hippopotamus amphibius.* L.
Dinka: Nyang.
Dyoor: Fahr.
Bongo: Habba.
Niam-niam: Duppoh.
Golo: Fyongoo.
Kredy: Mrungoo.
Sehre: Diffoh.

47. *Hyrax sp.*
Bongo: Mberedoo.
Niam-niam: Attaboo.
Lehsy: Keltoh.
Golo: Ngaffe.
Kredy: Ozo.
Sehre: Nogoun.

48. *Phacochœrus Aeliani.* Rüpp.
Dinka: Dyehr.
Dyoor: Kull.
Bongo: Bohdoo.
Niam-niam: Tibba.
Mittoo: Wadoh.
Kredy: Bonghoh, or Boddoh.
Golo: Vungbah.
Sehre: Badzo.

49. *Potamochœrus penicillatus.* Gray.
Niam-niam: Mokkuroo, or Djomborr.
Monbuttoo: Napazo.

50. *Camelopardalis giraffa.* L.
Dinka: Mehr.
Dyoor: Wehr.
Bongo: Killiroo.
Niam-niam: Basumbarrighy.
Golo: Ndakkala.
Kredy: Govisisce.
Sehre: Bagga.

51. *Sus sennaariensis.* Fitz.
Dinka: Angow.
Dyoor: Amayok.
Bongo: Mondoh.
Niam-niam: Gurrwa.
Mittoo Madi: Legyeh.

52. *Antilope Oreas.* Pall.
Dinka: Golgwall.
Dyoor: Odyerr.
Bongo: Mburreh.
Niam-niam: Mburreh.
Mittoo: Kehr, or Mburreh.
Bellanda: Odehr.
Kredy: Kobbo.
Sehre: Kovo.
Golo: Kobbo.

53. *Antilope leucophæa.* Pall. (*Ægoceros.* Ham. Sm.)
Dinka: Amomm.
Dyoor: Ommar.
Bongo: Manya.
Niam-niam: Bisso.
Golo: Vunnungoo.
Bellanda: Omahr.
Sehre: Dehngah.

54. *Antilope nigra.* Harris. (*Ægoceros.* Ham. Sm.)

55. *Antilope caama.* Gray. (*Acronotus.* H. Sm.)
Dinka: Alalwehl.
Dyoor: Purroh.
Bongo: Karia.
Niam-niam: Songoroh, or Soggumoo.
Mittoo: Borro.
Golo: Kotzo.
Kredy: Kreia.
Sehre: Dangah.
Babuckur: Borro.
Monbuttoo: Nakkibbee.

56. *Antilope leucotis.* Licht. Peters. (*Kobus.* A. Sm.)
Dinka: Teel.
Dyoor: Teel.
Bongo: Kalah.

Niam-niam: Tagba.
Mittoo: Kalla.
Sehre: Boddy.
Kredy: Ngaio.
Golo: Ngallah.
Monbuttoo: Nehpedde.

57. *Antilope defassa.* Rüpp. (*Kobus.* A. Sm.)
Dinka: Pohr or Fohr.
Dyoor: Ummoowoh.
Bongo: Booboo.
Niam-niam: Mbagga.
Mittoo: Lehby.
Kredy: Adyee.
Golo: Boggo, or Weendy.

58. *Antilope megaloceros.* Heugl. (*Kobus.* A. Sm.)
Dinka: Abohk.

59. *Antilope arundinacea.* Gray. (*Eleotragus.*)
Dinka: Kao.
Dyoor: Rohr.
Bongo: Yolo.
Niam-niam: Yoro.
Golo: Ngallah.
Sehre: Dyiang.

60. *Antilope scripta.* Pall. (*Tragelaphus.* Blainv.)
Dinka: Pehr, or Fehr.
Dyoor: Rohro.
Bongo: Tobbo.
Niam-niam: Boddy.
Golo: Kuffoo.
Mittoo: Ehboo.
Kredy: Leuje.
Sehre: Ya-oo, or Yavoh.
Bellanda: Rodda.

61. *Antilope Addax.* Licht.
Dinka: Anyidohl.
Bongo: Owel.

62. *Antilope senegalensis.* H. Lin. (*Dumalis.* Gray.)
Dinka: Tyang.
Dyoor: Tahng.
Bongo: Tanghe.

63. *Antilope madoqua.* Rüpp. (*Cephalolophus.* H. Sm. Hens.)
Dinka: Lohdy.
Dyoor: Nettyade.
Bongo: Heggoleh.
Mittoo: Kulleh.
Niam-niam: Bongbalyah.
Golo: Leffu.
Kredy: Kehdo.
Sehre: Ngogoh.
Shillook: Akony.

64. *Antilope grimmia.* Licht. (*Cephalolophus.* H. Sm.)
Dinka: Amook.
Dyoor: Nyepael.
Bongo: Deelg.
Niam-niam: Bafoo.
Mittoo: Lehloo.
Mittoo-Madi: Hecboo.
Sehre: Dee.

65. *Antilope pygmæa.* Licht. (*Cephalolophus.* H. Sm.)
Bongo: Mburrumoo.
Niam-niam: Mourrah.
Sehre: Nzerre.
Monbuttoo: Nelunbokoh.

66. *Antilope sp. minor rufescens.* (*Cephalolophus.* H. Sm.)
Bongo: Dongboh.
Niam-niam: Kohtumoh.

67. *Capra hircus.* L.
Dinka: Tonn (male); Tohk (female).
Dyoor: Byell.
Bongo: Binya.
Niam-niam: Wussindeh.
Mittoo: Oanya.
Golo: Orego.
Kredy: Ehne.
Sehre: Mvirry.
Monbuttoo: Memmeh.

68. *Ovis aries.* L.
Dinka: Amahl.
Dyoor: Rohmo.

Bongo: Romboh.
Kredy: Ndillimee.
Mittoo: Kameleh.
Sehre: Dzagga.
69. *Bos taurus.* L. (*B. Zebu*, var. *Africana*).
    Dinka: Wehng (common); Tonu (male); Ngoot (female.)
    Bongo: Shah.
    Niam-niam: Hiity.
    Mittoo: Ehshah.
    Golo: Moddoh.

Kredy: Modoh.
Dyoor: Dyang.
70. *Bubalis Caffer.* Gray.
    Dinka: Anyarr.
    Dyoor: Dyooy.
    Bongo: Kobby.
    Niam-niam: Mbah.
    Golo: Meende.
    Kredy: Sobbo, or Mbah.
    Sehre: Mbah.
71. *Manatus senegalensis.* Desm. M. Vogelii?
    Nubians: Kharoof-el-Bahr.

DOUBTFUL SPECIES, KNOWN ONLY FROM INFORMATION DERIVED FROM NATIVES.

72. *Sorex sp.?*
    Bongo: Higgeh Karia.

73. *Mus sp.?*
    Bongo: Mobiddy.

74. *Mus sp.?*
    Bongo: Highee Deeloo.

75. *Chrysochloris sp.?* (*Talpa?*)
    Bongo: Brumur.
    Niam-niam: Tundooah.

INDEX.

ABAKA, i. 189.
A-Banga, tribe of, i. 250; entertaining, i. 253; trophy of their heads, ii. 107; great body of, ii. 108.
Abbuloh, ii. 209.
Abd-el-fetah, ii. 1.
Aboo Dinga, ii. 237.
Aboo Guroon, i. 68; ii. 44, 173, 188.
Aboo Sammat (*vide* Mohammed Aboo Sammat).
Acacia-woods, i. 20.
Adiantum, ii. 91.
Adimokoo, ii. 69; his war-dance, ii. 70.
Agriculture, i. 62, 84, 117, 251.
Ahmed, ii. 142.
Ahmed Aga, ii. 212, 216.
AKKA, ii. 23; their country, ii. 36; height, complexion, and hair, ii. 79; appearance, ii. 80; dialect, ii. 82; treatment by Monbuttoo, ii. 83.
Albizzia, i. 46; ii. 230.
Allagabo, ii. 126, 263, 282.
Aloe, i. 225.
Alwaj, i. 64.
Ambatch, i. 25, 26.
Amomum, i. 221.
Amphistoma, i. 45, 61.
Ampularia, ii. 266.
Anona, i. 89.
Antelopes, i. 70, 170, 174; ii. 143.
Ant-hills, i. 33, 166; ii. 109.
Antinori, Marquis, i. 68; ii. 33.

Apostrophe, an, i. 70.
Arachis, i. 105.
Aristotle, ii. 67.
Arrows, i. 140, 255; ii. 105.
Artocarpus, i. 260.
Assika, i. 249, 252; ii. 111.
Atazilly, i. 231.
Atena, ii. 206.
Atoborroo, i. 217.
Auguries, i. 297.
Aulacodus, ii. 254.
Awoory, i. 177.

BABUCKUR, i. 99; ii. 36, 37, 129, 154.
Badry, ii. 142, 145.
Baggara Arabs, ii. 201, 223, 241.
Baginze, ii. 131.
Bahr-el-Abiad, i. 7.
Bahr-el-Arab, i. 34, 36; ii. 223, 237, 272.
Bahr-el-Dembo, ii. 203.
Bahr-el-Gebel, i. 7, 29; ii. 97.
Bahr-el-Ghazal, i. 29, 30, 34, 36 (*vide* Gazelle).
Bahr-el-Giraffe, i. 23; ii. 274.
Bahr-el-Kooroo, ii. 209.
Baker, Sir S., i. 25, 263; statement about Lake Mwootan, ii. 36, 96; peremptory measures, ii. 271, 276.
Balæniceps rex, i. 31; ii. 272.
Balanites, i. 53, 90.
Bamboos, i. 97; ii. 152.
Barabra, ii. 194.

INDEX. 301

Barth, i. 110, 215, 268; ii. 48, 92, 238.
Basket-work, Bongo, i. 133; Monbuttoo, ii. 61.
Bastard gemsbok, i. 99.
Batatas, i. 106.
Beads, i. 41, 51, 139, 239.
Beans, i. 105; ii. 154.
Bear-baboons, i. 75.
Bearers, i. 43; ii. 257; supply of, i. 200; consideration for, i. 220; feeding, i. 225.
Beer, i. 231, 281.
Beery, ii. 227.
Bees, attacked by, i. 11; a swarm found, ii. 99.
Behnky, i. 206.
Belanda, i. 76.
Belostoma, i. 45.
Benches, ii. 41, 58.
Bendo, i. 212, 214; ii. 144.
Benwe, ii. 86.
Berber, ii. 194, 281.
Bizelly, ii. 198.
Blessing, ii. 279.
Blippo (*Gardenia*), i. 209; used by Monbuttoo, ii. 51.
Blue Mountains, i. 267; ii. 36, 97.
Boddo, i. 221.
Bomby, ii. 71.
BONGO, their country, i. 112; vassalage, i. 113; complexion, i. 115; skulls and hair, i. 116; agriculture, i. 117; smoking, i. 118; goats, i. 119; dogs, i. 120; hunting, i. 120; dwellings, i. 123; weapons and ornaments, i. 125–8, 138; musical instruments, i. 130; pottery, i. 134; costume, i. 136; games, i. 140; funerals, i. 143; superstition, i. 144, 145; dialect, i. 147.
Bongwa, the chieftain, i. 261; his wife, i. 262; return to, ii. 90.
Borassus, i. 47, 176.
Boroo, i. 297; ii. 110.
Bread, i. 105.
Bruce, the traveller, i. 29.

Buffalo, attacked by a, i. 9; African species, i. 71; frantic herds of them, i. 203; ii. 157, 158; calf killed, ii. 205.
Bumba, i. 263; ii. 90.
Bunza, son of Munza, ii. 15.
Burckhardt, ii. 194.
Burton, i. 44.
Bushmen, ii. 78.
Butter-trees, i. 87, 184; ii. 127.

CALAMUS, i. 217, 221; ii. 115.
Calotropis, ii. 202.
Canavalia, i. 251; ii. 63.
Canis pictus, ii. 167.
Cannibalism, traces of, i. 55, 191; amongst Niam-niam, i. 274, 285; amongst Monbuttoo, ii. 42; instance of, ii. 138.
Canoes, i. 269; ii. 57.
Capparideæ, i. 87.
Caravans, i. 42, 201, 229.
Carpodinus, i. 87.
Cats, wild, i. 55, 153.
Cattle-diseases, i. 58; ii. 169.
Cattle-raids, i. 44, 66, 92, 169; ii. 267.
Caves, i. 94.
Cayenne pepper, i. 109.
Cecropia, i. 260; ii. 93.
Centropus, i. 165.
Cercopithecus, i. 232.
Chimpanzees in Wando's district, i. 136; skulls, i. 247; mode of catching, i. 249.
Chlorophytum, ii. 63.
Christ's thorn, i. 46.
Clappertonia, ii. 118.
Cogyoor, i. 62, 144.
Cola-nut, ii. 9.
Coldest day, ii. 185.
Colobus, i. 232.
Colocasia, i. 211.
Combretum, i. 165, 188; ii. 99.
Concerts, i. 131, 168, 231.
Copper, taken as exchange, i. 239; known to Monbuttoo, ii. 55; mines, ii. 224.

Cordia Abyssinica, i. 271.
Corn-magazines, i. 83, 123; ii. 179, 208, 225, 242.
Cowries, i. 140, 239.
Cranes, ii. 67.
Crocodiles, ii. 198.
Crosses, i. 288.
Crotalaria, i. 108.
Cubeba Clusii, i. 222.
Cucurbita, i. 107.
Cussonia, ii. 131.
Cyanite, ii. 134.

DAL KURDYOOK, ii. 267.
Damoory, ii. 203.
Dance, i. 185; ii. 29, 70, 132.
Danga, i. 175.
Dangabor (Bongo ornament), i. 127.
Dangadulloo, i. 175.
Dapper, ii. 75.
Dar Fertcet, ii. 219.
Darfoor, ii. 195, 224.
Date-palms, ii. 159.
Degbe, i. 174.
Degberra, i. 259; ii. 25.
Dehms, ii. 212, 219.
Deloo antelopes, i. 102.
Deraggo, i. 187.
Dialect, Dyoor, i. 76; Bongo, i. 147; Mittoo, i. 189; Niam-niam, i. 296; Monbuttoo, ii. 48; Akka, ii. 82; Golo, ii. 208.
Diamvonoo, i. 247; ii. 112.
Dimindoh, i. 174.
Dimmoh, ii. 197.
DINKA; territory and appearance, i. 48; ornaments, i. 52; weapons, i. 53; cookery, i. 54; dwellings, i. 55, 56; domestic animals, i. 57; population, i. 62; character, i. 63.
Dioscorea, i. 106.
Diospyros, i. 53, 89.
Distillery, i. 97.
Djee, the river, ii. 241.
Dogs, i. 59, 120, 283; ii. 23, 114.
Dogguroo, the river, i. 158, 205; ii. 162.

Dokkuttoo, i. 172.
Dubor, ii. 168, 184.
Du Chaillu, ii. 75, 83.
Duggoo, i. 161, 163.
Dugguddoo, i. 163.
Duisberg, German vice-consul, i. 4, 5.
Dyafer Pasha, Governor-General of Khartoom, i. 5; ii. 277, 280.
Dyagbe, the river, i. 238.
Dyoor, the river, i. 34, 69; ii. 132, 171, 190; fishing in, ii. 257.
DYOOR nation; name and dialect, i. 76; complexion and ornaments, i. 77, 78; spears and spades, i. 80; iron-smelting, i. 81; huts, i. 83; habits and character, i. 84, 85.
Dyoorab-el-Esh, i. 11.
Dyuihr, i. 64.

EARTH-NUTS, i. 105, 251.
Egyptians, i. 19; their troops, ii. 186, 212.
Elaïs, i. 260; ii. 39.
Elands, i. 169; ii. 149.
Elephants, wanton destruction of, i. 43, 207; traces of, i. 159; snares for, i. 187; present of a young elephant, ii. 169.
Eleusine corn, i. 104; beer made from, i. 281.
Elminia, ii. 191.
Encephalartus, i. 213; ii. 151, 159, 225.
Ensete (wild plantain), i. 213; ii. 133.
Entada scandens, ii. 18.
Entada sudanica, ii. 197.
Eriodendron, ii. 60.
Escayrac de Lauture, ii. 76, 222.
Etheria, i. 175; ii. 258.
Eulophia, ii. 133.
Eumenes tinctor, i. 154.
Eunuch, Munza's, ii. 11.
Euphorbiæ, i. 39, 89, 140.
Extract of meat, ii. 25.

FAKI, grave of a, ii. 177.
Fanekama, ii. 275.

INDEX.

Fans, analogy with Niam-niam, i. 286.
Farookh (black soldiers), i. 229; ii. 110.
Fashoda, limit of Egyptian government, i. 12; return to, ii. 277.
Ferns, i. 242.
Fever, immunity from, i. 38, 154; deaths from, ii. 281.
Ficus lutea, i. 164; ii. 249.
Fig-trees, ii. 49, 202.
Fire, alarm of, i. 151; in Seriba, ii. 175, 264.
Fish, i. 93.
Fishing, i. 80, 93; ii. 40, 225, 257.
Flags, i. 43, 201; ii. 31.
Flight before Shillooks, i. 22.
Fritsch, Gustav, i. 115; ii. 78, 81.
Frogs, i. 257.
Fulbe, affinity of Monbuttoo with, ii. 48.

GADDA, the river, ii. 89.
Galago, i. 144, 252; ii. 46.
Galleries, i. 240, 259; ii. 99.
Games, i. 140, 294.
Garden, my, i. 85; ii. 262.
Gardenia, i. 70, 75; ii. 63.
Gazelle (Bahr-el-Ghazal), i. 29; ii. 272.
Geer, the Seriba, i. 68, 93.
Gellahbas (slave-dealers), ii. 190, 215, 219, 240.
Genana, i. 68.
Gessi, ii. 85, 96.
Ghattas, contract with, i. 5, 7; his death, ii. 164.
Ghetty, the river, ii. 198, 247.
Giraffes, ii. 167.
Girkeny, i. 178.
Gneiss hills, i. 174, 234; ii. 235.
Goats, i. 59, 119, 190; ii. 24.
Goggo, i. 183.
Golo, ii. 207.
Gondokoro, i. 7.
Gourds, i. 96, 107.
Government contracts, i. 8.

Grass-barrier (El-Sett), i. 14, 24.
Grass-huts, ii. 139.
Graves, i. 129, 142, 198, 298.
Gresse, the river, ii. 229.
Grewia, i. 118.
Gubbehee, i. 96.
Gudyoo, ii. 228.
Guinea-fowl, i. 172, 232; ii. 135.
Guinea-hogs, ii. 32.
Guinea-worm, i. 63, 189.
Gumango, the hill, i. 212; ii. 144.
Gumba, i. 211; ii. 144.
Gum-arabic, i. 20.
Gun accident, i. 47.
Gurfala, i. 97.
Gurroogurroo, i. 251; ii. 34.

Habenaria, ii. 158.
Hailstorm, ii. 170.
Halls, Monbuttoo, ii. 5, 30, 32.
Hartebeests, i. 70, 72; ii. 143, 157, 159, 266.
Hartmann, Professor, i. 16.
Hegelig (Balanites), i. 46.
Hellali, the swindler, ii. 195, 212.
Helmia, i. 106.
Herodotus, ii. 67.
Heterometrus, i. 122.
Heuglin, Theodor von, i. 38; ii. 33, 199, 203.
Hexalobus, i. 182.
Hibiscus, i. 108.
Hippopotamuses in the White Nile, i. 25, 27; in the Dyoor, ii. 191; their fat, ii. 192.
Homer, ii. 67.
Honey, wild, i. 133; ii. 99.
Hoo, the river, i. 216; ii. 123, 139.
Hornblende, i. 69, 205.
Humboldtia (kobbo-tree), i. 159; ii. 158
Humboldt Institution, grant from, i. 2.
Hunger, ii. 121, 261.
Huts, Shillook, i. 16; Dinka, i. 56; in Seriba, i. 66; Dyoor, i. 83; Bongo, i. 123; Mittoo, i. 197; Niam-niam, i. 214, 287; Monbuttoo, ii. 62; crowded, ii. 174; Kredy, ii. 225.

Hydrolia, ii. 209.
Hyena-dogs (*Canis pictus*), ii. 167.
Hymenocardia, i. 134.
Hymenodictyon, ii. 133.
Hyphæne, ii. 112.
Hyptis, i. 105, 251 ; ii. 197.

IBBA, the river, i. 205.
Ibis, ii. 191.
Ibrahim Effendi, ii. 218.
Ichneumons, ii. 266.
Idrees (Ghattas's plenipotentiary), i. 65, 146 ; ii. 180, 264.
Idrees Wod Defter, ii. 206.
Indimma, ii. 35.
Iron-smelting of the Dyoor, i. 80; of the Bongo, i. 123; of the Monbuttoo, ii. 54.
Irvingia, i. 216.
Islamism, ii. 137.
Issoo, the Upper Tondy, ii. 130.
Ivory-trade, i. 6.
Izingerria, visit to, i. 264.

KAKA, i. 10.
Kahpily, the river, ii. 91.
Kambeley, the river, ii. 93.
Kamrasi, inquiries for, ii. 22.
Kanna, ambassadors from, ii. 14 ; territory of, ii. 34.
Karo, i. 182.
Karra, the magic tuber, ii. 205, 244.
Kashgar, i. 19 ; ii. 274.
Keebaly, the river, ii. 89, 94.
Kettle-drums, i. 131, 291.
Khalil, i. 70 ; ii. 184, 251.
Khareef, i. 155 ; ii. 170.
Khartoom, i. 3 ; return to, ii. 279.
Kigelia, i. 44, 88.
Kilnoky, i. 94.
Kirmo, i. 179.
Kishy, bridge over the, ii. 125.
Kokkorokkoo, the tree, i. 222.
Kölle, ii. 77.
Koolongo, i. 94, 157 ; ii. 163.
Kosaria palmata, i. 88.
Kotschy, ii. 199.

Krapf, ii. 77.
KREDY; their appearance, ii. 221 ; huts, ii. 226.
Kubby, ii. 93.
Kudy, village of, i. 47 ; ii. 268.
Kulenjo, i. 218 ; ii. 139.
Kuraggera, i. 183.
Kurkur, ii. 166.
Kurshook Ali, the Sandjak, i. 70 ; ii. 161 ; his death, i. 171.
Kussumbo, woods on the, i. 259 ; ii. 91, 98.
Kyt, *cul-de-sac* on the Gazelle, i. 36 ; ii. 272.

LAFARGUE, French vice-consul at Berber, ii. 281.
Lances, i. 53, 126, 292.
Lao, its water, i. 39 ; ii. 269.
Leather, i. 196.
Legby, i. 181.
Lehssy, the river, i. 158, 181, 205; ii. 152, 157.
LEHSSY people, i. 180.
Lepidosiren, i. 93.
Leucotis antelopes, i. 70, 73, 99 ; ii. 92, 143.
Lichtenstein, ii. 81, 82.
Limnicolaria, i. 165.
Lindukoo, last stream of Nile system, i. 230, 232, 233 ; ii. 117.
Lions, limited in number, i. 170 ; district infested by, i. 172 ; Bongo carried off by one, i. 226 ; traces of, ii. 92.
Lips, mutilation of, i. 138, 192.
Livingstone, Dr., i. 240, 277 ; ii. 113, 167.
Lollo, the river, ii. 275.
Longo, dirt in, ii. 201.
Loobah, i. 189, 195 ; ii. 155.
Lophira, i. 213 ; ii. 42.

MABODE, ii. 36.
Madi, i. 186, 194.
Madikamm, ii. 124.

INDEX.   305

Madoqua antelopes, i. 101; ii. 266.
Maia Signora, i. 26; ii. 273.
Maize, i. 105, preparation by Niamniam, i. 284; in Mbomo's district, ii. 154.
Makarakka, ii. 131.
Malzac, i. 159, 261.
Manatus, in the Keebaly, ii. 95.
Manga, ii. 151.
Manioc, bearer poisoned by, i. 226; cultivation, i. 251; ii. 41.
Manzilly, the brook, i. 217.
Maoggoo, cattle from the, i. 263; ii. 20; probable identity with the Malegga, ii. 37.
Maraboos, ii. 262.
Market, i. 24, 238; ii. 13.
Marra, i. 215; ii. 141.
Marriage portions, i. 141.
Marshes, crossing, i. 237; ii. 101, 117, 125.
Mashirr hills, ii. 159.
Massanza. ii. 36.
Matyoo, i. 164.
Mbahla Ngeea, i. 205; ii. 159.
Mbahly, nickname for Aboo Sammat i. 228; ii. 2, 107.
Mbanga, i. 208.
Mbarik-pah, the leaf-eater, i. 244; ii. 124.
Mbeeoh, ii. 119.
Mbomo, the Seriba, i. 190; ii. 149, 153.
Mrbwole, the river, i. 234, 236; ii. 115.
Merdyan, ii. 125.
Meshera, i. 7; arrival at the, i. 35; mode of anchoring in, i. 37.
Meteorological notes, ii. 170, 260.
Miani, the Italian explorer, ii. 9, 21, 47, 83.
Mimosa, ii. 157.
Miniscalchi, ii. 84.
Minstrel, i. 212, 296; ii. 146.
MITTOO; their dialect, i. 189; fertility of soil, i. 190; ornaments, i. 191, 192; music, i. 197; graves and weapons, i. 198.
Mofio, i. 224, 289.

VOL. II.

Mohammed Aboo Sammat, i. 22, 156, 162, 185, 200, 219, 228, 238; ii. 2, 26, 44, 60, 102, 107, 111, 136, 168, 172, 208.
Molmul, the river, i. 69; ii. 167.
Momvoo, ii. 24, 36.
MONBUTTOO; country and government, ii. 34, 35; fertility of soil, ii. 37; habits, ii. 40, 41, 42; cannibalism, ii. 42; potentates, ii. 44; complexion, ii. 47; *coiffure*, ii. 52; weapons, ii. 53; iron-smelting, ii. 54; tools, ii. 57; seats, ii. 59; handicraft, ii. 61; architecture, ii. 62; religion, ii. 64.
Money, i. 125, 232.
Mongolongboh, i. 204.
Mongono, ii. 206.
Monkeys, i. 188.
Morelia, i. 216; ii. 198.
Morokoh, the river, ii. 18, 152, 156.
Mossoolungoo, ii. 129.
Mummery, Munza's brother, ii. 26, 28, 72.
Mundo, i. 99; ii. 130, 155.
Mungala. Niam-niam game, i. 294.
Munza, ii. 1, 6, 29, 45.
Murahs, i. 56, 61.
Musa sapientium, i. 74, 213, 251; ii. 38.
Music, i. 131, 132, 197, 295; ii. 29.
Musical instruments, i. 130, 197, 295; ii. 58, 61, 248.
Mvolo, district of, i. 179.
Mwata Yanvo, i. 252; ii. 46.
Mwootan (Albert Nyanza), i. 265; ii. 96.
Mycteria Senegalensis, ii. 191.

NABAMBISSO, the river, i. 221, 225.
Nachtigal, i. 268.
Nalengbe. Munza's sister, ii. 16, 44.
Nalobey, ii. 96, 98.
Nambia, ii. 125.
Naporrooporoo, i. 235.
Nathalia, i. 212.
Ndoruma, ii. 174, 189.
Nduggo, ii. 222.

X

Nduppo, Wando's brother, i. 226; his death, i. 246.

Nembey, visit from, i. 259; arrival at residence of, ii. 90.

Ngahma, i. 174, 182, 194.

Nganye, a Niam-niam chieftain, i. 206, 210; ii. 147.

Ngoly, i. 203; ii. 156, 159.

Nguddoo, ii. 167.

Ngulfala, i. 97, 247.

NIAM-NIAM; first sight of, i. 206; visit from, i. 209; guides, i. 233; country, i. 274; appearance, i. 275; clothing and head-gear, i. 276, 277; weapons, i. 278; hunting and agriculture, i. 281; pipes, i. 282; dogs, i. 283; cannibalism, i. 285; architecture, i. 287; chieftains, i. 289; war-cries, i. 290; handicraft, i. 291, 293; greetings, i. 292; games and music, i. 294, 295; language, i. 296; auguries, i. 297; graves, i. 298; conjugal affection, ii. 113.

No, lake, i. 28.

Nomayo, ii. 26, 96.

Nomatilla, i. 71.

Nsewue, the Pygmy, ii. 23, 73, 110, 160; his death, ii. 281.

NUBIANS, i. 113; their stories, ii. 65; soldiers, ii. 111; cowardice, ii. 189; character, ii. 193.

Nueir, district of the, i. 30–33; ii. 272.

Nymphæa, i. 34.

O-BONGO, ii. 75.

Oil-palms, i. 260; ii. 39, 42.

Okale, i. 75.

Okuloh, ii. 200.

Ori, Dr., letter to Antinori, ii. 33.

Orycteropus, i. 138, 167.

Oryza punctata, i. 104.

Oysters, river, ii. 258.

Pandanus, i. 236.

Panicum, i. 207.

Papyrus, i. 24, 36; ii. 124.

Parkia-trees, i. 89; ii. 200.

Parley with Niam-niam, ii. 100.

Parra africanus, ii. 89.

Pelomedusa, i. 35.

Penceo, the behnky, i. 206; ii. 147.

Penicillaria, i. 104.

Pepper, i. 242.

Petherick, i. 38, 180, 181; ii. 130, 166.

Phacochærus, i. 68, 75.

Phaseolus, i. 105, 251; ii. 154.

Phœnix, i. 89, 221, 225.

Phrynia, ii. 117.

Phyllorhina, i. 95, 163.

Piaggia, i. 240, 273, 285; ii. 15, 21, 97.

Pipes, i. 56, 118, 283; ii. 9, 61.

Plantains, i. 74, 213; ii. 39.

Platinum, ii. 55.

Platycerium elephantotis, i. 242, 258.

Poncet, the brothers, i. 47, 175, 181; ii. 33, 35.

Pongo, the river, ii. 203.

Popukky-grass, i. 207.

Port Rek, i. 35.

Potamochærus, ii. 32.

Pottery, i. 134; ii. 40.

Prosopis, i. 128; ii. 98.

Protea, ii. 131, 206.

Psittacus, ii. 40.

Pterolobium, i. 252.

Pygmies, ii. 66 (*vide* Akka).

Pyrrhi Æthiopes, ii. 48.

QUININE, i. 12, 38, 154.

RAGOÛT, a, i. 243.

Rainfall, i. 154.

Randia, i. 46; ii. 51.

Raphia vinifera, i. 75, 260; ii. 5.

Rats, ii. 249.

Reed-rats, ii. 233, 254.

Reggo, i. 183.

Rek, Port, i. 35, 47; ii. 269.

Religion, i. 62, 143, 296; ii. 64.

Rhinoceros-bird, i. 147; ii. 136, 191.

Rice, i. 104.

Riharn, my cook, i. 8.

Rikkete, Wando's brother, i. 227, 231.

Rings, i. 52, 78, 139.

Roah, the river, i. 171, 172, 187.

INDEX.

Rock-rabbits, i. 180.
Rohl, the river, i. 177.'
Rokko coats of Monbuttoo, ii. 49.
Rye, the river, i. 202.

SABBY (Seriba), i. 167, 188; ii. 169.
Sabdariffa, ii. 197.
Salt, i. 16, 118.
Sanseviera, i. 133.
Scopus umbretta, ii. 191.
Scorbutic attack, ii. 230.
Seebehr Rahama, ii. 195; his court, ii. 216.
Sehre, ii. 241, 246.
Selaginella, ii. 133.
Seriba, i. 7, 65, 91, 152.
Sesame, i. 251.
Sett, i. 14, 24.
Shary, identity with the Welle, i. 268; ii. 96.
Shereefee attacks Mohammed, i. 162; shielded by the Aga, ii. 172, 214.
SHILLOOKS, first sight of, i. 9; villages, i. 10; population, i. 14; huts, i. 16; appearance and headgear, i. 17; domestic animals, i. 18; chased by, i. 22; market, i. 23; ii. 274.
Shoby, ii. 128, 135.
Shol, the Dinka queen, i. 40; her riches and influence, i. 39; presents to, i. 41; her death, ii. 200; remains of her huts, ii. 270.
Skins, i. 134, 227, 233.
Skulls, i. 116, 247; ii. 14, 107, 137.
Slaves, i. 173; ii. 231, 271, 276.
Slave-trade, ii. 186, 220, 277.
Smelting-furnaces, i. 81, 124.
Snares, i. 84, 120.
Sobat, the river, i. 7, 21.
Soldiers, i. 229; ii. 111, 145, 161.
Soliman, son of Kurshook Ali, ii. 258.
Solongoh, i. 76; ii. 236, 241.
Sorghum, i. 44, 96, 102; ii. 153.
Spades, i. 80.
Sparmannia, ii. 123.
Spathodea, ii. 99, 139.

Speke, i. 29; ii. 38, 68, 97.
Stanley, i. 269.
Stapelia, i. 291.
Stephegyne, ii. 204.
Steppe-burning, i. 164.
Steps, counting, ii. 183, 210.
Steudner, Dr., i. 38; ii. 198, 199.
Storm, ii. 243, 269.
Suakin, ii. 282.
Sugar-canes, i. 251, 264; ii. 90.
Surroor, Aboo Sammat's lieutenant, i. 214, 219; ii. 137.
Swamps, ii. 100, 117, 125.
Sway, the river, i. 215; ii. 132, 140.

TAKE, village of, i. 47; ii. 268.
Taya hills, ii. 243.
Tamarinds, i. 46, 171.
Tattooing, i. 77, 139, 194, 262, 276; ii. 51.
Tee, the river, ii. 159.
Teeth, mutilation of, i. 50, 135, 276; ii. 53.
Telegram, ii. 280.
Telphusa, i. 257.
Temperature, ii. 181.
Tephrosia, i. 40, 63.
Termes, i. 259.
Terminalia, i. 205.
Tetmoceras, ii. 126.
Tikkitikki, ii. 72, 87, 110, 160, 256, 281.
Tinné, Miss, i. 25, 41; her mother, ii. 199.
Tithymalus, ii. 151.
Tmetoceras, i. 147.
Tobacco, i. 109, 118, 251, 283.
Tondy, the river, i. 67, 156; crossing, i. 157; ii. 148, 163.
Transport, means of, i. 43; ii. 187, 257.
Travelling costume, i. 203.
Treculia, i. 252.
Trichilia, i. 216; ii. 198.
Troglodytes niger, i. 248.
Trumbashes, i. 278.
Trumpets, i. 131.

Tudyee, the river, i. 171, 202.
Tuhamy, i. 261; his Seriba, ii. 129.
Turks, ii. 161, 195, 215.

Uncaria, i. 68; ii. 57.
Uringama, ii. 149, 152.
Urostigma Kotschyana, ii. 49.
Usnea (beard moss), ii. 99.
Uzze, the river, i. 226.

Vallisneria in the Gazelle, i. 35; ii. 272.
Vasel, ii. 281.
Vatica, i. 158.
Vayssière, the French hunter, i. 68.
Vegetation, i. 86, 216, 240, 270; ii. 18.
Vigna sinensis, i. 105, 251.
Vitex, i. 89.
Voandzeia, i. 105, 251.

WANDO, animosity of, i. 227; Mohammed's interview with, i. 239 visit from, i. 242; his augury, ii. 110.

Wart-hogs, i. 68, 75.
Water, bad, i. 45, 117; ii. 168, 245.
Waterbock, i. 160.
Watershed of Nile, i. 234.
Welle, the river, i. 264; ii. 35.
White ants, i. 166, 258; ii. 122.
White Nile, i. 29.
Witches, belief in, i. 145.
Wod Shellay, ii. 278.
Wohko, i. 174.
Wounds, i. 146, 255; ii. 102, 105, 147.
Wow, the river, i. 70; ii. 196.

YADO, i. 225; ii. 118.
Yabongo, i. 225; ii. 118.
Yams, i. 106; ii. 90.
Yanga's grave, i. 129.
Yubbo, i. 226; ii. 118.
Yumma, Kurshook Ali's Vokeel, ii. 233, 237.
Yuroo, i. 253; ii. 101.

ZAWA-TREES, i. 213.
Zilei Mountains, ii. 130, 152.
Zizigium, ii. 198.

www.ingramcontent.com/pod-product-compliance
Lightning Source LLC
Chambersburg PA
CBHW021203230426
43667CB00006B/530